The New History of England

General Editors
A. G. Dickens and Norman Gash

Wars and Revolutions

Britain, 1760–1815

Ian R. Christie

Harvard University Press
Cambridge, Massachusetts
1982

Library of Congress Cataloging in Publication Data

Christie, Ian R.
  Wars and revolutions.

  (The new history of England)
  Bibliography: p.
  Includes index.
  1. Great Britain—Politics and government—1760—1820.
2. Great Britain—Foreign relations—France.   3. France
—Foreign relations—Great Britain.   I. Title.
II. Series.
DA505.C48   941.07′3   82-3009

ISBN 0-674-94760-6   AACR2

Contents

Preface

We cannot, from its nature, apply fully to the writing of history Burke's definition of society, as a partnership, 'not only between those who are living, but between those who are living, those who are dead, and those who are to be born'; but omit the last seven words, and the phrase is apt. He who writes a general book has particular obligations to salute the shades of past historians, whose thoughts may in some way have shaped his own; while he owes a more direct debt to his contemporaries. The list of authors and titles in the bibliography to this volume is far from a full acknowledgement of the reading that has contributed to it. Historical learning advances by a process of discussion and argument, and in a book of this kind there is too little room for all the arguments. Omission must therefore often mark my disagreements with other scholars. I can only apologize for this and for any inadvertent misrepresentation of their views.

I owe certain specific acknowledgements. Dr Roland Thorne, while unable to release prematurely findings of the forthcoming volumes of *The History of Parliament* for 1790–1820, kindly assured me that nothing in chapter 12 conflicted with them. Professor Norman Gash gave sound and helpful advice when I strayed into excessive length. And I am grateful to Miss Nazneen Razwi and Mrs Irena Leonessi for help in producing the final typescript.

Ian R. Christie
University College London

For
Joyce and John
whose kindness never fails

Introduction

The British national experience during the reign of George III was harsh and testing. In the small-scale, overall view of our national history, the glow of the golden Victorian age, a time of international peace and growing domestic prosperity, arising as it seemed out of years of triumphant warfare before 1815, has tended to cast its hue over the previous two generations. However, this is an illusion. There was nothing preordained about the victories of 1814 and 1815, and they came at the end of a half-century as fraught with danger and anxiety as any in the nation's history. Young men who, like George III, entered upon their adult years amidst the heady intoxication of success in the Seven Years War, in their early middle age beheld the empire for which that war had been fought torn asunder and feared the decline of their country into a minor satellite of France. Nor was there much comfort for their later years. For if revolution was momentarily to eclipse their formidable rival, it was but for that rival to rise again like a phœnix more bright and terrible than ever, so strong that continental Europe seemed unable to hold her in check. The French wars after 1793 were wars for survival, a survival doggedly pursued from one horizon to the next, always receding from the immediate grasp, never till the last quick turn of fate secured, and then more through the follies of Napoleon than the strength of Britain herself.

The storms and shocks of the international scene beat upon a people which was also facing its own severe internal stresses. A rapid growth of population brought in its train increasing movements of men and women in search of work, disrupting for some of them the calm routines of life in country parishes, and drawing them into unfamiliar urban environments, often under conditions in which social infra-structure had to be built up almost anew from the foundations. The onset of industrialization added to their problems, transforming the old frameworks of economic activity, enhancing the unpredictable effects of market forces, exposing trade and industry alike to the vagaries of international commercial and political relationships. The shadow of large-scale factory production began to loom over the textile industry, and metallurgical operations were carried on upon an increasing scale. Although the physical transformations of the environment foreshadowed by the first advances in technology had hardly begun to have their effect, nevertheless, before Waterloo was fought, parts of London were being lit by gas, a railway locomotive had proved its capacity to draw a train of trucks along a permanent way, and the age of the steamship had begun.

As always during times of change and stress men looked about them for reassurance and security. Some found these in the restoration of old faiths. Others sought them in new panaceas. At one extreme men like Wesley and Wilberforce saw safety in the renewal of zeal and earnestness in religious belief. At the other Jeremy Bentham claimed to find in rational understanding the key to all difficulties. A similar spectrum was to be seen in politics, ranging from Edmund Burke's intense conservative concern for traditional forms to the corrosive radicalism of Thomas Paine. The internal politics of the reign of George III were deeply coloured by these preoccupations. The seventeenth century had bequeathed a legacy of fear about the use of power and of anxiety to safeguard law and individual rights. The social and intellectual transformations of the eighteenth century diverted these fears and anxieties into new channels, giving rise to movements for the preservation or for the reform of the constitution.

And yet, buffeted by all these strains and forces of change, and despite the friction and conflict stemming from political or economic confrontation, the British nation remained on an even keel. At times men feared revolution, but revolution did not come. This volume tells the story of a nation's survival at peace with itself in an age of wars and revolutions. Somehow the tensile strength of British society resisted the forces making for disintegration. Some of the circumstances contributing to this outcome are clearly discernible, not least the astonishing advance in agricultural and industrial production which, overall, more than kept pace with population growth. But it has been borne in upon the author during the preparation of this book, that there is much about this process of survival that as yet remains unexplained. Historians have hardly begun to ask the right questions, which will lead to the proper elucidation of it. The successful emergence of Britain from the great power-struggle against France is at present more readily explicable than the emergence of British society unshattered from the age of revolutions. Subject to that reservation, it is the story of this survival which is outlined in the pages that follow.

1 The Nation and its Wealth 1760 – 1780

I

Land and people form the basis of national power. In the kingdom to which George III succeeded in 1760 the resources and potentialities of both were increasing slowly but steadily, though with as yet little sign of the extraordinary transformation which was to occur before his reign drew to its close. Population was rising. Agriculture was making steady progress, more clearly in the southern part of the island than in the north. The industrial revolution had not yet begun; but in the 1760s and 1770s a keen observer might have sensed the quickening pace of change. There is good ground for regarding the 20 or 30 years before 1780 as the seed-time of the industrial revolution which was to emerge with its full impact in the last 20 years of the eighteenth century.

Around the middle of the century the population of England and Wales was about six and half million and that of Scotland just over a million and a quarter. The sister kingdom of Ireland had rather over three million inhabitants. A further one and a half to one and three quarter million British subjects of European (not exclusively British) stock lived in the mainland colonies of North America, where they made an important contribution to the nation's economic life. In North America, with ample land available in many areas, there was little to check the natural growth of population which was visibly increasing as the years went by, fed by the addition of migrants from overcrowded areas of the British isles and a trickle of German settlers seeking a better life in the New World. At home the pace of growth was still modest in 1760. Even 20 years later some writers were speculating that the population was actually declining, but by that time parish clergymen, who kept a close watch on the local social scene, were finding clear indications that this was far from the case. However, in the absence of effective contemporary records, this growth remains difficult to define and still eludes clear explanation. Better diet, and an effective attack on the scourge of smallpox by the

Suttonian method of inoculation during the 1760s, may both have
been significant factors. The new trend showed itself earlier in the
north of England, where appreciable increase began in the 1730s; in
the south numbers were more stable until the late 1760s. In Scotland
expansion was still slow also. Nevertheless, in some areas, particularly
the Western Highlands and the Islands, the growth was sufficient to
press hard on the means of subsistence, to the point where migration
was the only means of salvation, and a movement of noticeable proportions to North America was occurring by the 1770s.

In most parts of the kingdom by the mid eighteenth century steady
advances in agriculture were underpinning and perhaps contributing
to the growth in population. Output was being increased and also
diversified both by the spread of improved methods of production
and by the extension of the lands under cultivation. Growing demand
and rising prices spurred farmer and landowner alike. Up till the
1760s the corn laws had encouraged farmers to keep wheat production slightly ahead of domestic demand as well as giving protection
against foreign competition. Export was encouraged with a bounty of
5*s*. a quarter so long as the domestic price was 48*s*. or less, which was
far above the normal, and importation was discouraged by high
duties so long as the price remained below 53*s*. 4*d*. But after 1764, as
demand rose, Britain ceased to have a marginal surplus of wheat for
export, and the pressure of a growing population upon subsistence
gave a decisive thrust to the already clear trend towards agricultural
improvement. Wheat prices which had averaged around 26*s*. to 30*s*. a
quarter in the 1750s moved up sharply in the period 1760–75, settling
down in the late 1770s at a level half as high again, as production
adjusted itself to the new demand. To reduce the risk of shortages the
corn law was adjusted in 1773, prohibiting export if the price rose to
44*s*. or above and permitting importation at a nominal duty if it
reached 48*s*. Meat prices showed a similar though less extreme movement, the rise in this case amounting only to about 25 per cent.

In England landowners looking to higher rents and farmers seeking
larger profits hastened to respond to the opportunities. Knowledge
about crop rotations, livestock breeding and improved methods of
treating land, gained by pioneers earlier in the century, were
promoted, popularized and more widely adopted. Arthur Young's
early farming manuals, including *The Farmer's Letters* and *Rural
Economy*, came into print between 1767 and 1771, and Nathaniel
Kent's *Hints to Gentlemen of Landed Property* appeared in 1775. A
sudden burst of parliamentary enclosures signalled an increase in
investment in farming. The number of enclosure bills rose from 137 in
the decade 1750–9 to 660 in the decade 1770–9. The areas mainly
affected were in the north and in the great midland area bounded

roughly by the Trent, the Severn, the chalk escarpments of Wiltshire and Hampshire, and the Great North Road, for the counties of East Anglia and south-eastern England were already largely enclosed. Part of the area enclosed after 1760 was already under cultivation, but a great deal, especially in the northern counties, was waste now for the first time made productive. In addition to parliamentary enclosure, an area nearly half this in extent may have been enclosed by private agreement. Rising profits could defray both the cost of enclosure and that of the improved farming then made possible, which could thereafter even double the yield.

In general, enclosures had four main objects. They promoted more efficient farming, by making farms more compact, larger and easier to work, by making possible a better balance between arable and pasture, by permitting the better care of animals and successful selective breeding, and by facilitating and encouraging the adoption of more effective methods of husbandry. They brought considerable amounts of waste and under-cultivated areas into production. Improvement tended to snowball, as increasing profits made available additional funds for capital spending. Inevitably the spread of enclosure was fairly haphazard, depending on all kinds of human and natural factors. Soil, climate, relief, the presence or absence of good communications were all factors determining where enclosure would take place. In general the initiative came from the large landowners, but in some cases the small men and even the tenant farmers could prove more keen to promote schemes than their social superiors.

Around 1760 Scottish agriculture lagged far behind that of England, and in many areas appeared to be little more than scratching for subsistence. In England the peasant had disappeared. In Scotland he was still very much a feature of the rural scene. Groups of tenants farmed lands in common with an open-field strip system — runrig — following practices which cropped the soil to exhaustion and required long unproductive periods in fallow to restore it. Farmers had no resources and little incentive to improvement. The main product for cash sale was cattle, for which there was a steady demand from further south: indeed it was cattle breeding alone which, over the country as a whole, lifted the rural economy from mere subsistence farming to farming for profit. For lack of drainage large areas of potentially fruitful land in the Lowlands remained waterlogged and useless. Generations of improvident use and the ravages of animals had almost stripped the country of trees, leaving fields unprotected from the winds and the people almost entirely dependent upon imported timber. Only in a few inaccessible areas of the Highland glens had substantial acreages of woodland survived the destructive activities of beasts and man. For the Scottish tenant farmer in general life was simple and near the edge of poverty, his dwelling primitive, his diet poor, and his chattels few.

During the next two generations Scotland moved from one of the most backward to one of the most advanced farming economies in Europe. During the 1760s and 1770s this process was only at its beginning. At this stage new farming methods were pioneered in the Lowlands by a small minority of leading landowners, mainly men whose involvement in public life caused them to pass part of their time in London and become acquainted with English practices. Their efforts were dictated as much, if not more, by the desire to modernize and to foster the prosperity of their native land, as by the sense of profit to be made. Resourceful in money as well as in ideas, they sometimes poured far more wealth into the improvement of their estates than they drew out. Under the influence of such leading figures as the third Earl of Marchmont at Polwarth, Lord Kames in the Merse, and the geologist James Hutton (who went himself to Norfolk to study farming methods and in 1754 brought a Norfolk ploughman to work on his estate), the county of Berwick, naturally endowed with fertile soil, had by 1780 become the most advanced agricultural shire in Scotland, with large numbers of consolidated, enclosed farms, improved farm buildings, and the use of adaptations of the Norfolk rotation. Vast programmes of afforestation began to restore windbreaks and lay down a future source of supplies of timber. Individuals were pioneering similar methods in other Lowland counties. In parts of the north a more corporate impetus to improvement was given by the commissioners for forfeited Jacobite estates. In 1774 they sent out instructions to factors enjoining the introduction of improved farming methods, the use of clover and grass in rotation, and the avoidance of overcropping. Building materials were specified and heath-burning without special sanction was forbidden. The Highland sector, with not much arable, benefited little during this period. The spread of cultivation of the potato, brought in from Ireland in the 1740s, led to a rapid multiplication of small crofts and in the short run contributed to overpopulation. Another innovation, sheep-farming, held out hopes of greater profits to the clan chieftains, but threatened depopulation to the clansmen, though this change had hardly begun to make itself felt before 1780.

II

It has been calculated that about the middle of the eighteenth century, something like half of the families living in England were primarily engaged in agriculture (contrast the modern figure of about 2½ per cent). The rest were involved in a great variety of manufacturing and commercial activities, and, at least outside London, many of these were closely linked with country life. Mid-century Britain was still mainly a rural country. Few people as yet lived in large towns. Only one very great city existed. London was unique. Including its suburbs it probably contained about 750,000 inhabitants at the accession of George III, and it reached about one million at the end of the century – that is to say, throughout the century it housed nearly one tenth of the country's population. The next largest town in England, Bristol, was less than a tenth the size, with a population approaching 60,000 in mid century, and close behind it stood the Scottish capital, Edinburgh, with slightly less than this number. The two future great western outports, both destined to overhaul Bristol by the end of the century, Glasgow and Liverpool, were flourishing towns of about 30,000 people. Norwich had about 40,000, Birmingham 30,000, Manchester with Salford a little over 20,000 inhabitants. Hardly any other town in England had a population of over 20,000, and some county towns were well below that figure. North of the border, with the exception of Aberdeen's 16,000 and Dundee with its 12,000 people, no town in Scotland except Edinburgh and Glasgow had yet exceeded 10,000 in 1760, though the linen and cotton-spinning centre of Paisley was soon to do so.

Britain in 1760 was still in the pre-factory age, and the typical unit of production remained small. The farm itself was in many cases run by the members of a single family, with only occasional hired assistance at certain seasons. The handloom weaver had his family production unit in his cottage. In some callings the unit was formed by the master craftsman with his two or three workmen and apprentices living in. Brewing and distilling involved slightly larger teams of people, but establishments with as many as 50 employees were probably unusual. In yet other sectors of the economy a master or entrepreneur might keep up to hundreds of people in employment, but through the putting-out system and not in his own establishments. London was exceptional in the great numbers of working people, including skilled craftsmen in an enormous diversity of manufacturing pursuits, living and following their trades cheek by jowl in an urban environment, flanked by an army of folk engaged in wholesale and retail trading on one hand, and on the other by men and women supplying necessities of life and providing transport services as wagon drovers, coachmen, ferrymen, and crews of coastal vessels. London's importance as by far the country's greatest port and trading centre was bound up with the fact that it was also the chief centre for manufactures of very many descriptions.

Developments in communications had much to do — perhaps more than is sometimes realized — with the growth of the urban industrialization which was to transform parts of the country during the reign of George III. Although much of the trunk highway system radiating from London into the provinces was turnpiked by 1750, the three following decades saw important advances. Between 1760 and 1774, soon after which a general slackening of the economy checked further enterprise, over 450 Acts were passed setting up turnpike trusts. In the north of England especially, the road system benefited from the genius of the engineer John Metcalf, now at the height of his powers, applying his skills to the improvement of road surfaces and the consolidation of highways passing through boggy country. In Scotland the commissioners for forfeited estates, as interested in economic development as in military strategy, contributed to the building of roads and bridges, and in particular, during the 1760s, gave grants totalling some £13,000 for the construction and upkeep of the nine-arch bridge built across the Tay at Perth. The new highways contributed to an increasing integration of economic activity and to social contact. By 1766 the coach journey from London to Manchester or Liverpool had been cut to three days. The breakdown of the isolation of the chief Scottish centres was even more marked. About 1760 one stage coach per month left Edinburgh for London, taking 15 days on the road, and the wonder is that anyone was prepared to travel by it, rather than make the journey by sea, or hazard the sloughs on horseback. By 1783 15 stage coaches were leaving Edinburgh for London each week, completing the journey in four days; and by then also the northern capital was linked by road services with every major town in Scotland.

Heavy haulage required a different sort of facility and acquired it through the great burst of canal building which continued through the 1760s and early 1770s, much of it due to the enterprise of the Duke of Bridgewater. A network of waterways was created linking the Mersey estuary with the Manchester area, the upper Trent, and the area of the Black Country and Birmingham, from which further connection was made at Kidderminster with the river route by the Stour and Severn to Bristol. By the late 1770s the development of this system had given Liverpool an easily accessible economic hinterland stretching almost a hundred miles to the south-east, which contributed greatly to the growth of this port during the late eighteenth century. In the West Midlands the ease of carriage of heavy and bulky raw materials and products underpinned the development of the iron industry and of the earthenwares industry in the Potteries. London ceased to be the main distribution centre for Birmingham metalwares, which were now dispersed in all directions along the canal routes. In Scotland the interest of the Carron Iron Company in cheap waterborne traffic was a driving force behind the initiation of the Forth–Clyde canal in 1768, which by 1777 had been carried as far west as Glasgow, and the first major works for deepening the river channel of the Clyde downstream from Glasgow were success-fully completed during the 1770s. The disruption of trade by the American war during the later 1770s put an end to this first canal boom, and a number of works which had been begun around 1776 and 1777 were not completed until the 1790s. Nevertheless by the end of the war, an important transport infrastructure had been estab-lished, of inestimable advantage for the future economic develop-ment of the country.

III

Iron and steel, and the cotton manufacture, formed the twin pillars of the British industrial revolution. Up to 1815 the transformed economy still remained narrowly based, although the developments in these two fields were drawing along other changes in their wake.

The role of technological innovation and invention in this process of change has been much debated. It seems probable that this was less important than economic factors. The inventors, so the argument runs, are always with us: of this the anticipatory works of Leonardo da Vinci stand as a supreme example. It was market opportunity which led to the application of men's discoveries. This is not to say that in individual cases the motive for invention was always commercial. Some at least of the men who made important contributions to the industrial revolution were lovers of knowledge and improvement, pursuing them for their own sake, and busying themselves with numerous projects other than the one or two which made their names. The other extreme was represented by Samuel Garbett, an entrepre-neur to his fingertips, backing the innovative enterprise of others, a central figure in the mid-eighteenth-century vitriol industry, a lead-ing light for a time in the Carron Iron Company, and a Birmingham manufacturer alert to commercial opportunity. This age was also a flood-tide for a number of remarkable men who stood somewhere between these extremes, having both a turn for invention and a keen sense of commercial advantage. Their success found a natural precondition in the scientific spirit of the time, the pervasive belief in the value of practical experiment, testing, observation, and categorization, on which the development of modern scientific culture is based, and they themselves, generally speaking, worked from a sound intellectual foundation, whether they were self-taught or had benefited from a good formal education. Josiah Wedgwood of pottery fame was not only an able businessman, but a practical scientist, an able research chemist, concerned with colours, glazing, the composition of materials, and the action of heat − he was the inventor of a ceramic pyrometer, which he marketed. The experiments of James Watt which led to the development of the steam engine were based on firm scientific knowledge and insight. The outstanding hydraulic engineers of the age − John Smeaton and John Rennie − were well grounded in mathematics and mechanics, and were notable for their application of the principles of scientific enquiry to the problems they tackled. The engineering profession which was in the process of formation in the late eighteenth century drew its personnel from the ranks of skilled workmen in many fields whose crafts required them to have competence in these areas and whose expertise was adapted to new uses: thus, precision-working in brass by clockmakers and toymakers long preceded the precision-working in the more intractable materials, iron and steel, which characterized the industrial revolution. However rudimentary it might be, the chemical knowledge of the day received keen attention from industrialists in the nascent chemical industry and from those, like potters, bleachers and dyers, who were working in associated fields. James Keir was not only a leading chemical manufacturer in Staffordshire but the compiler of a *Dictionary of Chemistry*. Science was associated with industry to an important degree through the training given in the Scottish universities, the influence of which on men like Lord Dundonald, James Watt, John Smeaton, John Rennie, James Keir or Charles Macintosh was of fundamental importance. It was involved also through the contacts made in local philosophical societies which flourished in a number of provincial towns, notably the Lunar Society of Birmingham: it is not unreasonable, one scholar has written, 'to claim the Lunar Society as an informal technological research organization.'[1]

There was no dramatic leap forward in industry up to the end of the 1770s, but the incentives revealed by the multiplication of patents are an indication of steady advance, and on the technical side

---

[1] R. E. Schofield, 'The Industrial Orientation of Science in the Lunar Society of Birmingham', in *Science, Technology and Economic Growth in the Eighteenth Century*, ed. A. E. Musson (1972), p. 140. See also Schofield, *The Lunar Society of Birmingham* (1963).

foundations were being laid in various ways for the rapid growth experienced in the latter half of George III's reign.

In mid century British iron-making was located in a number of areas determined by facilities of markets, water-power, water communication, and above all, the availability of charcoal which was required for the smelting and purifying processes. By 1760 the old-established iron centre of the Kent and Sussex Weald was operating under increasing fuel restrictions. Elsewhere smelting works and forges were established, particularly in the Forest of Dean, in the West Midlands around the valleys of the Stour and Coalbrookdale – reached from Bristol via the inland port of Bewdley-cum-Wribbenhall on Severn – in the Wrexham district of North Wales, in the Sheffield area, and further north around Newcastle. Foundries for the re-working of imported pig iron existed in the vicinity of the ports of London, Bristol and Hull. Dispersal was dictated by the limited availability of water-power required for driving bellows and hammers, and the dependence on wood fuel. But during the 1750s, through long processes of trial and error, the use of coked coal in smelting furnaces had been sufficiently perfected to become widespread in the Coalbrookdale and Wrexham areas, the new technique was carried to Dowlais in South Wales, and in 1760 its success was dramatically underlined by the establishment of the large purpose-built smelting works at Carron, near Falkirk, the first major plant in Scotland, and of the Seaton works near Workington in Cumberland. During the 1760s the new method came into general use in Staffordshire, South Yorkshire, and Northumberland, and its advantages spelled the end for the charcoal-based smelting in the Weald. War proved a compelling stimulus. Ten or 11 new smelting furnaces were brought into operation between 1756 and 1762, including those at Carron and Dowlais, and there was renewed rapid expansion after the outbreak of the American war.

Technical advances of various kinds increased the potential of the industry during the 1760s and 1770s. With the expert help of the engineer Smeaton, the Carron Company secured extra water by damming the river, improved the blast of the furnaces by the use of blowing cylinders powered with water, built to his design, and installed a boring machine devised by him to improve the production of guns and cylinders. By the mid 1770s it had developed an extensive export trade in cannon; and in the short-barrelled, large-bore gun which came to be known as the carronade its designers produced a formidable new weapon of naval warfare. Nevertheless, ordnance was not its main concern: by the early 1780s it had established a reputation for such peacetime requirements as spades, hoes, anvils, sad-irons, ovens, firegrates, and steam-engine components. The Staffordshire ironmaster John Wilkinson also developed a still more successful instrument for boring cannon early in the 1770s, which was soon pirated by his neighbours. While the superiority of the Midlands producers in making cannon by this means dealt the final blow to the Sussex gun-founders, the importance of the technique for general engineering was even more momentous, for it made possible the construction of the engines with close-fitting pistons using steam under pressure as the driving force with which James Watt had been experimenting for some years before 1774.

Another bottleneck successfully overcome during this period was in the production of malleable iron, where dependence on the scarce and expensive charcoal had continued longer than in the smelting process. In 1766 the brothers Cranage of Coalbrookdale took out a patent for refining pig iron in a coke-fired reverberatory furnace. There were still some flaws in the process. Although it produced a metal suitable for the manufacture of nails — a very important and extensive industry, especially in the Black Country — it proved inadequate for other purposes, and further experiment continued. The process was perfected principally by Henry Cort, whose trials led to patents in 1783 and 1784. At his works iron puddled in a reverberatory furnace was immediately purged of dross by rolling while at welding heat. By reducing dependence on hammering at this stage of manufacture, Cort immensely speeded up the production of malleable iron, and the metal made by his method was of sufficiently good quality to be substituted for charcoal iron in all uses except the making of steel.

At the hands of James Watt and his business partner, Matthew Boulton of Birmingham, the steam engine developed during this period mainly as a pumping machine. Its contribution to metallurgy was at first indirect, permitting the winning of coal and ore from the deeper levels of mines where drainage was a serious problem. By 1783 it was in almost universal use in the Cornish tin mines. But the new power unit could also be of service in other ways. It was soon used to add to resources of water power by recycling water into reservoirs. As early as 1780 John Wilkinson had four engines installed to provide more powerful blasts for his furnaces, and the example was quickly followed by his competitors. In the late 1770s Watt was busy with the development of ways to create rotary motion from the piston-stroke, which would give his engine still further, more vital industrial potential. His patents were taken out in 1781: their consequences belong to a later stage of this story.

By the early 1780s the output of British pig and bar iron had significantly increased, though the figures were not yet dramatic. More important, potentials for almost unlimited growth had been released.

Dependence on charcoal was ending. The ability to drive deeper mines meant that ample coal was available. Canals had made water carriage for heavy loads available wherever the industry required it. As yet the range of iron articles coming into use had not made a great impact, but the laying of 20 miles of iron railways in the Coalbrookdale complex and the building of the iron bridge over the Severn linking the Dale with Broseley in 1779 were portents of things to come.

IV

In the third quarter of the eighteenth century the woollen and worsted manufacture still ranked as England's (rather than Britain's) premier industry, accounting for about 40 per cent of the country's total domestic exports. Three areas were clearly pre-eminent: the West Riding of Yorkshire; the south-western clothing area extending from north Dorset through Wiltshire into southern Gloucestershire; and the East Anglian district with its business centre at Norwich. The only Scottish area noted for the supply of other than purely local needs was the north-east, where a sizeable stocking manufacture was centred around Aberdeen: otherwise any incipient Scottish woollen cloth industry had long been suppressed as a result of English competition after the Union.

In the south of England the business was generally dominated, even if it was not fully controlled, by merchant clothiers who owned the wool and put it out to domestic outworkers for all the successive processes of carding, combing, spinning, weaving, fulling and dressing. One or two of them, like the Fludyers of London and Wiltshire, made enormous fortunes. By contrast the Yorkshire clothiers were more independent master craftsmen, working with a slender capital, who owned their tools and materials, purchasing the wool, and with the help of up to six or seven journeymen carrying through the processes as far as the production of undressed cloth, which they then disposed of for cash at the cloth halls in Leeds, Wakefield, Bradford, or Halifax. The local merchants who bought it then saw to the fulling and dressing, and put the cloth on the domestic or foreign market. Their expertise in selling was generally greater than that of the Londoners. Between 1760 and 1780 the Yorkshiremen were finally consolidating their ascendancy and by 1775 were reckoned to be producing as much cloth as the rest of the country put together. Aiming at cheapness they were successfully penetrating one foreign market after another, and were so firmly established in the North American trade that they were able quickly to recover their position after the establishment of American independence.

The British linen manufacture has received relatively little attention from historians, being overshadowed at the end of the eighteenth century by cotton, which partly displaced it. Although occupying a much less important place in the national economy than woollens, it was nevertheless a subject of concern to governments, which disliked the partial dependence of the country on imports from abroad. The British and the Irish linen industries were encouraged both by protective tariffs and by subsidies on exports; and import duties on flax and on yarn, most of which had to be imported from the Low Countries, Germany and the Baltic region, had been abolished during the 1750s. In England some regional economies were largely dependent upon the industry, notably in parts of Yorkshire, Durham, Lancashire and Somerset. Proportionately to population Scotland contributed a substantially greater output. Here the main areas of the manufacture were the counties of Forfar, Fife, Perth, Lanark and Renfrew, and to meet the demand for yarn there was increasing putting-out for spinning in parts of the Highlands.

About 1760 the total annual consumption of linens of all kinds in Great Britain and the colonies was estimated at about 80 million yards. Of this Scotland supplied at least 12 millions, England rather over 25. Ireland provided a further 12 million yards, and the balance of rather over 30 million was contributed by imports from northern Europe. In the following decade the annual English output seems to have shot ahead rapidly, and may have exceeded 45 million yards during the 1770s. In the same period Scottish output increased by about 20 per cent. The industry satisfied an enormous range of requirements from furnishing and clothing to sailcoth. The fact that the domestic demand was rising distinctly more rapidly than the rate of population growth is indicative of an increasing absorption of consumer goods which was raising the standard of living of sections of the population and fits the view that a buoyant home market and an expanding domestic economy were major forces in the inception of the industrial revolution. Round Glasgow and Paisley there was specialization during the 1760s and 1770s in the production of fine cambrics, muslins and lawns: it was no accident that it was in this area of Scotland that the switch into cottons was beginning.

The emergence of cotton, the 'child-prodigy' of the industrial revolution, was becoming clear by about 1780. Before then its development was entwined with and dependent upon the linen manufacture. On the one hand it benefited from the protective

measures taken earlier in the century to protect the linen industry from foreign competition. On the other linen provided a cloak
behind which it developed half-concealed — for, in the interests
of the woollen manufacture, the making of cotton cloth had been
prohibited by statute in 1721. Nevertheless, cotton as a raw material
had too many attractions to be foregone, and it possessed two
enormous potential advantages over flax. It was capable of extensive cultivation, it was readily obtainable from the West Indies
and in smaller quantities and poorer quality from the Levant, and
it was more suited to mechanical preparation and spinning. For
many years before 1760 linen weavers had varied their products and
eked out their supplies of flax yarn by using cotton yarn for weft,
producing an array of smallwares, cotton-linen checks and fustians,
for which there were good markets at home and abroad. At times
the flax content became negligible, but the Act of 1721 was wholly
ignored.

However, only after release from the constrictions of a limited
supply of raw material and from the constraints of statutory prohibition could a fully fledged cotton weaving manufacture emerge. The
decisive advances came in the 1760s and 1770s. Richard Arkwright's
patenting of the water-frame in 1769 and James Hargreaves's launching of the spinning jenny in 1770 marked the culmination of years of
ingenious experiment to mechanize the process of spinning cotton, a
need which was more urgently felt in the '60s as the general adoption
of Kay's fly-shuttle increased the weavers' productive capacity. Moreover, both devices significantly improved the quality of the thread.
With Arkwright's water-frame the industry gained a spinning
machine which from the first was designed with the intention of
applying a power source to large-scale production of a thread sufficiently strong to form the warp. During the same period he also
perfected a power-driven carding engine which both cheapened and
speeded up the processes preliminary to spinning. His exploitation of
these inventions brought into the open the conflict between the cotton
manufacture and the statutory prohibition of 1721, and his success in
securing the repeal of this regulation in 1774 removed the remaining
obstacle to its free expansion. His processes, applied on a large scale in
factory buildings using water as the motive power, enormously
reduced the cost of cotton yarn while greatly increasing the quantity
available. A further advance was made with Crompton's 'mule',
launched in 1779, which combined various advantageous features of
the spinning-jenny and the water-frame, and permitted a thread
equally fine with that produced by the hand-jenny to be spun
mechanically. By the end of the American war of independence, with
ample supplies of high quality yarn available, the cotton industry

both in Lancashire and in the Clyde valley, was poised for revolutionary advance.

By contrast with the woollen and linen industries, the production of silk yarn and fabric formed only a small part of the national economy. Nevertheless it was of sufficient importance to attract the attention of the legislature. Men could move easily between this and the other weaving industries. In the second half of the century the silk industry was encouraged by the reduction of duties on raw silk from China and India, and in 1765 and 1773 Acts of Parliament prohibited the importation of wrought silks. Apart from the major concentrations of silk weavers in the Spitalfields and Bethnal Green areas of London, Coventry (for ribbons), Congleton and Macclesfield (for silk buttons), Nottingham (for stockings, gloves, scarves and lace), and Norwich (for crapes) were also important centres, and an important manufacture of silk gauze developed at Paisley. In the mid eighteenth century the supply of yarn proved the bottleneck in this as in other textile industries. The most dramatic development in the 1760s and 1770s — and the one of most significance for industrialization in textiles in general — was the growth of mechanized silk-spinning. The silk-throwing techniques developed at Derby by the Lombe brothers earlier in the century began to spread on a large scale in the 1750s. Silk-throwing mills were established in various parts of eastern Cheshire and Derbyshire and other districts, and their use of cheap water power and their greater productive capacity led to a decline of silk-throwing in the London area. Not the least important aspect of this development was the model set for the growth of the cotton-spinning mills of the late '70s and after: indeed, the Sheffield factory was later converted to cotton.

Among other economic developments of this period, one that stands out is the growth of the Potteries. Numbers of small firms were emerging from the level of somewhat poverty-stricken cottage-type production, in a trade buoyed up by the growing demand for good quality wares on the part of both the wealthy and the expanding middle classes, and helped by such changing social habits as the development of a taste for tea, coffee and hot chocolate. The boom owed much to the entrepreneurial abilities of Josiah Wedgwood, who not only aimed at the quality market but also directed his efforts to the mass production of popular earthenware lines. It was the latter that made his fortune, and the fortunes also of many of his competitors in the Potteries, and that helped to build up an extensive export trade, especially to North America. By the early 1780s the district of the Potteries had been transformed into a region of prosperity which was becoming a household word all over the country; by then, on Wedgwood's own account, the pottery workmen were earning nearly double the wage rates of 30 or 40 years before, housing had improved beyond all recognition, and instead of being relatively inaccessible, the area was well served with good turnpikes and canals.

V

A considerable proportion of the population of Great Britain derived a livelihood directly or indirectly from overseas trade — a trade which added to the country's resources, provided essential raw materials, and enhanced the general standard of living. In accordance with generally prevailing theories, this commerce was conducted on protectionist lines. British shipping interests functioned behind the shelter of the Navigation Acts, which excluded the merchant marine of any foreign nation from the coastal trade or from the role of common carrier, and the 'long haul' was totally reserved by the provision that goods of Asian, African or American origin could only be imported in British ships. The preoccupation with colonies as parts of a controlled economic system, providing raw materials and furnishing an exclusive market for manufactures, was never more intense than in the years following the Seven Years War, and was to contribute to crisis and revolution within the Empire in less than 20 years.

The West Indies — still regarded about 1760 as the most prized part of the Empire — supplied sugar, molasses and rum, which were either consumed in Britain or re-exported at considerable profit to the northern parts of Europe, and also most of the raw cotton forming the basis of the fustian and cotton-linen manufactures. In return they took a wide range of manufactured goods, a part of which found their way to the Spanish colonists in the Caribbean. But this commerce had reached the limits of expansion and was overshadowed by the opportunities offered by the American mainland.

The North American colonies with their rapidly increasing population provided a large and growing market for British manufactures of every description, and in return made contributions to the economic life of the home island which more often than not were indirect. The tobacco planters of Virginia and Maryland, and the indigo farmers of North Carolina stood in the most simple and direct economic relationship, exchanging for their wants their staple products, which under the Acts of Trade they could export only to Britain, and which

were there consumed or processed for re-export. The early prosperity
of Glasgow was almost wholly built up on the tobacco trade. By contrast, South Carolina paid its way largely by its direct export of rice to
southern Europe and, after 1764, to Latin America, deliveries being
paid for in Europe by bills of exchange on London which furnished
credits for purchases, or in the Spanish colonies by silver bullion or
tropical commodities disposable in London. The colonies north of the
Potomac sustained their economies by means of yet more complicated
patterns of trade. Their ships acted as common carriers within the
Empire. They shared in the slave trade between the West African
coast and the Caribbean and carried the silver-scaled harvest of the
Newfoundland Banks to markets in the West Indies and southern
Europe. They supplied foodstuffs, timber and draught animals to the
West Indies, and shipped small consignments of flour to Europe and
pig iron to Britain.

In Europe the trading area most prized by the British was the
Iberian Peninsula. Neither Spain nor Portugal had developed sufficient manufactures to meet their own needs, let alone those of their
extensive overseas possessions, and trade treaties with both countries
had included favourable tariff agreements. But after 1760 both
nations were seeking a greater degree of economic self-sufficiency,
with adverse effects on British export trade. A modest trade was
carried on with the Baltic countries, and a considerable boom in
Russian commerce developed after the end of the Russo-Turkish war
of 1768–74. Britain drew in return from all these countries various
essential imports: substantial quantities of timber and naval stores for
the maintenance of the navy and merchant marine; high grade bar
iron to supplement the inadequate domestic resources and to supply
the needs of the steel industries of Sheffield and Birmingham; and
Russian flax required for the linen manufacture. The Austrian
Netherlands took large quantities of British goods for local consumption, and Ostend was a major route for British commodities destined
for central Europe: between 1750 and 1775 this export trade
increased fourfold in annual value. Commerce with the United
Provinces was on a still larger scale, and the German states offered
substantial markets for both British manufactures and colonial
produce.

In contrast with the economic relationships with all these countries,
British trade with France tended to be minimal, not simply because
commerce was frequently interrupted by war, but through a concern
not to give support in any way to the French economy. The importation of French cambrics and lawns, silk stockings and gloves, was
forbidden by statute. Discriminatory duties were aimed against
French wines, silks and woollens, a tariff policy to which the French

responded in kind, with protective prohibitions against the importation of British cottons, hosiery, leather goods, glassware and hardware. According to the official figures (which are not exact) exports to France in the mid '70s were only about one tenth in value of those to the Austrian Netherlands and less than the trade with Denmark. Although on both sides the barriers were partly surmounted by extensive smuggling, it seems unlikely that this could greatly alter the general picture.

The only limited expansion and the fluctuating nature of British commerce during the first two decades of George III's reign give weight to the contention that it was not foreign trade but a buoyant domestic market which encouraged the initial outburst of invention and of capital investment marking the first stage of the industrial revolution. To a small extent the market was created by an increase in population, particularly with the lowering of child mortality from the 1760s. But, even more, several lines of evidence appear to converge to show that a gradually increasing proportion of the population enjoyed a modest but significant increase in purchasing power, that this created an additional demand for goods, and this in turn stimulated the development of improved modes of production. Since industrial production of various kinds was increasing steadily during the '60s and '70s, while overseas trade virtually marked time and even went into recession during the American war of independence, it seems evident that most of the additional goods were being absorbed by the domestic market. It has been suggested that whereas, at a rough guess, perhaps 15 per cent of the population had family incomes of between £50 and £400 in 1750, by 1780 the proportion may have risen to 20 or even 25 per cent, adding an extra 150,000 households which functioned as effective consumers of the products coming from the workshops and manufactories of the early industrial revolution.[2]

In all sorts of ways the economic pulse of Great Britain was quickening during the 1760s and 1770s, and the foundations were being laid for the country's industrial 'take-off' in the last two decades of the eighteenth century.

---

[2] D. E. C. Eversley, 'The Home Market and Economic Growth in England, 1750–1780' in *Land, Labour and Population in the Industrial Revolution*, ed. E. L. Jones and G. E. Mingay (1967), pp. 206–58.

2 State and Church

I

Whether made the subject of comment by political partisans, examined as an interlocking system of institutions by the admiring foreign observer Montesquieu, or discussed as a system of laws by the eminent native-born jurist Sir William Blackstone, the British constitution drew admiration for its apparent success in curbing the threat to the subject presented by the existence and growth of political power. It was generally believed that at the heart of this success lay the establishment of a durable balance of forces, each of which held the others in check. Men described in various ways these countervailing elements of the system. Some detected it in the constitutional separation and relative independence from each other of the executive, legislative and judicial elements in the state. However, this view could only be accepted with considerable reservations. The intermeshing of executive and legislature was apparent in the presence of ministers and placemen among the members of the two Houses of Parliament. Even the judiciary was not wholly separate from the other branches. Welsh judges sat in the Commons, and twice during George III's reign a lord chief justice acted as a member of the cabinet. To those steeped in classical learning, and this included most cultured men of the time, it seemed as if the British had succeeded in balancing the three potentially dangerous and destructive forces of monarchy, aristocracy and democracy, and some political commentators saw these elements as identified with the three elements of king, lords and commons which constituted the national legislature. If the legislature was, as Blackstone contended, legally omnipotent, nevertheless the liberty of the subject was protected by the divisions between its component parts.

As a matter of historical evolution the crown still remained the pivot of authority for all governmental action. The king was head of the state. Parliament and all public officials derived their motion from him. At the same time the king, the politicians, and the public (which may be taken to mean that part of the nation which took some intelligent interest in public affairs) all alike by this time accepted presuppositions encapsulated in the revolution settlement of 1689 and rationalized in the writings of John Locke and later commentators, that the monarch stood below the law and acted in trust for his subjects, whose rights he should be as sedulous to guard as his own. George III took these responsibilities seriously. Whereas the earlier Hanoverian kings had been nurtured in Germany and had had to adapt themselves to the British system of government, George III was the first of his line to have been trained from childhood in the history and the political traditions of his kingdom, and the exercises which he wrote during his early manhood under the guidance of his companion, the Earl of Bute, bear clear testimony to the lessons he had learned. The English, he wrote at this time, had 'created the noblest constitution the human mind is capable of framing' — a reflection to be often repeated in his letters of later years.[1] This careful drilling in constitutional theory perhaps helped to strengthen an innately conservative cast of mind, which led him to react strongly against political developments through which conventions of the constitution might have become modified; and his most conspicuous interventions in public affairs were invariably for the purpose of preserving the essence of the constitution as he understood it, whether in upholding the rights of Parliament against American colonists, the rights of the crown against factious politicians, or the position of the Church of England as a fundamental pillar of the British Protestant state.

The nature of limited monarchy and the absence of any clear statement entrenched in fundamental constitutional law regarding the functions of the respective public authorities in the state, made it inevitable that on some occasions the nature of the limits would come under debate, and that conflicts of interpretation were likely to arise between the king and Parliament. The Bill of Rights of 1689 had given certain precise directions about what the king could not or should not do, but as to what he could do otherwise the law laid down little in specific terms, and evolving customs of the constitution might be interpreted in varying ways. By the middle of the eighteenth century it was fully understood that ministers employed by the king assumed responsibility for the actions taken in his name, and it was equally fully understood that in extreme circumstances Parliament could withdraw confidence from the ministers and oblige them to resign; this last convention was so well established that no one any longer contemplated the necessity for processes of impeachment to enforce it. Between this limited right of veto on ministerial appointments on the one hand and the king's claim to appoint the men who

[1] John Brooke, *King George III* (1972), pp. 56–7.

conducted his public business on the other lay a penumbra of uncertainty, where either the king or the politicians in Parliament might seek to manipulate the rules to their advantage. The king's right to choose and retain ministers could not be absolute — though George III wished at times that it were — and on three occasions, in 1782, in 1783, and in 1804, he was obliged to part with men he wished to retain. But the fact that the king was constitutionally entrusted with responsibility for the executive branch of government created a presupposition that the choice of ministers should normally lie with him, and that the parliamentary veto should only be used in the event of gross maladministration and failure to forward the national interest. With this orthodox position George III firmly identified himself, and so did a large number of the politicians. Their stand was logical, for if the king was not to act as umpire between the politicians aspiring to office, who else could? The public neither had the information nor had it the electoral machinery at its disposal to enable it to make choice of governments. Unless the king were conceded some rights he would become a nonentity manipulated by aristocratic factions whose claims to power lacked any real legitimacy.[2]

This issue in part explained George III's intense and prolonged hostility towards Charles James Fox, whose pretensions in 1782 and 1783 appeared to him to amount to an usurpation by the House of Commons of the crown's prerogative of choosing ministers. While there was nothing morally reprehensible in Fox's attempting to change the balance of the constitution, he was in fact at odds with the precedents and, as the general election of 1784 showed, out of line with prevailing opinion among both the politicians and the public, and in resisting change the king was acting at least as correctly as Fox. To assume, by reference to the mid-nineteenth-century British parliamentary system, that Fox was on the side of the future in proposing to modify a relationship between the head of the executive and his advisers which, in fact, has not only survived within another branch of the Anglo-Saxon constitutional tradition but is actually entrenched there — by the written constitution of the United States — is to run the risk of anachronism and to adopt a stance at once too determinist and too parochial. In 1784 and on a number of subsequent occasions George III successfully defended his right, and during the opening years of the regency the calculations of the politicians continued to be based on the assumption that it still survived.

---

[2] For statements by the Earl of Shelburne, William Pitt, and Henry Dundas supporting this view see, *The Parliamentary History of England . . . to 1803*, ed. W. Cobbett and T. C. Hansard (36 vols., 1806–10) XXIII, p. 192, XXIV, p. 663; *Cobbett's Parliamentary Debates*, ed. W. Cobbett and T. C. Hansard (41 vols., 1803–20) IX, p. 256.

Government in the late eighteenth century dealt with only a very restricted range of activity: the administration of the revenue, diplomacy and defence, law and order, and the regulation of foreign trade. The machinery required was small, and the conduct of affairs was in the hands of a handful of ministers presiding over a group of departmental offices which were minuscule compared with the government establishments of the twentieth century. George III's reign saw only limited development and rationalization. The clumsy geographical division of the responsibilities of the secretaries of state was brought to an end in 1782, when the home and foreign offices began their separate existence. Colonial affairs were deemed to justify a separate department in 1768, but this was abolished in 1782 after the loss of the American colonies — though on political rather than administrative grounds. A board of control composed of various ministers was set up in 1784 to supervise the political affairs of the East India Company. The conflict against revolutionary France dictated the establishment of a secretaryship of state for war in 1794, and in 1801 this department also took over responsibility for colonial affairs from the home office which had conducted them since 1782. Nothing was done, however, to reduce the confusion of administrative agencies which in one way or another controlled the army.

After 1793 especially, the strains of war forced some expansion of the departmental establishments, though the extra workloads were met in part by use of temporary staff. Meanwhile, a gradual trend towards professionalism was apparent in the public service. At the beginning of George III's reign the clerks in the offices tended to be the employees of the minister rather than of the crown, and in some of the larger organizations the actual nomination of men for vacant clerkships was made some way down the chain of command. Once in post clerks were usually assured of permanent employment, save in cases of serious misconduct, and could expect gradual promotion by seniority. Salaries paid from the civil list were for the most part nominal, and the clerks' emoluments derived largely from other sources. A good proportion came from fees charged to the individuals for whom business was transacted. Numbers of departments also had sinecures or quasi-sinecures which were used to provide part of the rewards of their staffs, sometimes through the practice of deputization.

A first initiative to improve the service, at least within his own department, came from Lord North in 1776. A treasury minute laid down instructions for the proper training of the treasury clerks and specified that promotion would not as hitherto be simply by seniority but would be made in the light of 'ability, attention, care and diligence.'[3] Lord Shelburne took matters a stage further in 1782 when he not only reaffirmed the principle of the minute of 1776 but arranged for the pooling of the fees received in the department and their use as a fund from which to pay specific salaries to the secretaries and clerks. In 1783 Shelburne's successor took the further necessary step of ensuring that any deficiency in the fee fund would be made up, one third from the civil list and the other two thirds by parliamentary votes. As part of larger schemes of reorganization fee-funding was also introduced into the subordinate offices of the paymaster of the forces in 1782 and of the treasurer of the navy in 1784. In 1785, when Pitt in an attempt to improve the auditing of the public accounts abolished the exchequer auditors of the imprest and instituted a new office of audit, its officials were placed from the start on a salaried basis. These changes derived much of their impetus from the investigations of the board of commissioners appointed on Lord North's initiative in 1780 to examine the whole field of public expenditure and accounting. The commissioners reported critically on the fee system, and in 1785 Pitt set up a further commission to review it, which did the same. In consequence, during the 1790s systems of fee-funding and fixed salaries were adopted in the other main government departments, and were finally extended to the customs service in 1812. Between 1780 and 1815 the clerical service was also improved by the general application of the principles of grading of clerks, promotion by merit, incremental increases of salary, and more adequate schemes of super-annuation. Purchase of offices, mainly a feature in the navy depart-ments, was also brought to an end.

The effect of all these changes was to emphasize the role of the clerks as paid servants of the crown rather than as persons assistant to a minister who served members of the public in return for fees, and they strengthened the claims which Parliament might legitimately make to inquire into the size and working of the civil establishments, which it now had partly to finance from year to year. Although the full logical implications were not realized for some time, the rationale of the civil list as an institution had now been partly undermined. The pretence that the king paid for the civil administration out of his permanent revenue had become more transparent, and a situation had been created which in due course would lead to further change.

---

[3] J. C. Sainty, *Office-Holders in Modern Britain, 1: Treasury Officials, 1660–1870* (1972), p. 8.

II

This administrative machine existed to carry out the will of the central directing authority in national affairs, the king and the body of 'confidential servants' whom he appointed to assist him in this task. Technically ministers were no more than advisers and agents of the sovereign — 'tools', as George III in his brasher young days once unflatteringly described them. In practice their weight as great nobles, as political leaders commanding the confidence of Parliament, and often — by virtue of long tenure of office — as expert practitioners in public affairs, made them much more; and a great deal depended upon their initiative.

Soon after 1760 the system operating under George III's grandfather, of a small conciliabulum of five or six members making the important decisions while a formal cabinet council of up to 20 provided occasional endorsements, came to an end, and the cabinet took on a more recognizably modern form. The household officers dropped out, and it became a more compact body comprising the three great officers of state — the lord chancellor, the lord president of the council, and, usually, the lord privy seal — and the heads of the chief executive departments. Depending largely on political contingencies — coalitions usually entailed larger numbers — the size of George III's cabinets varied from seven to 13. The king's correspondence shows that he took very seriously his responsibilities as head of the executive and required a constant flow of information and consultation, but only on certain grand strategic issues, such as the retention of the American colonies, the preservation of the constitution, or the maintenance of the established Church, was he prepared to resist or even break with a ministry.

In such situations ministers claimed no more than that, while in office, they should be given full confidence: they accepted that if the king preferred to put his confidence in others he might do so. On such grounds the younger Pitt in 1783–4 had upheld the king's right of choice against the attempt of Charles Fox to circumvent it by insisting that a particular combination of parties and factions in a particular House of Commons could place a veto on any competitor for power. The crucial constitutional issue thus raised needs to be considered in the light of the role of Parliament.

Contemporary theoretical discussion of the two Houses of Parliament tended often to fix upon their functions as representatives of the two great competing forces of aristocracy and democracy (strictly 'polity' in the classical Greek sense) and as parts of the system of checks and balances which prevented either these forces or the monarchy itself from destroying the rule of law and diverting the powers of the state to selfish partisan ends. Because these views had common currency they naturally entered into the politicians' rhetoric and their rationalization of their actions; but at best they provided only a partial and crude picture of a constitutional and representative machine which had evolved and was evolving in ways the full implications of which were by no means clear.

In 1760 the British peerage numbered about 172, and total membership of the upper House, including 16 Scottish representative peers and 26 spiritual peers, was about 214. New creations and the addition of Irish members in 1801 had raised the number to about 367 by 1815. By then the House had come to represent a substantially greater proportion of the country's landed estate and a greater parliamentary electoral interest than had been the case in 1760: 20 of the peers Pitt created between 1784 and 1801 had influence or control over 41 parliamentary seats. Many peers carried great weight as leaders of political and social life in their counties; a few were able politicians with high pretensions to office and power; others served in court posts. The sprinkling of legal luminaries and bishops contributed particular qualities to the House and added to the conservative tone of its proceedings.

The House of Lords acted as an effective revising chamber for public bills. Its techniques for handling private and local bills became highly developed and the chairman of committees came to adopt a quasi-professional role as steersman and scrutineer. The inclination of most peers was to give political support to the king's government, but the House was far from acting as George III's poodle. A large proportion of the peers were prepared at some point to exercise their independent judgment, whether or not this coincided with what was understood to be the king's wishes, and then an administration could run into difficulties. Even so courtly a peer as the Earl of Bute led a revolt in 1766 against the American policy of the Rockingham administration in direct opposition to the king's canvassing of support for his ministers. Independent opposition contributed significantly to the defeat of Fox's East India Bill and the destruction of his ministry in December 1783 and to the worsting of his campaign against Pitt later that winter. Opposition by the peerage embarrassed Addington's ministry in 1804 and its loss of control over the handling of government bills in the House was a significant prelude to its collapse.

Peers also exerted political influence in various other ways. A county magnate might play an effective part in raising local political agitation which might affect the conduct of MPs and ministers. Personal intercession with ministers could carry weight. Through their local political and social prestige they could influence the conduct of members of Parliament, including those who were not strictly dependent upon their help with an electoral interest. Some commentators suggested that although the upper House had its clearly distinct functions of debate and legislation, its important checking role as one element in the balanced constitution was really conducted through the aristocratic interest which the peers projected by means of their relatives and clients in the House of Commons.

Be that as it may, the Commons was far from being a mere social and political extension of the House of Lords. Constitutional tradition stressed its function as representative of and defender of the liberties of the people; but much more emphasis was placed on its institutional role than on its derivation of authority from below. In practice the House appeared representative in the sense that it included men belonging to various significant groups and interests and both through them and by contact with others like them outside Westminster could speak on their behalf. Only a few extreme radicals thought in terms of a democratic representation of the people in the modern sense. Citizenship was equated with economic independence; the idea that the economically dependent should have the franchise was rejected on the grounds that such men would vote merely as the tools of others. As a matter of historical evolution the parliamentary electorate did not include even all those who had an independent livelihood. But this circumstance was not regarded as vitiating the role of the Commons, for the concept of virtual representation was invoked to explain and justify its status. According to this principle, those who did not enjoy the franchise were nevertheless represented in the Commons because their interests were shared by those who were able to vote. The prevailing habit of thinking of the nation in terms of communities, groups and interests — whether communal or economic — gave continuing vitality to this idea, which still dominated orthodox thinking about representation until long after 1815.

During George III's reign the electoral basis of the Commons remained much as it had been at the time of his grand-father's accession.[4] It is fairly clear that the number of voters was increasing, though by no means in proportion to the population. Moreover, the increasing urbanization of England between 1760 and 1815, limited as it still was, produced glaring anomalies of two sorts. In the first category, for instance, both Plymouth and Portsmouth were expanding industrial towns serving the war needs of the navy. In both the franchise remained confined to a narrow self-perpetuating corpora-

---

[4] For a brief description see *ante* in this series, W. A. Speck, *Stability and Strife. England 1714–1760* (1977), pp. 16–19.

tion. In the second, Manchester, Birmingham and Leeds were conspicuous examples of new commercial and industrial centres with crowded urban populations, which even in 1760 were larger than most county towns, and by 1800 had unimpeachable claims to representation. By 1815 these great towns, and the counties also, were putting into discordant perspective the many little ports and market towns, mainly in the southern districts and often with populations of well below 3,000, which returned a large proportion of members of Parliament. The growth of Glasgow, Paisley, Dundee and Aberdeen likewise made more glaring the anomalies among the Scottish constituencies.

Crewe's Act

There were two main changes in the general electoral framework. Crewe's Act for the disfranchisement of revenue officers − part of the package of 'economic reform' dictated by the Rockingham ministry in 1782 − had a small, not very easily defined effect in weakening the influence of the executive government in a few of the small seaport towns. The Irish Act of Union of 1800 increased the proportion of large open constituencies by adding 32 counties and two very large cities (Dublin and Cork) but only a relatively small number of insignificant boroughs open to influence or corruption. Perceptibly Parliament was thus more representative of large electorates after 1800.

The large open constituencies gave opportunities for electioneering along political lines and for the expression of a genuine public opinion on political questions, but it did not necessarily follow that this would occur. It seems to have done so most clearly in 1784 and in 1807, contributing in both cases to the defeat of groups of politicians who were at odds with George III.

In social composition the House of Commons remained overwhelmingly a body of landed proprietors, but commerce, banking and big business were increasingly represented, and one computation for 1812 puts the total of such members at almost one quarter of the membership. Nor did this signify the full representation of these interests, for numbers of leading landowners, by virtue of mineral rights or the development of urban properties, had an indirect stake of one kind or another in the prosperity of their districts and gave active support to it in Parliament. The great amount of local business, with which members of the Commons − like the peers − concerned themselves, underscored the role of the House as a body not riven by political divisions but acting together to promote the good of the nation or of particular sectional interests. The centripetal pull of this work has to be set against those centrifugal forces generated by conflict over national issues which tended to pull the House asunder into parties: it was perhaps one factor among many which tended to check the growth of political parties.

Much has been written during the last 30 years about the place of party in late-eighteenth-century British politics. It would be simplistic to suggest that any view at present expressed commands total adherence. At all events, the system after 1760 was different in a good many ways from that which had prevailed before. In particular, the first three or four years of George III's reign witnessed the final disintegration of the organized Tory party which had remained a marked and clearly recognizable feature in politics under George II, its members becoming scattered all through the political spectrum of the House — among the independents, among the members of the court circle, and among the followings of the various political factions. This development reflects the fact that, with the ghost of Jacobitism finally laid, a basic political consensus anchored upon the settlement of 1689 now united all the men in public life. From this time forward, right through to 1815, virtually all those engaged in politics were 'Whigs'. All accepted common basic assumptions about constitutional theory and practice, a fact superficially masked in public debate by the efforts of discontented politicians to magnify molehills into mountains in an attempt to demonstrate their constitutional purity as against their successful rivals. The historian here faces a real difficulty of nomenclature, for to accept at their own valuation the claims of the friends of Rockingham, or of Charles Fox, or of the second Earl Grey, that they were the Whigs, is by implication to deny to their opponents a political character which they continued to claim to the end of the period covered by this volume.[5] Many passages in parliamentary speeches and correspondence suggest the artificiality of the distinction which men like Fox sought to make between themselves as 'Whigs' and their opponents as 'Tories', that is, champions of prerogative power against the liberty of the subject; few of them more clearly than that in which Fox himself animadverted in 1794 against the impending junction of the magnates of his party with Pitt's ministry: 'Our old Whig friends are many of them worse Tories than even those whom they have joined.'[6] What Fox meant in this context by 'Tory' is perfectly clear, but his definition was not one to which the Duke of Portland and his friends would have subscribed. To Fox Pitt was 'Tory' because he had come to office by royal appointment and with royal support, not — as Fox had claimed to do — by the will of the House of Commons; because he was ready to use police powers to circumscribe liberties, such as liberty of the press and public meeting, which might open the way to revolution; and because he was

[5] See p. 283 below.
[6] *Memorials and Correspondence of Charles James Fox,* ed. Lord John Russell (4 vols., 1853–7) III, p. 70.

committed to war against what Fox persisted in regarding as a revolution in France based on the principle of 1689 — the overthrow of
arbitrary government. Portland still saw himself as a true 'Whig' in
1794 and as joining with Pitt in defending the 'Whig' revolution
settlement of 1689 against the excesses of democracy either at home or
abroad.

The impact of such skilful publicists as Edmund Burke, who very
ably extolled the principles of party in the abstract in order to justify
and benefit the particular party to which he for long belonged, has
tended to obscure for historians the fact that much prejudice against
party existed among the politicians. Detailed examination of the attitudes of MPs in George III's earlier parliaments has prompted the
remark that 'the number of members who in debate disclaimed party
connexions is legion'; nor were these mere disclaimers: many of these
references to party were distinctly pejorative.[7] Men might take up
common attitudes over certain questions such as the American war or
resistance to revolution, but this did not inevitably weld them into a
party. Those who had long voted together on one set of questions out
of personal conviction could easily find themselves on different sides
as the whirligig of time replaced one set of issues with another: conspicuous examples of this occurred in 1783, in 1794, and after 1800. The
fact that in contemporary parlance parties were so often referred to
by the names of their leaders is a true indication of their nature and
reflects the fact that at bottom they were chiefly composed of the
relatives, the friends and the admirers of leading personalities in the
Lords or Commons and were phalanxes to be used in the competitive
struggle for office.

In all ages party leaders have played the party game, partly in order
to attain power, partly to exercise it in what they deem to be the
national interest. In the eighteenth century they had to do so without
being able to appeal to any external sanction of national or majority
will, for the electoral system was not framed to give expression to it,
nor was the great majority of the electors sufficiently politically
sophisticated to express it. At the most, in times of crisis elections
could produce momentary vehement expressions of disapproval, as
was the case in 1784 and in 1807. But the normal primary task of the
electorate was seen as being to choose good men who would look after
the nation's interest, and this did not necessarily entail favouring
candidates who stood on one side or another over great political
issues. Through two generations of political life the followers of the
Marquis of Rockingham and of Charles Fox sought to overcome party
impotence by trying to identify their following with a single, simple,

[7] Sir Lewis Namier and John Brooke, *The History of Parliament. The House of Commons,
1754–1790* (3 vols., 1964) I, p. 192.

favourable political cause — defence of liberty, and opposition to the
power of the crown and to secret advisers. They never achieved sufficient credibility. Their efforts availed them nothing, and it was not as
a result of these appeals that first the one and then the other secured
brief tenures of office and power.

This absence of an external sanction for their performance
provides one explanation of the fact that the role of parliamentary
oppositions was inevitably conducted under conditions which were
frustrating and made it difficult to sustain the constitutional claims of
their proponents. In addition, it was out of the question for any particular group of politicians to aspire to a party following which would
extend to a majority of the House of Commons. In the 1760s only
about a quarter to a third of the members of the House were attached
to parties, and as late as 1807 the number had increased to only about
half. Even if the groupings in opposition were more numerous than
the parties in the government, which was often the case, the former
could not in normal circumstances command enough support from
the non-party sections of the House. The phalanx of minor office-
holders and courtiers would support the king's ministers as a matter of
course, and a large number of the independent country gentlemen
were likely to do the same. Only wholly exceptional circumstances
might produce a concurrence of groupings and break down the
normal independent support for government in such a way as to place
opposition leaders in a commanding situation. Without this they
could not establish a position compelling the king to turn to them by
blocking off support in Parliament for any rival party. If this exceptional situation did arise, then the opposition was still faced with the
difficulty that 'storming the closet' ran counter to fundamental
assumptions about the working of the constitution which were widely
held in parliamentary circles: the success of the Fox—North coalition
of 1783 in achieving this made them what one county MP afterwards
described as 'the just object of public indignation.'[8]

Working under all these handicaps parliamentary oppositions
during the reign of George III, as in that of his grandfather, had a
hard row to hoe, and under normal circumstances a confident monarch and a competent and reasonably lucky administration, secure
in the support of the independents and of the court circle (whom
Rockingham opprobiously described as Swiss — i.e. mercenaries),
would bid them defiance. The one sort of disaster which could upset
this situation was stress or humiliation in war. George II had been thus
thwarted in 1746 and 1756, and George III was likewise in 1782 and

[8] Sir G. A. W. Shuckburgh to William Pitt, 23 Apr. 1788, cited in Sir Lewis Namier and
John Brooke, *The History of Parliament. The House of Commons, 1754—1790* III, p. 437.

1783, but on all these occasions the normal equilibrium soon restored itself. Paradoxically, these circumstances may have given rise to another, in some ways more valid self-justification of opposition, that of acting as a watchdog over the administration and securing the correction or the rejection of unwise measures. Government pamphleteers, while condemning what they described as factious conduct, agreed that opposition could act usefully as a restraint. In the 1790s the Foxites on a number of occasions defended their activities in an apparently hopeless opposition, on the ground that they alone afforded any prospect of checking excesses of power exercised by the executive and of maintaining the balance of the constitution. Such pleas may have provided a psychological boost for Fox's followers, though to an ambitious man like Fox they were sour grapes indeed.[9]

Paradoxically also, apparently for built-in reasons, opposition became less successful after 1760 than it had been in the reigns of George I and George II. It may be plausibly suggested that the last success of the old-style opposition came in 1767, when the Bedford party secured its price for entry into the Grafton administration. The impotence of opposition has sometimes been attributed to the greater strength of character of George III by comparison with his predecessors; but this, and other explanations so far given, overlook a number of other factors. Some of these were purely political − notably the tendency of oppositions to run counter to national patriotic sentiment in time of war. But there were also factors of an institutional kind. One seems to have been, that after 1760 oppositions tended to become more broadly based, to include larger numbers of people, and to be involved with issues of greater concern. All these developments worked to arrest the pattern of political activity which before 1760 had led to small groups of malcontents forcing their way into office, usually in coalition with their former opponents. Possibly another decisive factor in this change of pattern was the disappearance of the old Tory party during the early 1760s. That party had been made use of time and time again by dissident Whig groups in order to push their way into office, while its members, politically proscribed, had scarcely any chance of obtaining office themselves and certainly not as a party. The absence after 1760 of Tory cannon fodder for Whig political battles perhaps helps to explain both the growing ineffectiveness of small opposition parties and the tendency of a single larger one to recruit a substantial rank and file of its own: the pawns in the game had to be obtained in some other way, since the Tories were no longer to hand. Indeed some former Tories became absorbed in self-styled 'Whig' opposition groups of the 1760s and 1770s: an MP like William

[9] See, for example, A. S. Foord, *His Majesty's Opposition, 1714−1830* (Oxford, 1964), pp. 322, 411.

Dowdeswell, right-hand man of the Marquis of Rockingham, no longer had a 'Tory' identity by 1770. But the politicians who recruited a larger opposition party paid a price: they might make too many demands to be acceptable. Thus, if in some ways opposition became more formidable, in others it became less powerful after the accession of George III.

III

'In a Christian Commonwealth the church and the state are one and the same thing, being different integral parts of the same whole.'[10] These words of Edmund Burke in 1792 sum up the view of the Established Church held by most reflective men in eighteenth-century England. Church and state were inseparably wedded together, each providing an essential support for the other, and both together furnishing the framework within which men might lead a godly life according to their Creator's will. All European tradition and experience pointed to the inevitability of this sort of arrangement − one which, in English experience particularly, seemed to be hallowed by the Reformation and the religious settlement of the sixteenth century and by the Revolution Settlement at the end of the seventeenth. Burke's comment was made at a time when experimentation with secular states lacking ecclesiastical establishments in North America had scarcely begun and could not compel attention by successful example. The grounds for doubt which lay within British − as distinct from English − example hardly obtruded themselves upon public attention. And yet there lurked an inherent contradiction in the circumstance that within the single British polity established in 1707 there existed not one but two established churches, different to some extent in their theology and still more different in their form of government. If Ireland, still a separate kingdom up to 1801, did not also present a contradiction, it did furnish an anomaly. A hundred years after the Revolution Settlement the bulk of the population still clung to the Roman Catholic faith, and the established Protestant Episcopal Church, in communion with the Church of England, commanded the loyalty of less than one sixth of the Irish people.

George III, subscribing as he did to the conventional belief in the

[10] Quoted in N. Sykes, *Church and State in England in the eighteenth century* (Cambridge, 1934), p. 379.

Church's role, took very seriously his duty to maintain it and displayed a keen interest in its leadership and vitality. He showed constant concern to secure the right men for the episcopate and to ensure that they performed their duties. But the amount that a royal gadfly might do was limited: the Church suffered from various inbuilt short-comings which were to require far greater pressures to remove during the course of the following century. Aristocratic insistence on a share of the plums was perhaps the least serious. A number of the cadets from noble families proved conscientious prelates and effective administrators, and there was still room for able directors of lower degree like Blomfield and Porteus and distinguished scholars of humble origin such as Warburton and Hurd. This was as well, for a burden of leadership fell on the episcopate all the greater because the suspension of the Convocations, which continued throughout George III's reign, deprived the Church of any dynamic impulse from the lower ranks of the clerisy. The political demands on a bishop's time were a serious disadvantage. Six to eight months' residence in London each year during the parliamentary session was almost *de rigueur*, leaving only four or five summer months for visits to sees. Episcopal supervision inevitably was less effective than it needed to be.

At parish level the great fault was clerical non-residence. No less than 7,358 incumbents were recorded as non-resident from the total of 11,194 benefices returned in 1809, and local studies suggest that for some time the figure had been getting worse. The situation was not quite so bad as the bare numbers suggest, for these conceal such circumstances as the holding in plurality of neighbouring small parishes which, in point of size, were mere hamlets incapable of pro-ducing a livelihood for a clergyman. While such instances did not seriously affect clerical ministry, the Church did accept a wide range of excuses for non-residence — school-mastering, university fellow-ships, chaplaincies to the great, membership of cathedral chapters — which were sometimes occasions of abuse, and had harmful effects. Over a fifth of the Devon parishes investigated in 1779 were in the care of resident stipendiary curates, a class of cleric generally among the most underpaid and overworked. About 1809 over a thousand parishes were without resident pastoral care. The clerical impact on parish life was well below the level that the bishops thought desirable, not merely in respect of the holding of services, but in regard to the multifarious activities of the clergy in relation to charities, sick-visiting, moral policing, unofficial arbitration of disputes, and educa-tion. To this problem another was added in parts of the north of England by the much larger geographical extent of many parishes and by the great increase in urban populations. The holder of a bene-fice could not possibly keep in touch with so many people; yet the obvious remedy, the creation of new parishes, owing to considerations of property rights, required legislation, and before 1815 there was no prospect of action on an effective scale.

In the later eighteenth century the mainstream theology of the Church still bore the scars of the Deist controversy, and had not wholly escaped the influence of ideas of 'natural religion' which it had been combating for the past two generations. One consequence of the persistence of Latitudinarianism was the growth of discontent over the Liturgy and the Thirty-Nine Articles, both among those like Archdeacon Blackburne, whose rational cast of mind drew them in the direction of Unitarianism, and a larger group who, while holding on to the essentials of Trinitarian belief, wished to render the doctrines of the Church less exclusive. Although the full Deist or Unitarian implications were rejected by mainstream Anglicanism, nevertheless 'natural religion' entered as a kind of bedrock into its theology, affecting the tone both of intellectual discussion and of the common approach of the clergy. The expositions of that leading thinker William Paley drew into harmony the rationalistic elements of 'natural religion' deriving from observations of natural phenomena and religion as revealed in the New Testament writings. Such theology combined acceptance of miracles in the past with a present which was ordered and predictable. It set at a distance the immanence of the divine, the idea of constant supernatural involvement in human affairs. Paley believed that credal formulas and articles of subscription should be as few and all-embracing as possible. His system also included other concepts typical of his generation – a belief in divine beneficence, which led in turn to virtual rejection of the doctrine of original sin and to the idea that the purposes of Christian faith included the promotion of happiness, in this world and the next.

The rational and formalistic tone thus imposed on the Church failed to satisfy a minority, whose psychological make-up sought satisfaction in a sense of immediate communion with a transcendent deity, and for whom the experience of believing in – to the point of 'knowing' with a deep inward emotional fervour and certainty – the Christian doctrine of redemption through Christ afforded a sense of personal salvation. This was the 'gospel', the 'vital' religion, which in the interest of 'saving souls' the evangelicals both within and outside the Church were concerned to promote. Fostered particularly at Cambridge by Isaac Milner and Charles Simeon, the Evangelical movement[11] commanded the loyalty of between 300 and 500 clergy by the turn of the century, and was making an effective impact among

---

[11] In this section 'Evangelical' is capitalized where reference is to the movement within the Church of England, otherwise not.

the ranks of the upper-class laity. Among the latter, William Wilberforce, Henry Thornton, and other members of the so-called Clapham Sect exerted a moral influence out of all proportion to their numbers, using it to foster the work of the Church, and to bring about civilizing improvements in the quality of life ranging from the abolition of the slave trade to the suppression of cruel sports.

Evangelicalism within the Church was paralleled by evangelicalism without and was insensibly influenced by it. The chief manifestation of this movement, Wesleyan Methodism, was very much the creation of one man, John Wesley, and was guided by him in almost autocratic fashion up till his death in 1791. More than half — and the more successful half — of Wesley's career as an evangelist lay within the reign of George III. By 1760 his movement was well-established. He saw it as essentially one for supporting, permeating and revitalizing the Church of England, and to the end of his life he firmly rejected the idea of secession. But its implications dismayed many churchmen, who found unacceptable its stress on justification by faith, on salvation and personal divine inspiration, and on the concomitant of this, continued miraculous divine intervention in human affairs. Although prominent clerics and laymen in the Church came to guide their lives by very similar tenets, the tensions between the Church and the Methodists were in the end too great for reconciliation. To many parish clergy the incursions of the zealous but ill-educated lay preachers employed in the Methodist movement were affronts not to be borne. While some Methodist congregations wholeheartedly obeyed Wesley's exhortations to stay within the Church, others, whether owing to the remoteness of the parish place of worship, the presence of an indifferent, bumbling parish clergyman, or some other reason, pressed for their own preachers to administer communion.

While the institutional legacy which Wesley had created thus faced pressures which were to transform it, it had become too strong to be destroyed. At the local level members were firmly drawn together in class and chapel, served by a strong cadre of class leaders, band leaders, helpers, stewards, and schoolmasters. Prosperous leading members of the local societies acted as trustees of chapels and meeting halls. Fellowship was maintained in band-meetings, class-meetings, quarterly meetings, and 'love-feasts', over and above the chapel services. National unity was secured by the annual meetings of the preachers in Conference, first established formally as an advisory body by Wesley in 1784, but after his death taking over a full governing role. In 1795 Conference took the decisive step towards separation from the Church when it decided to permit the celebration of the sacraments in its chapels, though not all societies immediately adopted this practice.

Spiritually Wesleyan Methodism derived its appeal and its strength from the extreme simplicity and optimism of the teaching of its founder. A true child of the Enlightenment, Wesley believed in the perfectibility of man, though unlike the secular philosophers he envisaged this in an intensely Christian sense. Partly for this reason he set his face against Calvinism, which he also distrusted for its latent antinomian tendencies. On one occasion he pronounced on it the dismissive epigram: 'The essence of Calvinism was that a man was damned do what he could or saved do what he would'.[12] Believing all could be saved, he sought, like the Evangelicals within the Church of England, to inculcate in men the immediate sense of personal salvation. Beyond that, his beliefs reflected a total lack of concern with the complexities of theology and biblical exegesis and left aside nine tenths of Christian doctrine to concentrate purely on its soteriological element.

Such an approach made a ready appeal to the poor, the simple and unsophisticated, to those of no or little education, to those who were insecure and sought support of an emotional kind, and it was to these that Wesley principally directed his mission, especially in the large and overpopulated parishes where the influence of the Church of England failed to penetrate; hence its strength both in Yorkshire and among the isolated mining villages of Cornwall. But by the turn of the century, some change in the balance of social composition was becoming apparent. A growing 'middle-class' element was emerging – though whether this came about chiefly because poor men made good and prospered, owing to the moral earnestness and stability of character instilled by membership, is difficult to say. Assured of their place in the next world, and in some cases at least prospering in this, the Methodists, as the drama of the revolutionary era unfolded, became increasingly a conservative force. The more radical groups of Kilhamites and Primitive Methodists, who split away from the main body after Wesley's death, carried off only relatively insignificant numbers. By 1816 the enrolled membership had risen to about 180,000, and Methodists formed an appreciable proportion of the population in some industrial and mining districts. Their rapid increase by no means reflects the totality of the Methodist impact on English society, for their influence upon dissent was considerable. Here they joined hands with Church of England Evangelicalism. This too made its contribution to dissent; for where a noted Evangelical – Henry Venn at Huddersfield is an outstanding instance – had built up a large and enthusiastic congregation, his death or departure sometimes caused a secession into nonconformity by part at least of

[12] Quoted in John Walsh, 'Methodism at the end of the eighteenth century', in *A History of the Methodist Church in Great Britain*, ed. R. E. Davies and E. G. Rupp (1965) I, p. 296.

his following in their search for continued spiritual guidance in the same style.

Earlier in the century the three main nonconformist sects — Presbyterians, Baptists and Congregationalists — had experienced the same diminution of religious zeal as the Established Church, had felt the effects of Latitudinarianism, and had suffered a decline in numbers of congregations and places of worship. The two first had also been influenced by socinianism. In the late eighteenth century some Presbyterian groups preserved their original character, aided sometimes perhaps by an influx of Scotsmen migrating to the south. Others continued to travel along the socinian road, attracting to themselves like-minded elements from both the Baptists and the Church of England and purging these of socinianism in the process. Emphasizing the rationalistic and intellectual approach to religion they thus pursued a course against the grain of the evangelical revival. They made no popular appeal, continued to decline in numbers, and tended to be confined to the intellectual middle class. By 1800 Presbyterianism and the now clearly Unitarian congregations with which it was enmeshed formed a mere twentieth part of dissent.

Both the Baptist and the Congregational churches derived new momentum from the inflow into their ranks of enthusiasts who had been influenced by Evangelicals within the Church of England, by Wesley and his preachers, and by men like George Whitefield preaching an evangelical gospel outside both the Church and Wesleyan movement. Of this influx the Congregationalists seem to have taken the lion's share. Not only did this recruitment have its effect in terms of numbers; but it tended also to temper, though not destroy, the Calvinistic spirit of these sects, and to submerge concern with doctrinal niceties under the pervading current of evangelical enthusiasm. In this respect these churches experienced a change of emphasis which was also discernible in the Church of England. Information about their growing numbers is difficult to assess; possibly by 1811 dissent and Wesleyan Methodism together may have enlisted about one in 10 of the population of England and Wales. Like the Methodists the Baptists and Congregationalists tended to carry a disproportionate weight in certain areas of the country, particularly the urban parts of Yorkshire and Lancashire, where the defective parish organization of the Church of England left much opportunity for infiltration.

Their growth led to a renewed collision with the Church. Dissenters once again began to press for legal concessions. In the early 1770s they sought the release of nonconformist ministers from the obligation to subscribe to the Thirty-Nine Articles, and in 1779 Parliament conceded their case by an Act substituting a declaration of acceptance of the Bible as the basis of Christian faith. In the late 1780s agitation was unsuccessfully renewed with the object of securing the repeal of the Test and Corporation Acts.[13] Both campaigns were spearheaded by the socinian Presbyterians, whose unitarian views received no legal protection under the Toleration Act. But the counter-revolutionary atmosphere of the years after 1790 not only blocked any concession but raised the spectre of harassment under other existing legislation, especially for those sects which relied partly on itinerant preaching. Magistrates, an increasing number of whom were Church of England clergy, began to refuse leave to preachers to take the declaration of 1779, to refuse the issue of licences to preach, and to evoke the Conventicle Act and the Five Mile Act against any who sought to carry on a mission without a licence. Eventually in 1811 and 1812 the influence of the Evangelicals in Parliament was thrown into the scale to end this campaign and secure the repeal of both Acts. In 1813 another statute extended the provisions of the Toleration Act to Unitarians.

Both within the Church and among the dissenters the evangelical spirit gave a powerful impulse to educational and missionary enterprise. In the years just after the French Revolution there was much effective inter-denominational co-operation over Sunday Schools, but rivalry between the two groups soon soured this relationship, and by 1810 the Church's National Society and the dissenters' Royal Lancastrian Society (later the British and Foreign Schools Society) had gone their separate ways. Wesleyans began organizing foreign missions from about 1787, the Baptist Missionary Society was formed in 1792, and the London Missionary Society, predominantly Congregational, in 1795. In 1799 Anglicans set up the organization which eventually in 1812 became the Church Missionary Society. Concern with the situation in England gave rise to the inter-denominational Religious Tract Society (later the British and Foreign Bible Society) in 1799.

A Roman Catholic community of some 80,000 survived in the 1760s, heavily concentrated in certain regions, chiefly in the north, lowland Lancashire (with the heaviest concentration) and Durham County having a Catholic element of over 20 per 1,000 in the population, whilst in five other counties — Northumberland, Yorkshire, Staffordshire, Worcestershire and Monmouth — the proportion was between 11 and 20 per 1,000. Elsewhere Catholics were thinly scattered, and in Wales and the two far south-western counties the numbers were negligible. A mere 10,000 were reported from London in 1767. In much of the south and east Catholicism was 'a

[13] Discussed in its political context, pp. 208–9 below.

nonconformism of the gentry.'[14] Overall there may have been around
1770 perhaps 200 Catholic heads of landowning families, whose
households were foci of congregations. A Catholic proletariat existed
in the north and west, in the 1760s still largely rural but including by
1815 considerable urban industrial elements, for both English
Catholics and Irish Catholic immigrants were attracted into the
growing industrial towns, where ready employment permitted early
marriages and large families, becoming established in districts where
they had hitherto been unknown, particularly south-east Lancashire
and the West Riding. At first the Irish element was relatively small
and does not seem to have outpaced English Catholic natural increase
till about 1810. By 1815 the total Catholic population in England
probably numbered between 200,000 and 250,000 and was much
more varied in social composition than in 1760. The gentry no longer
exerted much influence. Urban Catholics organized and supported
their chapels on a congregational basis — indeed there were many
organizational parallels with Protestant dissent.

By the turn of the century, for a number of reasons, Catholics had
experienced a growing public acceptance, manifested both informally and in changes in the law. Protestant evangelicalism tended to
submerge sectarian distinctions and yield answering echoes to the
spiritual preoccupations at the core of English Catholicism. Dissenters saw a common interest in fighting the remaining legal dis-
criminations imposed by the established order. After 1790 Christian
unity assumed a new importance in face of the menacing atheism of
the French Revolution. Clerical refugees found a sympathetic
welcome, and the dispersal of the English seminary at Douai to new
English centres at Ushaw, Oscott and Ware — slow as these were to
develop — provided native training centres for priests. The changing
attitude of the British political establishment may have been affected
also by its obligation ever since 1763 to come to terms with its responsibilities for the Catholic population of Canada. The tide of crude anti-
Catholic feeling, manifested at a popular level in the petitioning and
in the Gordon Riots of 1780, was on the ebb. Slowly the Catholic
priest's position, and that of his flock, was becoming more secure.
The Catholic Relief Act of 1778 removed the penal restrictions on the
activities of priests and ended other Catholic disabilities, such as the
prohibition on owning land. The further Act of 1791 granted full
religious toleration, though not political rights. With this situation
the Catholic community remained content for the next 16 years. Not
until 1808, with the encouragement of Lords Grey and Grenville, was
the Board of British Catholics established for the purpose of seeking
full political rights. This body made it clear a year or two later, that

[14] John Bossy, *The English Catholic Community, 1570–1858* (1975), p. 100.

Catholics accepted a position, 'as one among a plurality of bodies in a national community which maintained a Protestant establishment', eschewing any ultra-montane views.[15]

Strongly penetrated by Catholicism, Methodism, and by the reviving dissenting sects, the population of northern England, remote from the control of London and from the more solidly Anglican south, and shaken by the upheavals of industrialization, presented a greater degree of religious diversity than was to be found in any other region of the country. Beyond the Scottish border a somewhat similar, though simpler pattern presented itself, of an ecclesiastical regime with its power-centre in the local capital dominant in the nearer counties, but flanked with elements of dissent in the remoter areas of the north and west.

During the earlier Hanoverian period, tarred with the brand of Jacobitism, the Catholic church in Scotland had been almost pressured out of existence, and according to Alexander Webster's population counts in 1755 then had little over 16,000 adherents. The largest surviving concentration, about 10,000, lay around Aberdeen, where it depended on the protection of the Huntleys, and another 5,000 to 6,000 were scattered about parts of the Western Highlands and Islands. Although popular hostility survived longer in more virulent form in Scotland than in England, by the end of the century the community was showing signs of recovery and was being strongly reinforced by an inflow of immigrant Irish heading mainly for the industrial areas of the Clyde valley. The penal laws had for some time been a dead letter, and these were repealed in the year of the outbreak of war with revolutionary France. Estimates put the number of Catholics in Scotland in 1800 at around 30,000, and there was steady growth in the following years.

The Episcopal Church of Scotland also suffered from the self-inflicted wound of identification with Jacobitism. Its clergy were non-jurors, penalized by the Abjuration Oath of 1719, and victims after the '45 of further legal proscription under Acts of 1746 and 1748 which *inter alia* forbade them to hold services anywhere save in their own homes. In 1760 they still recognized the Pretender as their rightful sovereign, and not until the death of the Young Pretender in 1788 did they make their peace with the government in London. After prolonged negotiation the penal laws against them were repealed in 1792, and the 80,000 or so remaining members of their congregations could once again legitimately receive their spiritual services. During the next few years the Scottish bishops directed their attention to the recovery of control over the independent episcopal congregations which had come into existence served by clergy who had received

[15] Bossy, *Catholic Community*, p. 387.

ordination in England or in Ireland. At the Synod of Lawrencekirk in 1804 a formula was devised under which a number of these agreed to reabsorption.

Catholics and Episcopalians accounted for only small minorities of the Scottish people. Presbyterianism was massively predominant north of the Border. However, this did not mean that the great majority of Scotsmen all belonged to one church. From 1714 onward the Established Church had periodically been rent in schism over the question of lay patronage. Popular Presbyterianism insisted upon the overriding right of the congregation, or at least of the elders, to make their own free choice of minister. On the other hand the pressure from heritors, and from the agents of the crown which controlled at least a third and perhaps more of the patronage, was upheld by a narrow majority in the Church's General Assembly. As a result of these conflicts, in 1760 the Church was flanked by a number of break-away groups. The Sandemanians, who had separated off in the 1720s, condemned the church–state link laid down in the covenants. Burghers and Anti-Burghers faced each other as two mutually hostile factions of the Secession Church formed in the 1730s, both professing a rigid, puritanical Calvinism increasingly out of touch with the mid-eighteenth-century Scottish Enlightenment. The 'Relief Presbytery', which took formal shape in 1761, by contrast retained a markedly evangelical character stamped upon it by its founder, Thomas Gillespie. Its doctrinal positions remained very close to the moderate stance adopted by the Established Church.

This last was strongly influenced for much of the second half of the eighteenth century by the party known as the Moderates, which was headed by the historian William Robertson until his resignation from the General Assembly in 1780. Recent writers have emphasized that this party's control of the Assembly was always precarious and breaking down by the 1780s. Nevertheless, the guidance it gave to the Church set a stamp on it for over a generation. Its leaders had responded with enthusiasm to the learning of the European Englightenment, and Robertson himself achieved a European reputation. They fostered a latitudinarian outlook somewhat similar to that which had rather earlier overtaken the Church of England. While they were careful not to challenge the central position in the Church's system of the Westminster Confession, they tended to gloss over many of its implications in practice, and it has been observed that their somewhat isolated theological stance inhibited them from making any striking contribution to religious thought. Their writings and sermons eschewed the full-blooded Calvinism of earlier days, and their critics nursed not wholly unfounded suspicions that some of them were unsound on various central tenets of faith. In general they were impatient of the amount of attention paid to what they regarded as dogmatic trivialities. Like the English Latitudinarians they concerned themselves with 'placid addiction to duty and freedom from enthusiasm',[16] and they adopted a purely legalistic stance over the question of lay patronage: since this was the law, the law should be obeyed. In their eyes it had the advantage of securing the presentation of cultured and liberal-minded ministers like themselves, to the exclusion of the rabid Calvinists who were more to the public taste. By exerting their influence in favour of a church which was cool and rational in spirit and which had abandoned the puritanical censoriousness of old-fashioned Calvinism, the Moderates made it acceptable to the cultivated upper ranks of the Scottish laity, themselves steeped in the ideas of the Enlightenment, and thus — at least for the time being — bridged a potentially damaging gap between the outlooks of the upper and lower classes of Scottish society. In the process the Establishment was also made less unattractive to the episcopalian gentry who were forced in its direction when their old church came under the hammer of repressive legislation after the '45. Although the Moderates were faced in the General Assembly by a Popular party reflecting dogmatic Calvinism of the more perfervid sort and alert to guard against the incursion of Deism or socinianism, this party itself was checked from excess by a sense of the need to keep the Church to some extent in step with the intellectual spirit of the age.

The ecclesiastical polity which was the outcome of this balance of forces was in some respects ill-fitted to meet the strains thrust upon it by social change at the end of the eighteenth century. Like the Church of England it lacked proselytizing zeal. It was also similarly hampered by its traditional parish organization, which could not be readily adapted in response to movements and increases of population. The first of these weaknesses was compounded by an overconcern with dogma among those of less latitudinarian spirit, an attitude which had once come into collision with Wesley's simple creed and had drawn his fire with the remark: 'They knew too much, therefore they could learn nothing.'[17] In consequence, as industrialization brought social change in the middle and later years of George III's reign, the Established Church faced problems of competition from the independent churches similar to those encountered by the Church of England from Methodism and dissent, and in face of popular evangelicalism it showed a similar resentment. When in the late 1790s Charles Simeon and Rowland Hill came to preach the evangelical word in Scotland, and in their wake the brothers James and

---

[16] Andrew L. Drummond and James Bulloch, *The Scottish Church, 1688–1843. The Age of the Moderates* (1973), p. 65.
[17] Quoted in William Ferguson, *Scotland: 1689 to the Present* (1968), p. 229.

Robert Haldane set up an evangelizing mission and began to train lay preachers to serve it — they claimed to have 200 in service by 1805 — the first response of the General Assembly was entirely negative. In 1799 it passed an act restricting preaching to ministers and forbidding them to hold ministerial communion with any not qualified to accept a presentation to a parochial charge. Inevitably the result was to foster the forces of dissent. The efforts of the Haldanes led before long to the creation of both the Scottish Baptist and the Scottish Congregational Churches, and the Congregational Union of Scotland was formed in 1813. North of the Border as well as south of it, the situation towards the end of George III's reign was one of vigorous independent expansion and proselytizing activity, and of increasing challenge to the Established Church.

3 From Bute to North: Safety Abroad and Order at Home

I

In 1760 events were reaching a climax in the great conflict commonly known as the Seven Years War, but from the British point of view more accurately to be described as the Nine Years War for Empire which had broken out in the Ohio valley in 1754. In effect two wars were running concurrently. In the first Frederick the Great of Prussia fought for the existence of his kingdom against the combined forces of Russia, Sweden and Austria. In the second Great Britain, together with Hanover and its little group of west German allies, faced the French at sea, in the New World, in the Indian sub-continent and in Westphalia. In Germany the British and Hanoverians, as allies and auxiliaries of Frederick, stood back to back with him, each defending the other's rear. After the heavy Prussian defeat at Kunersdorf the previous year Frederick's fortunes were almost at their lowest ebb. By contrast the British had established an overwhelming supremacy over the French at sea, had liquidated the French empire in Canada, had stabilized a line of defence against the French armies east of the lower Rhine, and were poised to seize what remained of the French colonies in the Caribbean. At this stage British war aims embraced the annexation of Canada and the total exclusion of the French from the Newfoundland fishery, and the great war minister William Pitt attached the greatest importance to the second of these objects on the assumption that it would deal a fatal blow to the basis of French naval power thereafter.

French ministers attached a similar crucial importance to the Newfoundland fishery. It was mainly on this issue that peace negotiations hung fire during 1761, while in a further campaign the British took Belle Isle, to be held a pledge for the restoration of Minorca. French obstinacy was encouraged by hopes of assistance from Spain, whose new ruler, Charles III, was bitterly anglophobe, and nursed a series of grievances against Britain. Spain resented the British presence in Gibraltar, the British claim to the restitution of Minorca by

France, the existence of British logwood cutters' establishments in Honduras, and the favourable position British merchants enjoyed under existing Anglo-Spanish commercial treaties. Charles III also coveted a share in the Newfoundland fishery, and as France's empire crumbled under British blows, he feared for the safety of Spanish provinces in the New World. By October 1761 the threat of Spanish intervention in the war was becoming clear, and Pitt sought his colleagues' consent to a pre-emptive strike. On their refusal he resigned, only to be vindicated in the event, for early in January the British cabinet judged it necessary to declare war on Spain. During the campaign season of 1762 British military and naval might, now at its peak, smashed through Bourbon resistance to an almost unprecedented series of triumphs. In the Caribbean the British seized French Martinique, Grenada, and the neutral islands, and also Spain's leading island base at Havana in Cuba. From India an expedition was launched against the Philippines, and Spain had also lost Manila before the end of the summer.

In Germany the British and allied force maintained its position and the whole situation was changed early in 1762 by the death of the Tsaritsa Elizabeth of Russia and the accession successively of Peter III, and then of Catherine II as reigning empress. Russia and Sweden made their peace with Prussia, and Austrian enthusiasm for the war on Frederick began to be quenched by fears that Russia might enter the struggle on his side. In London the new first minister, Lord Bute, and his colleagues seized this opportunity to cut their financial commitments to Prussia, with all the more reason as help now had to be given to Portugal. The French and Spanish were well aware of the great value to Britain of Lisbon as a channel of export trade to Brazil and southern parts of Spanish America which brought in large returns of specie, and the British were bound to support this new front when Spanish troops moved over the Protuguese frontier in April 1762.

The partial collapse of France's eastern alliance system together with the British successes in the Caribbean and western Pacific, left the Bourbon powers no alternative but to submit, and peace terms with both were hammered out at Paris during the autumn of 1762. British sentiment was moving steadily in favour of peace. The mounting war debt caused growing anxiety; and the country's triumphs were so great there seemed no further objective for which to fight. In London a key role was held by Bute, who played off the hawks and doves in the cabinet against each other, and sometimes went behind the back of his colleagues in giving advice about concessions to the Duke of Bedford, the British negotiator at Paris. The Carthaginian terms which Pitt afterwards declared should have been imposed were not exacted, but both France and Spain paid heavily for their defeat. France resigned her rights in Canada and in what had remained of French Acadia, and also the Mobile district of Louisiana, east of the River Iberville. Cutting her losses in North America, she handed over the rest of Louisiana to Spain in compensation for the loss of Florida which the British demanded in return for the restoration of Cuba. Britain restored the chief French sugar islands, Martinique and Guadeloupe but annexed Grenada and the Grenadines, and the French abandoned their rights in the so-called neutral islands. French fishing rights in Newfoundland waters were conceded, together with the two islets of refuge, St Pierre and Miquelon, but Spanish pretensions in this area were brusquely rebuffed. Spain was pledged to pay a ransom for the return of Manila, and required to restore border districts seized from Portugal during the campaign of 1762. Her demands for a recasting of British commercial privileges in a new treaty were refused, and the old advantageous terms restored. The British agreed to destroy fortifications on the coast of Honduras, but Spain was required to concede the rights of British logwood cutters to do their business there and to set up permanent installations. In return for Belle Isle Britain recovered the valuable Mediterranean naval base of Minorca. France received back her West African trading centre of Goree but was obliged to cede her settlement on the Senegal river. In India the French trading settlements were restored, but France undertook not to build forts or maintain troops in Bengal and to recognize potentates friendly to Britain as rulers of the Deccan and the Carnatic. In west Germany the French yielded up occupied areas of Hanover and of allied German states and withdrew from Prussia's Rhenish territories, and British good offices helped to secure a peace settlement between Frederick and his remaining enemy, Austria, which was completed at Hubertusburg in February 1763. The representatives of England, France and Spain signed the final Peace of Paris on 10 February 1763.

In Parliament the government was fiercely denounced for deserting Frederick of Prussia, but this charge can scarcely be sustained. In fact the ministers could hardly be expected to underwrite plans for further aggressive warfare in eastern Europe, and the mature judgement on this episode is that, 'if there were any desertion in 1762, it was on the part of Frederick, who left the British for the Russians before Bute left him'.[1] His rear in west Germany had been protected up to the last.

It was not therefore ministerial perfidy, as has sometimes been suggested, which caused the diplomatic isolation of Great Britain in

[1] Frank Spencer, 'The Anglo-Prussian breach of 1762: an historical revision', *History* XLI (1956), p. 108.

the years after 1763. The simple truth was that the war left a legacy of irreconcilable animus on the part of the Bourbon states, and no other power in Europe had a compelling natural interest in a British alliance. Sixty years before, it had been the overwhelming military threat from Louis XIV which had drawn the Dutch (natural rivals) and the Austrians into a lasting combination with Great Britain. By mid century that threat no longer existed. After 1763 various British politicians, and even George III himself, hankered after the traditional Austrian alliance to counterbalance French power. But this was no longer practicable, for the Austrians saw their best security in a French alliance, the safest guarantee of Austrian possessions in the Low Countries and in northern Italy, also carrying assurances that the Turks would not cause trouble on their Balkan frontiers. Since 1748 the Dutch had been of no mind to expose themselves to French invasion for purely British interests. Secure in an understanding with Russia after 1763 Prussia had no common ground on which to act with the British, and in the interests of peace preferred to oppose their intermeddling in Europe. During the mid 1760s when first the Rockingham ministry and then Chatham made overtures for a renewal of the Anglo-Prussian accord, it was quickly made clear that Berlin had no interest in the proposal.

The other major continental power was Russia, and for years one British administration after another pursued the will-o'-the-wisp of a Russian alliance. Superficially such an outcome seemed 'natural' and had its attractions. Great Britain and Russia had a number of interests in common. The complementary nature of their economies was such that not even the circumstances of their fighting on opposite sides in the recent war had caused trade relations to be broken off between them. For Britain Russia was an indispensable source of naval stores and a valuable market for manufactures. After 1763 Russia shared Britain's enmity towards France, finding herself in collision with the French client states of Sweden, Poland, and Turkey, and nursing ambitions which led to conflict in particular with the second and third. The Empress Catherine II herself was strongly Anglophile, and apart from this a fund of goodwill towards Britain existed in Russia, fostered by the constant trickle of naval officers and agriculturalists under training who came to England in the 1760s and 1770s.[2]

Nevertheless an alliance was not secured. To some extent the personalities and the state of politics in London were responsible for this failure. Foreign statesmen, watching the instability of administrations and the rowdiness of British internal politics, rather naturally

[2] A. G. Cross, '*By the Banks of The Thames.*' *Russians in eighteenth century Britain* (Newtonville, Mass., 1980).

assumed, though in this they were wrong, that Britain suffered from a lack of continuity in foreign policy or even an absence of any settled principles of policy at all. Ministerial hands in London were indeed tied by particular popular prejudices and preconceptions voiced both in Parliament and outside − hatred of France and resistance to any policy likely to increase the burden of taxation. Foreign observers were also seriously misled by the wild denunciation of ministerial incompetence, corruption and secret influence by opposition politicians. From Chatham downwards their behaviour was factious in the extreme, and the French statesman Vergennes declared that he blushed for humanity at the folly which identified as virtue and patriotism action he considered 'le comble du crime et de la trahison'.

British ministers responsible for diplomatic business during the 1760s and early 1770s rarely commanded much respect in their own right. The Earl of Halifax was worn out, the Duke of Grafton young and inexperienced, interested in little but the affairs of the turf, the Earl of Shelburne inactive, confused, and indifferent, Lord Weymouth was drunk and indolent, leaving the envoys abroad almost entirely without guidance, and General Henry Seymour Conway suffered from a constitutional inability ever to make up his mind. The Earl of Rochford was the only real professional among them, a career diplomat with knowledge of Europe, but volatile and indiscreet. The Earl of Sandwich at the beginning of this period and the Earl of Suffolk later were business-like and reasonably efficient, but lacking in the experience, knowledge or imaginative grasp that would enable them to understand the designs of foreign courts. European ministers and envoys were not always very understanding on their side either; but in diplomacy success goes to the parties who make the fewest mistakes, and in this period the British made more than their fair share. It was essential to understand the general principles of policy as well as the particular views of individuals at foreign courts, and in this respect George III's ministers sometimes displayed an almost risible naïvety.

But the failure to make a Russian alliance also rested on broader grounds, and however obtuse ministers may have been, it is arguable that this failure best served British interests. The British sought help in curbing the Bourbon powers, but it was only in the Baltic that Russia could play any useful role in support of this aim, and her own interests in that region dictated that, regardless of any formal alliance, she would be working for the same ends as London. But after 1763 Russian preoccupations lay further to the east and south-east, in areas scarcely of concern to the British government. In 1763 Catherine II was anxious to strengthen her influence in Poland upon the next vacancy of the throne, by excluding the Saxon line and securing the election as king of her own candidate, but the British were disinclined to pour out money for electoral purposes in Poland, especially at such a time of financial stringency as that which followed the Seven Years War. Even more of an obstacle was the Russian insistence in the early 1760s, that the British must pledge themselves to give support in the event of a war with Turkey. Such a commitment seemed to have no connection with the balance against the Bourbons in western Europe, nor had the British government any comparable obligation it could press upon the Russian court in return for undertaking it. The proposals also raised fears (though the loss would have been no great one) that such remaining trade as the British still carried on in the Levant would be extinguished if they took a step likely to provoke Turkish enmity. This British indifference to Russian interests was reinforced in the early 1770s by apprehensions about the increase in Russia's strength, partly in consequence of her victories in the Russo-Turkish war of 1768, but still more after the first Polish partition of 1772. At Stockholm the British co-operated effectively if not always successfully with the Russians to combat French influence. At Copenhagen they set out to do so, but more often than not, owing to ignorance of local conditions, found themselves at cross purposes with St Petersburg. Their efforts had a dual motive. French influence was always to be countered wherever possible; but secondly, co-operation was seen as a possible way of smoothing the path towards an Anglo-Russian alliance on British terms. By the early 1770s the first of these considerations was losing some of its force and was being superseded by anxiety about Russian preponderance in the Baltic region. Two other circumstances stood in the way of the alliance. British ministers were adamantly opposed to entering into agreements to pay subsidies to foreign powers in peacetime. This was an insuperable obstacle to Russian proposals that the two powers should share the expense of dominating Sweden by a wholesale corruption of Swedish politicians. Ministers could conveniently plead that Parliament would never grant funds for such purposes; but in fact they themselves believed in the light of experience that allies who were subsidised in peacetime were likely to desert the ranks in the hour of need. Lastly all negotiations foundered on the belief of both British and Russians that their help was indispensable to the other party and could be had on their own terms: either side would have felt it was losing face if it conceded the demands of the other.

Nevertheless for most of the decade after 1763 British relations with Russia were more than cordial, and the common interest they shared in mutual trade was cemented by a commercial treaty of 1766. British naval circles took a paternal interest in the infant Russian navy, provided training facilities for its officers, and even furnished a squadron commander during the Russo-Turkish war. The movement of Russian naval units to the Mediterranean in 1768 and 1769 was greatly aided by the port facilities afforded in England, and their operations against the Turks were protected from French interference by threats of British naval intervention. However this could promise little in the event of a future clash between Britain and France, especially in view of the fact that after 1763 it was settled French policy not to combine a British war with one in Germany. Thus successive British governments vainly strove to find an ally on the assumption that Hanover would again need defending in a future Anglo-French war, while, unknown to them, the object of their policy had ceased to be of any relevance.

British front-line defence against France and Spain remained the fleet, and neither power was allowed to forget it. Towards France British policy was clearly defined as one of unremitting suspicion and hostility, and a determination, only once betrayed by incompetent statecraft, not to let France forge ahead in the race for power and influence. As already explained, the weapons of mercantilist policy were deployed to deny France commercial advantage and if possible to undermine the prosperity of her West Indian colonies, and direct trade with France was kept to a minimum on the assumption that France would gain more in war potential from such commerce than Britain.[3] Spain was exempted from this economic boycott, because the access to South American markets by way of her entrepôts at Seville and elsewhere was too valuable to be sacrificed. Within a short time Anglo-Spanish trade had regained something like the level which had obtained before the hostilities of 1762.

On three occasions the Grenville ministry brandished the big stick of naval supremacy to keep its recent enemies in awe. By a piece of unexampled obtuseness, the French naval commander D'Estaing provoked an incident in 1764 by removing British settlers from Turks Island on the ground that this speck of land at the east of the Bahamas belonged to Spain. Almost immediately afterwards the British government learned of action by the local Spanish authorities in Honduras against the British logwood cutters whose rights had only recently been reaffirmed in the Treaty of Paris. Both incidents provoked stern warnings that they were prejudicial to the good relations between the respective courts, the reinstatement of settlers and restoration of their property were demanded, and a naval reinforcement was sent to the West Indies to secure both these objects. A month or so later the French were again called to account for the misdeeds of their local agents, this time on the West Africa coast, where encroachments

[3] See pp. 18–19 above.

were being made at the mouth of the River Gambia, which the British regarded as their preserve. Once again a naval squadron was sent out with orders to take action by force if necessary against French frigates and troops understood to be establishing themselves in the area. Ministers believed that to show weakness in this instance would be fatal and only invite more serious detriment to British interest. 'All Europe has its eyes fixed upon us to observe how we bear that insult', Sandwich remarked of the Turk's Island affair, adding that the French would shape their future conduct according to the spirit or the weakness shown by Great Britain. Threats and menaces, he believed, were the best way to ward off a war.

This was a principle lost sight of during 1768, when government was in the weaker hands of the Duke of Grafton and his colleagues. Consequently the French were able to steal a march in Corsica which perhaps no other administration of the time would have tolerated. Ministers were slow to credit early rumours about the French purchase of the island from the Genoese who had failed to put down rebellion there for a number of years. When French intentions did become clear, a momentary warning was conveyed by the British ambassador that such an extension of territory could not be 'a matter of indifference' to France's neighbours, and at one stage in 1769 Grafton and his colleagues did cause hesitation and delay at Paris by ordering the manning of ships in reserve. But no determined attempt was made to warn off the French by a sustained campaign of diplomatic representations and threats of naval action, which would almost certainly have kept Corsica out of French hands without a war. The Duke of Bedford was no longer in office but, as in the years 1763–5, his influence, exerted through members of his party in the cabinet, was strongly in favour of conciliation with France. British naval experts gave it as their opinion that occupation of Corsica would be of little help to French naval power, and Grafton and his colleagues rejected the idea of challenging France on the ground that Corsica was not worth a war. The real measure of their incompetence lay in their failure to realize that the French were even less anxious for war and would climb down in face of pressure, and that their inaction would provoke the contempt of all the European courts and encourage the French to further challenges. An opportunity was missed of close and cordial co-operation with Catherine II, which would have significantly raised Britain's reputation and worthiness as an ally in Russian eyes. Instead, Catherine's confidence in the British was further lowered, despite the help then being received by her naval forces on their way to the eastern Mediterranean. Nor was she impressed by British attempts to act the mediator on her behalf at Constantinople, at a time when the victories of Russian armies were opening up extensive prospects of territorial expansion in the Black Sea lands.

By contrast North's ministry in the first year of its existence reacted strongly against the Bourbon powers in the crisis which blew up in 1770 over the Falkland Islands. France first among the European powers had established a base and made claim of sovereignty in 1764. In ignorance of this fact a British expedition had explored and set up marks of possession in 1765, as part of a drive to penetrate the hitherto Spanish-monopolized South Pacific. Regarding the French presence as an example which the British would soon emulate, the Spanish government persuaded the French to cede their claim to the islands and attached them for administrative purposes to the provincial government of Buenos Aires. Once the small British detachment in residence at Port Egmont had been located it was ordered to leave, and in 1770 a force of some 400 men was sent to remove the little garrison. The Spanish government considered it was expelling interlopers from its territory. To the British government this appeared an act of hostility against subjects of a friendly power occupying territory under British sovereignty. To demands for redress Spain remained obdurate, and increasingly outspoken threats of war from London were shrugged off in the knowledge that the French were sympathetic — for in the autumn of 1770 the French minister Choiseul had at last carried his warlike preparations to the point at which he believed British power could and should be challenged with a prospect of success.

In December 1770 the British ministers were by no means all enthusiastic for war with Spain, but they had become so cornered by events that a conflict appeared unavoidable. A surrender to the Spanish claims would have ruined them with Parliament and with the country. What saved them was a palace revolution in France. There is little doubt that the undeviating firmness with which they had carried out successive phases of naval mobilization had played a great part in bringing this about. Choiseul fell, the peace party gained the ascendant, and Charles III found that a war with Britain would have to be fought by Spain alone. Both sides were now ready for a compromise, which was rapidly achieved with the help of the good offices of France. North and his colleagues insisted on redress for the insult to the British flag, and required the Spanish to restore the settlement at Port Egmont. But neither side was to recognize any right of sovereignty in the Falklands on the part of the other, and by a secret agreement the British government pledged that its garrison would in due course be withdrawn, though without any undertaking that the islands might not be reoccupied at a later date.

After 1771 there was a short period when an Anglo-French

rapprochement and a new diplomatic alignment were just conceivable. The government headed by D'Aiguillon at Paris and representing the peace party at the French court was genuinely anxious for better relations with Great Britain, and events in eastern Europe were leading at least some British statesmen, and also George III, to look critically at the old diplomatic assumptions. Russian power seemed to be rising to dangerous heights. The Turks were at the empress's feet. In 1772 the first partition of Poland further consolidated her territorial position but at the same time set a new standard of international immorality, and Russian complaisance towards Prussian control of Danzig was particularly disquieting to the British because of possible interference with supplies of timber and naval stores drawn from Polish sources. The government faced with mixed feelings the diplomatic crisis which arose in 1772 over the Swedish king's successful *coup d'état* at Stockholm. His triumph represented the defeat of what the British and Russians had been striving for together for the past 10 years, the ascendancy of the anti-French party in Sweden. The situation seemed full of danger, perhaps appeared more dangerous than it really was. The prospect of a Baltic war into which France would be drawn as the auxiliary of Sweden seemed to present the possible necessity of a British intervention to prevent the establishment of French hegemony. In an effort to contain the crisis the government walked a diplomatic tightrope between Russia and France. On the one hand France was repeatedly advised that the British must react sharply to any French naval rearmament, and everything possible was done to counter Swedish aggressiveness. On the other hand, Russia was warned that she could not count on British assistance in the event of a war. Ministers hoped thus to prevent any Russian escalation of the crisis, though avoiding if possible driving Russia into the arms of France. These manœuvres involved assurances to France at one stage in the early spring that the British would not act if a French army were ferried to Gothenberg to support the Swedes, provided the warships accompanying it did not enter the Baltic. Russia was bluffed with rumours that the British might be on the verge of allying with France and giving her naval support, at the same time as the French were being firmly dissuaded by threats of naval intervention not to send the Toulon squadron against Russian vessels operating in the eastern Mediterranean. By these devious and half-secret manœuvres North and his colleagues may have contributed decisively to the resolution of the crisis, on the one hand by leading the Russians to accept the new situation in Sweden and on the other by preventing the start of a Franco-Russian war at sea. It was not to British interests to see either Russia or France win an ascendancy.

The Swedish crisis, coming on top of the Polish partition, finally ended British interest in a Russian alliance. At the same time it provided no real solid ground for the alternative possibility, an alliance with the ancient enemy, France. Whatever the extent to which the British had shown a limited sympathy towards the French concern with Sweden, throughout the crisis they had sought to confine French action with a high hand by threats of naval mobilization, and both British and European opinion believed in 1773 that the French had given way in face of British threats. Jingoistic pride north of the channel and national resentment south of it were no bases on which politicians in either country could hope to build diplomatic co-operation. The old animosity still prevailed. France and Spain continued to nurse their resentments and fears, and naval supremacy remained the only shield against their enmity.

II

At home the early humiliations followed by the spectacular successes of the Seven Years War had served to damp down political conflict, and at the time of George III's accession the fires of party controversy were burning lower than at almost any time in the eighteenth century. The Pitt–Newcastle coalition formed in 1757 was a 'national' or 'broad-bottom' administration in the fullest sense, for almost all the leading politicians were found a place in it, and it commanded support from the remains of the Tory party, which was soon to lose its separate identity. Up to 1760 the war itself was not a major issue of controversy. When in the next year or two the question how or on what terms to end it began to emerge, this cut right across the government groupings instead of becoming the issue for a party in opposition. Consequently the course of politics was determined more than usual by personalities, and although points of principle eventually arose they bore something of the quality of an artificial encrustation — they did not lie in the grain — and for that reason they proved disappointing in their results to those politicians who sought to exploit them for political action.

George III himself was very much the central political figure at the beginning of the new reign. His initial impact on the political system was partly determined by the fact that, in the preceding two or three years, he and his immediate circle had been almost the only figures in public life excluded from the Pitt–Newcastle 'broad-bottom' and reflecting a discordant attitude over war policy. In the effort to rationalize the bitter and otherwise inexplicable fact of their political impotence, the new king and his favourite, the Earl of Bute, had themselves developed an ideology of a sort, ravelled out of traditional opposition catch-phrases, and deeply coloured by the antipathies that tended to develop between a reigning sovereign and the young heir waiting to step into his shoes. George III had looked on his grand-father, George II, as a figure of contempt, a 'king in chains'. The ministers who surrounded him were regarded as evil men who had 'captured' the king and held him in thrall, in order to exploit the crown's authority to their own benefit. In this unjust caricature of the regime preceding October 1760, the Duke of Newcastle, because of his role as head of the treasury and therefore chief dispenser of patronage, ranked as the leading manipulator of corruption. The reputation of William Pitt the Elder, secretary of state and most suc-cessful British war minister for half a century, was in some respects even more clouded. Allying with Bute in 1755 Pitt had used the prince's court as a stepping stone to office, only to find after a brief and bitter experience that he could not at the same time serve both the king and the heir; thus to George III he appeared in the role of renegade, 'the blackest of hearts' and 'a snake in the grass'.

It was George III's misfortune that he came to the throne too young, without the knowledge of men and affairs which would have enabled him to tread a safe path through the political jungle in which he had to operate. His dedication to his royal duty was beyond ques-tion and made worse the wrenching anxiety about performing it, which both before and for some time after 1760 put him constantly on the rack. He was not highly talented, but he had a respectable endow-ment of abilities. His formal education had been good and left him with a sound taste and a wide if somewhat amateur range of intellec-tual interests. Well grounded in the British system of government and politics he believed that it represented the summit of human political wisdom. But, like even the most perfervid commonwealth man of the age, he saw it menaced on every side by human perfidy, and his responsibility for making it work and preserving it intact terrified him. A profound mistrust and contempt of all the politicians was hardly the best foundation for a harmonious reign. Newcastle was a man of 'dirty arts'; his followers were 'men of the most mercenary views.' Of George Grenville he commented: 'I have never yet met with a man more doubtful or dillitory.' Charles Townshend was 'that vermin', 'so fickle that no man can depend on him', 'the worst man that lives.' Henry Fox was a man 'void of principle', one he would 'rather see perish than at the head of ministry.' Two years after his accession he felt that, Bute apart, the ministry was composed of 'the most abandoned men that ever had those offices'; 'ingratitude, avarice, and ambition are the principles men act by.'

Past writers, viewing this psychological tension against a background of tutorial reports that as a boy the king was slothful and immature, and of his own admissions of hebetude in letters to Bute, have often coupled it with his illnesses in later life and assumed that it sprang from an inherent tendency to mental derangement. This explanation will no longer serve. The boxes of 'undergraduate essays' in the royal archives, written for and corrected by Bute, are evidence that the king's self-accusations should not be taken too seriously. The young prince who soon began the collection of books and pamphlets which became the nucleus of the British Museum library; who found time to talk with the great lexicographer Samuel Johnson; whose scientific curiosity made him the patron of one of the greatest observational astronomers, William Herschel; whose antipathy for radical London politicians like James Sharp melted away in their common enthusiasm for 'ancient musick'; whose conventional but deeply held religious convictions gave him strength and steadfastness in the face of both personal and political crises – in no way suffered from defect of the mind. The malady which on a number of occasions racked his body, and, during later manifestations, also disturbed his intellect, was physical in origin. Porphyria arises from an heritable genetic defect, as a consequence of which the bodily chemical reactions leading to the production of haemoglobin may become interrupted. Porphyrins so released, surging through the bloodstream, act like a poison with devastating effect on the nervous system, causing acute physical suffering and, in the more severe stages producing delirium with loss of self-awareness and self-control. As a young man George III suffered at least two sharp but purely physical attacks of this disease, in 1762 and in 1765. But there was nothing mentally abnormal about him. He brought to his task a sound mind, a keen sense of duty, an upright character and an intensely moral outlook. His weakness lay in the defective training he had been given for understanding the political world in which he must function.

The blame for this lay with his mentor and favourite, the Earl of Bute. Called in by the Princess Dowager of Wales to act as companion and guide to her eldest son when, at 18, he reached his majority, Bute achieved a striking success in establishing a rapport with a young man whose tutors had often found him unresponsive. In some ways he had much to offer. Aged at that time about 45, happily married and with a growing talented family held together by strong ties of family feeling, pious and upright in his personal life, and standing aside from the world of politics because he lacked the financial resources to play a part in public life, Bute had a fair share of intellectual curiosity, partook of the contemporary passion for botanical studies, knew something of his country's history, and not only had a reasonable smattering of learning but, being a Scotsman, also a genuine reverence for it. During the two or three years after he entered the prince's service he put him through a rigorous course in history and public affairs, some of which undoubtedly helped to prepare George III for his future role. But this education suffered from the serious drawback that Bute himself had no experience as a practising politician and substituted for it the prejudices passing for political doctrine which he had first picked up as a companion of George III's father, Frederick, Prince of Wales. He naïvely believed that a reign of virtue should and could replace a reign of vice and corruption. Under his influence the young prince was encouraged to think the worst of his grandfather's ministers and to understand that his task would be to cleanse the Augean stables of corruption. As George III's affection, admiration, and sense of dependence on Bute intensified, nothing seemed more natural, or indeed more necessary, than that Bute should guide him, should indeed take charge of the business, since there appeared to be no one else in political life who could be trusted to carry it out. The pedagogue must turn minister. Bute was not without ambition, nor was he modest enough to judge his capacity for such a task; but if he ever hesitated, he was overborne by the frantic pleadings of his pupil, who felt quite incapable of grappling alone with these responsibilities. Bute's greatest disservice to his master lay in his fostering this attitude of dependence and failing to create in George III some understanding of the merits and the dependability of the other politicians on whom he must rely for the conduct of public affairs. Consequently, in October 1760, Bute, who held the court office of groom of the stole, was immediately brought into the cabinet, and it was made clear that the king would depend heavily on his reports and opinions of what took place at cabinet meetings. A few months later, in order to avoid the appearance of exercising power without responsibility, he was promoted to the northern secretaryship of state. A year later, on the resignation of the Duke of Newcastle, he became head of the treasury and in effect first minister.

Bute was by no means lacking in abilities. No one who follows in detail the peace negotiations in the last year of the Seven Years War can fail to mark the common sense of his attempts to strike a middle course between those who would have driven France to desperate resistance by inordinate demands, and those who were prepared to make extensive — and expensive — concessions in the hope of achieving a peace of conciliation. However, even an extremely able politician suddenly thrust by royal favour from outside the charmed circle of politics into a central role among men who had been ruling the roost for the past several years would have found his task difficult enough, and that of Bute was made yet more intractable by the role the king sought to allot to him and by his own idealistic preconceptions and his defects of character. When George III insisted upon discussing with Bute all material — and many trivial — items of business brought to him by the departmentally responsible ministers before he dared give a yea or nay, and then very often used Bute to convey as his own wish the view that Bute had expressed to him, the ministers were slighted, feeling that Bute was undermining their positions by his engrossment of the royal confidence. Their resentment was kindled further on occasions when Bute intimated it was the king's will that certain things should be done, when it was patent that the decision was really Bute's rather than the king's. Perhaps a man of great tact and charm could have overcome such difficulties; but Bute was singularly lacking in these qualities, and his attempts to speak out for the king because the king lacked the self assurance and suavity to do it for himself perhaps added to the impression of arrogance which he created. Moreover, because Bute had swallowed the guiding assumptions of the Prince of Wales's court about the nature of politics, his own distaste and contempt for the professional politicians was as deeply rooted as that which he had inculcated into the king himself, and this underlying hostility inevitably coloured his personal bearing towards them and was naturally reciprocated. Its most conspicuous manifestation was the campaign by Bute's press hirelings against William Pitt, when the latter accepted a pension and peerage for his wife on retiring from office in October 1761. Rewards justly received for distinguished service were exploited to suggest to Pitt's followers that he was as open to corrupt inducement as anyone in public life. The riposte from Pitt's supporters, led by the witty journalistic frondeur John Wilkes, was a rude experience which did much finally to disillusion Bute about the attractions of public life. The handling of patronage and political management which centred on the treasury, so essential to the oiling of the political wheels, yet so much in conflict with the high ideals of the reign of virtue which he, and under his influence his royal pupil, aspired to create, sickened him — and also the king, witness his outburst in March 1763 against Henry Fox's management of the House of Commons: 'Has this whole winter been anything but a scene of corruption!'[4] As if the dice were not already sufficiently heavily loaded against Bute, it was doubly unfortunate for him that he was a Scotsman, for at the popular level he thus readily became a target for resentment

paranoia about scotch

[4] *Letters from George III to Lord Bute, 1756–1766*, ed. Romney Sedgwick (1939), p. 198.

on national as well as personal grounds.

Nevertheless Bute managed to keep a ministry working for over nine months after he became the head of it, and he did not lack for a majority supporting government business in both Houses of Parliament. His inner weaknesses, not political defeat, brought his career at the treasury to an end. By the beginning of 1763 he was wholly disillusioned about the possibilities of running politics on the high moral level he had predicted before 1760, and was being worn to the verge of a nervous breakdown by the pressure of business and the wrangling animosities he had created on all sides, and not least by the violent hostility of the London mobs. To George III's intense distress he insisted upon resigning in April 1763. For some months the king continued to bombard him with requests for advice, but during the autumn this contact seems to have been brought to an end on the insistence of the ministers, who naturally found it intolerable. With it ended Bute's importance as a leading political figure, though not the shadow which his name continued to cast for much longer over politics.

Of the older political figures in George II's last ministry, Henry Fox and the Duke of Newcastle were both near the end of their effective political careers. Fox had made his bid for the leading place, and had lost to Pitt in the mid 1750s. Thereafter he was content to enjoy the vast profits which an unscrupulous administration of the pay office could provide. His willingness, so contrary to the high example previously set by Pitt, to take for his own the sums of interest on the very large balances normally held in the paymaster's account, though the common form of the age, gave some colour to the king's and Bute's disapproval of him as one of the most corrupt of the politicians. Fox also mortally offended the king in 1761 by trying to arrange a liaison between him and his niece, Lady Sarah Lennox, presumably in the hope that large political advantages might accrue from it. In the winter of 1762–3 Bute felt obliged to fall back on Fox's expertise as a House of Commons man, to secure parliamentary approval of the Peace of Paris, but when he went further and suggested that only Fox could manage the profligate body of the politicians when he himself retired, the king struck altogether and vetoed the idea. Bute's insistence made him reconsider it, but fortunately for his peace of mind Fox himself declined on grounds of health a post for which he had by this time no inclination, and which the enormous fortune he had amassed made insufficiently financially attractive. For his help with the peace treaty Fox received a barony, and then went into retirement complaining that he had not been awarded an earldom.

Newcastle continued to hold the treasury for the first 20 months of the new reign. Although both he and Pitt were major targets of the new king's disapproval and dislike, these co-premiers of a successful war coalition ministry could hardly be thrown aside; in any case, who were to take their places? Newcastle had become a secretary of state in 1724, and by 1760 had an immense experience both of politics and of government. He had spent a fortune in 40 years of loyal service to the Hanoverian dynasty. Under a fussy, bumbling, emotional exterior, he concealed a good heart and a considerable measure of shrewdness; historians who have criticized aspects of his activities have rarely paused to consider whether any of his contemporaries without the advantages of hindsight could have done any better in the circumstances. Among the men who thought of themselves still as the 'Old Whig' corps he commanded great prestige, and though numbers of careerists were to desert his banner when he retired in 1762 a larger number remained faithful to him than some of his opponents had expected. Having been head of the treasury for most of the past six years up to 1760, Newcastle could hardly nurse higher political ambitions; but he was not yet ready to retire, for politics was his whole life. As the months passed, his position was gradually undermined. After Pitt's resignation in October 1761 he was more and more isolated in the cabinet and became the target of constant pinpricks. He finally resigned in May 1762, when George III, Bute, and his own chancellor of the exchequer combined to overrule him in his own department in order to secure economies in the subsidy policy towards Germany. With unexpected dignity Newcastle refused a pension on his retirement, though it would have been well merited and would have given some relief to his disordered private finances. The refusal clearly preserved his future freedom of action, and left it open to him to seek a return to power by means of critical attacks on some future ministry. Without activity and success he could hardly hope to retain his personal political following for long, and during the next three years, despite the difficulties of adjusting himself to the idea of conducting a systematic opposition, he gradually became more deeply engaged, together with a few remaining older friends and with a group of younger, discontented and ambitious associates, including the Marquis of Rockingham, and the Dukes of Grafton and Portland, against the ministries headed by Bute and his successor, George Grenville.

William Pitt, like Newcastle, resented Bute's sudden rise to power and intrusion into the cabinet in October 1760, but similarly accepted the fact that such changes could hardly be avoided in a new reign. Moreover, Pitt had less logical ground for complaint: he had planned in 1756 to become secretary of state with Bute as head of the treasury when the next reign should begin. However, the harmony then established between them had not survived Pitt's acceptance of office in coalition with Newcastle in 1757. To George III and Bute he appeared to have broken every pledge he had then given — personal pledges of service and political pledges against deep involvement in war in Germany. But in October 1760 the secretary of state who had created victory out of defeat was as nearly indispensable as a minister could be and there was no person who could supplant him. For the time being Pitt was prepared to put up with Bute provided he was left with a free hand to run the war. He resigned in October 1761, when not only the king and Bute, but also Newcastle and the majority of the cabinet, rejected his advice that Spain was only awaiting the most convenient moment to enter the war on the side of France and should be attacked immediately. During the following three years Pitt remained an incalculable quantity in politics. His impact in the House of Commons could be immense, but there are some grounds for thinking that by 1761 his contemporaries were mistaken in taking him at his past valuation and that his greatest force was spent. He could fall into disastrous errors of judgement. At the beginning of 1763 he emerged briefly from retirement to deliver a vituperative attack on the peace treaty, denouncing ministers for failing to strip France of the remaining shreds of her empire and of the remnants of the nursery of her seamen in the Newfoundland fishery. It fell flat in a chamber whose members were oppressed by the supposed threat of national bankruptcy. He was to betray a similar insensitivity three years later in the debates on American taxation. Ill-health, some-times manifested in intense fits of mental depression which reduced him to total inactivity and were to wreck the last phase of his public career, may already have been setting its curb upon him: there were long spells when he was absent from the Commons. His freedom of manœuvre was increasingly trammelled by the rise of other politi-cians. Aiming at the highest place if he should return to office, he could not contemplate co-operation in any ministry with previous lords of the treasury, and from the start this ruled out any close association with Newcastle and his friends. Though his marriage with Hester Grenville had brought him into an extensive family political connection which could have formed the basis of a substantial personal party, his temperament and his style of politics militated against his adoption of this tool as a means of rising to power. Perhaps his memory of the fatal effects on his prospects for many years of the personal dislike of George II made him anxious to avoid the appear-ance of faction. If there is any clear clue to his behaviour during the mid 1760s, it seems to have been a belief that a return to power must be at the king's invitation and sustained by the king's favour: he would not appear to force his way into the closet.

When Bute insisted upon retirement Fox, Pitt and Newcastle were

all thus for different reasons out of the running. On Bute's recommendation George III offered the treasury to Pitt's brother-in-law,
George Grenville, clearly hoping that Grenville would be willing to
conduct affairs under the tutelage of Bute. Thus the king's fear of
acting without his mentor had resulted in his setting up the very situation of government by an irresponsible adviser which he had himself
condemned two years before when he insisted upon Bute's becoming
secretary of state. Such a breach of constitutional convention could
not endure. Grenville — an able parliamentarian and man of business, with a wide experience in various branches of government, but
especially those concerned with trade and finance, and member of a
wealthy Buckinghamshire family whose leaders tended to have an
inordinate sense of their own importance — was not the man to
tolerate dictation from 'behind the curtain'. His cup was filled when,
within three months of his becoming head of the ministry, Bute and
the king took abortive steps to replace him by Pitt. From that time
onward he and his senior cabinet colleagues — the Duke of Bedford,
lord president of the council, and the Earls of Halifax and Sandwich,
secretaries of state — insisted that they would not serve unless George
III gave them his full confidence and Bute withdrew from active
participation in public affairs.

III

Grenville's ministry was to handle, with limited success, various diplomatic legacies of the peace settlement of 1763, and was to initiate a
bold and fateful policy with respect to the American colonies —
matters which are discussed elsewhere.[5] Its political strengths and
weaknesses were shown, and its eventual demise predetermined, by
various domestic occurrences of the years 1763—5.

During 1763 and 1764 the ministers came under fire for their handling of the affair of John Wilkes and no. 45 of the *North Briton*.
Wilkes, who was to be a thorn in the flesh of governments for the next
10 years, and to leave an indelible mark on British politics, was the son
of a wealthy London distiller, who by marriage to an heiress had
implanted himself among the country gentry of Buckinghamshire.
Politically ambitious, he had attached himself to William Pitt and the

[5] See pp. 51—2 above and pp. 86—90 below.

Grenvilles. Despite a hideous squint his vitality and wit made him attractive to company of both sexes, but he lacked the rhetorical talent to make his mark in the House of Commons. His genius lay in satirical journalism. Under the patronage of Pitt's brother-in-law — and George Grenville's brother — Earl Temple, Wilkes conducted in the *North Briton* a campaign in defence of Pitt against the press attacks made by Bute's newswriters and had gone over to scurrilous counter-attack with scarcely veiled innuendos to the effect that Bute owed his influence to an illicit relationship with the king's mother. It was a story that went down well with the London mobs, and the spectacle of a top boot and a petticoat strung side by side from a gibbet carried at the head of anti-ministerial demonstrations became a familiar sight in the streets of the capital. There was no truth in this: Bute was happy with and faithful to his wife, and George III, perhaps in exaggerated recoil from the reputation of his grandfather's mistresses, was adamant in excluding his womenfolk from any atom of political influence. His strong sense of his own virtues made him doubly resentful of the slur cast upon his mother's reputation, and in no mind to restrain ministers from action against its author. However, it was not the king's personal concerns which brought down the wrath of the government. A week after Bute's resignation, Wilkes published in no. 45 of the *North Briton* a comprehensive denunciation of the peace treaty. Much of it would be regarded by modern standards as legitimate, if unjustified, press comment; but in accusing the ministers of putting into the king's mouth falsehoods, to the effect that the recent treaty was 'honourable to my crown and beneficial to my people', it laid the author open to the charge of seditious libel. Constitutional lawyers of the time took a serious view of utterances likely to bring a government into contempt and to stir up popular action against it. Temple's patronage of Wilkes may have been an added aggravation to Grenville, who seized the chance to try to silence this formidable critic.

A comedy of legal errors ensued. Following traditional practice the secretaries of state issued a general warrant for the seizure of the author, printers and publishers of no. 45. From the testimony of some of the men picked up on the warrant, most of whom were quickly released, they secured firm evidence of what was already well known by common report, that Wilkes was the author. Then, reassured by the treasury solicitor that the procedure was in order, they gave instructions for the arrest of Wilkes on the same warrant.

This step was disastrous. Wilkes was a member of Parliament. According to the well-established privileges of the Commons, a member could not be placed under arrest except in cases of treason, felony or actual breach of the peace. The treasury solicitor had argued that the contents of no. 45 tended to a breach of the peace, but this could be a matter of dispute. Unlike past victims of government interference with the press Wilkes had powerful backing and funds to pay for legal advice were readily available. His friends immediately secured a hearing of his case on a writ of *habeas corpus*, and the court of common pleas discharged him from detention by virtue of his parliamentary privilege. Freed from gaol it appeared as if he might defy with impunity the attempts of the crown lawyers to bring him to trial on the charge of seditious libel and continue unscathed his campaign of press vilification of the ministers. The series of actions for damages which he and his associates began to bring against the ministers and their agents for illegal action involving wrongful arrest and the pillage of papers added to the provocation.

Throughout the summer the ministers were powerless to check him. The situation seemed sufficiently intolerable to drive them to have recourse at the beginning of the following parliamentary session to the expedient of stripping him of his immunity by securing his expulsion from the Commons. Further fuel for this purpose was provided when the law officers suborned one of Wilkes's assistants into furnishing them with one of a few copies of an indecent poem, *Essay on Woman*, which Wilkes had had struck off for the amusement of himself and his friends. As the scabrous editing had been attributed on the imprint to a reverend prelate Wilkes had laid himself open to a charge of blasphemy, which was soon approved when the secretary of state, Lord Sandwich, read out the text to a half-scandalized, half-convulsed chamber of peers. In the short session before Christmas 1763 it became clear that the government would gain its object of thus opening the way for a criminal prosecution, and Wilkes did not stay to face it. Wounded in a duel with the secretary to the treasury, Samuel Martin, over words flung across the floor of the House, he went to Paris at Christmas to recuperate and to visit his daughter who was completing her education there. When he failed to return he was expelled from the House, the prosecution took place in his absence early in 1764, he was found guilty on charges of both seditious libel and blasphemy, and on his failing to present himself for sentence a ban of outlawry was declared against him.

However, if the ministry had thus got rid of their most dangerous journalistic critic, they were by no means quit of the legacy of the affair. Since legal inquiry suggested that the use of general warrants was open to challenge, Wilkes and a number of his associates had begun actions for damages during 1763 directed against the secretaries of state, the under-secretaries, and the king's messengers who had executed their orders. The technicalities of the law dragged out some of these actions over the next two years, but during 1765 a series of decisions in the courts of king's bench and common pleas destroyed the general warrant as a means of harassing the press. Wilkes's case against under-secretary Robert Wood was settled by a verdict ruling that a general warrant against unnamed persons was illegal and could give no authority for search and seizure of papers. In the case of the printer Dryden Leach against the secretary's clerk, John Money, the perils of using such a warrant were underlined in a different way, since the arrest of anyone not involved in the activity specified in the warrant would be an action, 'not in pursuit of the warrant', which would entitle the victim to damages. In a third case, Entick versus Carrington, Lord Chief Justice Camden delivered an exhaustive judgment establishing that there was no precedent for the secretaries of state to issue warrants for the arrest even of named individuals save in cases of treason, nor for them in any event to authorize search and seizure of papers. Camden traced the probable derivation of the eighteenth-century general warrants from the search warrants issued legally under the late Stuart licensing Acts. He pointed out that once such specific authorization had disappeared with the lapsing of the Acts, there was no longer any ground for a procedure otherwise so opposed to the basic principles of organized society, among which he put foremost the preservation and protection of the subject's property. In one case after another sympathetic juries awarded swingeing damages to the victimized printers.

Although Grenville had secured ample parliamentary majorities for the expulsion of Wilkes, he was not spared difficulties in the Commons later in the session. Members became worried about the issue of parliamentary privilege, and the opposition seized the opportunity to attack the government for unconstitutional behaviour in the use of general warrants, putting down a motion declaring them illegal. Grenville undoubtedly adopted the correct course in opposing this, on the ground that the matter was then still *sub judice*. However, he gave undertakings that if court decisions left the warrant and its procedures intact, the ministry would not oppose legislation to curb their use. In the crucial debate of 17 February 1764 government spokesmen made the most of the fact that men now leading the parliamentary opposition had in their time issued large numbers of such warrants: among Pitt's there were two which mentioned no cause of commitment and were therefore a violation of the Petition of Right. But although it might appear that the opposition to government on this issue was factious, nevertheless many of the more independent supporters of the ministry in the Commons felt that a condemnation of the excessive discretion placed in the hands of executive agents by the warrants was necessary to safeguard the liberties of the subject. On a motion to put off the question for four months, to give time for the courts to reach a final decision, the ministry's normal majority of well over 100 sank to 14. Grenville was soon assured, however, that this did not mean any withdrawal of confidence, for at his next levee a great number of those who had voted against him came to pay their respects in order to make clear that they still supported him.

It was the weakness of Grenville's situation relative to the crown rather than to the Commons that was to prove his undoing. For this he was partly, but only partly, to blame. The role played by Bute at the king's insistence during the spring of 1763 ensured that relations between the king and Grenville started off on the wrong foot, and the damage proved to be irreparable. After the abortive attempt to replace him in June 1763 Grenville would not trust the king's assurances that Bute was no longer being consulted. He demanded complete control over appointments, even those involving most personal contact with the king, in order to build up his connection and to make it clear to all the politicians that he had no competitor for the king's favour. He bitterly resented George III's decision to give Bute's brother, Stuart Mackenzie, his office of privy seal for Scotland for life, with a controlling influence over Scottish patronage. His less attractive traits of personality increased the estrangement. His lectures to the king about the wisdom of his policies and the urgency of the king's duty to give him all the visible tokens of approval he sought were not taken in good part. 'When he has wearied me for two hours', the king once remarked, 'he looks at his watch to see if he may not tire me an hour more.' By the beginning of 1765 the king was beginning to find the relationship unbearable.

Early that year George III was stricken by a serious attack of porphyria, with severe pains in the chest and other symptoms. For some days his doctors were concerned whether he would live, and rumours began to go round that he was suffering from consumption. In two ways this illness contributed towards a crisis in the relations with Grenville. In the convalescent stage it left him feeling weak and irritable, in a state in which Grenville's lectures seemed all the more intolerable. It also made him anxious to provide for a regency in case another attack should carry him off while his heir was a child.

The plan for a regency produced a rich comedy of misunderstanding. George III instructed the cabinet to prepare a Bill along the lines of one enacted in 1751, but he broke with precedent in asking that the Bill should leave him the authority to nominate the regent instead of specifying the person to fill this post. George III's motive for this provision was to avoid creating contention within his family. He did not want the regency to fall to the obvious candidate, his brother the Duke of York, whom he mistrusted, but had no wish to have this exclusion made public so long as he himself lived. His own choice for regent was the queen. Since he desired to conceal his opposition to his brother's nomination, he declined to be explicit with Grenville. The hypersensitive minister, who shared the common suspicion that a special relationship existed between the Earl of Bute and the Princess Dowager of Wales, immediately jumped to the unpalatable conclusion that the king intended to nominate his mother as a means of ensuring the control of affairs by Bute in the event of a regency. Naturally Grenville for his part could not be explicit with the king, but after a series of hints dropped by him and other ministers about likely public and parliamentary disapproval of the procedure, the king unwittingly accepted a suggestion for the limitation of the choice of regent to the queen or to other members of the royal family 'born in England'. Only when the lord chancellor, no friend of Grenville, drew the king's attention to the matter, did he realize that this formula could be taken as directed against his mother and might be made a political issue. He then immediately demanded some formula which would retrieve the error and leave his mother among those eligible to be regent. Grenville felt this to be the fullest confirmation of his suspicions and declared that such action would be impossible; but his protestations that the ministers would not be able to carry a motion of this kind in the Commons were made a mockery when this was in fact done on the private initiative of a back-bencher. Grenville felt that the lack of confidence shown to him throughout the discussions of the Bill presaged an intention to remove him from office, and he was moved to protestations and reproaches which completed the process of alienating the king from him.

Early in April, while the planning of the Regency Act was getting under way, the king had begun to put out feelers through his uncle, the Duke of Cumberland, for a new ministry which would relieve him of Grenville's presence. A first attempt to enlist Pitt for this purpose failed. The result was a confrontation between the king on the one hand and Grenville, Bedford, and the two secretaries of state on the other, who all suspected (incorrectly) that Bute was behind the move to supplant them. For the moment Grenville and his colleagues had the whip-hand, since no other ministry could be found, and they made the most of it. They declared their continuance in office would be conditional on the proscription of both Bute and the Duke of Cumberland, that Bute's brother, Stuart Mackenzie, must be stripped of his post, and that the vice-royalty of Ireland should be given to Bedford's follower, Viscount Weymouth, whose profligacy made him in the king's view particularly unfitted to be the representative of royalty. During the next weeks there were renewed rows over patronage, and on 12 June Bedford in audience made further accusations against Bute and virtually faced the king with an ultimatum, that he would be left without a ministry if he did not within a month decide to fall in completely with the wishes of his present ministers. In desperation the king turned again to Cumberland and gave him a free hand. If Pitt would not serve — and he again refused since an offer had not been made to him direct — then the king would welcome back the Pelhams and Cavendishes, his *bêtes-noires* of three years before, in order to escape from the men for whom he had now come to feel a bitter animosity. He declared he would sooner see the devil in his closet than Grenville. For the next five years, until Grenville died, the king's politics were dominated by his determination not to have him in office again. Purely personal issues, not public affairs, spelled the end of this administration.

In June 1765 Pitt was no more willing to take office under the patronage of Cumberland than he had been two years earlier under that of Bute, and the royal duke turned perforce to the remnants of the Pelham—Cavendish connection and to such personal friends as the Duke of Grafton and General Henry Seymour Conway, brother of the Earl of Hertford. From the extent to which the new government had been put together during talks at Newmarket and Ascot it might well have been dubbed the racecourse administration. The Marquis of Rockingham, another of Cumberland's young racing associates, accepted the treasury, and thus became putative head of the ministry, although Cumberland was its effective chief until his death in October 1765. Neither Grafton nor Rockingham had any previous ministerial experience, and Conway but little as secretary to the lord lieutenant in Ireland. Newcastle, who had spent a lifetime in government, was now too old — and too little respected by his younger colleagues — to take an office of execution and entered the cabinet as lord privy seal. The Earl of Winchelsea, an aged nonentity, became lord president. The lord chancellorship and the Admiralty remained respectively in the hands of Lord Northington and the Earl of Egmont, who had served with Grenville but did not belong to his connection.

The Cumberland, or — as it became — the Rockingham ministry lasted for only a year. In that short period it made a strenuous effort, described elsewhere, to re-shape colonial fiscal and economic policy in a mode more acceptable to colonial susceptibilities: this was virtually the full sum of its achievements in the sphere of public policy[6] From the start it lacked cohesion and was hampered by the narrowness of its parliamentary base. The two secretaries of state, Grafton and Conway, both believed that no government without Pitt could endure and had agreed to serve only on the understanding that

[6] See pp. 91–2 below.

further attempts would be made to recruit him as first minister, a plan naturally disliked by Rockingham. At the outset the chief strength of the ministry lay in the prestige commanded by Cumberland and his ability to get ministers and the king to draw together. The duke's death shortly before the opening of the parliamentary session was a serious blow to its fortunes. One recourse would have been the establishment of a cordial relationship with Bute's followers, who were still active in both Houses of Parliament, a few of them holding minor offices. With the restoration to office of Stuart Mackenzie particularly in mind the king several times pressed this course on Rockingham and there is little question but that the ministers could have bought this much needed support cheaply enough. But Rockingham, Newcastle and their friends, haunted by memories of the years 1761−2, remained suspicious of Bute's supposed influence, and refused to have anything to do with him. In the early part of 1766 parliamentary debates on colonial policy went far to alienate the two groups, for the Bute party deplored concessions to the Americans, which they believed would destroy parliamentary supremacy within the Empire. Grafton and Conway despaired of the ministry unless Pitt was brought in and Newcastle gave similar counsel, offering to resign himself if Pitt raised objections to his remaining in office. However, Pitt was now playing for the highest stakes, and had no intention of joining a ministry already in being. Much of his parliamentary strategy during the early months of 1766 was devoted to making clear to George III that he had no commitment towards Grenville either, and he denounced Grenville's colonial policy in rounded terms. But at the same time Pitt sought to wear down the Rockingham group, and he achieved an important success in May, when Rockingham's refusal to make a further approach to him led Grafton to resign. About the same time Rockingham faltered in dealing with the unpopular task of finding funds for allowances for the king's brothers. George III rapidly came to the conclusion that he was a broken reed and that the ministry could not last. He put out new feelers to Pitt on his own account, and in July Pitt agreed to form as broadly based a ministry as possible, from which only George Grenville and his brother, Lord Temple, were proscribed.

IV

Although there were to be fresh ministerial crises in 1767 and 1770, and although Pitt himself failed to stay the course, in hindsight it can be seen that his assumption of the leadership in July 1766 heralded a return to a more stable system of politics. At the start his own declining state of health immediately introduced an element of uncertainty. By accepting a non-executive office as lord privy seal, and taking a peerage as Earl of Chatham on the ground that he could no longer face the hurly-burly of life in the Commons, he cast into the draught what everyone had thought to be the chief asset of the new ministry — his own great reputation as a House of Commons man. Apart from himself his cabinet was almost as inexperienced as Rockingham's. For the treasury he picked the Duke of Grafton, who was entirely his man, but whose experience was confined to a few months as Rockingham's secretary of state. Conway, who was in much the same case, stayed on as secretary of state. The other secretaryship went to the Earl of Shelburne, another young and untried follower of Chatham, who had served briefly at the board of trade, whose imprecision of mind has gained for him a somewhat unjustified reputation for duplicity. Another inexperienced supporter of Chatham, Lord Chief Justice Camden, took the office of lord chancellor. Other Chathamites, Sir Charles Saunders and the Marquis of Granby, took over the Admiralty and the Horse Guards. In fact this ministry, at least at cabinet level, was less 'checkered and speckled . . '. and whimsically dovetailed' than Edmund Burke afterwards alleged, or than many historians have assumed since. The chief odd-man out was Charles Townshend, whom Chatham recruited as chancellor of the exchequer and leading spokesman for the ministry in the House of Commons. Despite the wayward and erratic nature of his politics, Townshend's brilliance as a speaker led every aspiring premier to hope for his support, and once Chatham had left the Commons, he was perhaps the one politician who could outface Grenville. Next to Chatham he was by far the strongest personality in the government. During 1767 he displayed both firmness of purpose and serious errors of judgment in handling the great public questions of the session, finance, colonial taxation, and a settlement with the East India Company.[7] The mysterious mental malady which totally incapacitated Chatham from March 1767 onwards left Townshend the dominating figure in the cabinet until his death the following September.

At the outset this looked to be a strong, coherent ministry, solidly based on members of Chatham's circle, but with a reasonably broad basis of support in Parliament. Chatham knew that Bute had ceased to count with George III and was willing to make concessions to win

[7] See pp. 92–3 below.

over his former friends. Bute's brother was restored to the privy seal of Scotland, though without the Scottish patronage, and his daughter's father-in-law, the Earl of Northumberland, was made a duke. The minor placemen in this group were no longer treated with the veiled hostility they had encountered from previous ministers. Although Rockingham and his chief associates had lost office a number of this party kept their situations, at least for a time, and some of them settled down permanently in the ministerial ranks. Only the groups led by Grenville and Bedford were irreconcilable — small wonder, since the determination of George III and Chatham in 1766 to destroy faction was aimed primarily against them. It was not at first clear that Rockingham and his friends would go into opposition, but during the autumn Chatham's refusal to pay a sufficiently high price in patronage eventually made this inevitable. Thus, by the beginning of 1767 a new though temporary political alignment was emerging, with the Grenville, Bedford and Rockingham factions joined in uneasy alliance in an attempt to destroy the credibility of the government. The strength these groups could deploy in the House of Lords was formidable, and once or twice they came near to destroying the ministry's majority; but in the Commons the government managed to retain an adequate margin of votes despite the demoralization caused by Chatham's illness and withdrawal.

Four features of the political conflict of 1767 deserve emphasis. First, the ministry had the most wholehearted support of the king, for the very personal reason that he was determined never to let Grenville into his closet again. Second, co-operation in opposition between the followers of Grenville and Bedford on the one hand and the Rocking-hamites on the other was always overshadowed by the conflict of views between them over colonial policy. The former stood by the Stamp Act and condemned its repeal. The latter damned the Stamp Act and stood by their policy hinging upon the Declaratory Act of 1766. Concern for reputation and consistency forbade either to concede to the other. Third, neither Grenville nor Rockingham would yield their pretensions to return to the treasury.

Fourth, during 1767 the Rockingham party committed itself to belief in the 'Bute legend'. Chatham's concessions to Bute's former friends were taken to mean that he himself was merely a front-man for Bute, whose influence was thought to have been re-established through the agency of the Princess Dowager. This legend deepened and broadened until it took the form of the highly sophisticated theory, expressed in rounded rhetorical phrases three years later in Edmund Burke's *Thoughts on the Cause of the Present Discontents*. In this pamphlet Burke developed the view that Bute, or associates of Bute, were at the centre of a deeply laid plot to capture control behind the scenes and manipulate the activities of the ostensible ministers as a means of securing power based on a corrupt control of the Commons. As a result of these secret machinations the system of constitutional checks and balances was in train to be destroyed and British liberties placed in jeopardy. Nothing could have been more absurd or further removed from the truth. The circumstances surrounding the formation of Chatham's ministry had, in fact, finally destroyed the last remnants of the friendship between George III and Bute, and the earl's erstwhile followers were henceforth well content to be absorbed into the ranks of the parliamentary court and administration group. But Rockingham, Newcastle and their friends now rationalized their posture of opposition as one of defence of the constitution against a sinister conspiracy. It was a pose which was to have serious adverse implications for their future struggles to climb back into power. Their attempt to dramatize it as virtuous Whiggism in conflict with a resurgent authoritarian Toryism does not bear examination. Of the 104 men classed as 'Tory' returned for English constituencies in 1761 many died or lost their seats during the next seven years, but 49 were re-elected in 1768. Fourteen of these were independents of the purest sort, whose voting was entirely unpredictable. Only 13 of them could be regarded as friends of the government. Two could be classed as Chathamites and two as members of Grenville's connection. Eight voted regularly against the ministry, though not connected with any opposition faction. Eight had become regular supporters of the Rockingham party, including its leader in the Commons, William Dowdeswell, and the remaining two lay on the fringe between these two groups but not quite classifiable within either. The old Tory party was no longer a recognizable force; and, ironically enough, it had provided a substantial part of the support for the opposition group which set most store on the unadulterated Whiggishness of its political principles.

Momentarily the opposition's chances seemed bright. During the spring of 1767 they pressed the ministry hard with accusations of weakness in its handling of American questions and ran the ministers so close in the House of Lords as almost to destroy Grafton's confidence in the government's ability to survive. But the overtures he launched during the summer recess soon created rivalries and broke their ranks. George III steeled Grafton against any surrender, and the long parliamentary vacation gave a breathing space. By December Grafton — now fully in charge of the ministry owing to Chatham's incapacity — had managed to strike a bargain with the Bedfordites. Northington retired and Bedford's chief lieutenant, Earl Gower, took the presidency of the council. A secretaryship of state was found for Lord Weymouth, and minor places for a few of Bedford's other associates. Meanwhile, the death of Charles Townshend in September 1767 opened the way for Lord North to become chancellor of the exchequer and leading spokesman for the government in the House of Commons. In December North's position as a balancing force in the cabinet against the Bedfordites was strengthened by the recruitment of Lord Hillsborough as third secretary of state, with charge of colonial affairs.

North had long been marked as a coming man. Now aged 35 and with over 12 years' experience in the Commons he had briefly been considered as a replacement for Townshend at the exchequer the previous March. Because his father had at one time been tutor to the young George III, he and his elder step-brother, Lord Dartmouth, were among the very few younger men in political life whom the king had known personally from childhood, and the moral character of both had left nothing to be desired, even to the strait-laced views of the Princess Dowager. North's upright personality, his wit, good humour, and solid intellectual abilities had commanded increasing respect in the Commons, and it was soon to be seen that he yielded nothing to Grenville in his mastery of the nation's financial business. Hillsborough, now in his late forties, was a leading landed proprietor in Ireland, and an ambitious politician, who had established himself as one of the 20 or so leading debaters in the Commons before his elevation to the British peerage in 1756. For a time he had attached himself to a small political group led by North's kinsman, the Earl of Halifax, and following Halifax's example, he had developed a fully professional concern with matters of trade and colonies.

Grafton had thus succeeded in broadening the parliamentary basis of his ministry and probably no other course had been open to him if it was to survive. However, he had inevitably reduced the degree of coherence in the cabinet arising from Chatham's choice of men from his own circle, and this development proceeded still further in the autumn of 1768 when both Chatham and Shelburne resigned. Shelburne was replaced by a professional diplomat, the Earl of Rochfort, who seems to have begun to cultivate a connection with Earl Gower. Nevertheless, tessellated as the ministry had now become, it had the stability and resilience to face a series of tests, beginning with the general election of 1768, itself a quiet enough affair, and moving on into the fracas arising from the irruption into politics of John Wilkes.

V

For four years Wilkes had lain low in exile in Paris, condemned in the English courts for blasphemy and seditious libel, and with outlawry and threat of criminal sentence hanging over him should he return. His hopes that Grenville's fall would clear the way to a pardon and his rehabilitation had been disappointed, and the meagre goodwill payments sent across to him by Grafton and various members of Rockingham's circle were far from keeping him afloat in the style to which he was accustomed. By 1768 his outstanding debts made residence in Paris no longer safe, and to avoid a debtor's prison, he moved briefly to Leyden, enrolling at his old university as a student in order to secure protection against arrest for debt. But his only real safety seemed to lie in recovering a seat in the House of Commons, and to this end he bent all his efforts in the weeks before the general election. His arrival in England passed without official notice. No one in government circles wished to persecute him. He moved about the capital with impunity, and although he failed in his first objective to secure election for the City of London, his presentation of himself as an outraged victim of political chicanery won him the support of a majority of the voters in the Middlesex county election which followed a few days afterwards. Mass discontent due to economic recession and unemployment may have helped his cause: during the Middlesex poll crowds of weavers blocked the roads to Brentford and barred access to all who did not show his colours. But the political uneasiness of the middle classes of the metropolis mattered more. The baiter of the unpopular Scottish favourite in 1763 was in fashion in appealing to his reputation as a friend to 'Liberty' at a time when renewed rumours of Bute's secret influence were echoing both within and outside Parliament. Government officials noted as 'most dangerous and alarming' the reactions of 'sober discreet master traders and artificers' to his 'impudent assertions' of having a pardon or a promise of one, and their 'talk in cold blood of his sufferings and his merits in the cause for which he suffered'.[8]

A pardon and a place were Wilkes's objectives, and he now offered an olive branch to the ministers. Having won parliamentary immunity he waived it and gave himself up to justice. Mobs and tumults greeted his progress. While he lay awaiting sentence in the king's bench prison there were intermittent disturbances in the adjacent St George's Fields and on 10 May troops attempting to keep control of rioters fired, killing six people and wounding another 15. However, the law took its course, and he found himself under sentence of a fine,

[8] British Library Additional Manuscripts 38457, fos. 259.–60.

22 months'imprisonment, and an obligation to give sureties for future good behaviour, for the crimes of which he had been found guilty in 1764. Sign of pardon there was none. His riposte was to mount a renewed campaign of self-justification and of calumny against members of the government. Such were the visiting and other facil- ities in the king's bench prison that his incarceration imposed prac- tically no limitations upon his journalistic activity. The shootings on 10 May – the 'massacre of St George's Fields' – were made the grounds for violent denunciation of the ministers. As the winter session of Parliament approached he prepared a comprehensive petition outlining his grievances.

To the ministers it appeared that Wilkes was determined to raise a dust, whatever the consequences; and in an age when, in the absence of any civil police, rioting could only be checked by gun and sabre, they became increasingly alarmed about the maintenance of law and order. It began to seem as if the only way to discredit Wilkes was to expel him once more from the Commons, so that he could be brought before the courts again on new criminal charges of fomenting sedition. In May the ministers had thought such a course inexpedient. By November they believed it unavoidable. Late in the year the situa- tion was further aggravated by the massive turnout of Middlesex voters at a by-election in favour of Wilkes's legal adviser, John Glynn, and by Wilkes's own election as alderman of the London City ward of Farringdon Without with a poll of 1,300 out of 1,500 votes.

On 3 February 1769 the ministry carried Wilkes's expulsion by 219 votes to 137, but at the ensuing by-election he was returned without opposition. The House again expelled him, and this time declared him incapable of being elected to the present Parliament. This was an unwise step, for while the House had an undoubted right of expul- sion, eligibility for election arguably was a matter determined by the common and statute law and not by the law and custom of Parlia- ment. A second time Wilkes was re-elected without opposition, and once again the House expelled him. At a third by-election in April, a government candidate, Henry Lawes Luttrell, was found to oppose him. The ensuing poll was exceptionally low, reflecting the circum- stances that Wilkes himself could pull out less than a third of the Middlesex voters, perhaps little over a quarter, that fear of distur- bance kept many from the hustings, and that Luttrell, an unknown with no stake in the county, was able to attract only the votes of a handful of government supporters. After the return had been reported with 1,143 votes for Wilkes and 296 for Luttrell, the House of Commons declared Luttrell duly elected on the ground that as Wilkes was ineligible the votes cast for him had been thrown away.

The seating of Lutrell raised an issue which critics of the government and of the established order could pursue with passionate conviction. How could the House of Commons declare an ineligibility which was not known to the law of the land? Was this not destructive of the whole principle of representation? Might not a ministry controlling a corrupt majority in the Commons use this technique to pack the House as it pleased? While to sophisticated politicians who knew the facts of political life these suspicions were ludicrous, they were real enough to many of those out of doors who were already half-convinced by the public prints, that the king's mother, the Earl of Bute, and their myrmidons were playing some unconstitutional and sinister role behind the scenes. Men cast about for both short- and long-term solutions. At the end of 1769 an abortive campaign of addresses and petitions was whipped up demanding a dissolution and the election of a new Parliament, on the ground that the existing one was no longer truly representative. Leaders of the Rockingham party took the first step towards their future programme of 'economical reform' by demanding the disfranchisement of revenue officers in order to reduce executive influence over the members of the Commons. Chatham emerged from retirement to blast the ministers. Behind a cloak of anonymity Junius denounced them in biting phrases. The heat was more than some of them could bear. Chatham's influence led Camden to court dismissal by denouncing the expulsion of Wilkes, brought Granby to resign on the same issue, and created a situation in which Grafton, deprived of his more congenial colleagues, sick of press abuse, uneasy himself at what had been done, and also at odds with some ministers over other issues, insisted upon throwing up the treasury. Nevertheless, purged of its Chathamite element, the ministry survived. Accepting the treasury Lord North inaugurated a period of stable government which was to hold firm for over a decade. Within a year he was able, following the death of Grenville, greatly to strengthen the administration by recruiting a number of able men from that connection, and the forces of opposition led by Chatham and Rockingham found themselves powerless to make any impression against its parliamentary foundations.

The affair of the Middlesex elections had lasting political consequences in the metropolis. It brought into focus a mass of fears and discontents which laid the foundations of both a new reforming tradition and a radical organization. In late 1769 a small group of young lawyers and merchants banded themselves together into the Society of Supporters of the Bill of Rights. Their initial object was to support John Wilkes and pay his debts, but before long they emerged as champions of extensive reform programmes embracing the form and administration of the law on one hand and the nature of the representative system on the other. General warrants and American taxation alike fell into the scheme of things which they condemned and sought to change, and which they diagnosed in the broadest sense as abuse of power. Their agitation struck chords in the mass discontents of elements of the metropolitan middle classes and skilled craftsmen, scattered throughout the areas of the City, Southwark, Westminster and the other urban parishes of Middlesex, who began to coalesce in one movement as never before.

Starting from the experiences of Wilkes and the London printers in the *North Briton* affair of the early 1760s, the Bill of Rights men began to demand what was in effect a generalization of the general warrant decisions, that those in authority should be brought fully within the law. They campaigned against the legal short cuts available to government through the attorney general's privilege of *ex officio* informations, which deprived those indicted for seditious libel of the right to a preliminary hearing before a grand jury. They criticized the refusal of judges to let juries decide what constituted libel, and they opposed imprisonment for contempt or breach of privilege on the part of the courts or the two Houses of Parliament. In a more general way they pressed for various improvements in the criminal law and its administration, and those of them who became aldermen and magistrates in the City tried to achieve reforms by their own example.

They also took up reforms of a more specifically political nature. Borrowing from Tory traditions of a previous generation, they called for a sweeping Place Act excluding all office holders from the Commons, for a repeal of the Septennial Act and shorter parliaments, and for an effective oath against bribery at elections. They aired the idea of secret ballot, called in question the existence of the rotten and pocket boroughs, and under the designation of a 'more equal representation' threw out suggestions for increasing the number of MPs elected by the metropolis. With this last point they appealed to a great urban public well aware of the enormous contributions it made through customs and excise to the national revenues and by no means inclined to underestimate the importance of its interests or of its role. Their more radical ideas reflected a profound urban mistrust and dislike of the aristocracy and hostility towards the minority of big businessmen in the capital who allied themselves with the aristocratic regime and profited from it. Such attitudes made co-operation with the Rockinghamite parliamentary opposition virtually impossible. In 1770 Burke's call in his *Thoughts on the Cause of the Present Discontents* for all good men to support Rockinghamite resistance to the suspected secret cabal of Bute or others was denounced by the metropolitan republican blue-stocking Catherine Macaulay as a smokescreen for 'the more complicated and specious, though no less dangerous manœuvres of aristocratic faction and party, founded on and supported by the corrupt principles of self-interest.'[9] As the writings of radical propagandists in the metropolis ranged increasingly widely over the issues raised by the Middlesex elections, they also drew in for good measure the American colonists' defence of their right to be free from taxes imposed by Parliament, and the metropolitan and colonial campaigns in defence of constitutional liberties became increasingly fused together.

Perhaps the most important triumph of the popular movement was the successful campaign masterminded by Wilkes at the beginning of 1771 to defeat the efforts of the two Houses of Parliament to curb reporting of debates by arresting and disciplining printers for breach of privilege. When agents of black rod and the sergeant-at-arms found themselves arrested by constables of the City, and bound over by its courts, for molesting freemen and members of the Livery, the game was up. Like the challenges to general warrants after 1763 this success marked an important step towards greater freedom of the press, more open government, and the exercise of greater popular influence over the actions of the politicians. In all this the Wilkites were perhaps building better than they knew. Contrary to their claims that they were fighting off the onset of a Tory authoritarian reaction, Wilkes and his friends in various minor ways were extending the range of civil liberties, liberalizing the constitution, and opening the way for developments that would only mature in the years after Waterloo.

[9] Catherine Macaulay, *Observations on Burke's Pamphlet, On the Cause of the Present Discontents* (1770), p. 7.

4 Imperial Problems in British Politics 1760 – 1773

I

The details of British enterprise in India and of colonial development in North America lie outside the scope of this volume, but both impinged upon British politics, and the latter had calamitous consequences for the country's standing in international affairs in the 1770s.

Up till the Seven Years War the East India Company had functioned solely as a great and successful monopolistic commercial organization, with trading bases at Bombay, Madras and Calcutta, a posting station at Bencoolen in southern Sumatra, and an important stake (but without any permanent local base) in the Chinese tea trade at Canton. Thereafter a combination of factors – Anglo-French rivalry on the Indian sub-continent, and the hostility of native rulers – impelled it into becoming a local power in India in its own right. By the mid 1760s it had emerged as the paramount force in the lower Ganges valley, controlling the provinces of Bengal, Bihar and Orissa. In the south-east, though controlling directly only small enclaves of territory, it had become closely enmeshed in a patron–client relationship with Muhammad Ali of Arcot, the ruler of the extensive province of the Carnatic. In order to maintain these positions, it had been forced to build up a considerable and expensive native army under British officers and willy-nilly to become entangled in the diplomacy and the rivalries of the major Indian principalities.

As a result disturbing problems spilled over from East India House in Leadenhall Street to the national political arena at Westminster. Not only did various factions among the Company's servants in India – notably those of Robert Clive and his rivals – come into conflict over their competing financial interests and seek to establish defences for them by deals with the politicians in the House of Commons. The king's ministers also became concerned about the implications.

The first of these to be perceived was financial. The Company had secured what was happily assumed to be a vastly profitable administration of revenues in Bengal. Should not some of this be channelled into the nation's coffers? No politician as yet had any thought for the impact on Indians of corrupt, oppressive, or maladroit Company administration: 'The first parliamentary incursion into the affairs of the Company began [as indeed it largely ended] as a predatory raid on the Company's new riches rather than as an attempt to impose reforms upon it.'[1] At the outset of Chatham's administration in 1766, a financial settlement with the Company seems to have been regarded as the most important business before it, with the clear purpose of obtaining a substantial contribution which might help to reduce the frightening level of the national debt. No concern was shown for the population of Bengal. Admittedly the scope for manœuvre was limited. At this stage the assumption by the crown of any direct administrative responsibility in India was out of the question. For one thing, no eighteenth-century British government disposed of the necessary personnel or the special knowledge and administrative expertise required. For another, such an enlargement of the patronage and resources at the disposal of the crown might seem to threaten the balance of the constitution, giving the crown a basis of independence from the financial control exercised by the Commons and a fund of political influence by means of which that control might be sapped from within.

Throughout 1766–7 the ministry, though agreed on the main object, was split over tactics. Chatham's own policy was to insist that the Company had no right to territorial revenues, all fruits of political authority being the perquisite of the crown, but then to concede to it a share of the revenues in consideration of its administrative commitments. This simple stand had some warrant in the Company's charter, but it was not wholly consistent with powers to dispose of conquered territories in India which Chatham himself, as secretary of state, had conceded to East India House in the 1750s. Some of his colleagues feared a challenge which might place them in the dangerously invidious posture of attacking chartered rights. They preferred the alternative policy pushed by Charles Townshend, that an amicable agreement should be negotiated with the Company, with no recourse to parliamentary definitions of right except as a last resort. Chatham's breakdown early in 1767 gave them their head, and so it was on this basis that the Company won a temporary respite from governmental and parliamentary interference with its position in Bengal at the cost of an agreement to pay £400,000 annually to the exchequer during the next two years. The directors' attempt to fight this demand as excessive was blocked at East India House by factions which hoped by concession to stave off parliamentary interference with the

[1] P. J. Marshall, *Problems of Empire. Britain and India, 1757–1813* (1968), p. 30.

proprietors' freedom to fix the dividend; nevertheless an upper limit of 10 per cent was fixed by statute.

Having once secured a tribute from the Company the government was inevitably drawn into measures to confirm the state's claim to a share in the revenues, to maintain the Company's financial stability, on which its capacity to pay depended, and therefore to set a curb on speculation. The Dividend Act was renewed in 1768. The major pre-occupation, however, was the contribution to the exchequer, and since a head-on collision with the Company over its charter was politically inexpedient, the alternative course was adopted of building up a ministerial party within the court of proprietors as a means of securing an agreed settlement when the Act of 1767 ran out in 1769. Various ministers and government servants became stockholders, and the Earl of Sandwich, who entered the ministry as joint postmaster-general at the beginning of 1768, began his career as manager of an extensive proprietorial interest.

This policy had a certain success. By an agreement between the government and the Company in 1769 to last for five years, confirmed by Act of Parliament, the former secured a continuance of the payment of £400,000 so long as the dividend remained at not less than 10 per cent, but with a provision that the amount would be scaled down if the dividend fell, and payments would cease altogether if it dropped as low as 6 per cent. Ministers conceded the Company's right to raise the dividend to a maximum of 12½ per cent, but by not more than 1 per cent in any one year. The government also required that any surplus cash in the Company's hands after the paying off of its simple contract debts and the reduction of its bond debt to an agreed level, was to be lent to the state at 2 per cent.

Almost immediately after the completion of this settlement the second important implication of the Indian situation came home to the ministers. Financial stability must be secured in India also, and this meant control over the political and diplomatic activities of the Company's servants. In mid 1769 the news that the Company had become involved in a war with Mysore caused a slump in stocks and the near-ruin of many shareholders. At the same time a rumour that the French were massing ships and troops at Mauritius with a view to intervening on the side of their old ally, Mysore, drew the ministers' attention with renewed urgency to the dangers of leaving the Company free in its handling of Indian diplomacy. Fifteen months later the war scare over the Falkland Islands, raising afresh the spectre of a French attack upon India from Mauritius, underscored the continued military vulnerability of the Company and forced additional expenditure for defence upon it. In 1771 the impoverishment of Bengal by famine added further to its difficulties.

The agreement of 1769 lapsed in 1773. When, during 1771 and 1772, Lord North and his colleagues began a leisurely contemplation of a new arrangement, the airing of scandal about the administration of Bengal ultimately involved some redirection of their concern. Opinion was stirred in the Commons and the House appointed a select committee of inquiry in 1773. But more crucial to the ministers' thinking was the impact on the Company of the general financial crash of 1772. Ahead of this the proprietors in the general court had pursued a reckless and unjustifiable policy of raising the dividend at a time when Indian trade and territorial revenue yield were alike in recession, and the crash brought the Company itself to the verge of disaster. As its cash-flow dried up the government faced a default on its tribute under the 1769 Act and also the prospect of a further shattering blow to the nation's credit if the Company failed altogether. General public indignation in September at the sudden fall of East India stock put pressure on the ministers to take effective remedial action and greatly weakened those forces within the Company which were hostile to government intervention.

In November, on North's initiative, the House of Commons set up a secret committee to secure full information on the Company's financial affairs. With the nine penetrating and informative reports it produced during the next six months the ministry began for the first time to acquire knowledge which was indispensable for any effective intervention in Indian affairs. The prospect of this inevitably brought the Company into the political arena. An unholy alliance developed between the more anarchistic and disreputable elements in the general court, anxious to stave off retribution for past malversations, and the parliamentary opposition led by Rockingham, who feared the growth of executive power in the hands of the supposed secret cabal behind the scenes. As Rockingham put it in October 1772: 'All thinking men must already clearly acknowledge that the influence of the crown and the means of corruption are become very dangerous to the constitution and yet the enormous addition of power which the government are aiming at by subjecting the . . . Company to their control does not strike and alarm so much as it ought.' Public outcry against misrule in Bengal merely played into the hands of the secret advisers: 'The interior cabinet laugh in their sleeve at the pretence with which this helps to furnish them in their object of more control over India affairs.'[2] A proposal by North for a royal administration of Bengal would have been political dynamite, and would have been avoided on this score alone, even if it had not been

[2] *The Correspondence of Edmund Burke* II, *July 1768–June 1774*, ed. Lucy S. Sutherland (Cambridge, 1960), pp. 344–5.

considered impracticable on other grounds. North was bound to feel his way towards forms of indirect control. By this course he probably disarmed much of the opposition that might otherwise have rallied round Rockingham against his measures. He attempted also to secure as much agreement within the Company as possible. But while he obtained reasonable co-operation from the directors, whose appreciation of the financial disaster overshadowing them made them malleable, the proprietors proved truculent, and in the end legislation had to be forced upon the Company against the clamorous indignation of the general court.

North's Regulating Act was framed to secure reform both in London and in India. One clause, aimed against the uncontrollable 'democratic' anarchy of the general court, doubled the qualification for a vote in the court from £500 to £1,000 of stock, and laid down that the stock must be held for at least twelve months, not six, before the shareholder became enfranchised. About 1,600 proprietors lost their voting rights. The size of the court was greatly reduced, and a considerable check set upon the much abused practice of creating faggot votes by the splitting of stock. The possibilities of government 'management' of the court were correspondingly enhanced. Another clause ended the rule whereby the 24 directors were all elected annually by the general court, and provided that tenure should be for four years, six directors retiring by rotation each year. A much greater degree of stability was thus secured for the direction, and the chances of its being diverted from sober reforming policies were greatly reduced. Government oversight of its activity was partly secured by a clause requiring the directors to transmit as appropriate either to the treasury or to the secretary of state copies of all correspondence from India within 14 days of its arrival. The Act said nothing about outgoing despatches, over which the directors retained complete formal control, but some consultation about policy seems to have become the practice.

Other clauses of the Act were intended to strengthen the control of both the directors and the government over the Company's servants in India. The elevation of the chief post in Bengal into a governor-generalship with supervision over the presidencies of Madras and Bombay was intended to secure an overriding check upon relations with native states; the governor-general and his four members of council were to be nominated by the crown. A supreme court of judicature was created with four judges nominated by the crown, to take cognizance of criminal or civil actions brought against British subjects resident in Bengal, Bihar and Orissa, or against their agents. It was designed to give some protection to the native population against oppression and exploitation of the kind recently practised by some Company servants, and to support efforts to improve the Company's rule.

Administratively the new arrangement had serious defects. It imposed heavy responsibilities upon the new governor-general, Warren Hastings, but gave him no clear discretion to act without referring back to London for instructions which might take two years to arrive. He lacked adequately defined powers over the other presidencies and could be frustrated by his council where decision lay with a majority. The relationship between the executive government and the new supreme court had not been thought out and defined. In particular, the ministers were so preoccupied with misrule in Bengal, that they ignored the dangerous situation in Madras, where the relations between the Nawab of the Carnatic and his creditors on the presidency council virtually committed the latter to following the Nawab's interests rather than those of the Company.

Having forced these measures of reform upon the Company, the ministry was ready to bail it out of its financial difficulties over the heads of the recalcitrant proprietors. Acceptance of a loan of £1,400,000 was made compulsory. The dividend was restricted to not more than 6 per cent until such time as the loan had been repaid and the Company's bonded debt reduced to £1,500,000. The practice of British personnel lending money to the Company in India in order to bring funds home and so adding to its debts at the London end was put under severe statutory restriction. For the time being the government abandoned its claim to a contribution to the exchequer: this point would be reviewed when the five-year term of the Regulating Act expired.

The ministry also responded to requests for help over the tea trade. By its charter the Company had to dispose of its stocks of this as of other commodities at public auctions in London. Heavy customs duties had so raised the price that it was calculated that half the country's consumption, about seven million pounds, was smuggled, to the loss of both the revenue and the Company's profits. A reduction of duties in 1767 had greatly benefited sales, but this concession ended in 1772, and in 1773, on top of its other difficulties, the Company faced a slump in home sales of about four million pounds. In this extremity the directors sought leave to dispose of stocks abroad with full drawback of customs duties to make the price competitive. Plans to dump large quantities on the European market were considered but abandoned when it appeared likely that the only result would be to stimulate an illegal return traffic from Channel ports in smuggled tea. The one overseas outlet which did not entail this risk was North America. By the Tea Act of 1773 the government conceded that the Company might arrange directly for the sale of some of its stocks in the North American colonies, appointing its own agents on commission. The grant of full drawback, plus the reduction in handling charges to middlemen, would, it was hoped, bring the selling price so low that smugglers would be beaten out of the North American market — a somewhat dubious assumption. The government refused to abolish also the colonial import duty of 3*d*. a pound imposed in Charles Townshend's Revenue Act of 1767. The consequences of this refusal require discussion in the American context;[3] but the effect so far as the Company was concerned was to render null this scheme for improving its trade.

II

During the Seven Years War North America had made a significant contribution to British victory. The war kindled a quickening realization in London that the colonies constituted an essential pillar of strength in the perennial rivalry with the Bourbon powers. At the same time ministers and officials came to feel that American resources were only partially and ineffectually tapped, leaving an excessive burden on the subjects in the metropolitan country, and that the causes of this lay in the institutional weaknesses of the Empire.

The need to rectify this state of affairs seemed all the more pressing since the end of the war imposed increased commitments. British claims to territories ceded by France and Spain could hardly be sustained without at least an effective token occupation. St Augustine, Pensacola, and Mobile in the Floridas were easily accessible by sea and presented few problems, but to maintain even small detachments in such remote interior outposts as Detroit, Mackillimackinac on Lake Superior, or Kaskaskia and Fort Chartres on the upper Mississippi, was exorbitantly expensive. The presence of 80,000 or more French Canadians in the St Lawrence valley dictated the retention there of a substantial military force until such time as a large population of non-French immigrants had been established. Interwoven with this question of the effective occupation of conquered territory was that of Indian relations, one made pressing by the outbreak of the great Indian rising known as Pontiac's conspiracy

[3] See p. 95 below.

in the upper Ohio valley in the summer of 1763.

During the two years following the Peace of Paris, British policy towards North America was to a large degree improvised to meet immediate circumstances. Nevertheless, at the same time, much of it was moulded by a general viewpoint, the various parts of it linked together into a coherent whole, and it carried various distinct implications for the future.

An attempt to conciliate the Red Indians involved cordoning off the whole area of the Great Lakes and the Ohio basin as an Indian reserve. This idea dovetailed well with another ministerial concern — to channel the flow of new settlement into Canada, Nova Scotia, and the Floridas, in the interests of both commercial and strategic objectives. Remote settlements in the interior were regarded askance on the ground that it would be difficult to maintain either commercial or political connections with them. By royal proclamation in October 1763 the government forbade further settlement beyond the watershed of the Alleghany Mountains and west of the Ottawa valley. Commerce might continue, but traders were to be licenced by their respective provincial authorities, and their activities were to be restricted to the vicinity of military posts or of Indian villages, where fair and lawful intercourse could be guaranteed by a military commandant or an official Indian agent. In particular the Indians were to be protected from British sharp practice. The army was thus allotted the role of police in addition to its other functions. Its commitments involved the stationing of four regiments in the St Lawrence valley, and the scattering of a number of detachments in the Floridas and the American interior, while resting stations for a reserve of three regiments were fixed in the colonies of New York, New Jersey and Pennsylvania, where the climate was healthy and food supplies were most readily available. Altogether 15 regiments were allotted to the new North American establishment. The estimated upkeep was in excess of £200,000 (though it proved to be much more). To the politicians in London the equity of placing part of this defence expenditure on the shoulders of the colonists seemed indisputable. Since the record of the colonial assemblies in providing grants for war purposes in response to royal requisition had been uneven, it seemed best to do this by parliamentary authority.

Planning for economic benefit converged with planning for taxation during 1763—4. For a century, running back to the Navigation and Trade Acts of Charles II's reign, British thinking about colonial relationships had been dominated by the principles of what is loosely described as mercantilism. The Grenville ministry was following orthodox doctrine when it sought to maintain and extend the usefulness of the colonies as a captive market for British manufactures and also to encourage the production of strategic materials for the navy and raw materials for processing and consumption in Britain or for export. But it approached these tasks with a new sense of urgency, because by 1763 both the trade and the extent to which the rules were broken were much greater than they had been earlier in the century. A tightening up of administration began in 1763, and this was soon followed by legislation. Grenville's Plantation Act of 1764 (the 'Sugar Act') was largely devoted to the problem of trade control. It introduced new, highly complex, and not easily evaded rules enforcing the documentation of cargoes and the movement of ships, and systems of bonds to ensure compliance. Various additions were made to the list of enumerated commodities which could be disposed of only in Britain or another colony − coffee, pimiento, coconuts, whalefins, deerskins, and timber, and pig and bar iron. Other supporting legislation provided bounties for the production of hemp and flax, raw materials for a whole range of goods required by the navy. The Act secured a preference for various British manufactures in the colonial market by terminating or reducing the drawbacks (repayment of duty on re-export) on competing European products. The other object of raising a revenue in America to help pay defence costs was achieved by imposition of duties on foreign textiles and on wines from Madeira and the Azores entering colonial ports, and also on colonial imports of sugar and sugar products.

The northern colonies imported vast amounts of molasses, a by-product of sugar extraction, from both the British and the foreign West Indies. British supplies were limited and the bulk of the requirements were met from the French islands. By far the greater part was distilled into rum, a major industry in New York and the New England colonies. This spirit was the staple of a far-ranging traffic. It provided an almost indispensable support for health and life in the brutally raw weather conditions under which men worked in the Newfoundland fishery. It was a highly marketable commodity in the exchanges for slaves, gold dust and palm oil carried on along the West African coast. It sapped Indian bargaining ability in the trading for furs along the Great Lakes. Rum brought wealth to the North Americans and was a lubricant for British trade all over the Atlantic world. And yet, paradoxically, the molasses traffic contravened one of the most basic principles of eighteenth-century British commercial policy, because it appeared to sustain the French sugar trade, which had a dominating hold on the European markets that British merchants found themselves powerless to challenge. British West Indian sugar interests would have liked to see the French islands totally deprived of the North American foodstuffs, timber and draught animals for which they bartered their molasses, believing that if the

French planters were forced to rely on more expensive European supplies the competitiveness of French sugar on the European market would be undermined.

The imperial government realized that the molasses and rum trade was too valuable to be placed in jeopardy. Instead, it evolved a policy directed against the prosperity of the French sugar trade which was of such Machiavellian ingenuity that the point of it seems never to have been grasped by its colonial critics. An Act of 1733, which had remained almost a dead letter, had imposed a prohibitive duty of 6*d*. per gallon on foreign molasses entering British colonial ports. Now in the Plantation Act the government reduced the duty to 3*d*., but set out to enforce it. This step was taken on the understanding that the North American supplies of foodstuffs and other requirements were so indispensable to the French planters that the British colonists supplying them would be able to recoup themselves for the molasses duty by charging higher prices. In effect the British would tax French sugar production, with the Yankee merchants acting as tax collectors. As part of the attempt to strike a balance between different compet-ing interests, British West Indian planters were given the sop of a high discriminatory duty on non-British sugar imported into the colonies, and the New England distillers were given a near monopoly of their home market by a total prohibition on the importation of foreign rum. The molasses duty which lay at the heart of these arrangements was expected to yield a substantial revenue. In 1765 Grenville rounded off his programme of taxation with his Stamp Act, imposing a series of duties on playing cards, dice, newspapers, and a wide range of legal and business documents.

In two other enactments of 1764—5 Grenville dealt with problems raised for British debtors by the depreciation of colonial paper cur-rency and for the British commander-in-chief by his need to feed and shelter troops on the march in the colonies. The Currency Act of 1764 forbade the issue of colonial bills of credit as full legal tender and required the rigorous redemption of such bills as were in circulation. The Quartering Act provided that magistrates, on requisition by a military officer, should find billets and also obtain barrack supplies, and pay for them, the money so spent to be reimbursed by the local legislatures.

Grenville's legislation provoked an imperial crisis of major propor-tions, as much because of its implications as its immediate effects. The colonists had on the whole accepted in principle the system of the Acts of Navigation and Trade. In practice the rules had been treated in happy-go-lucky fashion. The fact that this provided loopholes for a fair amount of smuggling was just unfortunate. When the govern-ment imposed a new harshness and rigidity of regulation, intended to stop the smuggling, colonists found this a serious impediment also to legitimate trade. Merchants in the northern colonies were thrown into something approaching a panic over the possible commercial consequences of the 3*d*. duty on molasses. But far more serious was the constitutional issue almost immediately injected into the imperial dispute. To British politicians it was axiomatic that Parliament exercised sovereign powers in all respects over all British subjects in the king's dominions, and might lay such taxes and regulations as it pleased. Colonists insisted that their legislatures were miniature parliaments with full and exclusive powers over their internal policy, and that the colonial inheritance of all the rights and liberties of Englishmen precluded their property being subjected to taxation except by an assembly in which they were represented. They had little difficulty in rebutting British suggestions that they were virtually represented in Parliament as much as the many residents in Britain who had no right to choose its members. Although comparatively few of the protests against the Act of 1764 raised the complaint of taxation without representation, the undertones were clearly heard in London and stiffened the attitudes of both government and Parliament during the passage of the Stamp Act. To imperial statesmen this colonial opposition was profoundly alarming. It seemed to strike at the whole conception of a united empire. Without the universal acceptance of Parliament's authority, how could the Empire gird itself for defence? How could it pursue a coherent commercial policy? How could it effectively carry on the economic warfare against France which had been traditional since 1689? Would not British resources in North America inevitably be diverted to the enrichment of dangerous European rivals? Was it not even possible that the sovereign, secure in the receipt of financial grants from colonies which were not under parliamentary control, might maintain a standing army with which he could defy the constitutional claims of Parliament? Seen in a glass darkly, the shadow of a commonwealth of quasi-independent states subject to a single prince whose prerogative powers had little substance unless backed by legislative support — the outcome towards which it seemed in London colonial pretensions would lead — presaged only disaster, and almost unanimously the politicians set their faces against it.

And yet to the British colonists in America also the prospects opened by Grenville's legislation seemed fraught with menace. If representation guaranteed life, liberty and property — and this belief stood at the heart of current British constitutional doctrine — where did they stand? In practice their guarantee would be gone. They felt that if they gave way to Parliament they would be no better than slaves. This was an argument which perhaps struck with partic-

ular force among members of communities which had slaves among them
and knew from first-hand experience what existence without liberty
or property could mean.

And so, during the second half of 1765, after news of the passage
of the Stamp Act had reached America, a furious gale of resistance
blew up all along the Atlantic coast. One assembly after another
reaffirmed colonial claims to all the constitutional rights and liberties
of Englishmen. One or two ordered local officials to disregard the
Act. Complaint extended to the loss of the right of jury trial involved
both by the extension of the functions of local vice-admiralty courts in
revenue cases under both the Acts and by the government's decision
to set up an imperial vice-admiralty court at Halifax. Nine assemblies
sent delegates to a congress at New York to draw up a joint assertion of
their claims. In all the main seaport towns systematic violence successfully frustrated the implementation of the Stamp Act and secured the
resignation of stamp officials. Royal administration in the colonies
proved helpless in face of the massive display of public sentiment, to
which even members of the magistracy gave countenance. To add still
further to the impact it was hoped these developments would have in
London, colonial merchants combined to impose a virtual boycott of
British trade. They also agreed to delay repayment of their debts to
British suppliers, a course of action powerfully assisted by the virtual
stop put to court actions once the obligation to use stamped paper on
legal documents became law. The immediate pretext for these steps
was, as it could plausibly be, economic. Taxation, it was said, so
drained the colonies of specie and sterling credits that merchants
could not afford either to buy or to pay outstanding debts. British
ministers and officials could be in little doubt, however, that these
arguments were specious and face-saving, and that the ultimate
object behind the colonial non-importation agreements was political.

The resolution of the Stamp Act crisis fell to the administration
headed by Rockingham. He and his colleagues ignored the fire-eating
cries of Grenville for suppression of colonial rebellion by military
force. Responding to, but also moulding, pressures from the British
business community, they accepted the pleas for lightening taxation
of the colonies on economic grounds and by these arguments justified
their repeal of the Stamp Act. The excesses of colonial resistance were
quickly ended. But thoughtful men on both sides of the Atlantic saw
that the essential point of conflict still remained. In Britain no politician could have survived who appeared to abandon the supremacy of
Parliament, and to satisfy the political convictions of almost the whole
of the parliamentary corps, Rockingham had coupled the repeal with
the passage of a Declaratory Act, which reaffirmed Parliament's

power to legislate for the colonies 'in all cases whatsoever'. Nor, even in his hands, was this a wholly idle threat. For while the government proceeded to repeal, on economic grounds, some of Grenville's revenue duties of 1764, it substituted for the protective duty of 3*d*. on foreign molasses entering the American colonies a flat rate of 1*d*. per gallon on all imports whether from British or foreign sources, making the charge purely a revenue measure. Various other customs duties were left in force, notably those on wines. In the Plantation Act of 1766, by which these adjustments were made, the government also introduced some intelligent improvements to the laws of trade, but it added further restrictions on the movement of shipping intended to prevent any vessel outward bound from American colonial ports from visiting European mainland ports north of Cape Finisterre, where it might pick up goods to be smuggled into the colonies. Another Act introduced a system of free ports in the West Indies, with the object of tapping the local production of foreign colonies, with provision for handling foreign sugars, coffee and indigo without charge through bonded warehouses if they were brought to a colony for onward transmission to a British port. This gave some encouragement to trade both in the West Indies and in North America, but it did not allay discontent. Within less than a year New York merchants were petitioning for extensive relaxations of the laws of trade.

In 1767 there was tension over colonial opposition to the Quartering Act. This blew over; but a much more serious confrontation arose out of the decision of the chancellor of the exchequer, Charles Townshend, to raise further revenues in the colonies by customs duties. His policy was a clear response to the mood of the House of Commons, whose members were appalled by the high level of expenditure on the army in North America; but he broke new ground and further exacerbated the Anglo-American dispute by his decision to make provision for a colonial civil list a first charge on the revenues he planned to obtain. The Stamp Act crisis had seemed to show that imperial officials would be set at naught by the assemblies unless they secured an independent financial provision similar to the king's civil list in Britain. This weakness in the imperial structure must be eliminated. To this end his Revenue Act of 1767 imposed American customs duties on a small variety of relatively unimportant manufactured products – glass, paints, lead, and paper – which the colonies were bound to import from Great Britain, and also on tea, brought to England by the East India Company and re-exported in considerable quantities to the colonies. A number of ancillary measures added further fuel to the flames of colonial discontent. A clause in the Revenue Act specifically validated the use of writs of assistance by customs officials to facilitate searches for smuggled goods in premises ashore, a device which had been rendered null by colonial obstruction in the law courts since 1761. By a separate enactment the government instituted a commission of customs in America, to give high-powered direction, support and discipline to the colonial section of the customs service, and fixed its location at Boston, apparently the most stubborn focus of resistance to imperial authority. Early in the following year the ministers' determination to enforce the trade and revenue laws was made still more clear by the establishment of four district vice-admiralty courts in place of the single court previously set up at Halifax.

None of these measures attracted any serious obstruction from opposition parties in the House of Commons. Townshend's American revenue policy was in no way save in its purpose distinct from that which had been pursued by the Rockingham administration after the repeal of the Stamp Act. The only criticism — voiced by Grenville — was that the provisions were not sufficiently extensive. No party at this time espoused the colonial cause, but all were ready to use American issues to score points against the ministers.

The chief colonial riposte was a second boycott of trade, but this was less well concerted than that of 1765 and made less impact. Spasmodic harrying of customs officials, including the customs commissioners at Boston, caused the government to send four regiments to the town to assist in the maintenance of law and order; but as the governor of Massachusetts could not get approval from his council to use them, they served no purpose save to provoke public irritation. Unemployed and bored, the troops continued to be the target of general animosity evinced in a series of violent incidents culminating in the King Street riot of 5 March 1770, when a squad of redcoats, fearing danger to life and limb, killed or fatally wounded five Bostonians and injured several more. In America thenceforth the 'Massacre' became a salient piece of colonial mythology, a dramatic incident in the contest between liberty and 'military tyranny', and annual commemorative orations were used to whip up popular enthusiasm against the imperial government.

The ministers for their part, from an early date, had doubts about the wisdom of Townshend's Revenue Act on commercial grounds, and his death late in 1767 removed an obstacle to its repeal; but they felt unable to yield in face of renewed colonial claims that Parliament had no right to impose taxation in America. In May 1769, by a majority of one in a meeting attended by nine ministers, the cabinet agreed to abandon all the duties except that on tea but to defer legislation till 1770. Both the delay and the retention of the tea duty were intended to make clear that the government's return to an orthodox commercial policy was in no way a concession to the colonists' constitutional claims and marked also a ministerial intention to hold on to an American fund for civil-list purposes. Such partial concession did nothing to reconcile differences. Tension remained and on the American side especially growing uneasiness and suspicion. In a manner which is difficult to discern and has not yet been systematically explored, but which the indications place beyond doubt, domestic politics in Britain exacerbated this situation. The storm over real or alleged abuses of executive power and influence in the affair of Wilkes and the Middlesex elections, the reformulation in specific and particularly readable form in Edmund Burke's *Thoughts on the Cause of the Present Discontents* of the theory that the British constitution and British liberties were being undermined by the manipulations of a secret cabinet or inner cabal, which ruled the ministers and diverted patronage and power to its own malignant purposes, all this made American patriot leaders place the most sinister interpretation on every move by the British government and its agents in North America.

And in the atmosphere of apprehension that prevailed almost every action was suspect. In three southern colonies the very principle of representative government appeared to be threatened: in Georgia, where the governor in 1771 made an almost unprecedented use of the power of dissolution; in South Carolina, where the activity of the assembly was almost brought to a standstill by its refusal to bow to ministerial demands that it rescind an appropriation for the defence of Wilkes and Liberty; in North Carolina, where a somewhat similar situation of deadlock developed over ministerial hostility to a proposal by the legislature to empower the local courts to attach all property owned by non-residents in the province against debts they owed to inhabitants. During 1770–1 renewed agitation among Anglican clergy for the appointment of an American bishop raised a storm among both Congregationalists and hostile Episcopalians throughout the tidewater from the Chesapeake to Maine. Sporadic outbreaks of violence by smugglers culminated in 1772 in the destruction of HMS *Gaspée* by Rhode Islanders while she was stranded on a sandbank, and the ministers' decision to set up a commission of inquiry roused colonial leaders in Virginia to institute committees of correspondence to scrutinize the nature and authority of this and other actions taken in London. In late 1772 the grant of salaries, financed out of the tea duty, to the governors of New York and Massachusetts, and to the lieutenant-governor and the judges of the high court in the latter province, fired the suspicions of the patriots at Boston and was used by them to whip up popular support for a comprehensive statement of colonial rights and a strongly-worded list of infringements and violations. The Massachusetts radicals condemned parliamentary legislation and taxation affecting them without their consent, the imperial challenge to their control of officials, the presence of troops unauthorized by their assemblies, the casting of revenue cases into the admiralty courts with the consequent denial of trial by jury, and the threat to trial in the vicinage implied in the establishment of the imperial district vice-admiralty courts. They claimed the full powers of a sister legislature equal to Parliament for their General Court.

Both the assembly and the council of Massachusetts upheld these popular grievances in a well-publicized controversy with governor Thomas Hutchinson, drawn out over several months at the beginning of 1773, which defined with ever-increasing clarity the popular party's repudiation of Parliament's claims to authority in America. This threat to the legislative unity of the Empire was duly noted by the ministers, although, preoccupied with the affairs of the East India Company and by a European diplomatic crisis, they let it slide. But by the end of 1773 they could ignore Massachusetts no longer. First, the disclosure of private correspondence of Hutchinson and his brother-in-law, the lieutenant-governor Andrew Oliver, the carefully edited version implying that in past years the men now in high office had misrepresented and maligned the province, followed by a petition seeking their removal, posed a direct challenge to executive control through the king's representative and produced a case with which the privy council was bound to deal. Second, the renewed campaign against the importation of tea, made cheaper by the legislative arrangements accompanying the settlement with the East India Company, which culminated in December 1773 in the destruction of cargoes worth £10,000 in Boston harbour, raised questions of law and order and of parliamentary authority in the American colonies which, for fear of the parliamentary repercussions, the government dared not neglect. The stage was set for the climax of the imperial crisis in North America.

III

In the early years of George III's reign Ireland, in theory a sister king-dom, in practice occupied a position of colonial dependence more thorough-going than that of the American colonies.

Under legislation passed in Tudor times the Irish parliament could not even be assembled until the bills which the executive in Dublin proposed to refer to it had first been approved in London. The application of this procedure even to money bills, for which in Britain the Commons claimed the sole right of initiation, was regarded as particularly objectionable by Irish political leaders. If measures were initiated during the session in either House they might be suppressed or amended by either the Irish or the British privy council before legislative stages in the other chamber could be completed. All bills approved in both Houses were subject to either veto or amendment in the British privy council. If they were returned in altered form to Dublin the Irish parliament had no right of amendment and could only accept or reject them as they stood. The Irish parliament's authority was also diminished by the British parliament's assumption of the right to legislate for Ireland, reaffirmed in the Declaratory Act (Ireland) of 1719; and while legislation passed at Westminster related mainly to commercial regulations of the kind imposed also on the American colonies, occasional conspicuous exceptions such as the Irish Mutiny Act were a clear interference in internal Irish affairs. Ireland had no Habeas Corpus Act, the judges still held office at pleasure, and under the Act of 1719 Irish legal cases on appeal were resolved by the British courts.

Irish politicians were not in a strong position to challenge this state of affairs, since they represented only that small land-owning minority of the population, perhaps a tenth, which belonged to the Protestant Episcopal church of Ireland, and depended on British support for both their political and their economic ascendancy. Roman Catholics, who constituted some three quarters of the population, were entirely excluded from participation in political life. On paper they were still subject to crippling penal laws, and the anomalies between laws which reflected the political and religious tensions of the seventeenth century and practice corresponding with the greater tolerance and enlightenment of the eighteenth, aggravated rather than soothed the feelings of this substantial section of Irish society. Although much less numerous the Irish Presbyterians formed another under-privileged element of the population, and one all the more significant because of its heavy regional concentration in the north-eastern counties of Ulster. Presbyterians lived under far fewer disabilities than their Catholic fellow-subjects, but the operation of the Test and Corporation Acts debarred them from active participation in municipal government and thereby largely also from influence in parliamentary elections. Their close connections with Scotland, where to be a Presbyterian was to be usually a member of the Established Church with full political rights, emphasized the anomaly of their situation, and their sensitivity over it led Irish administrations, with some justice, to regard them as the most serious potential source of political disaffection.

The role of the Irish politicians as a mere minority of a minority was underlined still further by the nature of the institutions through which they worked. The representative system reproduced to an extreme degree the anomalies and abuses of its British counterpart. In the lower House of 300 members over 170 of the 236 borough seats were under the control or influence of a relatively small number of landed proprietors. General elections occurred only upon a demise of the crown: George III's accession put a term to a parliament which had lasted for 33 years. By tradition parliament was summoned not annually but biennially, and voted supply for a two-year period. Easily manipulated by a clique the system was run by a small circle of Irish peers, the 'undertakers', who struck their bargains with Whitehall for pensions, places, and honours, and provided a body of lords justices or regents, since the lord lieutenant made only occasional appearances at Dublin when parliamentary sessions were due. Irish places and pensions formed part of the British political gravy train: it has been calculated that Englishmen placed on the Irish list were receiving rather under 4 per cent of the total Irish budget.

Despite exclusion from the colonial trade and the operation of a British protective policy against some Irish manufactures, Irish commerce was prosperous and increasing. In social terms this was of importance in encouraging the growth of an urban commercial class in Dublin, Cork, Waterford and Belfast, where men of different churches mingled on common ground – a class which, in some degree occupying the social gulf between Protestant landowners and Catholic peasantry, could provide at least a limited new impetus for Irish political development. Lower down the social scale the problem of a desperately poor society of peasant cultivators remained intractable. Absentee landlords, sub-letting, rack-renting, and the rapacity of land-agents, seem to have been mainly responsible for this state of affairs, which caused many rural areas to be in a state of chronic insurrection. But the peasants' welfare was not an issue in which the landowners dominating the Dublin parliament interested themselves, nor at this time did it present itself as a problem to the British government.

In Ireland, as in Great Britain, the advent of a new sovereign kindled expectations. Various groups hoped that under a new regime a more liberal attitude towards their interests might emerge. Catholics raised a growing agitation for the repeal of the penal laws. As this pressure gathered momentum during the later '60s and early '70s, advocates of Catholic relief laid stress on the economic and political advantages of enabling Catholics to invest freely in land; it was suggested that farming would benefit from injections of capital and that landownership would increase the Catholic stake in the established order. The Protestant political nation showed a growing desire to reaffirm Irish constitutional rights in precisely the same terms as those prevailing in Britain. This involved a general challenge of the various arrangements for British control of Irish legislation. The workable balance achieved in the relations between the British government and the Irish 'undertakers' came under increasing strain. The Anglo-American debate over constitutional rights did not pass unnoticed: it was two Irishmen, one of them the enthusiastic Earl of Charlemont, who publicized William Pitt's vehement defence of the rights of the colonists against the claims of Parliament to impose the Stamp Act.[4] A small but increasing number of young Irish politicians began to express resentment at the denial to them of elementary constitutional rights and liberties, and in the persons of Henry Flood and later of Henry Grattan the Irish House of Commons produced two champions of unsurpassing rhetorical power. From 1763 onwards the Irish Commons began to demand the passage of a Habeas Corpus Act and of a Bill for limiting the duration of the Irish parliament. In 1765 it added to this programme a Bill for securing the tenure of judges during good behaviour.

It was in this very delicately poised situation that the British government embarked on a series of steps which first encouraged then thwarted this incipient Irish national movement. The occasion arose out of the problems of American taxation. Casting round for means to pay for imperial defence after the repeal of the Stamp Act, Charles Townshend turned to Ireland. The Irish parliament financed a military establishment at a nominal strength of about 12,000 men, normally stationed within the kingdom for purposes of internal security and defence: if the king ever withdrew troops for foreign service, they were then placed on the British payroll. But might the Irish agree to raise another 3,000 or so men *and* pay for them while they were on overseas service, if in return some of their constitutional aspirations were met? This was Townshend's proposal in 1767, and that summer his elder brother, Viscount Townshend, was appointed lord lieutenant with instructions to arrange a bargain: but for Charles's unexpected death some three months later, the history of the British Isles in 1768 and perhaps for some years might have been dominated by these two talented brothers working together in the two key offices on either side of St George's Channel. As a price for the additional troops, Lord Townshend carried over a package of offers: a statutory limitation upon the duration of the Irish parliament;

---

[4] Ian R. Christie, 'William Pitt and American Taxation, 1766: A Problem of Parliamentary Reporting', *Studies in Burke and his Time* 17 (1976), pp. 167–8 and n. 5.

security of tenure for judges; favourable consideration for a Habeas
Corpus Bill; an Irish militia; and a reduction of pensions on the Irish
establishment.[5]

Matters at first progressed well with the passage of the Irish
Octennial Act, but Townshend encountered a degree of reluctance
on the part of Irish MPs to vote the larger military establishment just
before the general election which must now ensue, and he did not
obtain it until the new parliament met in 1769. Then British obstruction proved fatal to the fulfilment of the remaining part of the bargain. A law granting security of tenure to the judges was blocked by a
British insistence that petitions for their removal might come from
the Westminster parliament as well as the parliament at Dublin.
London had second thoughts about *Habeas Corpus*, owing to the
difficulties of dealing with peasant unrest. Irishmen's interest in
having their own Mutiny Act was not even discussed.

Irish political hopes had thus been raised only to be dashed, and
Townshend's troubles in Dublin increased. Part of the odium for
resistance to Irish pretensions fell upon him. The disappointed
'undertakers' whom he had superseded as manager of Irish politics
turned patriot and joined the parliamentary opposition. A few Irish
MPs at least discovered that the Octennial Act had made them
vulnerable in a new way to popular electoral pressure. Parliamentary 'management' became increasingly difficult and expensive.
Townshend's remodelling of the administration in 1771 in order to
exploit the potential patronage of the revenue boards for political
purposes led to a vote of censure at Dublin carried by the casting vote
of the speaker. In 1772 he handed over the lieutenancy to Earl
Harcourt, leaving the political scene at Dublin in a state ⌐f tension
and uncertainty. Places, pensions, peerages, and promises for the
future were a cobweb structure on which to found a ministerial
majority. In the Irish Commons commitment to government as a
matter of principle hardly existed; indeed, principle was only too
likely to weigh in the opposing scale. During 1771 Benjamin Franklin,
leading agent for the American colonies in London, had visited
Ireland, and in conversation with the leaders of the Irish opposition
had declared his hope that 'our growing weight might in time be
thrown into their scale, and, by joining our interest to theirs [there]
might be obtained for them as well as for us, a more equitable treatment from [England]'.[6] The materials were not wanting for Ireland to
make its contribution to the general combustion which faced Great
Britain in the mid 1770s.

---

[5] For a just-published revision on this episode, see Thomas Bartlett, 'The augmentation of
the army in Ireland, 1767–1769', *English Historical Review* XCVI (1981), pp. 540–59.

[6] *The Papers of Benjamin Franklin*, XIX, ed. W. B. Willcox (New Haven, 1975), p. 21.

5   The Loss of America

I

It would not be altogether wrong — though it would be an over-simplification — to see in the growing difficulties faced by Lord North's administration during the 1770s a general confrontation between a national government trying to discharge imperial respon-sibilities and irresponsible sectionalism and self-interest assum-ing rather different forms in different sectors but linked by similar problems and deploying similar arguments and tactics. In both the eastern and the western extremities of the sphere of British enterprise defence problems arose, created partly by the activities of uncon-trolled frontiersmen, partly by international tensions centred in Europe, which brought financial pressures to bear upon the central authority. The attempts to deal with these created strife over char-tered rights and raised conflicts over constitutional practice and principle which found an echo much nearer home, across the Irish sea. Irresponsible forces at home — the Rockingham opposition and the Wilkite radicals — worked upon these disputes for their own particular ends, and by identifying themselves to some extent with sectional interests added to the burdens the imperial government had to bear.

About the end of 1773, the East India Company had been success-fully brought to heel, Irish relations stood in a state of uneasy equili-brium, and the most pressing difficulty was that presented by the North American colonies. However, it is with regard to this last area that the limitations of the simple scheme depicted above appear most forcefully. The older American colonies were no longer a peripheral frontier region but mature political communities which had drifted far along the course towards a federal relationship with the parent state. The just comment made upon one minister of the time really applies to the whole British administration — that they 'held fast to the belief that [their] task was to check a civil broil within the Empire, when in fact [they were] attempting to check the historic development of more than a century.'[1]

During the months after the Boston Tea Party the ministers' attitude was strongly coloured by the belief that a small group of conspirators at Boston was set upon destroying the imperial government's control over the affairs of America in the service of their own personal ambitions. Governors' letters over the years had complained repeatedly of the manœuvres of the 'faction'. Ministers were also convinced that to let things drift would be to allow the poison to spread unchecked throughout the American continent. In this, of course, they misjudged the depth of the concern and the sincerity of the convictions held by the leaders of the popular party in the colonies. They underestimated the extent of American resentment against parliamentary claims to powers of taxation, a resentment shared by many who were to emerge a year or so later as loyalists. Also they failed to foresee the degree of support which would be given to Boston from other provinces. They believed that sharp measures to bring Massachusetts firmly under control would have a salutary effect throughout the rest of the American empire, and just as much as Samuel Adams and his friends, they were carried along by a sense of the righteousness of their cause. Law and order must be maintained. That colonists should expect the home population to take the whole weight of the burden of imperial defence was inequitable. The king's subjects everywhere owed obedience to the laws and statutes. The well being of the whole British nation on both sides of the Atlantic depended upon a unified control of trade and defence. Separation would spell the economic and political ruin of both. And yet this was exactly what appeared to loom ahead. To allow a handful of factious men at Boston to bring general ruin in consequence of their endeavours to crow on their own dunghill would be a betrayal of the responsibilities which an imperial government owed to all those whom it governed. Ministers did not think most colonists sympathized with such wrecking activities and believed that a firm reassertion of parliamentary authority in Massachusetts would halt the movement in its tracks. Diagnosing the evil in classical terms of political science, they deduced that in that province the careful balance between the different elements that constituted the ideal of a mixed polity had been destroyed by the predominance of the 'democratic' element, and their answer was to seek a restoration of this balance. In their approach to the problem posed by the Boston Tea Party they reflected the general attitude of the political nation in Britain. Here dissident minorities

[1] Gerald Saxon Brown, *The American Secretary. The Colonial Policy of Lord George Germain, 1775–1778* (1963), p. 179.

were vocal; but no ministry which had shown weakness in face of colonial contumacy at the beginning of 1774 could have survived for long in face of feeling in Parliament and in the country at large.

Acting on these premises, in the early months of 1774 the ministers brought before Parliament the string of proposals which became the 'Coercive' or 'Intolerable' Acts. At first judicial action against patriot leaders on the charge of treason under Henrician legislation was contemplated, but the law officers advised that this could not be sustained, and instead faith was pinned on the resources of statute law.

The first object was to restore Boston to order. The Boston Port Act closed the port as from specified dates in the following June, except to vessels carrying in fuel and food supplies and materials required by the armed services. The custom house was removed to Salem, where the officials would be out of immediate reach of the town mob, and Boston's overseas trade would thereafter have to be carried on with the interposition of an overland carriage of about 17 miles. Activities relating directly to the waterfront would virtually come to a halt. The crown was empowered to lift these restrictions as soon as the people of Boston had reimbursed the East India Company for its lost cargoes of tea and had satisfied the government that in future customs officials would be able to perform their duties without hindrance.

The government's main measure, the Massachusetts Charter Act, was intended to restore the balance in the colony's constitution, by setting checks on the 'democratic' element, which appeared to have got out of hand, and by strengthening the executive and judicial authority, bringing the form of government more into line with that in other 'royal' provinces. It conferred on the governor greatly increased powers over the appointment of judges, and over the appointment and removal of justices of the peace, sheriffs, provosts, and other minor officials. The powers of the council in these matters were drastically curtailed, and the Act specified that the governor himself might act as a justice of the peace. The appointed sheriffs were henceforth to select the panels of jurymen, who would thus be less responsive to popular pressures than they were under the existing system of local election. It was assumed that with these powers the governor would be able to secure the service of magistrates who would co-operate zealously in the maintenance of law and order, and who would not hesitate to use troops to put down rioting in accordance with the well-known rules and conventions already established in Britain. Once the mob was suppressed everyone from the rank of magistrate to juror would cease to fear victimization by popular violence, recover confidence, and act vigorously to support the law.

By a crucial decision at a late stage in the preparation of the Bill, the government decided to remodel the upper chamber of the general court. For years governors had criticized the consequences of the annual election of the council by the assembly. In 1769 the then colonial secretary had discussed bringing it to an end. Now the Act prescribed the setting up of a nominated council, which would deprive the popular party of its leverage. The excess of 'democratic' influence in the politics of the province was also attacked in a clause which closely circumscribed the functions of town meetings and restricted the occasions of their assembling. The main purpose of this provision was to end the role of the Boston town meeting as a focal point of resistance and agitation.

The ministers rounded off their coercive measures with an Administration of Justice Act and a Quartering Act. The former permitted trials on capital charges arising out of the suppression of riots to take place in another province or in Great Britain. Its immediate purpose was to protect loyal supporters of law and order from legal harassment. The ministers also believed that the witness of their intention provided by the Act would of itself operate as a powerful check on disorder. The Quartering Act added to the powers of the governor or of magistrates to station troops where they were most needed to deal with expected riots.

In Parliament the opposition became warmer as the ministers' legislative programme unfolded, but the government's majority was never at risk. The Tea Party so offended against the strong feeling of the age about the sanctity of property that even Chatham's follower, Isaac Barré, gave a qualified approval to the Port Bill. Only members of Rockingham's party showed themselves sharply critical of any action likely to lead to military coercion of America; but even some of the Marquis's friends were taken aback at the anarchy let loose in Boston, and not until the last stages of the proceedings on the Charter Bill did they gather their forces for an outright attack. It was no good augury for them, however, that in mid April the Commons had rejected by a large majority a proposal to abandon the tea duty. On 2 May, after a prolonged debate, it approved the Charter Bill by 239 votes to 64. In the Lords the Rockinghamites denounced the Bill as an inadmissible attack on chartered rights without due process of law, as a dangerous 'strengthening [of] the authority of the officers and ministers of state, at the expence of the rights and liberties of the subject', and as abandoning the principle which the party claimed (falsely) to have upheld since 1766, that parliamentary taxation, because it alienated the affections of the colonists, should be resorted to only on extraordinary occasions. But they could muster only 20 votes against a ministerial phalanx of 69 peers present plus 23 proxies. The general feeling of both Houses was against any concession that could be taken as a weakening of the will to maintain parliamentary authority over the colonies.

As the agent of enforcement the government picked the most experienced military commander in North America. The replacement of Hutchinson as governor of Massachusetts by General Thomas Gage had much to commend it. A long career in America, including 12 years of service as commander-in-chief, had given him an extensive knowledge of the colonies and a wide acquaintance. His wife was American and he was personally not unpopular in the colonial circles in which he moved. There appeared to be clear advantage in placing in the office of governor of this province, which ministers regarded as holding the key to the whole American situation, the man who in his other capacity disposed of the full resources of the American military command. The point was emphasized by the despatch of additional troops. However it was generally understood that military force would be used in Massachusetts only as an aid to the civil power. The government did not yet contemplate the need to employ it against rebellion, an outcome which at this stage they never seem to have considered in the least probable.

It was unfortunate for the ministers that this crisis coincided with the implementation of their decision to solve the problem of ruling the French Roman Catholic population of Canada in a mode which broke with British constitutional precedent. Their plan dispensed with the representative assembly projected as an ultimate objective in 1763, virtually conceded a Catholic church establishment, and also appeared to threaten the pretensions of other colonies to lands in the interior of the American continent. The Quebec Act of 1774 placed the province under a governor and a nominated council on which a careful balance of Canadian and British councillors was prescribed. Since it was thought improper to give this truncated legislature powers of taxation, certain revenues to be raised in Canada were imposed by a separate Act of Parliament. The Quebec Act introduced English criminal law but left French civil law in force with provisions for adaptation, which might bring about a progressive degree of anglicization. In order to satisfy the small minority of British settlers, it was laid down that civil cases might be tried with a jury if either the plaintiff or the defendant so required.

Coinciding as it did with the controversy over the Massachusetts Charter Act, the Quebec Act drew fire both from the parliamentary opposition and from the American colonists for its creation of an authoritarian form of government, its grant of full rights to Roman Catholics and its recognition of the status of their church. The redefinition of the boundaries of the province to include lands north of the Ohio as far west as the Mississippi also aroused a storm of protest. The people of New York, Pennsylvania, Maryland and Virginia all felt their claims to western lands denied by this ruling, and the government was obliged to give undertakings that the charter claims of these colonies would not be regarded as extinguished. And yet the policy was a rational one. It satisfied the political, religious and legal aspirations of most articulate French Canadians. It brought under the control of the provincial government scattered groups of French settlers, whose very existence had not been known when the original boundary of the colony was fixed in 1763. It gave political unity to a territory which was linked together by the river system of the St Lawrence and the Great Lakes, and connected commercially by the fur trade. And to some extent it marked a return to the abandoned policy of protecting the Indians from European exploitation. A well-meaning attempt to deal with multifarious problems, it did not deserve the vicious onslaught made upon it by the parliamentary opposition, and Chatham's denunciation of it as erecting a tyrannous and papal system displays one of the least reputable sides of his complex character.

II

Before long the ministers were rudely undeceived: the response in North America was very different from what they had expected. Early in the summer the news of the Boston Port Act evoked a remarkable display of American solidarity. From townships in Massachusetts, and from centres in other provinces all along the Atlantic coast came assurances of support and gifts in footstuffs, goods, and cash, to ease the port town's difficulties. Even before the texts of the other Coercive Acts had reached America moves were afoot to bring together a Continental Congress to co-ordinate resistance. In New England and in Virginia there was enthusiasm for another non-importation and non-consumption agreement of the kind which many colonists thought had forced the government to make concessions in 1766 and 1770. New Yorkers on the contrary backed a congress in the hope that it would make such a ruinous interruption of trade unnecessary. With the news of the remaining Coercive Acts American opinion rapidly hardened. As the nature and the implications of Parliament's pretensions became more clear the determination to resist them grew. William Drayton of South Carolina declared the question had now become, 'not whether Great Britain has a right to tax America against her consent, but whether she has a constitutional right to exercise despotism over America.' John Dickinson's *Essay on the Constitutional Power of Great Britain* denounced as illegal any power in which the people had no share, and conceded to Parliament only the right to regulate colonial trade. James Wilson's *Considerations on the Nature and Extent of the Legislative Authority of the British Parliament* denied it even this power, though he was prepared to see it legislate on trade by agreement with the colonies; and Thomas Jefferson, in his *A Summary View of the Rights of British America*, articulated a theory of an Empire of free and equal states connected only by common loyalty to the same sovereign. To many of the most able leaders of colonial society the issue had now crystalized into simple black and white, slavery or liberty, with slavery as the apparent alternative to full self-government under the king. By the time the Congress assembled at Philadelphia in September 1774, the prevailing tide of articulate opinion in the colonies was thus flowing strongly against the position which the British ministry had committed itself to uphold.

Both at Boston and at Philadelphia the rift deepened during the autumn. Massachusetts displayed flat defiance of the Charter Act. Men nominated to the new council were hounded and threatened till many of them resigned. Mass refusals of service as jurymen closed the courts of law. A public meeting of Suffolk county, in which Boston lay, threw down the gauntlet by calling for regular training of the militia and by declaring that no obedience was due to statutes violating the constitutional rights of British subjects. A provincial convention replaced the suspended general court, and began to assume the reins of authority, encouraging military preparations throughout the colony. Militia officers loyal to the royal administration were forced to resign. Town meetings carried on their defiant proceedings regardless of the ban on them written into the Charter Act, using as pretext the argument that meetings called before the Act was passed had merely been adjourned. By late autumn governor Gage could exercise no authority beyond the gun-range of the warships in Boston harbour.

The delegates who assembled in September at Philadelphia from various colonies soon showed that their sympathies were firmly behind Massachusetts. If the legislation of 1774 could be enforced then no provincial charter seemed safe, and early in the proceedings the Congress endorsed the Suffolk resolves. In the following weeks the delegates rejected a compromise plan put forward by the Pennsylvanian politician Joseph Galloway, under which Parliament and an all-American council representing the provincial assemblies would have exercised joint control over legislation pertaining to

America, each body having a right of veto. They resolved to exert pressure on Great Britain by means of a non-importation and a non-exportation agreement, and to recommend to the provinces the formation of an association to enforce it, backed by local committees which would place a social stigma on the recalcitrant. They approved a Declaration of Rights, and in a petition to the king and an address to the people of Britain they called for a repeal of the Coercive Acts and of all Acts imposing taxation in America. They demanded also the rescinding of the Quebec Act, doubly objectionable for its concessions of public status to Roman Catholics and its establishment of a non-representative provincial government. The maintenance of a military force in any colony without the consent of its assembly was declared to be contrary to law. To the king members of Congress complained also against grants of salaries to judges whose appointments still stood at the king's pleasure, against the extended powers given to customs officials and the increases in official fees which they might claim. The extent to which Burke's theory of a conspiracy by a secret cabal had entered into the thinking of colonial leaders is perhaps indicated by their attribution of blame not simply to ministers as such, but to 'those designing and dangerous men, who daringly [interposed] themselves' between the king and his 'faithful subjects' in America.[2] In their address to the British people the colonial leaders made clear that they claimed full constitutional equality and conceded no right of superiority to their fellow subjects on the eastern side of the Atlantic.

These developments were watched in London with anxiety but also with determination. What Congress was demanding in effect was the recognition of a confederation of commonwealths bound only by allegiance to a common sovereign. British politicians could see that the idea of executive unity under such conditions was a pure illusion. The strength in trade and defence derived from a unitary system would be destroyed, for the fulcrum of that system was no longer the king but Parliament. By November George III and the ministers were convinced that Massachusetts and the adjacent New England provinces were in a state of rebellion, and only force could 'decide whether they [were] to be subject to this country or independent.'[3]

It was with a new House of Commons behind them that ministers faced the next stage of the now rapidly escalating American crisis. By law a dissolution was unavoidable by the end of March 1775. But the disruption of the parliamentary session might be highly inconvenient in the midst of the further trials that might lie ahead. Moreover, although eighteenth-century elections rarely turned on great issues of

[2] Quoted in Ian R. Christie and Benjamin W. Labaree, *Empire or Independence, 1760–1776* (1976), p. 212.

[3] Quoted, Christie and Labaree, *Empire or Independence*, p. 227.

political controversy, and the unresponsiveness of the electoral system to popular opinion ensured a high degree of continuity of attitudes in the Commons, nevertheless the existence of a new Parliament would give more assurance of continued support for any policies approved during the autumn and winter. However, America was not the only consideration. The international situation seemed increasingly uncertain with the winding up of the Russo-Turkish war of 1768, and with readjustments at the French court following the death of Louis XV which made French policy less predictable. All these factors contributed to the decision to dissolve which the ministers finally took at the end of September.

The debate on the Address in the new House of Commons on 30 November made clear that so far as Parliament was concerned North and his colleagues could face the future with confidence, and during the next few months a series of decisions emerged in response to the developments in America. The law officers confirmed that the situation in Massachusetts was one of rebellion, and a proclamation calling on subjects to return to their allegiance was prepared. Limited reinforcements were scraped together for Gage, who was instructed that with the estimated 4,000 men he would then have he was expected to put down the rebellion. This step was taken despite urgent warnings. The secretary-at-war gave his expert opinion that the projected force could not possibly perform the service required of it, and this judgment was backed by Gage, who advised the recruitment of mercenaries and the establishment of a force of 20,000 men. But the ministry still grossly underestimated the extent of American resistance.

Congress's recommendation that committees should be set up to enforce the Continental Association produced immediate orders to governors that these combinations should be suppressed. A legitimate government, under obligation to safeguard its citizens in the pursuit of their lawful avocations, could hardly do less: it could not tolerate the activities of organizations seeking to impose their own peculiar restrictions on what citizens might do. If colonists voluntarily adhered to the Association, this was not the government's affair: but if self-appointed groups pressured colonists under threat into subscribing and then adhering to the association, this was a very different matter. It became action incompatible with the established rule of law and an usurpation of power. The protection of subjects from such coercion, by the use of whatever force might be necessary, then became an absolute duty; and in the following months ministers and their supporters began to talk in terms of succouring their colonial fellow-subjects from the 'tyranny' of Congress.

The economic warfare threatened by Congress's Continental Association provoked an equivalent British riposte with the Non-

Intercourse Act of March 1775. Initially this measure was directed only against the provinces considered to be in rebellion: it excluded the New Englanders from participation in the Newfoundland fisheries, or from trading with any area outside Great Britain, Ireland, and the British West Indies, forbidding them direct access for instance to their sources of supply of molasses from the French West Indies and to their markets for fish, grain, and lumber in southern Europe. An embargo on the transport of war stores to North America from other parts of the Empire had been ordered the previous autumn, and a major purpose of the Act was to interrupt the flow of similar supplies reaching New England from European or foreign Caribbean sources. As other colonies threw their weight behind New England during the following months the Act was progressively applied also to them.

During the winter the king and the ministry also sought to undermine American opposition by holding out prospects of favour to any province which, like New York, seemed inclined to remain in obedience, and by trying to formulate compromises which would drive a wedge between moderates and extremists. The most significant of these moves took shape in Lord North's conciliatory propositions put before Parliament in February 1775. This scheme made no concession to the demands of Congress. In particular it maintained Parliament's rights regarding taxation, merely conceding that the colonists should pass their own tax Bills provided the substance of these had received approval in London. From the colonial viewpoint this was wholly unacceptable. Ministers however believed the scheme to offer real practical concessions, since it was envisaged that colonial assemblies would retain full power to regulate the size of their civil establishments, and that colonial military contributions, once fixed, would be geared in exact proportion to the defence expenditure voted in Britain by Parliament. As the colonial secretary emphasized, the colonists would have 'full security that they [could] never be required to tax themselves without Parliament's taxing the subjects of this kingdom in a far greater proportion.'[4] Informally the proposal contained an offer of a 'compact' to the colonists, ruling out for the future arbitrary parliamentary assessments and establishing that link between the tax burden of the subject at home and of the subject in the colonies, the lack of which had been one of the most vulnerable aspects of British colonial revenue legislation since 1764. To the ministers this was both a genuine offer of compromise and a means of bidding for the support of moderate opinion in America. Perhaps even under the most favourable circumstances this proposal had

[4] Circular to governors, 3 March 1775, *Documents of the American Revolution 1770–1783* (*Colonial Office Series*), ed. K. G. Davies (21 vols., 1972–81) IX, pp. 61–2.

come too late, was unacceptable on principle, and rendered useless by the dissipation of trust due to the vagaries of British policy over the past 12 years. But in the event any hope of its making a favourable impact was cut short by the outbreak of hostilities at Lexington and Concord on 19 April 1775.

Three days earlier Gage had received his instructions to strike down rebellion. On 19 April he thrust at what he believed to be the main rebel supply dump at Concord. The object of the expedition was only partially fulfilled, and the consequences were catastrophic. The British columns extricated themselves only with heavy loss during a running battle over most of the 17 miles of their retreat. Within a few days thousands of New England militia, including many men from neighbouring Connecticut, had closed in on Boston. Gage was faced with exactly the situation against which he had warned the government more than six months before. Hostilities had been provoked when the army available in America was heavily outnumbered and incapable of controlling the province. All the moral advantage of success in the first armed clash had gone to the colonists.

During the weeks before this decisive event, both the wings of the parliamentary opposition had offered their solutions only to have them derisively rejected. Both Chatham in the Lords and Burke in the Commons called for the abandonment of any attempt to coerce the colonists and for a return to the legislative situation of 1763. Chatham's scheme proposed certain conditions which would have amounted to a clear colonial recognition of the essential unity of the Empire, including royal control of the army and the payment of a defence contribution. Burke's went far further in its concessions to provincial demands, laying down the principle that parliamentary supremacy should only be exercised when there was a general agreement within the Empire on the issues concerned: in this respect his vision anticipated solutions ultimately to be achieved in the Empire of the late nineteenth century. But even Burke's ideas were incompatible with the intellectual positions staked out by colonial leaders by 1775, and to most British politicians both schemes seemed to imply a total destruction of the essential bases of British safety, strength, and prosperity.

During the next 12 months events moved steadily towards breaking point. Faced with rebellion not only in New England but along the whole Atlantic coast, the government at last roused itself to take appropriate measures. A naval blockade of the whole coast was instituted. Sir Guy Carleton, the governor of Canada, was instructed to raise up to 3,000 troops from the local population. In December Parliament passed a further Act prohibiting all intercourse with the colonies while they remained in a state of rebellion, making their ships liable to seizure and their crews to impressment, and authorizing the crown to appoint commissioners to receive submissions, grant pardons and restore normal government and commercial intercourse to communities which returned to their allegiance. During the winter the ministry invoked subsidy treaties in force with Brunswick, Hesse Cassel and other German principalities and took into pay over 17,000 German mercenaries. Since the blockaded army at Boston was helpless and the place ultimately indefensible, the decision was taken to withdraw it, though this was not effected till March 1776. A great striking force of British and German troops was assembled during the spring, with the control of the lower Hudson valley as its main objective.

On the American side Lexington and Concord brought about a similar hardening of purpose. Everywhere opinion crystallized in favour of Massachusetts. Moderates who still hoped for compromise were shouldered aside, and the elements in New York which had hitherto held out against the Continental Association were overwhelmed. Supporters of the Association seized power and royal governors found themselves isolated and helpless. In the north the Green Mountain boys led by Ethan Allen seized the fort of Ticonderoga commanding the southern end of the route to Canada via Lake Champlain. Congress recommended the establishment of a provincial legislature to take over government in Massachusetts, authorized the movement of militia from the Middle Colonies to serve in what was now termed the Continental Army outside Boston, and appointed Washington to be its commander-in-chief. In July it formally rejected the British 'conciliatory propositions'. It also prepared a final 'Olive Branch' petition to George III, calling for the redress of the grievances listed the previous year. Once more it made clear that colonial leaders wished to remain within the Empire on their own terms and did not regard themselves as seeking independence. But if necessary these terms would be obtained by force, and this point was rammed home during the autumn by the despatch of expeditions which took Montreal and came near to capturing Quebec: as a result British troops intended for the New York campaign of 1776 had to be switched to the St Lawrence. In isolated clashes British governors were chased out of the southern colonies, the town of Norfolk, Virginia, being razed to the ground in the process.

Twelve months of war and the threats of war following upon Lexington and Concord drove the leaders of colonial resistance inexorably towards independence. 'Dependence' in their view meant loyalty to George III, not to Parliament, and as the British political tradition of the last hundred years informed them, this loyalty was contingent upon the king performing his appropriate role of safeguarding law and order and the constitutional liberties of his subjects. George III's rejection of the 'Olive Branch' petition in the winter of 1775 was seen as proof that he refused to fulfil this role, and months before Congress formally considered the question, a swelling tide of squibs and pamphlets was pointing the moral. In January 1776 Thomas Paine's *Common Sense* summed up in simple, vivid phrase the already widespread hostility to the monarchy, and in attacking kingship as an institution and not merely the person of George III, he focussed attention on the republican alternative to the form of state organization hitherto familiar to British Americans. In the early months of 1776 Congress began to act increasingly as the representative of a group of associated independent republics. It launched a mission to seek succour from France. It authorized operations by American privateers against the British. In defiance of the Prohibitory Act, it declared the ports of America open to foreign shipping. Early in the spring the delegates from Virginia and the New England provinces were ready to press for independence, and the reluctance of the Middle Colonies, particularly of New York and Pennsylvania, was gradually overcome. On 4 July, while British forces were massing at the mouth of the Hudson, Congress adopted the Declaration of Independence. Revolt had merged into revolution, and the sundered parts of the British Empire hovered on the verge of a major war.

III

When George III and the North Administration lurched into war with the American colonists, few men if any in official circles foresaw the intensity or the extent and duration of the conflict. In 1776 and again in 1777, and occasionally even later, ministers believed one, or one more campaign would finish the business.

Their assumptions were not without some grounds, although in the end they were to be proved mistaken. In the first place they believed in the existence of a considerable fund of loyalism in the colonies, which might well be fuelled by the 'tyranny' of the Continental Association. Officials from the areas south of the Potomac foretold this, and the flood of submissions in southern New York and central New Jersey in the autumn of 1776 seemed to confirm their impressions. The role of the armed forces was seen not as one of conquering a hostile population but of 'helping the good Americans to overcome the bad'. In

London rebellion was still regarded as the work of a minority only, though the obduracy of a large proportion of the New Englanders was recognized. Only with time did it become clear that loyalism was less strong than had been anticipated, and that the forces of rebellion were determined and powerful enough to crush it inexorably in any area not heavily guarded by regular military units. In particular, the rebel musters of militia faced men with the inescapable choice of immediate ostracism and ruin or of commitment against the armies of King George.

The initial miscalculation about the attitude of the population led inevitably to others. Military movement in North America proved to be much more difficult than expected, because local supplies of food, forage, kindling, and land carriage were virtually unobtainable. An army charged with the rescue of a loyal population from rebel task-masters could not simply live off the land as if it were a foreign terri-tory, though some of the German troops in British pay occasionally forgot this fact and alienated potential loyalists by their plundering habits. From the end of 1775 the army in America was almost totally dependent on supply organization in the British Isles linked to it by an Atlantic crossing of 3,000 miles. Its maintenance over the next six years was a staggering achievement by eighteenth-century standards, but even so the scale of effort was insufficient, and the inactivity of British forces, which has often been blamed simply on the inade-quacies of the commanders, was often due to failures of supply. The reasons for this were multifarious, and not all under human control. Orders placed in England for flour could be held up by lack of rainfall and water to drive the mills. On two or three occasions vital convoys of provisions were scattered and partly destroyed by Atlantic gales. But the human shortcomings were also important. Ration and strength returns from America were never adequate. Commitments to feed civilian or Indian auxiliaries were often overlooked. For the first three years at least, government efforts to enforce delivery dates on provi-sion contractors were half-hearted and the control over the quality of deliveries inadequate. The inefficiency, perhaps the corruption, of a single official in a key position, the commissary-general at Cork, con-tributed greatly to American provision shortages, as a large propor-tion of badly packed and rotten biscuit and meat slipped through into the supply pipeline. Above all, treasury parsimony prevented the provision of an adequate margin of supply of either transport tonnage or foodstuffs to allow for the wastage of war. Its refusal to sanction the maintenance of a reserve of tonnage meant further delays while the necessary ships were hired and collected for particular services. In the early years of the war national resources could well have sustained a more lavish policy, which would have given British military forces in

America a freedom to strike hard and early in the campaign season which they rarely enjoyed. But the army had no advocate within the governmental machine whose task it was to oversee its logistical interests. Only in 1781, the year of defeat, did it have an ample reserve of provisions, and by that time a growing serious shipping shortage ruled out further transportation of supplies on such a scale.

It was a combination of miscalculations about the nature of the war, an under-estimation of the scale of effort which it would require, and in the end formidable foreign intervention, that led to failure, rather than incompetence in conducting it. From the autumn of 1775, when Lord George Germain succeeded Dartmouth as colonial secretary, he was virtually minister for war. In the judgment of modern scholars he was an efficient administrator and a good strategist, and not guilty of various errors of omission and commission which have often been laid at his door. He certainly lacked the dynamism and personal ascendancy which the elder Pitt had shown as a war leader in the 1750s, but he was not a bungler — and Britain was to come through a far greater war crisis without a charismatic war leader in the 1800s. At least one historian has concluded that he, of all the ministers, had the soundest appreciation of the possibilities of naval action when the French first entered the war in the spring of 1778. But without Pitt's volcanic force of will, Germain could not sweep his colleagues into acceptance of bold and effective strategies.[5]

In 1776 the government planned a triple assault. A small force was to go to the south to restore loyalist control in Georgia and the Carolinas, and was then to hasten north to join the major expedition launched under the command of the Howe brothers to seize New York and the lower Hudson valley. A third force under the command of Carleton, the governor of Quebec, was to strike at the Upper Hudson Valley and the interior of New England by way of Lake Champlain. Successful operations by the two forces in the north would, it was hoped, isolate New England, regarded as the hard core of the rebellion, force the Americans' Continental army into battle under conditions chosen by the British generals, and lead to rapid collapse of the revolt.

None of these expectations was fulfilled. The expedition to the south found conditions far less favourable than the government had been led to expect. After some abortive probing, it moved on to New York, but its late arrival was one of many factors which delayed the start of operations there. In Canada, as a result of the American offensive the previous winter, Carleton, instead of commencing a

[5] For this interesting reassessment see Gerald Saxon Brown. *The American Secretary: The Colonial Policy of Lord George Germain, 1775–1778* (Ann Arbor, 1963), *passim*. Cf. Piers Mackesy, *The War for America 1775–1783* (1964), pp. 50–4.

campaign from bases at the northern or even the southern end of Lake Champlain, had first to advance to the lake and build vessels to wrest naval control of it from the Americans. But the vital factor which precluded for that year the capture of Ticonderoga at the south end of the lake and the exertion of pressure on the Americans in the Hudson valley was supply. While the treasury had sent over the provisions for the 12,000 men calculated to be on the army establishment under Carleton, the governor's Canadian militia, Indian auxiliaries, and several thousand civilian cart drivers and boat-builders nearly doubled the force his commissaries had to feed. Canada could provide no reserves. Lack of food and equipment, as well as the advancing season, ruled out the establishment and provisioning of a base south of the lake before the winter.

At New York General Howe lost two months of the campaigning season owing to the delays in shipping his provisions and camp equipment. The loss of opportunities to bring Washington to a decisive action can only be conjectured. In late August he swiftly secured the city and the surrounding area, including Long Island; but through fear of suffering too many casualties he missed the one chance which offered of destroying the Continental Army in its inadequate entrenchments on Brooklyn Heights. Outmanœuvred and pursued, Washington eventually retreated hastily westwards, keeping open his communications with the granaries of Pennsylvania, and the British pursuit brought Howe's troops to the Delaware, 'liberating' the population of central and western New Jersey. But to protect the loyalists Howe over-extended his forces in scattered detachments, giving Washington the opportunity for a small but decisive success on Christmas Day at Trenton. American morale soared; new enlistments for the Continental Army multiplied. Howe for his part accepted the necessity to shorten his lines and abandon western New Jersey, a move which cast a fatal damp on loyalist confidence in British protection. Meanwhile, to the east a detachment under Sir Henry Clinton occupied Rhode Island.

The campaign of 1777 began in an atmosphere of heady overconfidence and ended with one moderate triumph and a serious disaster. General Howe's decision to go for Philadelphia was expected to yield various advantages. The lure of strong loyalist support once again beckoned. The city was the largest in North America and, as the seat of Congress, had become in some sense the rebel capital, though its importance as such was greatly overestimated. Howe was not wrong, however, in thinking that Washington would be bound to offer battle in its defence, and thereby he might be forced into a situation in which his army could be destroyed. If a large part of Pennsylvania could be brought under control, New Jersey and Delaware would also be secure, and the army's provisioning problems would be solved whilst those of the Americans would be intensified. By moving the theatre of action to the westward Howe might also hope to separate the American forces and reduce any opposition to the second intended prong of the British attack, the expedition from Canada, which was now resumed under the leadership of General Burgoyne. Neither Howe, Burgoyne, nor the government in London believed there was any need to concert action by the two British armies at either end of the Hudson valley. Once again fallacious calculations were made about numbers of loyalists who were expected to rise in the back country of New England. Burgoyne believed that the few thousand men of his own command would be sufficient either to master the Hudson valley and so cut off New England, or to crush the heart of rebellion by a parade down the valley of the Connecticut River.

Howe's plans were hampered at the outset by the surviving Continental Army on his northern flank. Unable to trap it in a decisive action, and rightly fearing attacks on his communications if he marched westward, he opted for a seaborne attack on Philadelphia: his supply lanes by water would be secure. An attack up the Delaware River might have reaped great gains from the element of surprise, for Washington, groping totally at a loss, was then a hundred miles away. But Howe was put off by erroneous reports of the near approach of his army and of the strength of American fortifications up the Delaware and thereupon elected to sail round into the Chesapeake and approach Philadelphia from further west. By the time he landed in late August, his men had been seven weeks at sea, Washington had arrived, and the British cavalry mounts had been decimated by lack of forage on the voyage. Thus although Howe won his expected battle at Brandywine, lack of cavalry made pursuit and destruction of the fleeing Continentals impossible. Washington was able to rally his troops, received reinforcements, and managed to mount a counter-stroke at Germantown. Though this attack was a failure and did not shake the British hold on Philadelphia, it was not a disaster, and American morale remained high. The Continental army was still in being and could fight, and while this was so no extensive British occupation or pacification of territory would be possible.

Although to this extent the Philadelphia campaign was indecisive, decision elsewhere cast the scales heavily against Great Britain. On the northern front Burgoyne quickly seized Ticonderoga with éclat, and then with growing difficulty thrust his way through to the Hudson River. But a series of errors of judgment followed. Horses which should have been used to carry up provisions were instead employed to haul an excessive artillery train. Although the disastrous raid

Burgoyne ordered on Bennington in the hope of acquiring rebel supplies revealed no expected loyalists, only a dangerous concentration of American patriots which destroyed two British detachments totalling some 1,400 men, the general failed to act thereafter with due circumspection. In face of superior numbers of Americans blocking his road southward to Albany, while the militia from the Green Mountains threatened his extending line of communications, a sensible commander would have revised his plans, accepted that his information had been false, and returned to the comparative safety of Ticonderoga. Not so the amateur dramatist Burgoyne, who plunged rashly forward, to be surrounded and forced to surrender by superior forces at Saratoga. Although the army thus lost was relatively small, the episode had deep significance. It emphasized once more the fact revealed at Boston in 1775, that at a crisis hordes of militia, especially with a small stiffening of Continentals, could swallow up substantial British forces and destroy them by sheer weight of numbers. No small professional army could fight a war indefinitely on those lines. Howe's drawing off Washington to Pennsylvania had availed nothing. Above all, the American victory persuaded Britain's European rival, France, that the time had arrived to redress the reverse suffered in the Seven Years War.

The two years of warfare in which the British faced only the Americans revealed a further important limitation of British arms. American seaborne contact with the outer world could not be checked. This was work for frigates and lighter craft, and the British navy simply did not dispose of enough of them to set up an effective blockade of the long American coastline. A full naval mobilization in American waters was never contemplated, not only because of the expense, but for the two much more compelling reasons, that the English Channel had to be guarded, and that such a step would undoubtedly have been treated as a *casus belli* by the French, who understandably would not have dared to leave their Caribbean empire unprotected when a large British fleet was loose in the western Atlantic. There were rarely more than 70 ships of war on the American station, and many of these were often otherwise engaged, protecting British supply vessels jeopardized by the *guerre de course* waged by American privateers, or assisting in the amphibious operations of the army. American tobacco and other commodities continued to find their way to the neutral West Indies or direct to Europe, and brought in the funds for purchases of arms and munitions the Americans could not fully provide for themselves. Nine tenths of the gunpower available to the Americans up to the end of 1777 was imported by sea. A small but useful balance of *matériel* was gained from prizes taken by privateers. These circumstances were no good augury for the British conduct of the widening struggle in the years to follow.

<h1 style="text-align:center">IV</h1>

During the winter lull a diplomatic race ensued, which the French won with the signature on 6 February 1778 of a treaty of commerce and alliance with the Americans. This inevitably involved them in an armed collision with Great Britain, formally as an auxiliary, in effect as a principal, although no declaration of war was made by either side. For the Americans the treaty represented a recommitment to outright independence and ruled out any possibility that they would negotiate on the rather less favourable terms North's ministry was preparing. The launching of the Carlisle Peace Commission in the spring of 1778, with offers of almost every concession Congress had demanded in 1775, but not independence, and coupled with an Act of Parliament abandoning parliamentary claims to impose taxes for revenue on colonial possessions, was thus abortive. The Commissioners reached Philadelphia at the beginning of June but found Congress adamant against any discussion save on the basis of an immediate British military withdrawal or a recognition of independence. The Americans were all the less concerned to parley owing to the immediate relief from British pressure brought about by the French intervention.

For war with France not only thrust upon the British government the expensive burden of a full naval mobilization. It also dictated changes of plan, for two new preoccupations immediately came to the fore. A naval screen had to be maintained in the Channel against invasion and for the defence of trade; and the commercially valuable West Indies had to be secured. The Admiralty headed by Lord Sandwich successfully provided a guard for the Channel, but an indecisive action against the French fleet off Ushant at the end of July made clear that the British were far from holding naval superiority. Safety in the Caribbean depended upon local naval ascendancy and a pre-emptive strike against French bases, and while the warships could be provided from Great Britain, troops for such an enterprise could only be found in North America. The conquests of 1777 perforce had to be abandoned: at the end of June General Clinton, the new British commander in America, withdrew his forces from Philadelphia, losing thus also all hold on New Jersey and Delaware. Between Nova Scotia and Florida only the two enclaves at New York and Rhode Island remained under his control. Then, as the hurricane season in the Caribbean came to an end, the military reserves thus made available were launched to the southward. In December British forces seized the strategically important island of St Lucia overlooking the main French base at Martinique. The British position on the northern flank of the Caribbean theatre was strengthened by the dispatch of a small force to east Florida which succeeded early in 1779 in occupying Savannah and regaining control of much of the colony of Georgia.

This success shaped the British North American initiative for 1779. The recovery of Georgia held out the promise that British authority might be established piecemeal in one colony after another, especially in the more isolated southern territories distant from the centres of American strength. The restoration of loyalist control and of civil government embodying the concessions of 1778 would act as an encouragement to a return to allegiance elsewhere. Where rebellion was more obdurate the population was to be harassed by coastal raids intended to generate popular pressure on Congress to accept British terms.

But as the year progressed the intervention of hostile European naval power placed growing restrictions on British initiative. For lack of naval supremacy the troops which had taken St Lucia in December 1778 could not be switched back to Clinton's command and were permanently lost to the North American theatre of operations. Indeed, the West Indies could not be fully protected: before the hurricanes broke, both St Vincent and Grenada had fallen into French hands. In April Clinton mounted a successful raid on Portsmouth, Virginia, destroying large quantities of military stores, tobacco awaiting export, and about 150 ships of various sizes; but by September a French fleet under D'Estaing was off the coast of Georgia, paralysing all troop movements in the southern part of his command and blocking an intended campaign into South Carolina. With naval superiority temporarily lost Clinton felt obliged to withdraw to New York the substantial garrison at Rhode Island which might otherwise be cut off and overwhelmed. His attempt in June to force Washington into a pitched battle by threatening his lateral communications across the Hudson at King's Ferry ended in a repulse at Stoney Point which discouraged him from any further venture in the Hudson valley.

By mid 1779 the British navy had to contend with the forces not only of France but also of Spain, and even before the Spanish declaration of war on 16 June, ships of the line were being held back from the western theatre in order to secure the Channel. Spanish statesmen hoped for a short war which would secure them Gibraltar, Minorca, Jamaica and the Honduras, and believed that the only way to achieve this was an invasion of England which would rock British commercial credit and destroy the country's capacity to fight. From their insistence sprang the invasion project of 1779, and as the combined French and Spanish fleets greatly outnumbered the British home fleet in ships of the line, the threat of it imposed stringent restrictions on British naval deployment, and set a pattern which was to be repeated in succeeding years. So long as the Channel was menaced ships could not be sent in adequate force to the West Indies or North America, any naval superiority established in those areas proved to be only temporary, and in the long run the safety of British possessions could not be guaranteed. A further strain was placed upon the navy by the need for an expedition each year to revictual and reinforce Gibraltar. In 1779 the allied invasion project itself collapsed through bad timing and the inefficiency of the Spanish fleet, but the general pattern of the war now became increasingly adverse to Great Britain.

At the beginning of 1780 diplomatic feelers failed to disclose a way out of the difficulties in which the British government now found itself. Knowing that Gibraltar was the real point of Spanish grievance which kept the Bourbon alliance in being, ministers toyed with the idea of abandoning it, George III himself was not averse to the suggestion; but the Spanish were not yet ready to be bought off even by this concession, and later events suggest that North and his colleagues might have been overwhelmed by a storm of public opinion for offering it. In a desperate search for an alliance to counter the French, the ministers persuaded George III to offer Minorca to Catherine of Russia; but Catherine had her own preoccupations in eastern Europe and was in no mind to become entangled in a war in the west on Britain's behalf.

In these circumstances only the preoccupation of the French with the West Indies in the winter and spring of 1779−80 made possible the illusory British success of 1780 in the southern colonies.

D'Estaing's departure for the Caribbean enabled Clinton to embark 6,000 men for South Carolina in December 1779, three months later than originally planned. Owing to bad weather and other factors this expedition was unable to commence operations at Charleston till 1 April, but it scored a striking initial triumph. On 12 May the city was captured with a large haul of prisoners and war material. Small surviving groups of American troops were broken in a series of battles, and the way seemed open for the pacification of the province. Leaving General Cornwallis with 4,000 troops to secure it, Clinton returned with the remainder to New York. To divert American attention from the far south he then launched a further expedition of 2,500 men into the Chesapeake. But thereafter the year brought increasingly adverse developments, both in America and in Europe. In July 1780 a French expedition established itself firmly in Rhode Island. In South Carolina, despite a second decisive victory over an American force at Camden, Cornwallis began to discover, as Howe had done in New Jersey in 1776, that the approach of any American army would act as a magnet to formidable forces of patriot militia, that loyalists could not hold the ground, and that detachments were vulnerable. He concluded that South Carolina could not be held unless the enemy were driven out of North Carolina also, and made plans to strike north, but in doing so he overlooked the strength of patriot feeling in the interior. In October a loyalist militia force about a thousand strong operating up country was surrounded and destroyed at King's Mountain, and all offensive operations had to be halted.

In Europe the burdens upon the navy multiplied more rapidly than the navy itself, for in December a new enemy, the United Provinces, entered the ring. Ever since the French entry into the war the British, regardless of Dutch protests, had systematically intercepted and purchased supplies of Baltic naval stores consigned to France in Dutch vessels. Under pressure from the French the Dutch took what appeared a way out of this impasse in the latter part of 1780. For reasons which remain obscure but which probably related more than anything to national prestige, Catherine of Russia organized a league of neutral northern states to uphold the principle of freedom of transport in neutral vessels and deny the rights of search and seizure asserted by Great Britain. The states concerned, including Russia, had only small merchant navies, and the naval stores France and Spain might receive by way of them caused the British no concern. But if the Dutch who had most of the Baltic carrying trade secured the protection of the Armed Neutrality the gain to France would be great. When reports arrived that they were negotiating to accede to it, the British government hastily declared war on the pretext, to which captured documents gave some semblance of colour, that the Dutch were negotiating a commercial treaty with the Americans. This step involved a heavy new naval commitment in the North Sea. Moreover French attention was drawn to the Cape of Good Hope and to South Asia, where the Dutch disposed of a first-rate naval anchorage at Trincomalee, and in reaction to French initiatives the British were forced to divert warships and some troops to the east.

As a consequence plans drawn up in London for attacks on the Spanish empire had to be abandoned, and in 1781 the overstrained navy could no longer meet all necessary commitments in the Caribbean and western Atlantic. The results were first apparent in the

Caribbean. Although the Dutch island of St Eustatius fell into British hands with a rich spoil of war contraband on its way to the Americans, the French were able to occupy Tobago, and to the west the Spanish took over west Florida. Ultimately British operations in North America faced the increasing hazard of the rupture of sea communications. Before this came to pass, Cornwallis resumed his northward campaign at the start of 1781, but his hopes that a decisive victory could be gained which would consolidate British control of the southern colonies was dashed by the partisan activity in his rear. His march northward through North Carolina in the early months of 1781 brought him victories in the field but no control of territory, and failed to draw the American forces back from the southward. In the summer, once his onward advance had taken him out of reach, the detachments left to secure South Carolina and Georgia were driven back until only the provincial capitals were left in British hands. Nor was any advantage derived from his further summer advance to Richmond, Virginia, where he linked up with the force sent to Portsmouth in the Chesapeake the previous year before moving to the Williamsburg peninsula, where Clinton instructed him to hold a base for future operations. Clinton's orders were predicated on the assumption that British naval control of American waters would continue; but it was now the end of the campaign season in the West Indies and the threat of decisive French naval action on the American coast at last became a reality. British naval and military reinforcements from the Caribbean arrived too late and in inadequate strength, and in September a British naval challenge in inferior force was unable to drive D'Estaing from the Chesapeake. The British army in Virginia was isolated both by land and by sea. By forced marches the main American and French army under Washington swooped down from the north and cut off Cornwallis's position at Yorktown on the landward side, while D'Estaing's fleet took control of the Chesapeake, blockaded it to seaward, and made possible the waterborne delivery of Washington's siege train to the scene of action. Cornwallis's field fortifications were pounded to pieces before a relief force from New York could reach him, and in mid October he surrendered his army.

Less than 4,000 troops were lost at Yorktown. The main British army in North America was still in being. But this disaster came on top of reverses in the Caribbean, losses of valuable convoys off home waters, and a critical straining of the nation's resources. For the time being New York and other British seaport bases in North America were safe, for as soon as Yorktown was won the French fleet under D'Estaing returned to the West Indies. But the dangers of the situation were obvious. Although the king could not reconcile himself to the thought of losing America and believed it must spell the end of the existence of Britain as a major power, among the politicians the opinion steadily gained ground that the colonies were irrecoverable, and that the only sensible course was an all-out war against the French in hopes of saving the West Indies and India. Divided in opinion, pressed on one side by the king and on the other by its dissident supporters, the cabinet fell into a state of inanition on American business. In the end the direction of national policy was decided in Parliament. On 27 February the House of Commons voted against the continuance of offensive operations in America. On 20 March it threatened a vote of no confidence which North only escaped by announcing the ministers' resignations. The task of salvage and peace-making passed to their successors, and in circumstances which were not wholly desperate; for in the last weeks of its existence the North ministry had pressed vigorously forward with the vital rein-forcement of both the East and West Indian theatres, action which was to avert complete disaster in the last year of the war.

V

Three themes stand out in the history of British affairs in India during the later years of the North administration: the increasing, often war-like, involvement of the presidencies with the country powers; the efforts of Hastings to grapple with this situation at the same time as trying to improve the administration of Bengal; and the frustrations of the ministry in its relation with the Company.

In 1775 the Bombay presidency had fished in the troubled waters of Maratha politics with the object of securing the strategic island of Salsette and the district of Bassein. Since London approved, Warren Hastings had been obliged to exert supporting pressure on the Peshwa at Poona. His threats of hostilities brought about the treaty of Purandhar in March 1776, which settled terms neither side felt inclined to observe. After 1778 the claims to Salsette and the cause of Ragunath Rao involved the presidency in further inglorious military ventures which had to be supported by a campaign mounted across the centre of India from Bengal. By 1782 the Company's troops had gained sufficient success to secure an acceptable general peace with the Marathas and their allies by the Peace of Salbai.

The financial interdependence of the Arcot creditors on the

Madras council and Mohammed Ali, the Nawab of the Carnatic, brought still greater troubles upon that presidency, entailing further demands for financial and military help from Bengal. The support given by the council to the aggressive designs of the Nawab in Tanjore roused the suspicion and hostility of the two major south Indian principalities, Hyderabad and Mysore. Although the directors in London ordered the abandonment of this policy, they were helpless to check it. The Arcot creditors were so much in command of affairs that when a new governor, George Pigot, was sent out to carry out their instructions, he was deposed and imprisoned by the majority on the council. His successor, Sir Thomas Rumbold, involved himself in further quarrels with both Hyderabad and Mysore, repudiating treaties which had been made in the past with the rulers of both states, and he gave great umbrage to Hyder Ali of Mysore after the entry of France into the American war by occupying the French factory at Mahé, which Hyder Ali had declared to be under his protection. In 1780 Hyder Ali invaded and laid waste the Carnatic. During the next two years it became evident that while his army could not stand up to the Company's troops in a set battle, they on their part could not round up his forces and expel them from the Nawab's territories. French intervention on the Coromandel coast in 1782−3, including the landing of soldiers to support the forces of Mysore, created a perilous situation for the Company's troops in the Carnatic, from the consequences of which perhaps only the signing of the peace preliminaries at Paris saved them.

Hastings's most creative reforms in Bengal had taken place before 1775, but in one area there was a steadily growing improvement in the later 1770s. The number of British personnel engaged in administration increased, and their emoluments began to be raised to a realistic level. The Company's assumption that its servants should receive only a nominal salary and look after themselves by private trading had been abandoned by Clive; but if private trading was no longer admissible, then adequate remuneration had to be provided in some other form. Hastings extended the practice of payment by commission for the Bengal civilians engaged in revenue administration. While both this trend and the enlargement of the service partly reflected the pressures of demands for patronage coming from London, the scaling up of emoluments also stemmed from the governor-general's genuine concern to create a body of officials whose financial security would conduce to integrity in their handling of Company revenues.

His policy placed additional charges on the revenues. The amounts were relatively small, but this coincided with the very great additional burdens caused by the wars against the Marathas and Mysore, and later against the French. Some indication of this increase is given by the figures revealing the growth of the Company's forces. Whereas in 1763 about 8,000 Indian sepoys had been enrolled in the Company's Bengal army, by 1784 the number had risen to nearly 40,000 and by then the Company also had in pay a swollen European officer corps of over 1,000.

By the end of the 1770s heavy military expenditure was having a two-fold effect on the Company's affairs. As in the late 1760s, the surplus of Bengal revenue available for the Company's investment disappeared, and the trading activities with which the directors in London were chiefly concerned fell into disorder. As the Company became unable to meet its liabilities, the government also became concerned. In Bengal Hastings was driven to extraordinary expedients in his search for funds, which were later to form some of the most damaging articles of an impeachment against him. His demands for war contributions upon Chait Singh, the Raja of Benares, ultimately drove that potentate into revolt, and the charges imposed by Hastings on his successor were excessive and damaging in relation to the productive capacity of the principality. Hastings' withdrawal of protection of the jaghirs and treasure of the Begums of Oudh for the purpose of tapping some of this wealth in contributions from the reigning Nawab, may have had some political justification, but was undertaken without the preliminary judicial inquiries which would have been appropriate. His calls for troops from the ruler of Rampur were undoubtedly in excess of treaty stipulations.

By the late 1770s both the government's own timetable and the course of events in India made the business of the Company one of pressing concern. North's ministry had regarded the Regulating Act of 1773 as a rescue operation to be reviewed when the Act expired in 1779. Before the six years had elapsed those responsible for working the system, especially John Robinson, North's secretary to the treasury, had good reason to be dissatisfied. The attempt to manage the Company politically had failed. The limit of this method was demonstrated most conspicuously by the proprietors' resistance to demands for the recall of Hastings in 1775. When Robinson in 1778 began to rough out plans for a new settlement, he plumped for greater powers of control. While a direct takeover by the crown was still out of the question, he began to think in terms of government nominees in the direction, of a full control over outgoing correspondence, and more power for the crown over the appointment and dismissal of the chief officers in India. But any airing of such plans immediately encountered strong resistance both from the directors and the proprietors. In dealing with this the government was greatly weakened by the hostility of the parliamentary opposition led by Rockingham.

Members of this party had taken sides against the Arcot creditors as partisans of the Pigot family. The party as a whole remained extremely suspicious of any growth of the power of the crown fed by resources from India, and was at this time grafting on to its myth of the secret cabal the further myth of the secret influence wielded over the ministry by the Nawab of the Carnatic. Early in 1781 its pre-occupation with these questions gave rise to the establishment of a new House of Commons Select Committee on Indian affairs, in which Edmund Burke became the driving force. The government for its part also faced other pressing problems in America and in Ireland, was rent by internal dissension in 1779, and was diverted by a general election in 1780. In these circumstances the existing arrangements had to be extended temporarily in 1779 and 1780. Serious action was deferred till 1781, by which time news of the war in the Carnatic had prompted the ministry to set up its own Commons Secret Committee on the Company's affairs. In face of all these various difficulties the settlement with the Company in 1781 inevitably bore the character of a compromise and left much to be desired from the point of view of the treasury officials.

The India Act of 1781 renewed the Company's charter for a further 10 years. It perpetuated the compromise of 1773, by which the question of the crown's right to the territorial revenues was evaded, the revenues being left in the Company's hands. The Company was to make a down payment of £400,000 in full discharge of its tribute obligations for the period 1773–81. Henceforth, after payment of a dividend of 8 per cent any surplus was to be divided in a ratio of three quarters to the exchequer and one quarter to the Company. The maximum dividend payable out of the Company's share was to be 12½ per cent, and the former restriction that the dividend might not be raised more than 1 per cent a year was retained. The treasury was to receive annual accounts of the territorial revenues and of the disbursements charged against them. The Act renewed the government's powers in relation to the appointment of the governor-general and the council in Bengal, but no attempt was made to follow up recommendations from the treasury advisers for a clarification of the authority of these officials over the other presidencies or for any strengthening of the governor-general's powers in relation to the council. In response to difficulties which had arisen between Hastings and the supreme court of Bengal, and applying policy emanating from the opposition through the Commons Select Committee rather than from the government, the Act constrained the court by exclud-ing from its jurisdiction anything done by the governor-general and council in their public capacity, any matter concerning the revenue and its collection, and any Indian acting in the capacity of landholder or farmer of rents. This thwarted attempts by the court to prevent oppression of *ryots* by *zamindars* or by the native agents of Company officials. The court's jurisdiction over all inhabitants of Calcutta was confirmed, but Hindu or Moslem law as appropriate was to be administered in cases of inheritance, contract, or succession. In an attempt to prevent foreign interests from benefitting at the Company's expense, British subjects in India were forbidden to lend money to foreign companies. This practice had been frequently followed as a means of remitting funds from India once the treasury, after 1773, had imposed checks on the amounts in bills of exchange from India which might be honoured by the Company.

Politicians on both sides in Parliament remained dissatisfied with the situation of the Company. Their anxieties increased as the exigencies of war in India made it clear as early as December 1781 that the Company would be unable without financial help to meet its obligations to shareholders or to the treasury. Its growing financial embarrassments made further political interference almost inevitable, but the next developments were to take place under the new political dispensations that followed the collapse of the North administration.

6 The Years of Crisis

The British defeat at Saratoga, the intervention of France in the American war, and the failure during the summer of 1778 of the peace mission sent to negotiate with the Americans under the leadership of the Earl of Carlisle, ushered in a prolonged period of high political crisis not finally resolved until 1784, and after four changes of administration within 21 months. Although Lord North survived in office till early 1782 confidence in the ministry and within the ministry was severely shaken. As one European power after another was added to the list of Britain's enemies, hopes of recovering America or even emerging from the war without serious disaster grew increasingly unrealistic, blame was heaped on North and his colleagues for bringing the country into such a sorry situation, and their whole war policy came under mounting fire.

Such circumstances demanded a war leader of genius. None was to hand. No politician had the charisma to rally the nation's forces as the war passed into its most critical stage. Any faint − and highly unrealistic − hopes that Chatham might re-emerge to play this role were extinguished by his death in May 1778. Germain, capable as he was, could not force his war policy on his colleagues, came into constant conflict with Sandwich over naval deployment, and grew unhappy with his situation. North was even less capable of providing a lead. Under the strain of trying to co-operate with feuding colleagues and face a growing opposition in the Commons he seems for some months to have teetered on the edge of a nervous breakdown, and was only prevented from resigning by the insistent refusal of George III to let him go. In 1779 with one secretaryship of state left vacant by the death of the Earl of Suffolk, the problem of filling it apparently beyond North's power to resolve, and two other senior cabinet ministers − Earl Gower, the president of the council, and Lord Weymouth, the southern secretary of state − moving towards a decision to resign on the score of North's failure to settle the Irish question, the administration almost collapsed. It was saved by the king's resolution and also perhaps by an upsurge of confidence arising from the recovery of Georgia. Two new secretaries of state were found. Hillsborough, who had been out of office since 1772, returned to take the southern department. The northern department was accepted by Viscount Stormont, a nephew of Lord Chief Justice Mansfield, a hard-working professional diplomat, whose abilities soon introduced a new order and efficiency into cabinet proceedings. But neither of them brought any additional parliamentary support for the ministry, and still less did the sexagenarian professional lawyer, Earl Bathurst, an ex-lord chancellor, who agreed to fill the void of the presidency.

Attempts to recruit from the parliamentary opposition were not neglected, but all proved fruitless. Ministers would have liked to detach to their own side the Duke of Grafton and his friends and the members of the Chathamite circle, led after Chatham's death by the Earl of Shelburne. The imperialist sympathies of the Chathamites and their known repugnance to the idea of American independence kindled a faint hope that they might agree to take office and support the war, but this they were not prepared to do. Rockingham was even less ready to compromise with or give countenance to the present ministers. About 1774 it had seemed as if his party was isolated, frustrated, and on the verge of dissolution. The re-emergence of clear-cut, divisive political issues during the ensuing years had consolidated it and brought it new recruits. Edmund Burke's *Thoughts on the Cause of the Present Discontents* had given it a clear ideological base. Its leaders saw themselves as the potential saviours of the nation's liberties and believed that this cause would be jeopardized by the success of British arms in North America. From the spring of 1778 they were reconciled and committed to the idea of American independence. The uncompromising nature of their attitude became evident in the early summer of 1780 when North put out feelers for a coalition. Rockingham made clear that his terms included full freedom to negotiate peace even at the cost of independence for America, the passage of legislation curbing the parliamentary influence of the executive, and a clean sweep of the existing cabinet. To George III, committed to the hilt to the recovery of America, and insistent on his prerogative right to choose ministers, such terms were wholly unacceptable, so long as any alternative course remained. North and his colleagues perforce continued in office past the eleventh hour, to grapple with a desperate war situation, growing diplomatic difficulties, and mounting pressures of discontent both in Ireland and in Britain itself.

II

The American war was Ireland's opportunity, and during the late 1770s North encountered growing difficulties in Dublin on both commercial and constitutional questions. Among members of the Protestant political class in Ireland the American crisis roused conflicting feelings. On the one hand loyal Irishmen had no wish to let the colonists secede. On the other they felt a common interest with them in defence of constitutional principles against the claims of the British parliament, especially on the issue of taxation. Although British politicians tried to indicate that taxation of Ireland from Westminster was not really on the cards, they could not hide the fact that the over-riding claims to supremacy of the British parliament, in defence of which they were fighting the Americans, included that function in principle. If Irish establishment support for British policy in America was thus cool and shot through with reservations, the attitude of the Ulster Presbyterians was distinctly hostile. By contrast the politically aware element among the Irish Catholics supported the imperial authority and gave assistance with recruiting — a development which Protestants regarded with distaste and suspicion.

With growing economic prosperity over the past 30 years, Irish society was becoming both more self-assured and more ready to react sharply to any setback. Hardships caused by the American war soon led to protests. At the commencement of the rebellion the Irish lost an important section of their overseas market for linen, and also the benefits of a substantial illicit trade carried on with the colonies. Emigration, which had helped to relieve unemployment, was cut short. In 1775−6 their provisions trade was affected by a British embargo intended to ensure that sufficient supplies were available to meet military and naval requirements in America; but this check was only temporary, for the American war produced a continuing demand for thousands of tons of barrelled beef and pork and butter. The business fraternity raked in fat profits, but the consequent rise in food prices created difficulties of a different kind for those lower down the social scale and increased the general discontent. Private profiteering by the dishonest British commissary at Cork, Robert Gordon, aroused much indignation. During 1776 Irish resentments were strongly echoed in the House of Commons in Dublin, and the administration was reduced to a lavish distribution of peerage creations and advancements in order to ride through the storm and secure support for supply for a further 4,000 men on the Irish military establishment destined for service in North America.

A more long-term threat to Irish commercial prosperity came from the loss of European markets due to the entry of France and Spain into the war, with an accompanying dislocation of the trade routes to those parts of Europe which remained open to Irish commerce. Bankruptcies multiplied, unemployment increased, and the lord lieutenant began to foresee the time when yields of taxes would fail and the country become a financial liability to Britain. The opening of new channels of commerce became imperative or the Irish administration itself might face bankruptcy. In face of the French threat an Irish militia Act had been put on the statute book in 1778 but it remained inoperative for lack of money.

North and his cabinet colleagues did not lack for information on this deteriorating situation, which was hammered home by such unofficial spokesmen as the MPs Lord Nugent and Lord Midleton, as well as by the lord lieutenant and his staff, and they were not unwilling to make concessions. The embargo on provisions was relaxed during 1778 and finally lifted at the end of the year. An investigation by a committee of the British House of Commons ended with recommendations that Ireland should be granted a direct export and import trade with the colonies in all articles except woollen goods and tobacco, and that Irish sailcloth, cordage, and cotton yarn should be freely admitted into Great Britain. The government introduced Bills to this effect but they were blocked as a result of a flurry of petitions from British commercial interests which felt themselves threatened, and the proposed concessions were then so whittled down as to be of little help to Ireland. The refusal to let Ireland import goods direct from the colonies made valueless the leave given to export to them. Except for the admission free of duty of Irish cotton yarn − a commodity in rapidly growing demand in England − British protective legislation remained intact, and it was small help that Irish ships were given the benefit of the British fishery acts.

But the dam would no longer hold. The logic of the British case for refusing Irish commercial demands had been destroyed by the sweeping offers made to the Americans within the terms of the Carlisle Peace Commission of 1778. To no avail the North ministry made small concessions during the spring of 1779: the prohibition on Irish tobacco entering Britain was abolished, a bounty was granted on imported Irish hemp, and the government agreed to shoulder the charges for the Irish regiments serving in America. This was no longer sufficient. In Ireland it now became a fixed idea that only terms similar to those offered to the Americans would preserve some measure of commercial prosperity and compensate for the high levels of war taxation. Public agitation increased. A county meeting at Galway in March 1779 adopted the American example of a non-importation agreement directed against British manufacturers and this movement soon obtained wide support elsewhere. In Dublin the radical leadership known as the committee of the aggregate body systematically blacklisted merchants handling British goods. The gestures of meetings of grand juries and counties were reinforced by expressions of opinion from the newly raised bodies of Volunteers which, in the absence of the proposed militia, began to make an almost spontaneous appearance in face of the Bourbon invasion threat of 1779. Though primarily confined to the Church of Ireland gentry and their Protestant tenants, and the middling ranks of society in town and country, the Volunteers proved to be a highly responsive sounding board for Irish discontent, and their connection with the influential part of the parliamentary electorate had its effect in due course on the proceedings of the Irish House of Commons. Under the guidance of Charlemont and Henry Grattan the movement began to act as a bridge between Protestant and Catholic Irishmen, and political awareness spread rapidly among its members. Constant reference to it by opposition spokesmen at Westminster helped to create an exaggerated sense of its importance and to speed recruitment among those who were prepared to use it to attain political ends. By the autumn of 1779 it was thought to number over 40,000, and bade fair to become a rallying point for national feeling.

Throughout the summer the lord lieutenant sent frequent warnings to London that in face of the public excitement and discontent the usual management of the Irish Commons by traditional modes of influence was bound to break down. In the autumn his forebodings proved fully justified. At its first meeting to debate the Address on 12 October, the House ran wild and passed a motion declaring the necessity for free trade. Before long, in response to addresses from the constituencies and harassment by public demonstrations, it took the decision to vote supplies for six months only, instead of the usual two years, in order to enforce the demand for commercial concessions.

These acts of defiance were encouraged by the knowledge that the parliamentary opposition in Britain was sympathetic and ready to harass the ministry. The situation they created was critical. Unless concessions were made, either the Irish administration would break down for lack of funds or else the British authorities would have to shoulder the fiscal burden of maintaining it. In face of the threat of a refusal of supplies, of the rapid growth of the Volunteer movement, of widespread bankruptcies in Ireland, of growing disorder and fresh public manifestations of Irish discontent, and with British commercial opinion sobered by the threat to its Irish markets from the non-importation agreements, the British government hastened to act. By a series of statutes passed at Westminster at the beginning of 1780 the restraints on the export of Irish wool, woollens and glassware were removed. Acts prohibiting the carrying of gold and silver into Ireland were repealed. The Irish were conceded freedom to trade with the British colonies on the same terms that the British themselves enjoyed, that is to say, duties equal to those payable in British ports were to be imposed by the Irish parliament on the imports and exports of Ireland. Membership of the Levant Company was opened to Irish merchants. The Irish, in fact, had been granted a system of commerce corresponding to that offered by the Carlisle Commission to the Americans.

But now the momentum of Irish discontent could no longer be checked, and almost without a pause Charlemont, Grattan and their friends turned to the constitutional grievances which might be held to have underpinned the recent adverse economic situation. Once again they took comfort from the situation in Britain, where the agitation of the Yorkshire Association and the Westminster Committee was at its height and the ministry was coming under pressure from the parliamentary campaign for economical reform.[1] In the belief that a sinister conspiracy underlying British administration must be destroyed the Rockinghamite opposition did not blench even from supporting the Irish constitutional demands. In April 1780, in response to a new wave of carefully orchestrated public agitation in county meetings, Grattan moved a series of resolutions in the Irish Commons amounting to a declaration of Irish legislative independence, and although they were defeated by the lord lieutenant's majority, the situation was highly unstable. Irish justices of the peace struck a more resounding blow against the British parliament's pretensions to authority in Ireland by refusing to take action against military deserters under the British Mutiny Act, and the need for an Irish Act immediately became acute. Even some of the lord lieutenant's advisers, especially on the military side, took the view that such an Act was now essential, although the very passage of it would amount to an assertion that in Irish internal affairs the powers of the Westminster parliament were of no account. The ministers in London accepted the necessity. They tried to restrict its implications as much as possible by amending the Bill in the privy council so as to make it perpetual. In this form it was eventually passed at the end of the Irish parliamentary session.

Such an outcome simply made more plain to Irish patriot leaders the need to free their parliament from British control. Their agitation for this purpose became steadily more unrestrained. Early in 1780 it was still believed at Westminster that the Protestant politicians, conscious of the vulnerability of their position in Irish society, would not

---

[1] See pp. 135−8 below.

dare to push matters to extremes. 'However distressing a quarrel between the two kingdoms might be to England', the lord lieutenant wrote in February 1780, 'it would necessarily in its consequences be subversive of the Protestant interest here and completely ruinous to Ireland.'[2] During the summer he was further encouraged when a Combination Act and a Tenantry Act drove wedges into the forces of Irish radicalism. Middle-class agitation in Dublin for political participation alarmed the gentry just as the metropolitan activity during the spring had done in England. Radical attacks on Irish pocket boroughs also gave pause to some of the great landowners who had espoused the popular side. But the effects of these developments were limited and for the time being the patriot members of the Ascendancy seem to have ceased to feel any danger from a Catholic challenge. All that mattered to them was the winning of full constitutional rights. Throughout 1781 county meetings, grand juries, and assemblies of Volunteers, in a swelling chorus, demanded that all constitutional restraints upon the Irish legislature should be removed and the British parliament's claim to legislate for Ireland be withdrawn. The movement reached its culmination in a convention of delegates of Ulster Volunteers assembled at Dungannon in February 1782, representing some 25,000 men in arms, and its lead was rapidly followed all over the country. That month the lord lieutenant and the ministry in London conceded the passage of an Irish Habeas Corpus Act, but the government vetoed any further concession, and the lord lieutenant, the Earl of Carlisle, predicted that the situation might 'ultimately be productive of very serious and calamitous consequences.' At the moment of North's fall from office the Irish situation appeared to have reached a critical stage, and the insistence of Charlemont and Grattan upon immediate satisfaction of Irish demands held out a daunting prospect to North's successors.

Apart from wrestling with these two major issues, North and his colleagues took action to defuse yet another element of Irish discontent, that of those underprivileged on the score of religion. They pushed the Protestant Ascendancy at Dublin rather further along the road of toleration than it clearly desired to go. Relief for Irish Catholics required legislation by both parliaments, and at first when Catholic representations were made in 1778 the Irish parliament declined to grant the right to hold property on long lease. However, both ministerial and opposition politicians in Britain were more favourably disposed, and by legislation in May 1778 the British parliament cleared the decks for action in Ireland and set an example for the Dublin politicians. One Act lifted the penal laws from English

[2] Quoted in Edith M. Johnston, *Great Britain and Ireland, 1760–1800* (Edinburgh, 1963), p. 297.

Catholics. A second repealed two statutes of Queen Anne's reign prohibiting Catholics from buying forfeited Irish estates. In both instances the initiative was taken by leaders of the opposition, Sir George Savile and Lord Rockingham sponsoring the first of these Bills, Lord Richard Cavendish and Lord Effingham the second. The Irish parliament followed suit with a limited Catholic Relief Act, which permitted the purchase of land on leases of 999 years or for five lives and conceded full testamentary rights. The rule of gavelling was ended, and so was the right of a conforming eldest son to take control of an estate in his father's lifetime leaving him merely a life tenant. These proposals provoked considerable dissension among the politicians at Dublin. Grattan and a number of other Irish patriot leaders had strong reservations about the policy, and there was sufficient hostility to it to prevent legislation going the whole way with the sanction of freehold purchase by Catholics, a concession which was delayed until 1782. At the same time the discontents of the Irish Presbyterians were recognized. Some of the discrimination from which they suffered was removed by an Irish enactment of 1780 repealing that part of the Irish Test Act of 1704 imposing a sacramental test which debarred them from holding local appointments or offices under the crown. None of these measures was characterized by any sort of finality, and the concessions thus made merely strengthened resentment against other legal restrictions and inequalities which still remained.

III

Distrust and discontent with the government's poor showing in the American war, suspicion about financial waste and war profiteering, resentment over heavy taxation, fear of an imbalance in the constitution — all these factors contributed at the end of 1779 to the growth of a political reform movement in England which added further to North's difficulties. For years the aristocratic opposition in Parliament had been trying to use public opinion as a lever against the administration. Now, suddenly, it appeared they might be successful. Unlike the agitation of a decade before, the new movement had a provincial origin. It was master-minded by a Yorkshire landowner, the Reverend Christopher Wyvill, who in his own way was as much concerned as the Wilkites had been with the dangers of an overmighty executive. While one of his objects was undoubtedly the elimination of financial waste, he coupled this with the objective of a substantial reduction of crown expenditure, on the assumption that this would help to free Parliament from executive influence; but he believed two further constitutional reforms would be necessary to safeguard the independence of Parliament: an addition to the Commons of 100 county representatives, and a requirement to hold general elections more frequently than was dictated by the Septennial Act of 1716.

Wyvill's initial moves drew a ready response from the metropolitan area, where Wilkite radicalism had flagged in face of national patriotism after the commencement of the American war. Enthusiastic county meetings in Middlesex took up the Yorkshire cry for economic reform, and a well-attended meeting in Westminster gave Charles Fox an ovation when he called for a public rallying of forces against the government. Committees of association were voted into being by Westminster, Middlesex, Southwark, by the county of Surrey, and by the Common Council of the City of London, and within less than two years they were to establish such a close-knit collaboration that they came to be known in reforming circles as the Quintuple Alliance. Although it proved to be less sustained, considerable initial support also showed itself in the provinces. In various constituencies local political leaders secured the election of corresponding committees, set out to co-ordinate their agitation, and carried on propaganda; by the beginning of April 1780 nearly 40, including over half the English counties, had petitioned Parliament for 'economical reform'.

Both the Rockinghamites and the small Chathamite group led by Shelburne were quick to exploit this public unrest, and sought to move into a commanding position at the head of it. Much to the annoyance of Wyvill and his circle, who were suspicious of the magnates and wished to preserve their movement as exclusively one of the independent country gentry, Rockingham and his friends attended the launching meeting at York in force. They were however outmanoeuvred when Wyvill persuaded his audience that neither peers nor members of parliament should be elected to the committee set up to manage the county petition and to instruct Parliament about the wishes of the people. On the basis of their town residence many of Rockingham's friends did secure election to the very large and influential committee elected in February by a meeting of the householders of Westminster. This committee might have become no more than an instrument for the forwarding of Rockinghamite party policy but for the presence of a small group of extreme radicals, including Major John Cartwright and Dr John Jebb, who tried without very much success to make it a vehicle for their own schemes. As its chairman, Charles Fox laid the foundations of his popularity in his new role as 'man of the people' and won the loyalty of a great proportion of the electorate of Westminster constituency, which he was to represent from the general election of 1780 till the end of his life.

Exploiting the public head of steam for economical reform the opposition was able during the late winter and spring of 1780 to press North hard in the House of Commons. Rockingham's friends brought forward an elaborate set of Bills for 'economic reform', commonly known by the names of the men who took charge and successfully piloted them through on to the statute book two years later. Sir Philip Jennings Clerke introduced, for the third time, a Bill to debar government contractors from the Commons. John Crewe, MP for Cheshire, took up the proposal first made in 1770 for the disfranchisement of all men holding posts in the revenue services, whose votes were believed to give the executive an excessive influence in a number of constituencies. Edmund Burke's Establishment Bill was framed to dismantle, by the abolition of various court posts, sinecures, and quasi-sinecures, together with the now assumedly superfluous offices of the board of trade and the secretary of state for the colonies, the apparatus by which the ministers were supposed to achieve a packed majority in the Commons. After a hard struggle North fought off these schemes either in the Commons or, in the case of the Contractors' Bill, in the Lords. And in March he neatly stole the thunder of the Chathamite Isaac Barré by substituting for Barré's proposed parliamentary committee for the examination of the public accounts a royal commission of inquiry. There was no question which proposal was the most valuable. All past precedents showed that a committee investigation would have been a partisan and also futile muckraking political exercise. The commission opened the way to a sustained and methodical investigation of shortcomings in the financial administration. North's 10 years at the treasury had left him in no doubt that such an inquiry could produce useful results; but, easy-going as he was, it is doubtful if anything but a major political crisis would have pushed him to take action.

By the end of April the ministers had fended off the parliamentary attack. Dunning's momentary success on 6 April in obtaining a majority for his motion that 'the influence of the crown has increased, is increasing, and ought to be diminished' had no significant effect, and his attempt to follow it up with a motion for an address against any prorogation or dissolution of Parliament until the complaints in the petitions for economical reform had been satisfied was thrown out by a ministerial majority of nearly 50. Meanwhile the fissiparous tendencies in the popular reform movement were beginning to show themselves and the movement itself to run out of steam. In March a conference of delegates from various county committees, organized by Wyvill, agreed upon the two objectives of adding 100 knights of the shire to the Commons and of instituting annual dissolutions of Parliament, but on reference back to county meetings these proposals were generally considered too extreme and unacceptable. In March the Westminster Committee of Association set up a sub-committee to examine the state of the representation, whose suggestions soon began to scare the country gentry. Strongly influenced by the former Cambridge don John Jebb, whose Unitarian convictions had obliged him to make another career in medicine, and by a young member of the republican 'commonwealth' group, Thomas Brand Hollis, this body produced during the spring a series of sweeping recommendations, calling for annual parliaments, single-member and equal electoral districts, universal male suffrage with secret ballot, payment of MPs, and the exclusion of all placemen from the House of Commons. The views of these men were also supported and circulated by a new propagandist association, the Society for Promoting Constitutional Information, founded in April on the initiative of John Cartwright, Dr Jebb, Brand-Hollis, Thomas Day, and other enthusiasts.

Nothing could have been more calculated to alienate both the Rockinghamites and the independent landed gentry, and their aversion to any move likely to stir up the populace was sharpened by the anti-Catholic disturbances commonly known as the Gordon riots which caused a complete breakdown of law and order in parts of the metropolis for several days at the beginning of June. Rifts also appeared between Rockingham and the county association for reform which Wyvill had launched in Yorkshire, some of whose members were almost as opposed to aristocratic as to crown influence in politics. By mid summer the government's hand was also being strengthened by news of military success in the southern colonies. Except in Yorkshire and in the London area, the results of the general election in October 1780 gave little encouragement to reformers. Wyvill's attempt in March 1781 to renew pressure on Parliament by a petition presented by a conference of deputies from the counties convened in London drew only a weak response from the country and aroused resentment both in ministerial circles and in Parliament as an action only too reminiscent of the American Continental Congress and Association of 1774.

IV

North's resignation at the end of March 1782 in face of the threat of withdrawal of support in the Commons opened up a period of political crisis and uncertainty extending over two years, only finally resolved by the general election of spring 1784. The crucial factor in the situation in March was that the balancing force of independent MPs, usually favourably disposed to the king's ministers, who were now convinced that the American war was lost, could only bring it to an end against the wishes of George III by withdrawing their confidence from his ministers and obliging him to accept others who were pledged to make peace. This the king did with ill grace, and subsequent events were deeply affected by his convictions and prejudices. The disappearance of the North ministry destroyed the typical pattern of Hanoverian politics presented by an almost impregnable ministerial phalanx impotently assaulted by opposition like a great cliff with the sea waves washing harmlessly around its base. As after 1761, the restoration of stability was a work of time.

The new administration was a coalition of the two opposition parties led by Rockingham and Shelburne, an arrangement which kindled immediate jealousies over patronage and offered easy opportunities for intrigue. The king regarded Rockingham's group with particular distaste. It appeared to him to be the archetypal example of an aristocratic faction out to dictate to the crown. Its nonsensical theories about hidden cabals and secret influence appeared to him to be directed against his exercise of his few remaining legitimate constitutional functions, one of the chief of which he took to be the selection and appointment of ministers. The disreputable personal character of Charles Fox, whose father had earlier caused deep offence to George III, his reckless ebullience in debate, his association with the wilder flights of political radicalism in Westminster, and, before long, his growing (apparently corrupting) friendship with George, Prince of Wales, fuelled a deeper animosity. Fox was one of the only two politicians throughout the reign to provoke real hatred in the king.

George III therefore looked to the Shelburne group in the ministry to keep the Rockinghams in their place, and his partiality towards them increased the strain and disharmony which soon arose over both patronage and foreign policy. Unfortunately for him, in Shelburne George III had picked a loser. Shelburne's unpopularity and the distrust of him on all sides are beyond doubt, though the reasons for this have often puzzled historians. Most politicians are devious, but it appeared that his deviousness exceeded the common level of tolerance. It is possible that, at bottom, it arose out of a constitutional inability to articulate his thoughts without confusion: Bentham, for many years his friend, noted at the beginning of their acquaintance in 1781 the 'prodigious deal of ambiguity' which marked his conversation on general as well as political mattes. Too many people fell victim to it over the years. The higher Shelburne climbed the wider and more damaging the ripples of alienation which spread around him.

The main domestic achievement of this administration in the three months of its existence was the implementation of its programme of economical reform. The Bills which had been drawn up in 1780 were brought out of file and refurbished, and in due course Crewe's Act for the disfranchisement of revenue officers, Clerke's Act for the exclusion of government contractors from the Commons, and Burke's Establishment Act abolishing a number of government and court appointments found their way to the statute book. If nothing else, Fox felt, the ministry held office long enough to give 'a good stout blow to the influence of the Crown',[3] whether it was exercised by a secret cabal or by the king himself. By these measures the Rockinghamites sought to exorcise what they thought to be the factor behind their fall in 1766. But as a means of making the political world safe for the sort of meritocracy the Rockinghamites conceived themselves to be the Acts fell far short of expectation. The assumed evils were largely paper tigers. Government contractors were few and had not always been biddable, and the numbers of enfranchised revenue officers were far less than estimated in Rockinghamite circles. Later calculations showed that, if necessary, numbers of existing offices could be made available to members of the Commons to replace those swept away by Burke's legislation; and Burke's rules for controlling pensions did far more damage to the legitimate purposes of this institution than service in cleaning up a minor unsavoury corner of politics.

The ministers' entry into office immediately raised the hopes of political radicals both in the metropolis and in Yorkshire, and before long the Yorkshire leader, Christopher Wyvill, was besieging the doors of both Rockingham and Shelburne. But a ministerial undertaking about parliamentary reform was out of the question. Shelburne was discreetly sympathetic. The rising young star, William Pitt, favoured it, as did a small number of independent members in the Commons. Fox too was deeply involved through his activities in the Westminster Committee. But most of his party was hostile, though some of them were prepared to support a motion to consider the matter. Probably less than a fifth of the House of Commons were committed supporters of some kind of reform of the representation. When a motion for a committee to consider the question was introduced by Pitt on 7 May, its defeat by only 20 votes (161 to 141) gave a wholly misleading impression, for the great phalanx of opponents of

[3] *Memorials and Correspondence of Charles James Fox*, ed. Lord John Russell (4 vols. 1853–7) I, p. 316.

reform constituting North's parliamentary following were absenting themselves after their rejection in March. No better fortune attended the efforts of Pitt's young cousin, Lord Mahon, heir of Earl Stanhope, also emerging at this time as an energetic supporter of Wyvill and a canvasser among the politicians for the cause of reform. In June he unsuccessfully promoted a Bill for the strict suppression of bribery at parliamentary elections and the reduction of expenses by the institution of district polling centres in county constituencies.

Ireland and the war were the government's most pressing problems. In Ireland the upthrust of the Volunteer movement appeared to create a perilous situation in which that country might go the way of America. In mid April, only two days after the arrival of the new lord lieutenant, the Duke of Portland, the Irish Commons at the instigation of Grattan reaffirmed the principle of Irish legislative independence, giving no time for the consideration of a tempered, comprehensive and reciprocal settlement, which was the aim of Charles Fox and such Irish advisers as Edmund Burke. Perhaps the likelihood of the 'Protestant garrison' really exposing their position by quarrelling with their British power-base was small, but a ministry still faced with a great war in which command of the Irish coasts was not secure could not afford to take the risk. With reluctance Rockingham and his colleagues agreed to concede immediate full and equal British constitutional rights to the Irish subjects of George III. The Dublin parliament was permitted to repeal the Tudor legislation by which, two centuries and more ago, it had shackled itself completely under the control of the privy council in London: it now acquired full powers of initiative and legislation. At the same time it passed Acts giving judges of the Irish superior courts tenure during good behaviour and affirming the right of the Irish House of Lords to act as the sole and supreme court of appeal, and it asserted its authority in military matters by adopting the principle of an annual Mutiny Act. But in addition it reaffirmed the association with Britain, voted £100,000 towards the cost of raising men for the navy, and empowered the administration to withdraw 5,000 troops from Ireland for foreign service. In the general euphoria Protestant prejudice was overcome by the sense of solidarity with Catholics as Irishmen, which liberal leaders had been doing their best to promote, and the Catholic Relief Act of 1782 not only abolished remaining restrictions on land tenure but also repealed the laws banning Irish Catholic bishops and clergy.

In London the ministry pushed through the British parliament a repeal of the Declaratory Act of 1719, wiping out, it was assumed, the claims of Parliament to legislate for Ireland and of the British House of Lords to act as a final court of appeal in Irish cases. But as early as

May Flood raised doubts at Dublin about the effectiveness of a measure which might be held merely to cancel a declaration of a situation and not the situation itself, which was presumed to have existed before it was made; and he called for a specific renunciation of British legislative authority. The continuance of the hearing of an Irish case on appeal before the British King's Bench later in the summer reinforced these suspicions, and a series of resolutions from bodies of Volunteers backed Flood's demand. At the beginning of 1783, coerced by the threat that the Irish Commons might otherwise fly out of control, the British government secured the passage at Westminster of a Renunciation Act.

Regarding this settlement the observation has justly been made that, 'unlike the American colonies Ireland had managed both to win legislative independence and maintain its connection with Great Britain; and it had obtained its objective without using military force'.[4] The union of the crowns preserved elements of subordination at administrative level. The lord lieutenant's patent of appointment continued to pass under the British great seal and it was clear that he was a member of the British administration. Royal warrants counter-signed by three British lords of the treasury were used to notify the crown's decision on various Irish administrative matters − the issue of public money, appointments, grants of pensions, and the regulation of public departments. Irish opposition attempts to legislate against these administrative practices in subsequent years were doomed to failure. Although the Irish legislature had won almost complete independence, the British great seal was also used to give royal assent to Irish Bills. Moreover in theory the crown in privy council retained a right of legislative veto as in the case of colonial legislation, though political realities made its use exceedingly unlikely: in the event it was to be employed only once during the 18 years before the Union. Thus the persuasive influence of the king's representative, the lord lieutenant, remained almost the only instrument for keeping British and Irish measures in harmony. In this period of weakness the British had conceded to the kingdom of Ireland the sort of constitutional relationship which James Wilson and Thomas Jefferson had demanded for America nearly a decade before and to preclude which the British had unavailingly fought the American War of Independence.

In the matters of war and peace the Rockingham ministry made little progress before its demise. Its members were in general agreed upon the need to cut loose from the American war and also to wind up

---

[4] R. B. McDowell, *Ireland in the Age of Imperialism and Revolution, 1760–1801* (Oxford, 1980), p. 288.

the conflict with the Bourbon powers as soon and with as little loss as possible, but they were not averse from another campaign if Bourbon demands were pitched too high. About means there was less unanimity. In the spring of 1782 Rockingham, Fox and their friends wanted an immediate recognition of American independence in the expectation of splitting the Americans from the French, but they were unable to carry with them a group in the cabinet led by Shelburne. The latter hankered after the preservation of some sort of special relationship with the Americans, and wished to use independence as a bargaining counter to secure it, or even to create it within a framework of some federal type of connection, with which independence might not be strictly compatible. Between April and June the situation within the ministry was further confused by the fact that Fox and Shelburne, according to the formal division of their responsibilities as secretaries of state, both had agents in Paris negotiating separately with the French and the Americans respectively; for while America was not yet recognized as independent, its business fell within the sphere of the secretary of state for home and colonial affairs. This real conflict on a question of diplomatic tactics, on which the cabinet could not make up its collective mind, added greatly to the stresses within the administration, and to the rivalry and mutual distrust of the two secretaries. The effect would have been much more serious had the negotiations made more progress; but up till July the combatants on both sides were uncertain what the current campaign would bring, the French and Spanish especially were reserving their position, and little more was done than obtain preliminary extreme statements of claims from the allied powers.

V

Unified control of negotiations was only achieved on the British side after Shelburne succeeded Rockingham at the treasury. George III had already been working actively to this end since the beginning of April, and on 1 July the death of Rockingham seemed to place the game in his hands at the same time as it threw Rockingham's party into disarray. Fox, Burke, and the Cavendish clan, with their immediate connections, refused to serve under Shelburne and withdrew from the administration. But Fox's uncle, the Duke of Richmond, and Keppel, the head of the Admiralty, remained in their posts, and

Shelburne could also count on the support of Grafton and his friend General Conway, at least for the time.

The pursuit of peace now became the most urgent task of the administration. The new home secretary, Thomas Townshend, put forward no pretensions to conduct the American part of these, in which Shelburne was already deeply immersed, and Shelburne and his foreign secretary, Lord Grantham, a well-qualified professional diplomat with years of service as ambassador at Madrid behind him, worked closely together, with Shelburne conducting the most vital exchanges. By the late summer the last legacies of the North ministry in the way of naval expansion and reinforcement were somewhat strengthening his hand. Although in the early months of 1782 the Spanish had occupied the Bahamas and the French had had various successes, recapturing St Eustatius and mopping up sundry British islands, St Lucia had stood firm against them, and in February the arrival of the British reinforcement commanded by Rodney established naval superiority in the Caribbean. D'Estaing's fleet was mauled at the Battle of the Saints and he himself captured. Rodney's triumph foiled the great Bourbon design for the year in this theatre, an expedition to seize Jamaica (it was with red faces that the members of the Rockingham ministry heard this news, for they had just superseded Rodney in favour of one of Fox's impecunious friends, Admiral Pigot, and they could now do no less than confer on him a peerage and pension.) While Rodney's success eliminated one aspiration sustaining Spanish and therefore French determination to continue the war, the other disappeared in September and October 1782, when the garrison of Gibraltar first repelled a grand Franco-Spanish assault launched by floating batteries and then received its next annual provision fleet with next to no loss. Minorca had gone, however; in February 1782 a scurvy epidemic destroyed the garrison's power of resistance.

During the same period an element of realism also crept into British ministerial attitudes towards their European enemies. In the spring Shelburne had talked loudly of a great transfer of forces from America to the West Indies and stout blows against Spain's empire. But neither he nor his colleagues had the slightest idea how this might be done. The men who knew how to run the war machine had gone. As one historian has phrased it, 'the bridge between conception and execution had vanished, for no one in the new administration knew the procedure for executing a strategic decision.[5] Ministers did not even realize that a vast transport tonnage would be required to evacuate the bases on the North American coast, and the severity of

[5] Piers Mackesy, *The War for America, 1775–1783* (1964), p. 484.

the shipping shortage ruled out the possibility of amassing it in 1782. General Carleton, sent to New York with orders to evacuate and swing the British forces to the southward, soon made it clear that the most he could undertake with the tonnage at his disposal was the minor withdrawal from Savannah, which was successfully completed in July. Other movements would have to wait till 1783. Hopes of striking at the Spanish empire thus evaporated.

On the British side the peace terms were largely the work of Shelburne, though modified at various stages at the insistence of his cabinet colleagues. In recent years his achievement has attracted extremes of comment, on the one hand unduly favourable, on the other unnecessarily harsh. The claim that owing to his efforts the important gains in the Seven Years War remained substantially intact is not borne out by the terms of the resulting treaty. But too much has been made of the friction arising between him and his colleagues, to which parallels can easily be found in 1762. A cabinet cannot negotiate. Only an individual can conduct diplomatic bargaining and at the end of an unsuccessful war the negotiator can hardly be expected by ministerial colleagues to avoid setbacks imposed by the enemy. Peacemaking in defeat was bound to set up exceptional strains among the ministers, and the most that can be said is that the general distrust which Shelburne engendered added a good deal to the tensions.

By the autumn Shelburne was hardly negotiating from strength, but the failure of the allied plans against Jamaica and Gibraltar gave him a leverage the government had lacked in the spring. Moreover, the financial exhaustion of France was far greater than that of Britain, and Shelburne cleverly exploited the fissures between the allies. The logic of the situation almost immediately forced him into the position taken up in April by Fox. American complaisance was won with the concession of independence, a generous boundary south and west of the Great Lakes, and favourable terms for American shipping entering British ports. By November the interest of the Americans in the war was over, and the French and Spanish faced the danger that the anti-British war front would begin to crumble. The French leaders had at least gained their main point – as they thought – the cutting of Britain down to size by the loss of her North American empire – and they were in no position to fight for a reversal of other provisions of the Peace of 1763 which had been among their original war objectives. Spain too by late 1782 was ready for peace even without Gibraltar – though so far as George III and Shelburne were concerned she might have obtained it, and only the outright hostility of the rest of the cabinet, responding to widespread jingoist feeling in the country, prevented it. Britain fared badly enough — 'plucked like a chicken', one French diplomat declared — losing Minorca and the Floridas to Spain, yielding Senegal back to France and ceding Tobago, but she recovered her other West Indian losses in return for St Lucia. The French also gained some extension of their fishing rights on the Newfoundland coast and the restoration of trading posts in India. The Dutch, whose misfortune it had been to find themselves squeezed between British and French, lost their Indian factory at Negapatam and had to concede British demands for freedom of navigation in the Spice Islands: throughout 1783 they protested bitterly but, deserted by their allies, were obliged to subscribe these terms early the following year. Although the loss of the 13 American colonies had torn a great gap in the edifice of the British Empire and separated from it almost one quarter of the nation, the important gains made at the expense of France in the Seven Years War did remain substantially intact — Canada, the Maritimes, the Newfoundland fisheries. Despite the pessimism of George III and the politicians the basis remained for the creation within a generation of an imperial polity far more powerful than the nation's enemies could have conceived in 1783.

While the problems of the peace and dissensions over patronage caused growing fissures in Shelburne's administration, the chief threat to its existence came from Parliament. The long summer and autumn vacation gave a breathing space, but the blow fell soon after the Houses reconvened and as soon as the peace preliminaries were submitted to them. The personal followers of Shelburne and of his chancellor of the exchequer, William Pitt, constituted only a small group in the Commons, and from the first it seemed clear that only the support of all or most of North's following would give the ministry a safe majority. In six months the turn of the political wheel had brought North from the nadir to a commanding position. When Parliament should reassemble the 120 votes he commanded in the Commons could secure Shelburne's ministry or damn it to limbo. More knowledgeable than Shelburne of the conditions in the Commons, Fox was quick to seize the initiative with pressing invitations to co-operate. North, torn in either direction by conflicting advice from different groups within his own following, urged by the king to support Shelburne, hesitated until the peace terms came up for discussion in the Commons, and then threw his weight in the adverse scale. He did so with much doubt and under the stress of various considerations. The most immediate, perhaps, was his genuine disgust at Shelburne's failure to secure compensation for victimized American loyalists, a matter over which the emissaries of Congress had disclaimed any authority on the ground that it lay within the competence of the state governments. Less important perhaps was North's hostility to the commitment of Pitt and Shelburne to parliamentary reform. Of more substance may have been his concern with his own future: he faced political extinction from Pitt's veto on his inclusion in any ministry in which he himself served, a veto Shelburne dared not challenge. This last factor may have been the more pressing, because of the extreme financial insecurity into which North had been plunged by George III's repudiation of election account debts exceeding £20,000: without a ministerial salary he faced near ruin. By this niggardliness the king had lost all claim to sway North's conduct. Meanwhile Charles Fox continued to urge that all differences with North were now sunk and that he was prepared to enter into cordial collaboration. As effective leader of the Rockingham party he was now able to force upon its members the policy of coalition which he had preached in vain to Rockingham between 1778 and 1782. It seemed clear to North that if he had any political future it was to be found in alliance with Fox. Accordingly in February their followers combined to berate the peace terms in the Commons and to outvote the ministry with a narrow but sufficient majority. A popular minister might have rallied enough strength from the independent members to beat them, but the widespread underlying mistrust of Shelburne was fatal to his chances. The votes of censure on the peace cemented the Fox — North coalition and condemned Shelburne's ministry to extinction.

VI

For the second time in 12 months George III found himself faced with the necessity of taking into administration politicians to whom he was utterly opposed on both personal and political grounds. His hostility towards Fox as a turncoat and a factionmonger intent on forcing his way into office — a man without principle, he had called him in 1780 — was spiced by his knowledge that Fox had passed on his discarded mistress, Mary (Perdita) Robinson, to the Prince of Wales, with the result that he had had to expend £5,000 on the recovery of compromising letters written by his son which the actress had threatened to publish. For nearly six weeks every alternative expedient was attempted, and the king himself was half-persuaded that the denial of his essential prerogative of choosing ministers would leave him no honourable alternative but abdication. Appeals to William Pitt, to the leaders of the old Bedford party, and to North himself, all fell on deaf ears. For the moment no politicians except the leaders of the coalition could command a majority in the Commons. But the king was at length persuaded that a surrender might not be irretrievable and so brought himself to bow to the inevitable. At the beginning of April the coalition ministry came into being under the nominal headship of the Duke of Portland, with Fox and North as the two secretaries of state and a cabinet in which the Foxites were favoured by a balance of four to three. From the moment of its formation the king was determined to get rid of it as soon as he could.

During the last crucial debate on the peace terms William Pitt, defending the Shelburne ministry in the first outstandingly brilliant speech of his career, had referred to the 'unnatural coalition', and this charge has in general been echoed by historians. Such a combination, it was implied, inevitably carried within it the seeds of its downfall. More recently the view has been strongly urged that there was nothing inherently unnatural or reprehensible about it. Some recombination of parliamentary groupings was essential if a ministry soundly based on a majority in the Commons was to be established, and Pitt himself later accepted the logic of this with his merger with the old Bedford party at the end of 1783.

But for many contemporaries the issue could not be so simply resolved. It was true that a great source of difference between the two groups in the new coalition — the American war — had now disappeared. But it was disingenuous of Fox to stress this fact and to gloss over a more fundamental issue. For at least 10 years the members of the Rockingham party, both in their private correspondence among themselves and in the speeches by which they appealed for public support, had denounced the North ministry as a collection of men either manipulated without realizing it by a vicious and sinister secret cabal or else as consciously conniving at such manipulation. On the eve of North's fall Rockingham had reaffirmed his proscription of 'obnoxious ministers, or of those who were deemed as belonging to a sort of secret system, from which many attributed all the evils of the reign.'[6] By this assumption either North and his friends were political imbeciles or they were political villains committed to a conspiracy against British liberties at home and in the Empire. In neither case should they be tolerated in office.

These circumstances explain the peculiar distaste with which some members of the Commons and still more people outside watched Fox hobnobbing with North in the cabinet and acquiescing in the admission to minor court offices of such associates of his as Lord Sandwich

---

[6] Albemarle, *Memoirs of the Marquis of Rockingham and his Contemporaries* (2 vols., 1852) II, p. 453.

and his son. Because the Rockinghamites had protested too much, they had created an atmosphere in which the coalition was vulnerable. Some people inevitably asked the question, if Fox could do this, how on earth was he to be trusted? Of what avail his protests about defending and securing the balance of the constitution? Was he not just one more unscrupulous politician on the make? By contrast, William Pitt was to make a deep impression on some politicians and on a wide section of the public outside Parliament by his uncompromising stand against the return to office of North and his friends: his own alliance with Earl Gower in December 1783 did not arouse the same suspicions because Gower had been out of office since November 1779. Thus, to the implacable enmity of the king towards the coalition a degree of public suspicion of the motives of half its leaders and outright hostility towards the other half added a second, heavy liability. Neither from above nor from below was the position of the new administration secure. From the outset the king made known his hostility by declining any creations or promotions in the peerage — a move which torpedoed plans for North to act as home secretary in the Upper House and for the purchase of political support from borough owners. George III's official dealings with Fox and North were conducted in the coldest personal terms compatible with formal courtesy, and he declined to enter into active discussion of departmental business.

The situation of 1783 was not one in which the ministry could easily consolidate a reputation for achievement to counter-balance these disadvantages.

The conclusion of the peace treaties held out no hopes. Although the coalition leaders had censured the terms obtained by Shelburne, they had been obliged to declare their acceptance of them in order to avoid the imputation of war-mongering, and a resumption of hostilities was out of the question. In America the levers had been thrown fully into reverse. In England several regiments were in mutiny for want of pay or at the prospect of posting to India, where the war in the Carnatic was still a source of anxiety. Fox could hope for, and gained, scarcely anything in the way of concession during the final negotiations which converted the preliminaries into a formal treaty of peace.

Pitt's motion for parliamentary reform, rejected on 7 May by a resounding majority (293 against 149) drawn largely from North's following and rallied by his able denunciation, emphasized the split over this issue within the coalition, and brought the ministry no credit in the eyes of those activists in the constituencies who wanted reform. This was not Pitt's original intention. The motion came as the culmination of plans he had begun to concert with Wyvill nearly a year before, in the genuine belief that the Rockinghamite programme of economical reform was not sufficient to cleanse the constitution of its dangerous defects. Both men had hoped for a massive public demonstration of support by way of petitions comparable to that expressed in favour of economical reform in 1780. They were disappointed. Solid support emerged only in Yorkshire and in the metropolis, and it seems doubtful if more than 20,000 signatures in all were appended to the petitions submitted during the opening months of 1783. In the country as a whole the defeat of reform probably did no damage to the coalition; but in a small number of important constituencies it contributed a further trickle of suspicion and hostility to the flood which was to break loose early the following year, and added to the reputation of the only politicians who, as events were to show, could mount an effective challenge to the coalition. In Yorkshire Wyvill made the coalition the target of a sustained and strident campaign of press denunciation for months before its fall. It was in just these constituencies also that a damaging impact may have been made during May by two debates over Edmund Burke's ill-judged reinstatement of two pay-office clerks facing prosecution for malfeasance. Pitt and various independents had good grounds for their attack, and soon afterwards the suicide of one official and the criminal conviction of the other vindicated their stand.

The need to set up an establishment for the Prince of Wales on his attainment of his majority raised a more material issue at the beginning of the summer. Fox, as the prince's friend, pressed for generous treatment, and despite the reluctance of North and of the coalition's chancellor of the exchequer, Lord John Cavendish, the cabinet agreed to find him an income of £100,000 and pay his debts. After hesitation they suggested that £50,000 of this allowance should come out of the civil list. There are indications that George III sought to make an issue out of the matter with the hope of forcing the government out of office. Such generosity at a time when the tax-payers were burdened by the aftermath of heavy war expenditure and an enormously increased national debt could easily be set in an invidious light before the public. But Pitt's cousin, Earl Temple, counselled caution, and the king drew back, having won his point that £50,000 for the prince out of the civil list was quite sufficient.

Before long the ministry had created a more favourable excuse for their dismissal. By the summer of 1783 the affairs of India had been for several years the subject of comprehensive study in parliamentary committees, a vast fund of information had been acquired, and the politicians in general were agreed that reform was urgent. Despite the work of Warren Hastings, the machinery of a great trading company was not geared to provide good government for the enormous area in India which had fallen under its sway, the failure to control its country policies was capable of producing serious international complications, and the warfare it stirred up in India was making it a financial liability instead of the asset everyone expected. Action was urgently needed, and a successful attack on a problem which had dogged administrations for over 15 years could ground the new ministry firmly in the public esteem. While Fox looked to reputation and political advantage, Edmund Burke was also driven by humanitarian considerations and a burning, crusading indignation against injustices committed upon Indians by the hand of the Company's power. His answer — the armchair administrator's answer — was to centre all control of Indian affairs in a parliamentary commission.

Burke was the chief author of the East India Bill which the ministry prepared to bring before Parliament in the short autumn sitting. It is arguable that this scheme would have broken down anyway, owing to its attempt to deprive the men on the spot of any freedom of action. But in the event what destroyed the Bill, and with it the coalition ministry, was the vulnerability of other of its provisions. North had warned against the danger, and a more cautious cabinet might have re-shaped their measure with better lines of defence; there were not wanting suggestions from East India House for a Bill more like that which Pitt was to produce the following year: but Fox's impetuous temperament too often inclined him to stake all on a gambler's throw, and now this defect of character brought him not for the first or the last time to disaster.

The Bill constituted a head-on attack on chartered rights. Although some of the directors at East India House were willing to support it, almost as many opposed it, and among the numerous proprietors there was widespread hostility to such government interference. Since the Company did not unanimously and voluntarily submit itself to the wisdom of Parliament, the Bill could be represented as a unilateral act of power on the part of the legislature, violating rights and liberties which had been secured by charter. The recent history of America suggested that at least there might be a certain moral turpitude in action of this kind, and in any case the protection of individual and corporate rights and liberties was an incessant preoccupation of eighteenth-century Englishmen, to whom the preservation of property was the principal end of government. Thus a strong revulsion could be stirred up against the Bill, regardless of its real merits, on the basis not merely of vested interests but of constitutional principles. Before long a hostile majority of the proprietors was up in arms appealing to the public in defence of their rights, and the City of London with its own chartered liberties in mind sprang to their aid, petitioning with a nice choice of words in exactly the same terms the Rockinghamites had used to protest in the Lords in 1773 against North's Regulating Act.

The Bill was also highly vulnerable because of its patronage provisions. Control of Indian affairs, including all appointments, was to be vested in a board of seven commissioners. These were to be appointed in the Act by name for a term of years — four was proposed. Subsequent appointments would be in the hands of the crown, that is to say, of the ministers of the day. All the seven commissioners nominated in the Bill were members of the coalition parties.

Contemporaries fastened upon the apparent threat to the balance of the constitution presented by this commission's control over East India patronage. Nonsense though this was, it was seriously believed by many, especially outside Parliament, that this provision would make it impossible for the king ever to get rid of the ministry and would deliver the kingdom into the hands of Fox and his friends in perpetuity. Wyvill straitly declared: 'The man who wanted the patronage of the Indies wanted to govern by corruption'.[7] The commissioners were expected to gain more influence over the Commons than any possible alternative ministry could acquire through the control of all the other patronage at the crown's disposal. Chatham's old ally Lord Camden believed that this advantage would have made Fox 'too powerful to have been turned out, and . . . perpetual dictator'.[8] When such a prominent politician as North's supporter William Eden could boast at a private dinner party of 'the infinite advantages of this politic expedient for infallibly securing the permanency of the present administration for seven years at least, by their possessing such an unbounded and lucrative patronage', less sophisticated observers might be forgiven for fearing the worst.[9] At the end of four years the appointment of any new commissioners other than members of the coalition might be blocked by action in the Commons. It appeared that the royal element in the balance of the constitution would be rendered impotent, and all power would accrue in the hands of the coalition leaders. In effect, ministry and commission would be self-perpetuating and irremovable, because no alternative government could ever get support from the Commons. Were Charles Fox's fine flourishes about dealing a 'good stout blow to the influence of the Crown' merely a prelude to the erection of a new empire of influence for himself? On the whole politicians in Parliament were not over-impressed by this sort of argument, but a very different impression developed out of doors, and the mounting revulsion against the coalition came to display an element of hysteria scarcely

[7] Christopher Wyvill, *Political Papers* (6 vols., 1794–1802) IV, pp. 379–80.
[8] Camden to Robert Stewart, 19 Dec. 1783, Camden MSS.
[9] John Courtenay, *Incidental Anecdotes and a Biographical Sketch* (1809), pp. 135–8.

observed in Britain since the campaign against Walpole's excise Bill of 1733.

VII

By the end of November the sense of outrage of the East India proprietors, the ambitions of William Pitt, and the inveterate determination of George III to destroy the coalition ministry converged in plans for a political coup, for which the determination of Pitt and his friends to provide an alternative ministry were crucial. Two possibilities were discussed, each of them leading to the dismissal of the coalition under conditions which would justify this by reprobation of its measures. The idea that the king should use the royal veto after the passage of the East India Bill through Parliament was considered but rejected on the sensible ground that this prerogative had not been used for 80 years and would lay him open to attack. The alternative course was adopted of ensuring the rejection of the Bill in the House of Lords, where a government measure would normally be treated as deserving of assent. Recent research has established that Pitt himself was responsible for the plan to instruct peers to oppose the Bill, and it was his cousin, Lord Temple, who undertook to pass on a message that the king would regard as his enemy any peer who voted for it. This step ensured its rejection. This in turn provided the pretext for George III to call for Fox and North to return their seals of office; and in mid December Pitt in accordance with his pledges formed a new administration.

From the start George III's action in influencing peerage votes invited controversy and has commonly been condemned as contrary to constitutional convention; and according to the normal rules and precedents established by the eighteenth century to ensure the independence of parliamentary proceedings, this was certainly the case. The one justification for the king's action lay in the assumption that the constitution had already virtually broken down as a consequence of the encroachments, actual and intended, of the coalition politicians upon the powers of the crown. Their actions could only be defeated by others equally unconstitutional. George III has sometimes been blamed in this case for refusing to bow to constitutional limitations which his grandfather, George II, had been obliged to accept. But the parallels are not quite exact; for in 1746 George II

had tried to keep a favourite minister rather than reject an object of
his dislike, and though he had attempted the latter in 1757, the
person concerned had not become the centre of an acrimonious controversy already beginning to stir up public protest. That feature of
the situation held out the prospect of *post facto* justification of an
extreme measure: without that it seems unlikely that Pitt, and therefore George III, would have dared to act as they did in December
1783. In George III's defence it can be said that large numbers of his
subjects thought that he was right and that a threat to the balance of
the constitution had been averted. Recent work on the House of Lords
has shown that a revulsion against the Bill was already developing
among the peers before the king's feelings became known to them.
The general extent of public approval of his action became fully
apparent in the early weeks of 1784, when a demonstration of opinion
on a wholly unprecedented scale in the form of addresses to the crown
revealed unexpectedly massive popular support for the dismissal of
the coalition.

With the new ministry installed the first battle had been won, but
George III and Pitt still had to consolidate their position. According
to the normal conventions of the constitution the ministers appointed
by the sovereign could expect to receive adequate support in the
House of Commons. But while elements of the normal pattern slowly
began to emerge, for some time the abnormal situation created by the
formation of the coalition prevailed. Pitt faced great difficulties in
the Commons in the early weeks of 1784. His ministry was largely
recruited from young untried men or men with few political connections. At the outset it had to face the immediate withdrawal of Earl
Temple, whose association with the royal message to the peers put the
ministry in jeopardy when it was found that an immediate dissolution
of Parliament would not be possible. To have had the leading secretary of state the target of a successful motion of censure in the
Commons would have been an invitation to disaster. Parliamentary
support had to be attracted by painful degrees. Pitt's own friends and
the connections of other ministers provided a limited block of votes
in the Commons. To these were added the votes of many independent members who had regarded the Fox — North coalition as
unprincipled from its commencement, and also those of members of
the court and administration group who had given support to
Shelburne's ministry and then found themselves pushed out of office
in February 1783. Feverish canvassing by the king and the ministers
brought over another 40 or so members of this group during the
Christmas recess. Prospects of peerage favours were held out to
borough patrons. Even so, when the Commons reassembled after the
Christmas holidays, Pitt's voting strength at its best was 20 or so short

of that of the coalition, and some divisions were carried against him by much larger margins. A bid to make it clear that he could and would offer an effective alternative to the previous administration was brushed off by the rejection of his own Bill for the regulation of the East India Company's affairs.

The king vehemently urged the expediency of an early general election; but while this was the course ultimately adopted in March, the ministers were more aware of the difficulties. Perhaps least among these was an address against a dissolution carried by the coalition's majority. Many other considerations gave ground for delay. In early January numbers of members had not attended the House since the previous summer, and Pitt was correct in expecting that many of them would prove to be friends. To subject members to the expense of seeking re-election three years earlier than expected, unless this was clearly shown to be necessary, would be bound to provoke resentment: indeed, reluctance to face such expense seems to have been one of the motives prompting a large group of independent members meeting at the St Albans Tavern to try to arrange a compromise and coalition between Pitt and Fox. By-elections gave a few opportunities to bring in committed supporters. The sheer task of activating the machinery of elections, of making contact with patrons and lining up candidates for seats required some weeks. Finally, the parliamentary timetable made an immediate election difficult, and a dissolution had to be postponed until the supplies had been voted. Even facing an initially adverse House of Commons Pitt could reckon that mere survival would gradually bring over support and dishearten some of the coalition's following. There are indications that by February these were becoming discouraged by the growing public demonstrations against them, and that some members began to abstain from voting in response to public opinion in their constituencies. The event proved that Fox had not sufficient confidence in his position to take such extreme steps as blocking financial supply. By early March his majority on obstructive tactical divisions had dwindled to one, and it was clear that in the event of an election Pitt's position would not rest merely on the use of crown electoral influence.

In fact, his extraordinary triumph at the ensuing elections held during April and May 1784 derived from both crown influence and a remarkable wave of public support. The arrangements made by the treasury in government boroughs and in some of those under private influence resulted in a general clearing out of the men whom North had brought into those seats in 1774 and 1780. Mainly as a result of these operations over 40 of North's friends were excluded from the House; others had already gone over to Pitt; and after May 1784 North could contribute a following of only about 70, instead of 120, to the parliamentary opposition. Several of these died or deserted during the next two or three years. Many of the remainder soon merged into Fox's following, and the opposition came to consist to all intents and purposes of a single large party based mainly on the former Rockingham connection.

The Rockinghamite party weathered the elections with rather more success, but it lost a significant number both of party members had also of friendly independents through the public revulsion in those constituencies where an effective public opinion could operate. Coalition candidates were beaten out of the field in Yorkshire, where grotesque misrepresentations of Fox as a would-be Cromwell were circulating among the freeholders. In Norfolk, Suffolk, Berkshire, Buckinghamshire, Dorset and Gloucestershire, the electors were hot against them. Pitt's apparently more sincere commitment to parliamentary reform may have been an important factor in his sweeping victory in the London metropolitan area, where sympathizers took 10 out of 12 seats, and something of this same urban radical spirit seems to have spilled out into neighbouring counties.

While the number of newcomers elected to the House in 1784 was much the same as usual, a more direct indication of the disruptive effect of the crisis on established parliamentary interests is given by the increase in the number of such men who were not predestined to a political career. Fifty-nine, or not far short of half the newcomers were to have no legislative career in the Commons except in this Parliament (the previous comparable figures had been 43 in 1774 and 38 in 1780). The importance of the unique impact which public opinion had in this general election is beyond doubt. By March over 200 addresses had reached the king thanking him for dismissing the coalition. Had the popular tide run the other way, not only would it have followed that Pitt would not have gained 12 seats for English counties and about 16 in the 30 boroughs with large electorates; he would also have been at risk over some, though not all, of the 36 county seats which were held during the elections by his well-wishers or at least kept out of coalition hands, and over some of the 24 seats held by them in 'large' boroughs — indeed some of these MPs and also other independents would probably have been voting against him during March. Furthermore, under the peculiar political stress of this period, boroughs under influence — even 'government' boroughs — proved unreliable, and victimization of the kind actually encountered by coalition supporters in one or two constituencies might well instead have befallen Pitt's friends. It is also quite likely that fewer of the great borough-mongers would have done trade with Pitt had the flood-tide of opinion been against him. The opposition to North in 1780 of Edward Eliot and Sir James Lowther, mustering some 15 seats between them, is evidence of what could happen when a minister stood under a cloud. In such adverse circumstances Pitt might have fared worse than North had done in 1780. As it was, the elections inflicted on the coalition a loss variously estimated at between 70 to 90 seats, having double this effect in divisions. In the new Parliament Pitt thus had an ample and assured majority.

The general election of 1784 was a deliberate appeal by George III and Pitt against an existing adverse majority in the Commons. This was their response to the challenge made by Fox, that the will of the Commons should prevail. Undoubtedly this conjuration of a new balancing force in the constitution was an innovation, and one of much more significance for the future development of the constitution than Fox's insistence that a party majority in the Commons should dictate the composition of the ministry. So long as, under eighteenth-century conditions, any particular 'party' majority represented only the fortuitous concurrence of certain political groupings, it could not have the sanctity later conferred on parties by electoral majorities in a two-party system. Meanwhile Pitt and the king had turned against Fox and the Rockinghamites the very weapon of public opinion which in the recent past that party had vainly sought to use as a counterpoise to 'the influence of the crown'. In thus ignoring the so-called 'septennial convention' which had crystallized in practice since 1714, they had ironically enough adopted a radical principle, one which in the rather different form of 'short parliaments' had been demanded for years by radical reformers. The experiment was to be repeated in 1806 and 1807, and again though less blatantly in 1812. In 1784 the potentialities of this new expedient were still limited; but with the growth in the early nineteenth century of a wider and more constantly alert public opinion stimulated by a more mature press, it carried important implications for the development of constitutional practice.

7   The Sinews of Recovery

I

To many observers both at home and abroad the British defeat in the American war signalled the end of a chapter — wrote *finis* to the brief episode of British ascendancy achieved in 1763. The king himself believed that, bereft of the colonies, Britain would sink into the position of a minor power and that nothing would stand in the way of Bourbon world preponderance. European governments wrote off Britain as finished, no longer to be seriously reckoned with in the balance of power and the calculations of diplomatic combinations. London had lost command of the quarter of the British nation planted in North America and with it much more than a quarter of the Empire's potential economic resources. That within 30 years the nation's destiny would give it a leading role in Europe and an unquestioned oceanic ascendancy seemed scarcely conceivable in the conditions of 1783. Nevertheless, the grounds of recovery lay barely hidden, in the country's mounting population, in the skills it could evoke and command, in the energies with which economic advantage would be secured, and not least in the safety from invasion which the Channel and an indefatigable attention to sea-power made good.

By the 1780s the upward surge of population was making its impact upon the economy and upon war potential, adding to the labour force, enlarging the domestic market, and yielding a greater margin for military and naval recruitment. From an estimated total of some 9.4 millions in 1780, it had risen to over 10.7 millions by the time of the first census in 1801 and to 12.25 millions by 1811. Ireland, incorporated with Britain in the United Kingdom in 1801, added at that date a further 5.2 millions, which had become nearly 6 millions by 1811.

Urbanization continued, though its extent must not be exaggerated. It has been estimated that no more than 25 per cent of the populace was living in concentrations of over 5,000 at the turn of the century. But a small number of very large provincial towns emerged during this period. Outside the unique expanse of greater London, which passed the million mark soon after 1801, eight British cities and towns had a population in excess of 50,000 in 1780, of 70,000 in 1801, and of 85,000 in 1811. The most remarkable urban phenomena of industrial England in the early nineteenth century were Manchester and its great outport at Liverpool, each with about 100,000 people in 1815. Both Edinburgh and Glasgow had just topped this mark by 1811, and the latter had become the capital of an industrial region extending over much of the counties of Lanark and Renfrew, which together now contained between one seventh and one eighth of the population of Scotland.

The increasing demand from this growing population for food-stuffs, together with occasional uncertainties about foreign supplies in times of war, all reflected in rising prices, provided ample incentive for British agriculture to expand production. More capital was laid out, and the improvements already adopted in various areas early in the reign were taken up more widely.

In England much waste land continued to be brought into culti-vation and more cultivated land farmed more efficiently as a result of enclosure. Between 1793 and 1815 some 2,000 Acts of enclosure were passed, double the number enacted between 1760 and 1780. They involved slightly over three million acres and possibly as much again was enclosed by private treaty. The districts mainly affected were in eastern England, running from East Anglia northwards through Lincolnshire and Yorkshire, and in a southerly belt extend-ing through Berkshire, Wiltshire, Somerset and Gloucestershire. Thousands more acres were reclaimed by drainage in the Fens and around the Humber. Everywhere there was an increased adoption of improved crop rotations, a considerable expansion of potato culture, and the raising of a more prolific strain of oats. Winter feed for animals became more abundant with the widespread cultivation of the swede after about 1800. Recent scholarship has shown that enclosure entailed much less victimization of the small cultivators than was once alleged and the demands for extra labour which it created were considerable.[1] Rural poverty, found mainly in the south, including districts where enclosure had largely taken place a century earlier, was due in part at least to local over-population. Agricultural wage rates were consistently rather higher in the north of England, where the reclamation of waste could absorb the labour available and was in competition for it with the textile manufacture of Lancashire and the multifarious industry of the Black Country. At times during

[1] On this controversy see J. D. Chambers and G. E. Mingay, *The Agricultural Revolution, 1750–1880* (1966), pp. 86–99, and G. E. Mingay, *Enclosure and the Small Farmer in the Age of the Industrial Revolution* (1968).

the long French wars a widespread shortage of agricultural labour became noticeable as a result of calls upon manpower for the army, navy, and militia. As a result farmers began to turn to mechanical aids — machines for drilling, reaping, mowing, haymaking and winnowing were the subjects of numerous patents in the years 1789–1815 — and there was a move towards lighter ploughs and more efficient wagons and carts. In some areas threshing machines, often horse-driven, were in common use by 1815. Agricultural expansion made a general contribution to the economy by its generation of a growing demand for iron for tools of all descriptions, for building materials, and for labour.

Scottish farming underwent a dramatic transformation as a result of the general adoption of the new techniques between 1780 and 1815, and with a speed that justifies the description 'revolutionary'. Over the lowlands in general the new farming brought solid prosperity — and to all classes. Rents doubled between 1783 and 1793, and doubled again between 1794 and 1815. The rental of land in Scotland was estimated at rather over £2,000,000 in 1795; by 1815 it was reckoned at £5,000,000. The labourer's wage seems to have more than kept up with the rising cost of foodstuffs: wage levels about 1790 may have advanced to two and a half times what they had been 40 years before, and figures for Ayrshire indicate a three-fold increase between 1780 and 1810. Everywhere solid well-built farmhouses were replacing the old peasant cabins, and by the last years of George III's reign many Scottish tenant farmers were men of education and substance, and vied with the townsmen of Edinburgh in the material comforts and refinements of their dwellings.

The remote Highlands and Islands with their poor soil and high rainfall by contrast saw relatively little agricultural improvement, and the major change during this period, the switch from cattle to sheep, proved highly disruptive to the traditional Celtic way of life. In many districts the mountain straths which now became the centres of great sheep-farms were cleared of all or part of their inhabitants, the clan-chieftain landlords to whom they were tenants allotting small plots for subsistence elsewhere. Many of those displaced either emigrated to the New World or drifted away in search of the better employment opportunities of the industrial lowlands. Some found a living from kelp-gathering or from the herring fishery.

As a result of all these various developments, the growing supply of foodstuffs produced in Britain roughly kept pace with demand, although there were slight shortfalls, particularly in bad harvest years. Estimates for England and Wales indicate that the net output of grains rose from 16,700,000 quarters in 1780 to nearly 22,000,000 quarters in 1810 — a year when net imports stood at about 1,200,000 quarters. Between 1800 and 1815 the country supplied nine tenths of its own needs in wheat and all but 4 per cent of the needs in grains overall. The average importation of wheat was about 600,000 quarters — more or less, depending upon the quality of the harvest — much of it coming from Prussia and north-west Germany; and about the same quantity of oats, of which Ireland was a major supplier. In normal years the minor shortfall could always be made good by importing if necessary from outside Europe, by reducing consignments to the colonies, and by cutting grain consumption in distilleries and breweries. Hardship, nevertheless, might be caused by fluctuations in price, by panic buying, and by farmers holding grain off the market in hopes of a further advance in price. In the mid 1790s, in 1801, and again in 1810 and 1811 bad harvests gave rise to serious distress and social unrest.

Various additions to the road and canal system were made between 1780 and 1815, underpinning an expanding industrial economy which made great strides during the period 1780 to 1806 but thereafter ran into a period of checks and fluctuations due in part at least to disruption of trade caused by the Napoleonic war. Considerable as were the effects of industrialization, in 1815 Britain was still predominantly a rural rather than an urban industrialized society, and the greater part of the population was still engaged either in agriculture or in all the small-scale limited manufacturing, commercial and service activities which supported life in the countryside. Various rough estimates suggest that at the time of the 1811 census perhaps a quarter of the total population was deriving its livelihood from the main export industries and the transport and marketing services which were involved with them. The total range of the cotton-spinning and weaving industries and their ancillary and finishing branches may have supported over 350,000 people, metallurgy another 300,000, the manufacture of woollens a further 200,000. During the later part of the Napoleonic war, from about 1806, there seems to have been relatively little addition to productive capacity in either the metallurgic or textile industries. Indeed, capacity was more than sufficient to meet a demand which came under irregular check, partly due to the business cycle, but also from the closure of European markets by Napoleon's continental blockade and the non-intercourse policy adopted by the United States. Furthermore, a strong inflationary pressure generated after 1808 by British war expenditure abroad created a monetary situation increasingly unfavourable to industrial investment.

Freed by the technological discoveries of the previous decades from its old dependence on charcoal, the iron industry expanded rapidly. In 1760 the number of coke furnaces in blast had been a mere 17. By

1788 there were 53, by 1790 81, and in 1805 the total number of furnaces, mostly coke-burning, was around 200. The annual output of pig iron reached some 60,000 tons by 1788. By 1805 it was estimated to be about a quarter of a million tons, two fifths of this being produced in Shropshire and Staffordshire. From the late 1790s onwards production was running surplus to domestic requirements, and substantial quantities of pig iron were being exported. After about 1800 periodic breakdown in Anglo-Russian relations and the general difficulties of trading in the Baltic in wartime made the traditional sources of supply of imported high-quality bar iron increasingly precarious, adding to the advantages of the home industry which also benefited from the high duties on imports imposed by Pitt for revenue purposes. Although a certain amount of Swedish bar iron was always in demand for the manufacture of steel, the trade figures clearly reflect the progressive liberation of the industry from dependence on Baltic supplies. The application of steam power at all the various stages of the industry contributed greatly to its development. Industrialists, no longer tied to the river courses, and able to use one fuel for all purposes, could bring smelting furnace, foundry, forge, and rolling-mill together in one industrial complex and integrate their businesses, with direct savings in transport and administration.

The ending of the American war was followed by a brief depression, but recovery was not long delayed. The American market for nails and small metalwares of all kinds soon picked up, a demand for steam engines of various sorts created new business, and the Wilkinsons secured contracts for the supply of iron water pipes for Paris and for New York. The building of the iron bridge over the Severn near Coalbrookdale in 1779 proved only a foretaste of the versatility of the new material: in 1787 John Wilkinson launched his first iron barge on the Severn, and the unfinished Forth and Clyde canal carried its first steam-driven vessel in 1789. From this time on there was a rapid proliferation of uses, aided by the improvement in the quality of cast iron obtained through William Wilkinson's invention of the cupola. The mushroom expansion of the cotton industry created a demand for larger and more robust spinning machinery than the wooden machines which had satisfied the needs of domestic outworkers a generation before. The demand for weapons increased, especially after the permanent French occupation of the Low Countries cut off access to the small-arms manufactures of Liége, and the Carron Company became one of the great arsenals for Europe: about 1805–6 it was casting cannon at the rate of over 5,000 a year.

Power-unit manufacturers created an important new demand for iron. The versatility of the steam engine, as developed by Boulton and Watt and their competitors, gave it a market in various industrial fields, not merely the iron industry. The tin miners of Cornwall found the pumping engine almost indispensable as an aid to winning ore from the deeper seams they were now forced to exploit. The steam engine found its way into the pottery industry, where it drove machines grinding down flint; into brewing, where mechanical power could be used for mashing; into flour-milling; and even into the West Indian sugar industry, where powered machinery came to be used for crushing sugar cane. At least up to the expiry of Watt's patents after 1800 his rotary engine was slow to penetrate the cotton industry. His charges made it relatively expensive, and many spinning mills were sufficiently small to find water-power satisfactory – and cheap. But more enterprising mill-owners turned to steam-engines of other kinds. Throughout the last 20 years of the eighteenth century a number of firms in Lancashire were specializing in the manufacture and installation of inexpensive power units based on the Newcomen or Savery engine, usually for the purpose of recharging reservoirs above water wheels and thus freeing factories from the vagaries of water supply due to frost or drought.

In the years after 1780 cotton was the miracle-product of the industrial revolution, the commodity which contributed most to the growth of overseas trade, and which provided employment for additional thousands of working people. The technological advances in spinning before 1780 had created a situation in which the supply of cotton yarn was almost unlimited so long as the raw material was available, and the rise in the import figures for cotton wool provides dramatic evidence of the expansion of the industry.[2] The general use of Crompton's mule also brought enormous economies in production due to reduction of waste and other technical advantages: yarn which sold for 38 shillings the lb. in 1786 was down to 5s.2d. the lb. in 1813. The development of a substantial export trade in yarn to the Continent in the early 1800s indicates that productive capacity had outrun domestic demand, and relatively little further increase took place during the Napoleonic war.

Up till 1815 weaving remained almost entirely a handloom occupation. Though experiments with power-looms were proceeding from the 1780s onwards, the quality of the product was poor and only about 2,000 had by then been brought into use. Labour for handloom weaving was cheap and abundant, and the expansion of the labour force was made all the easier through the facility with which men

---

[2] Importation of cotton wool, millions of lb.

1780	— 6.8	1800	— 56.
1785	— 15.4	1805	— 59.
1790	— 31.4	1810	— 132.4
1795	— 26.4	1815	— 99.3

could switch from woollen or linen weaving to the new trade. Indeed, from the late 1790s overmanning was leading to a decline in real wages, one factor of many which contributed to the cheapening of cotton goods. Costs were also being cut in the final stages of bleaching and dyeing. Cylinder printing was introduced in 1785 and brought various economies. Also important was the development after 1799 of the efficient and conveniently handled bleaching agent chloride of lime, the common bleaching powder.

Overall demand for cotton cloth was strong and encouraged rapid increase in productive capacity. The gross annual value of output, about £4 millions at the end of the American war, had reached £11 millions by the turn of the century and was approaching £30 millions by 1815. An importance part of this output went to the home market, which may have been of relatively greater importance until the mid 1790s, and the strength of which lay in the appeal of the product of the loom to a very wide social spectrum. Its cheapness and adaptability for fashion made it attractive to the upper and middle ranks of society; but Sir Robert Peel the elder estimated in 1786 that three quarters of the printed goods 'were consumed by the lower classes of the people.' It was remarked about 1810 that 'a pretty muslin gown' was obtainable by the village girl for as little as 10 shillings.[3] The crucial expansion in the export trade began in the 1790s and continued almost unchecked until the major recession of 1811. In the mid 1780s the value of exports at current prices was less than one fifth of the gross value of cottons (£900,000 as against £5,400,000). By the years 1801−3 it had reached three fifths of a vastly increased total (£9,300,000, out of £15,000,000). Within a decade, by the years 1811−13, both figures had nearly doubled. By 1790 the then fairly substantial sales to Africa had reached saturation point and soon became a relatively insignificant proportion of the whole, but for the next two decades the United States offered a voracious market. As growing tensions over neutral rights led to interruptions of this traffic after 1807 much of it was switched to the South American empires of Spain and Portugal, opened as a consequence of the Iberian national revolts against Napoleon's domination. By 1815 the value of cotton exports was more than twice that of woollen exports, and was approaching 40 per cent of the declared value of all British exports.

The woollen industry continued to expand during the middle and later years of George III's reign, though at a slower pace than cotton. The raw material was less amenable to mechanical processes, and although numbers of power-driven mills were established for the preliminary operations of scribbling and carding, the hand-operated

---

[3] Quoted in M. M. Edwards, *The Growth of the British Cotton Trade, 1780−1815* (Manchester, 1967), pp. 30, 48.

jenny continued to predominate in the spinning branch throughout this period. The pre-eminence of the West Riding became steadily more marked, and the weaving industry there continued to be organized mainly in small workshops controlled by master weavers. English linen production scarcely increased at all after the 1770s. On the other hand Scottish linen nearly doubled between 1780 and 1800, to about 24 million yards. At the same time it became increasingly concentrated in the eastern Lowlands, especially in the counties of Fife, Perth, and Forfar. Employment in the domestic production of linen yarn became an important ancillary source of income for rural families during the winter months over much of the Lowlands, and also in parts of the eastern Highlands. But the largest producing region in the British Isles was northern Ireland, with a main concentration in the Lagan valley; Irish weavers and entrepreneurs moved into the markets abandoned by English — and to some extent Scottish — producers who were turning over to cotton, and in the period of the Napoleonic war may have been supplying about as much as England and Scotland combined. Circumstances were less favourable for the silk industry. Catering always for a luxury market, this expanded slightly during the early 1780s but for the most part stagnated during the last two decades of the eighteenth century and made little advance during the next 15 years. Marginally at least it suffered from the competition in cheap accessories offered by the manufacturers of cottons, and its production costs were adversely affected by the difficulties placed by the French invasions of Italy in the way of securing supplies of the raw material.

A generation after its early beginnings in the 1750s the chemical industry was beginning to emerge after 1780 as a recognizably separate branch of the economy, concerned with the production of industrial chemicals, and linked directly or indirectly with more and more of the multifarious manufacturing processes to which the industrial revolution was giving birth. The demands of the soap and glass manufacturers led to the establishment of several plants in Staffordshire and in the north-east for the purpose of supplementing traditional vegetable sources of potash with supplies of soda, an alternative raw material. Various experiments with bleaching agents required for the textile trades were undertaken, leading to the discovery of bleaching powder in 1799. Industrial chemists also assisted textiles by stepping up the production of alum, a material which played an essential part as a mordant in dyeing, but which also had other industrial uses in the production of tallow, of fire-resistant paper, in tanning and in metal-cleaning. Improvements were also made in the cheap production of other mordants, copperas, sugar of lead, and aluminium acetate. The Scottish entrepreneur Archibald

Cochrane, Lord Dundonald, developed the process of extracting tar from coal. His process was found to yield also a range of other materials which could be put to various industrial uses: lamp-black, ammonia, sal-ammoniac, Glauber's salt, and fossile alkali. Nor was it long before the potential uses of the most volatile distillates were grasped. The engineer William Murdoch, Boulton and Watt's agent in Cornwall, lighted his own house at Redruth with an experimental coal gas system in 1792. In the early 1800s gas began to be used to light factories, theatres, and other large buildings. The Gas Light and Coke Company was chartered in 1812 with the role of providing street lighting in the metropolis, and by 1815 there were already some 26 miles of gas main laid in London serving about 4,000 burners. In 1814 the police commissioners of Manchester obtained legal powers to run their own gasworks for the same purpose.

In 1814 the Scottish politician Sir John Sinclair noted: 'At present there are a greater number of intelligent practical chemists in Scotland, in proportion to the population, than perhaps in any other country in the world.'[4] In the development of new processes, and in the exchange of expertise in various fields in agriculture and industry which characterize the economic development of George III's reign, it is noteworthy that the Scots contributed quite disproportionately. This was undoubtedly due in part to the superiority of the Scottish over the English universities in the field of scientific study at this time. Numbers of the pioneers of the more scientific aspects of the industrial revolution had been trained there, particularly at Glasgow and Edinburgh, and notably under the guidance of the distinguished scientist Joseph Black. More than half the leading members of the Lunar Society of Birmingham had Scottish connections and most of these men were interested in various applications of chemistry. Despite the prejudices which national politics had demonstrated so clearly in the early 1760s, the peoples of north and south were coming together, and the industrial revolution was neither an English nor a Scottish but a truly British phenomenon.

British trade relationships underwent a series of adjustments in the years after the war of American independence. A strong 'mercantilist' sentiment in Britain, typified by Lord Sheffield's pamphlet of 1783, *Observations on the Commerce of the American States*, ensured that the newly independent Americans would preserve little of the trading advantages they had formerly enjoyed within the British Empire. In particular, while bowing to some extent in practice to the needs of the situation, the British government and Parliament were intent on denying to the Americans their old favoured position as suppliers of

---

[4] Quoted in Clow, *The Chemical Revolution* (1952), p. 199.

timber and foodstuffs to the British West Indies. Direct trade with the former colonies on a most favoured nation basis was quickly resumed and in the year 1784 exceeded in value the annual average for the last normal trading years of the colonial regime, 1771–3. Trading relations were placed upon a sounder footing by the Jay treaty of 1794. This reduced the extent of American discrimination against British shipping, conceded the right of American vessels to trade at the bases of the East India Company in South Asia, and permitted direct trade with the West Indies in small vessels of not more than 70 tons – a provision intended to check direct transit of British West indian commodities in American ships across the Atlantic. Although this last clause was rejected by the American senate, the principle was unilaterally extended by order in council in the interests of the West Indian planters. Thereafter the American trade became of increasing importance as the French wars closed markets in Europe. Between 1793 and 1801 British exports to the United States doubled, and in the early 1800s they accounted for about one fourth of total exports, until diplomatic disputes and finally war diminished and then brought them to an end. Some goods also passed into the United States by way of the Canadian provinces, and these later became a not insignificant trading area in their own right, taking British manufactures in return for timber and furs and marginal importations of wheat.

Trade with Europe soon returned to normal after the American war. The most remarkable development was the new connection with France under the terms of the Eden treaty of 1786. The Pitt administration initially saw no reason to abandon the traditional policy of denying to France as far as possible the benefits of commercial intercourse, but the French for their part were determined to secure them, and Vergenne's threat of commercial retaliation at a time when the British were diplomatically isolated and vulnerable, brought Pitt to the negotiating table at the moment when the changing economic circumstances were tipping the balance of advantage in an Anglo-French commercial agreement to the British side. By this treaty both countries temporarily abandoned their long-standing intent to damage the economy of the other and sought to suppress smuggling in the interests of their national revenues. In general they agreed to the importation of each other's products on payment of moderate duties ranging from 10 to 15 per cent. The French gained particularly by the very substantial reductions of British import duties on wines to the level then applying to wines from Portugal (though this did not preclude further preferential concessions on the Portuguese trade). On the other hand they yielded to the British insistence that all goods containing silk be prohibited on either side; in no other way could the

survival of the British silk industry have been safeguarded. The ships
of the two nations were to enjoy the rights of a most favoured nation in
each other's ports, alien duties being abolished. Each government
conceded liberal rights as trading residents to nationals of the other.
The agreement was made for a term of 12 years (though in fact it was
abrogated by the French revolutionary leaders in 1792). The balance
of advantage was soon proved to lie with Britain, and during the late
1780s, for the first time, British exports to France reached a level
comparable with those to other major European trading partners.

Although commercial negotiations with other European countries
between 1783 and 1793 came to nothing, and the British government
failed to obtain advantages which it sought, the interest of those countries in exchanging goods with Britain was strong and ensured that
traffic would continue. It was the renewed wars after 1793 that
created problems, as from time to time parts of Europe dominated by
a hostile France ceased to be open to commerce. In the early 1800s
Europe took about a third of Britain's total exports, a rather larger
proportion than did the United States, and was the major market for
cottons and cotton yarn. The breakdown of either of these trading
systems could have serious consequences. But not all sections of the
economy were equally vulnerable. It was chiefly the textile industries
which were threatened by Napoleon's continental blockade and by
tension with the United States.[5] The cotton industry was most liable to
damage for it exported more than half of its output, sent three
quarters of its exports to Europe and the United States, and obtained
half of its raw material from the latter country. The two fifths of
British export trade that went to customers other than Europe or the
United States included a great measure of the important lines of
metalwares of all kinds, glassware, china, and coals. Fairly important
in this trading sector were the areas of the Spanish and Portuguese
empires, and the fortunes of war gave the British particular opportunities in both. The Latin American region made up to some extent
though by no means completely for the losses of trade inflicted after
1807 by the non-intercourse policy of the United States and
Napoleon's blockade of Europe.

Between 1793 and 1815 Great Britain was engaged in a series of the
greatest wars the country had ever experienced. What effects did this
have on economic development? While numerous particular effects
of war can be discerned, it would seem as if historians are as yet far
from being able to suggest any final, balanced, general answer to this
question. In part this may be because measurement of the economic

---

[5] The economic warfare between Britain and Napoleonic France is treated in the context of
the war, pp. 307 seq below.

effect of war is too shot through with the imponderables of what might have been.

If Napoleon's continental system brought dislocation to British trade and industry, and for a while European markets became almost inaccessible, at the same time the pattern of hostilities enabled the British to dominate trade over wide areas outside Europe to the detriment of their European rivals. France lost millions of pounds worth of overseas trade to Britain as a result of the British conquest of most of her West Indian colonies and her loss of Haiti through its winning of its independence. There was also a permanent loss of French trade to Britain in the Levant, and French overseas enterprise in other parts of the globe was checked by the omnipresent operation of British sea-power while that of Britain thrived. Both the Spanish and the Portuguese colonial trading systems were smashed during the course of the wars, and upon their ruins was founded the dominant position of British export trade to Brazil and to large parts of Spanish America. Taking the figures of 1788−92 as a base, British imports increased by over 50 per cent by 1798−1802 and were nearly doubled by 1814. Re-exports trebled by 1798−1802 and were up by between five and six times by 1814. Nevertheless, it seems impossible to say whether these figures would or would not have been exceeded had there been no war. Some trade channels would not have opened as they did; on the other hand, the British might have held for longer and on a greater scale their markets for manufactures in the United States.

Producer and consumer alike were affected by the interruptions of supplies of raw materials for industry and the destruction of profits through the haphazard closing of markets. In the 1790s especially, the pressure from the government in the money market drove up interest rates and created difficulties for investment. Shortages of goods caused increases in price; but in this connection it has to be kept in mind that the serious problems which arose over food prices in the years after 1793 had little to do with the war and were largely due to vagaries of the climate, which seems to have become slightly less equable during this period. On the other hand the war brought certain compensatory advantages. The abandonment of cash payments by the Bank of England in 1797 removed a restraint affecting both military and civilian spending, and for the next 15 years the country experienced a steady mild inflation. Between 1800 and 1811 the monthly average value of Bank of England notes in circulation increased by approximately 50 per cent, and this circulating medium was supplemented by the very substantial total issues from the country banks. It has been estimated that the face value of money and money instruments in circulation in Britain may have more than doubled during the French wars. This was not wholly inflationary: population, capital assets, industrial production had all greatly increased, and it appears also that the rate of growth of both overseas trade and of the gross national product was proceeding faster than the general growth of population. But there was an appreciable inflation which, over the same period, amounted to about 20 per cent. Under these circumstances the government's monetary policy in effect provided a flexible credit base, not only for the expansion of industry, but for the creation of other very substantial capital assets, docks, canals, roads, and urban properties in the growing industrial towns.

By these means, whether knowingly or not, the government underpinned the livelihood of countless people, whose lot otherwise it is difficult to imagine. Moreover, it offset to some degree the fact that, at least after 1797, war taxation fell largely on the consumer and on the landed interest and was less discouraging than it might have been to the industrial investor. Government spending created some positive advantages for both the textile and the metallurgical industries — the armed forces had to be both clothed and equipped with weapons. Not only was the government thus providing employment, but by its maintenance of large armed forces it guaranteed a large consumer demand for foodstuffs and other necessaries; and by removing into the services a number of men which, by 1811, amounted to some 9 to 10 per cent of the total adult male labour force, it not only eliminated a possible source of large-scale unemployment, but actually caused shortages of labour which tended to encourage the development of alternative mechanical methods of production. It may be, that in important ways the wars helped to promote essential preconditions for industrial 'take-off': sustained consumer demand, and a labour force not too numerous and cheap to make technological developments not worth pursuing. Whether these conditions would have been maintained in some other way had there not been war seems difficult if not impossible to judge. Faced with such imponderables, perhaps the only conclusion can be, that war despite the dislocations and difficulties which it caused, did in important ways stimulate and foster the British economy during the 20 years before 1815.

II

It is beyond doubt that for considerable sections of the population conditions became more adverse during the 30 or 40 years before 1815. Town life sometimes meant unhealthy overcrowding on a scale not hitherto experienced outside London. Changing conditions of work often brought a lowering of the quality of life. The daily round was losing its leisureliness, and increased effort was called for to gain a livelihood. This pressure was felt even where industry remained largely domestic, but it pressed most upon the small but growing section of the workforce involved in factory industry. The drafting of pauper children into the cotton-spinning mills posed this social problem in its most acute form, leading to the first tentative and hardly successful attempt to bring it under public regulation by the Factory Act of 1802.

For a large part of the population making a living had always been an acute problem; and yet it is probably true that the proportion was much smaller in 1800 than it had been in 1700.[6] The question whether the standard of living in general was rising or falling appears hardly susceptible to elucidation, at least in the present state of historical knowledge. With regard to some particular groups the picture is rather more clear. Craftsmen like those in the building and clothing trades in the metropolis seem to have been relatively successful in defending their interests, preventing over-recruitment and securing advances in wages which at least more or less kept up with the falling purchasing power of money. On the other hand, the enormous boom in the various weaving trades between about 1780 and 1800 ultimately created a situation of heavy over-manning and under-employment at a time of falling demand. Cotton weavers who had been prospering with earnings of up to 30 shillings a week in the 1780s and early 1790s thereafter found their wages declining in money terms, and still more in real terms as bad harvests forced up the price of foodstuffs, and as the competition for employment intensified. The ending in 1807 of a general wage agreement which had stood for the last 20 years in the east Midlands stocking manufacture proved the prelude to wage cuts of as much as a third. A significant fraction of the total labour force was thus subjected, during the latter part of the French wars, to a descent from a comfortable competence to what was often dire poverty.

Various forms of mutual help existed among working people. Friendly or benefit societies proliferated. Ministers and Parliament concurred in 1793 in the passage of an Act which enabled such societies registering with the local magistrates to secure protection of

---

[6] Writing in 1969 Gregory King had estimated that over half the population spent more than they earned and occasionally or regularly depended on parochial or charitable assistance. W. Speck, *Stability and Strife. England, 1714−1760* (1977), p. 34. Returns for 1802−3 suggest that about one eighth of the population was dependent on the poor law in that bad year. J. R. Poynter, *Society and Pauperism. English Ideas on Poor Relief, 1795−1834* (1969), p. 189.

their funds against default by their officers. This measure was of service so far as it went, though it did not save societies from the disasters arising from unsound amateur actuarial calculations, and in any case an unknown but certainly large number of short-lived societies never took advantage of it.

While association in friendly societies for mutual self-help was recognized as legal, the combination of men to forward their industrial interests usually was not. There were exceptions. The Spitalfields Act of 1773 virtually gave sanction to delegates of employees in the silk manufacture to present their case about wages periodically to the magistrates. More generally, combinations to seek enforcement of laws governing trades, however obsolete these might be, do not seem to have been regarded as unlawful by the authorities. But apart from such cases, any banding together 'in restraint of trade' was a criminal offence indictable as conspiracy at common law. An accused man convicted on indictment before quarter sessions or assizes faced penalties up to a maximum of two years' imprisonment or seven years' transportation. Also, the Elizabethan Statute of Artificers of 1563 laid down penalties for men who left work unfinished.

As legal delays made these laws largely inoperative, the Pitt ministry secured the passage of the Combination Act of 1799 giving magistrates summary jurisdiction to deal with combinations which engaged in strike action. The grossest defects of this statute were redressed by a second Combination Act in 1800. This required that two magistrates, not merely one, should exercise jurisdiction, and it barred a justice who was an employer in a particular trade from hearing any case arising in connection with it. It also declared illegal combinations of employers formed to determine levels of wages or hours of employment. In an interesting way, the Act looked further, towards conciliation and not merely to the suppression of combinations. Almost for the last time for many years, here was a statutory articulation of older ideas about the responsibility of public authorities to interfere in labour disputes. The Act established a set of rules for arbitration in disputes over wages or hours of labour, with the provision that, failing agreement among the arbitrators, either party might require them to lay the points in dispute before a magistrate, who should himself make an award. One practical limitation soon rendered this provision ineffectual. For many small employers walking the tightrope between solvency and bankruptcy a decision against them inevitably dictated the suspension or the total abandonment of their business and the disappearance of any employment they might otherwise be able to offer.

If the legal situation of workmen's combinations was parlous, nevertheless the bite of the English criminal law was much less fierce than its bark. Magistrates and employers were alike loth to evoke it, unless actual violence occurred. In many trades a customary body of procedures had evolved for the handling of questions of hours and wages, conducted usually by committees which theoretically, and perhaps often in practice, had only a temporary *ad hoc* existence. In favourable circumstances such combinations frequently did force employers into granting advances of wages, and it is a travesty of the facts to suggest, as has occasionally been done, that the machinery of the law was invoked to defeat a union whenever it appeared about to be successful in such a campaign. In fact the extent to which unions escaped the theoretical rigours of the law was quite remarkable.[7] In the early 1790s the journeymen in the metalware trades at Sheffield provide an example of a flourishing combination able to keep wages at a level which yielded them a livelihood from three days work per week. The financial resources eighteenth-century unions could command were sometimes considerable. The croppers and weavers of the West Riding, then acting in unison to defend their interests by representations to Parliament, were said in 1806 to have raised between £10,000 and £12,000 for legal expenses and attendance in London over the previous three years; and in 1812 the carpenters of London claimed to have a standing fund of £20,000.

In certain specific contexts unions opposed the introduction of machines. Attacks against spinning jennies during the 1770s seem to have been inspired more by a dislike of factory industry than the machine itself, for appliances with up to 24 spindles which were suitable for cottage industry were exempt; only the larger machines became the target for riotous destruction. However, the rapid spread of mechanization in the cotton-spinning industry from 1780 onwards seems to have caused little unrest, perhaps because the enormous increase in the quantity of yarn available meant an employment boom on the weaving side and labour displaced from hand-spinning was relatively easily absorbed. There were no major factory riots against factory spinning after 1779, though there was an occasional incident in defence of local interests. The attempt of Joseph Brookhouse to adapt Arkwright's techniques to the mechanized spinning of worsted yarn at Leicester in 1787 provoked such a violent outbreak of rioting and machine-breaking that he abandoned it. The local domestic spinners kept the town clear of mechanized spinning for a further 20 years. This was probably to the detriment of the users of yarn, who had to bring in part of their supplies from Worcester and other Midland towns where Brookhouse was able to establish mills. By

---

[7] For the situation in one industrial centre, Nottingham, see Malcolm I. Thomis, *The Town Labourer in the Industrial Revolution* (1974), pp. 138—9.

contrast, Arkwright's enterprise was welcomed at Nottingham, since his factory-spun thread supported rather than threatened the interests of the local hosiery trade, and the hosiers also welcomed the establishment of one of Brookhouse's mills, since this relieved them from the necessity of bringing in supplies of worsted yarn from other areas.

The threat to skilled crafts from the development of gig-mills and shearing frames in the finishing stages of woollen cloth manufacture gave rise to serious disputes which eventually merged into the Luddite machine-breaking of 1811–13. In Wiltshire in 1802 workers in these branches of the trade refused to undertake the 'dressing' of cloth on gig-mills, despite the fact that the speed of the operation created a greater amount of work for the shearers and the cloth so treated had a preference in the market. Strikes by the shearers initially held back the introduction of mechanical dressing but the ultimate consequence was recourse by the clothiers to mechanical shearing also. By threats of strike action the Yorkshire croppers were able to keep shearing frames out of the Leeds area well into the early years of the nineteenth century, but the machine-breaking in which they indulged in 1812 in neighbouring districts where their direct influence was less strong likewise in the end hastened their disappearance and the advent of the machines.

As economic distress increased after the resumption of war in 1803, working people increasingly sought protection through the enforcement of ancient statutory provisions or through fresh enactments. A few remnants of ancient practice did survive into the opening years of the nineteenth century. Hours, wages, and rules of apprenticeship were subject to public regulation for the journeymen tailors of London under a statute of 1768 and for the Spitalfields silk weavers by the Act of 1773 which was renewed in 1792. Wages were subject to determination in both cases by the local justices — in the case of the silk weavers by the JPs of Middlesex acting in concert with the magistrates of the City of London, in that of the tailors by the City authorities alone. But in other callings, where appeal lay only to obsolete Tudor legislation, which had long been ignored, employers and authorities alike turned a blind eye.

In the early 1800s workers and small masters of various descriptions in the woollen cloth industry mounted an extensive campaign to secure the enforcement of old statutory restrictions, if necessary with confirmation of them anew by Act of Parliament. Their agitation covered wages, apprenticeship, limitation of individual master's employment of looms, and the prohibition of gig-mills. A committee of the House of Commons on the woollen trade in 1806 heard evidence from both the men and the employers, but eventually came down in favour of the more go-ahead employers' contention, that the old restrictions were unworkable, would only bring the industry to a standstill if enforced, and ought to be repealed. Eventually all legal restrictions regarding apprenticeship, gig-mills, and the number of looms that might be employed were swept away by statute in 1809. In 1803 and 1804 the calico printers agitated for an Act to reintroduce the system of apprenticeship into their industry, together with a limitation on the numbers that might be admitted, but found it blocked in the Commons. In 1807 the privations of the Lancashire cotton weavers led to approaches to Parliament for legislation. According to some reports as many as 100,000 men signed a petition seeking the establishment of statutory minimum wage levels, in order to prevent a minority of employers from undercutting wage and price levels voluntarily agreed by a majority. Spencer Perceval, the chancellor of the exchequer, was sympathetic, but insisted that Parliament could only legislate if there was sufficient agreement among the employers. This proved to be unobtainable, and accordingly men on all sides in the Commons united in rejecting a minimum-wage Bill for the industry introduced in May 1808 by the vice-president of the board of trade. MPs feared that the proposed regulations might have adverse effects on employment by driving many entrepreneurs out of business altogether. The workmen were left to see what widespread strike action might achieve. They were able to secure for a short time a 20 per cent advance, but it is possible that the cost in part-time working outweighed the benefits.

The controversy over public control reached its climax in the years 1812 and 1813, when it was brought to a head by various disputes. In 1812 the Nottinghamshire framework knitters, organized in their Society for Parliamentary Relief, petitioned Parliament for a comprehensive package of regulation, including wage rates, apprenticeship, and the prohibition of 'cut-up' articles. At the same time came the strike of weavers in the Lanarkshire area, intended to force employers to comply with the wage rates awarded by the arbitration of the Glasgow magistrates. The lord provost himself reported from Glasgow that the employers could not afford to pay the rates awarded. The growing awareness, not only in connection with this case but also with others, of the impracticability of putting masters in this position, led in the following year to the repeal of the clauses of the Elizabethan statutes relating to the fixing of wages. In 1814 the apprenticeship clauses of the Act of 1563 were similarly repealed.

While in relation to wage regulation, apprenticeship and use of machinery public authority was gradually becoming more disengaged from the world of labour and industry, in one sphere it remained firmly in contact with it — that of the poor law. Relatively little poor-law legislation was passed in the late eighteenth century, but this is not to say that politicians were indifferent to the question. Four parliamentary inquiries took place between 1775 and 1815, as well as several private investigations. But it was the local authorities, especially the magistrates, who bore the chief responsibility, and the fact that there was so little recourse to action by higher authority in part reflects the very flexibility and adaptiveness of the system.

As a safety net for the indigent the poor law undoubtedly had many imperfections, but even if it was only geared to provide mere subsistence, the very fact that it existed was important, and it was not without effect. At this time receipt of relief bore little of the stigma which came to be associated with it after 1834. The practice of more than one and a half centuries had firmly planted the assumptions that the helpless poor were entitled to support, and that the able-bodied who came upon the parish should be helped back to economic independence as effectively as possible.

Increasingly the parish gave aid to men encumbered with large families who were unable to earn enough for their subsistence. This in effect meant the subsidizing of wages, a practice formally authorized by the poor law statute of 1782 commonly known as Gilbert's Act. Initially, recourse to this expedient seems to have been envisaged as a temporary measure in times of dearth. In 1785 the Cambridgeshire justices responded to a deficient harvest by ordering all wages in the county to be made up to a standard fixed level. Similar decisions were taken in Dorset in 1792, and then in Buckinghamshire and Oxfordshire early in 1795, three months before the much publicized declaration by the Berkshire justices meeting at Speenhamland, after which the practice came to be named. The 'Speenhamland Act' was neither new nor original. What eventually proved novel was the continuance in perpetuity in parts of the country, as a result of bad harvests, inflation, and high prices, of a system at first thought of as merely temporary. Its adoption amounted to an outright declaration in many localities, chiefly in the agricultural south and east, that every man had a right to a minimum of subsistance, to be made up if necessary from public sources. The practice has been described as 'an alternative to and a method of evading the payment of a minimum statutory earned wage.'[8]

The problem of the law of settlement was treated with increasing flexibility, made more and more necessary as the growth and relocation of industry brought with it considerable − if only short-distance − migrations of labour. In theory, to move about in this way men still required a certificate of settlement from their parish of origin if they

---

[8] J. D. Marshall, *The Old Poor Law, 1795–1834* (1968), p. 13.

were to avoid the risk of being hastily expelled from the parish in which they sought work before they could establish a legal domicile. But at least in the industrial districts, it was becoming a common practice by the 1790s, in cases of unemployment, for the overseer of the parish of residence providing poor relief to secure reimbursement from his opposite number in the parish of settlement. An immigrant temporarily out of work was therefore able to remain in a district where his labour was likely soon to be again in demand. A statute of 1795 gave legal extension to this system in two ways. It made the inter-parish financial settlement obligatory in cases where relief was given to sick persons unfit to travel back to their parish of settlement, thus reducing what had been one of the most callous and inhumane aspects of poor-law administration; and it laid down that an immigrant without a certificate of settlement could not, nevertheless, be sent back to his parish of settlement before he had become actually chargeable upon his parish of residence. Thus employers gained increasing freedom to recruit labour, and the workman's freedom to look for work was also enlarged.

Between 1760 and 1815, in whatever way it was effected, the community in fact shouldered a large and increasingly heavy financial responsibility for the upkeep of the poor. In the mid eighteenth century the total annual poor-rate charge for England and Wales was estimated to be about £1 million. There was a steady rise thereafter, only in part to be discounted by inflation. The first official estimate made in 1776 set the figure at £1½ millions. It was £2 millions in 1785, about £4 millions in 1801, and £6½ millions by 1812. The proportion of the population of England and Wales which at one time or other had recourse to poor relief during the 12 months commencing at easter 1811 has been estimated at about 11 per cent. But probably not much more than 2 per cent were able-bodied: a large part of the rest were made up of orphan children, the sick and the impotent.

There was also charity. The supplementation of the poor law by charity schools, the endowment of almshouses, of dispensaries and hospitals, was a regular feature of eighteenth-century British life. In addition, in periods of serious economic crisis extremely large charitable resources were available. Contemporaries estimated that in the death of 1794−5 charity contributed some £6 millions to the relief of the poor, more than the poor itself, and that in the similar crisis of 1801−3 well over £3 millions were provided.[9] Indeed, the dividing line between public and private assistance was never so clearly drawn then as it later became. The churches and the religious spirit helped

[9] J. R. Poynter, *Society and Pauperism. English Ideas on Poor Relief, 1795−1834* (1969), pp. 114, 203.

to bind them together. While on the one hand clergy and evangelicals stressed the moral duty of helping the unfortunate, on the other the clergy, and not least the clerical magistrates, were often among those zealous to ensure that the poor-law services were properly performed. Charity operated from a mixture of motives. In the eyes of some it was a fulfilment of spiritual obligation, to others a matter of secular but no less obligatory humanitarianism, to yet others a form of social reinsurance. But whatever the motives of the donors charity made its contribution to the quality of life.

From time to time historians have given consideration to the view that during the reign of George III there emerged a social confrontation in which class lines began to assume importance. The picture is one of working people victimized and defeated by a class of employers intent on keeping wages at starvation levels, with a capitalist-controlled apparatus of government condoning and supporting this development, both by its police action and by its abolition of legislative protection for working men. Some criticism may perhaps be made of such an approach, which ignores not only the external pressures of international events, but also the propensity of people at that time to worsen their own condition by breeding too fast, and which takes no account of the fact that had not the gross national product been greatly increased by the stimulus of private enterprise in the period 1784—1815, the privations of the people might have been very much worse than in fact they were. There is, furthermore, a good deal of evidence to controvert the picture of systematic confrontation or of victimization.

In numbers of industrial disputes the conflict was not between workmen and employers as two exclusive, antagonistic groups, but between two groups, each comprising both workmen and employers, who were locked in disagreement about the way of carrying on the business. Nor in the one conspicuous example of an industrial town which has been investigated — Nottingham — did any clear class division spill over into parliamentary electoral politics; all the indications are to the contrary. Authorities were not constantly on the alert to suppress trade unions; on the contrary they showed a remarkable tolerance of them. The confidence with which skilled craftsmen in London were handling their relations with employers and maintaining fighting funds for the purpose strikingly belies the impression of victimization.[10] Magistrates and landowners often showed sympathy with workmen engaged in industrial disputes. The weighty accusation has been made against Pitt's government that the decision taken

---

[10] See for instance the passage quoted in E. P. Thompson, *The Making of the English Working Class* (1964), p. 238.

in 1792 to build military barracks was motivated primarily by a desire to hold down a potentially revolutionary industrial proletariat. But apart from the fact that available information about the public discussions of this decision during 1792 provides no indications that a repressive policy was in view, the latter-day suspicions of the government's intentions are not borne out by an examination of its performance. By the end of the long French wars, in 1815, about 160 barracks had been erected. Only about a dozen of these were situated in the main industrial areas of the north and Midlands, and the position was still the same in the 1830s, when there was great difficulty in accommodating troops drafted in to overawe the Chartists. It is also observable that a later government showed great reluctance to send in troops during the Luddite disturbances of 1811 – 12, and the military commanders involved, like their naval counterparts on the River Tyne on other occasions, showed a much more commendably moderate sense of realities in assessing the situation than either the magistracy or the employers. Army commanders denounced the attempts of the latter to exploit the military presence in reaching settlements with their workmen. There was no fear of an industrial proletariat at the time of the French invasion scare in 1804, when the rush of volunteers embraced all sections of the population: by the end of the year almost every adult male was involved in some form of training in arms. The idea of two nations facing each other in Britain in the period of the French Revolution is far from reality.

How in this connection should the agitation of the Luddites be judged?

The Luddite outbreaks which began in the winter of 1811 – 12 and were repeated sporadically up till 1816 involved three distinct areas of the country: the cotton districts of south Lancashire and the Cheshire border; the West Riding, especially in a region round Leeds; and that part of the east Midlands hosiery district that lies round Nottingham. In each the issues were different. In the east Midlands, attacks on new and on old machinery were used as a means of coercing employers into making concessions on wages, working conditions, and other specific grievances, including the manufacture of 'cut-ups'. In the West Riding machine-breaking expressed a direct hostility to such labour-saving machinery as gig-mills and shearing frames, which were threatening to produce technological redundancy for certain hitherto favoured groups of craftsmen. In south Lancashire the generalized discontent of the handloom weavers focussed upon what was still a relatively distant threat, the power-driven loom. In all these districts workmen's grievances had been, or were being also brought to notice in other ways, by strike action, by appeals to magistrates, or by petitions to Parliament.

The view most generally taken of this agitation is that it was purely a movement of industrial protest with distinct regional variations. There appear to be some difficulties with an alternative view which has been put forward, that apart from economic motivation, Luddism had a real political significance as a 'quasi-insurrectionary movement which continually trembled on the edge of ulterior revolutionary objectives.'[11] There is no support for it in local reports, apart from the often suspect scare stories put out for their own advantage by professional informers. Neither the editors of the *Leeds Mercury* nor of the *Nottingham Review*, journals catering for the property-owning employing class, took seriously local rumours of revolutionary intent. In both Yorkshire and Nottinghamshire part of the employing class identified itself with the objects, though not the methods, of the Luddites, and associated with the craftsmen to try to promote them by peaceful, constitutional means. Rumours that Yorkshire Luddites were seizing arms with revolutionary intent appear unconvincing in face of the evidence of the Sheffield food riots of April 1812, when the participants raided a militia arms depot but seemed more concerned to destroy the weapons than to purloin them. That some subversive groups existed in Yorkshire and made use of the Luddite oath seems evident, but their centres at Halifax and Barnsley were not associated with the croppers' attacks on cloth-dressing machines. Neither the home secretary in office in the years 1809−12 nor the general commanding the Lancashire district in 1812 believed Luddism was involved with anything more than industrial disputes. Employers as a class revealed nothing of the fear of social disruption which might have been expected had they sensed a revolutionary intent in the Luddite movement. No dumps of arms, no wide network of organization, no plan of revolution could be unearthed by the authorities. There is much more ground for accepting the view that the economic distress in the Luddite districts helped to stimulate a peaceful, constitutional movement for radical reform which began to take shape in 1812 in parts of both Lancashire and the West Riding.[12]

---

[11] E. P. Thompson, *op. cit.*, p. 553.

[12] For a judicious reassessment of northern Luddism, see John Dinwiddy, 'Luddism and Politics in the northern counties', *Journal of Social History* 4 (1979), pp. 33−63.

8   The Ascendancy of Pitt

I

From the end of 1783 British politics settled down into a duel between two great men of commanding stature, who for more than 20 years were to face each other across the floor of the House of Commons. There had been nothing quite like it before in the eighteenth century: even the rivalry between Walpole and Pulteney had not been fraught with such drama, caught up in issues of such major importance for the fate of the country, or continued for such a length of time.

At the beginning of 1784 William Pitt was aged 24 and Charles James Fox was just 10 years older. The two men had much in common – not least, perhaps, an element of mutual admiration which persisted despite the bitterness of their political conflict. Both boasted family backgrounds closely linked with the nation's top political leadership. Pitt's position indeed was unique: both his father and his uncle, George Grenville, had preceded him in the role of First Minister, and his first cousin, William, Lord Grenville, was to succeed him. Fox's father had legitimately, if unsuccessfully, aspired to that role, and from further back in his pedigree, through his Lennox ancestors, Fox could claim – perhaps to his misfortune – a dash of the genetic inheritance of Charles II.

Both men had a surpassing ability to absorb information and to manipulate it through the spoken word, though their styles in debate appeared to be very different. Almost from the beginning of Fox's career observers noted the aggressive assurance with which he would attack the whole body of argument put up by his opponents. By contrast the great characteristic of Pitt's oratory was its massive, ordered presentation of information and argument. Yet this rhetorical contrast was not a fundamental one, and it derived largely from the fact that the one almost always spoke in opposition whilst the other was concerned with the exposition of government policy. Fox was just as capable of mastering a brief, as appeared for instance, from his introduction in the Commons of the East India Bill of 1783;

and Pitt's rapier thrusts against the weak points of his opponent's armour were never better displayed than in the fulfilled threat to 'unwhig' Fox in the debates during the Regency crisis of 1788—9.

At the outset also at least, there were important similarities of personal character. Both men were highly cultured and widely read. Both could give a dazzling display in social intercourse and were capable of winning devoted friendship among their close associates. But as the years passed the picture changed and the contrast sharpened. Fox remained always the genial extrovert, with an attractive sympathy for youth which spilt far beyond his immediate concern for the welfare of his favourite nephew, Lord Holland, and continued to win him new friends and followers to the end of his life. Pitt early developed a coldness and aloofness of manner, by which he held the great part of his wide acquaintance at arm's length. This was not the real man: in the small circle of his intimates he could display a charm and sympathy and human concern that could make them his slaves for life, and the suppressed romance with Eleanor Eden shows that he shared the normal human passions albeit tempered by a highly sensitive conscience and kept under rigorous intellectual control. But towards the wide world he presented a social artifact which, while he commanded respect and even admiration on the score of his talents, denied him the power of magnetic attraction exerted by Fox, and sometimes made him enemies. Perhaps a very young man thrust so early into a position of great power could do no less. At 24 Pitt was first minister, the only commoner in a cabinet of peers, and almost the sole top-ranking spokesman for the government in the House of Commons. The pressures on such a man from those seeking all kinds of favours which the administration could provide were enormous. A hard shell of resistance was essential, of a kind with which an older and more experienced politician could have dispensed. Fox never had occasion to develop it, and a row during the coalition ministry over army patronage illustrated the difficulties that could result.

With this contrast between the two men we begin, perhaps, to reach towards the inner explanations of Pitt's success and Fox's failure. Both men were ambitious in the highest degree. Both were devoted to a public career — if Fox's ambition and devotion flagged latterly, this is no more than might be expected after long years of frustration and failure. Yet, after December 1783 Pitt was prime minister for most of the remaining 22 years of his life, while Fox achieved high office only for the last seven months before his death. If anything, Fox with a 10 years' lead in age and experience, should have had the advantage. That Pitt gained it instead seems almost certainly explicable in terms of personal character.

Pitt was impulsive, erratic, a man of improvisations, ready to drop schemes which presented unforeseen difficulties, and as devious as anyone in political life (a fact clearly shown by his carefully concealed involvement in the king's pressuring of the House of Lords in 1783). Nevertheless his politics, including his deviousness, were always directed within the confines of carefully controlled guidelines which corresponded to the realities and beliefs of the eighteenth-century political world. If in part his ambition was served by cold calculation, it was also guided — and this perhaps mattered still more — by an icy self-imposed intellectual discipline. Pitt always displayed in the highest degree powers of discrimination which, for most of the time, enabled him to avoid creating situations he could not control. Not until 1800 did he run into an unavoidable confrontation with George III; and even then, although he felt obliged to resign, he resolved it in a way which did not preclude his ultimate return to office. Fox, by contrast, never displayed this discrimination or self-control in his politics. If the evidence of his closest friends is to be believed, it was personal pique that first carried him into opposition in 1774. In the early 1780s he overdramatized his career in terms of personal conflict with George III in ways which reached the ears of the king and helped to make him irreconcilable towards him. In the mid 1780s and afterwards he adopted an anti-monarchical posture and attributed his failures to unconstitutional behaviour on the part of his opponents, charges which they and the majority of their supporters could easily dismiss. And on various occasions in the 1790s his behaviour verged on the unpatriotic.

The roots of Fox's failure may perhaps be found in an indiscipline fundamental to his nature and given full play owing to the defects of his upbringing, which marred all his splendid gifts and generous impulses. As a young man he developed the gambler's indifference to people and to circumstances; and as almost invariably happens in such instances, before long realities caught up with him. Because he was constitutionally ill-adapted to come to terms with people and circumstances, his political judgment was blind and disastrous for himself and his followers. Not all his febrile energy, fertile intelligence, personal attraction, mental ingenuity and dexterity with words could compensate for this defect. As a politician Fox was his own worst enemy.

II

Even more than most ministries of the century Pitt's administration initially lacked inner coherence. Pitt himself, its chief spokesman in the Commons, disposed of a personal following eventually to grow to some 50 or more among the young men in both Houses, but he was not the focus of a great political connection. In the cabinet he was flanked by colleagues not closely associated with him, forceful in personality, and in some instances men of much longer political experience. Nevertheless, in all departments the government came to feel the sure touch and quickening energy of his hand, and such coherence as was achieved derived largely from his formidable energies and initiative. He gave vigorous leadership on the three boards which between them carried responsibility for the range of financial and economic questions of primary importance in a period of post-war retrenchment and reconstruction. At the treasury he had the active backing of personal friends. On the reconstituted committee or board of trade, Charles Jenkinson, Lord Hawkesbury, was his right-hand man. On the board of control for the affairs of India he was ably seconded by Henry Dundas, who rapidly became one of his two or three most intimate friends and allies. For great affairs of state — Ireland, foreign policy — the cabinet itself was the effective committee, and in this sphere his relations with the foreign secretary, Lord Carmarthen, and with George III became increasingly influential from about 1786.

In the immediate post-war period the administration had to deal with three major issues: the re-ordering of the national finances; the promotion of national prosperity; and the re-establishment of an effective British presence in the international scene.

The first of these problems, lying particularly in Pitt's department, was grimly symbolized by the national debt, nearly doubled during the American war, and now standing at about £243 millions. Somehow funds had to be found to meet an annual interest charge approaching £9 millions, on top of over one million for civil government and several millions for the fighting services. In 1784 expenditure exceeded income, so that the debt, already viewed with alarm, was still increasing. Either expenditure must be cut, of which there was little immediate prospect, or greater yields must be found from taxation.

One obvious answer was to undercut the smuggling which had been stimulated to unprecedented levels by high war-time taxation. A low tax which could be collected with certainty might yield more than a high one systematically evaded. By the Commutation Act of 1784 Pitt lowered the duties on tea from 119 to 25 per cent *ad valorem*, making up the temporary loss of revenue by an increased graduated window tax. Government support for the East India Company's marketing of its tea completed the discomfiture of the smuggling interests. To the same end, during the next few years Pitt reduced the duties on imported wines and spirits and transferred collection on wines and tobacco from the customs to the excise list, thereby greatly improving the efficiency of the collection. The defeat of smuggling was one of his major arguments in favour of the commercial treaty negotiated with France in 1786 which provided for a general reciprocal lowering of tariffs: in the previous year over a third of the brandy estimated to have entered the country had done so illicitly. Other reductions of duties were effected in 1787 in the legislation setting up the consolidated fund. Stronger measures of preventive action against smuggling were introduced.

Pitt raised still further funds by ringing the changes on various familiar forms of taxation on luxuries ranging from hair-powder to servants and horses. But he also sought to bring other forms of business activity into the treasury's net, sometimes causing considerable difficulties for his victims as well as for himself, and the final impression left is one of rather desperate and unsuccessful improvisation. In 1784 increases in excise duties on calicos, muslins and other cotton textile products brought down a storm from the manufacturers which led to rapid repeal. Another Act of 1784 compelled bleachers, printers, and dyers to take out licences at a charge of £2 per annum, and a tax was laid on all printed and bleached textiles. This was represented as so injurious to the industry that it had to be abandoned the following year. Likewise a tax on coals had to be given up the following year under pressure from the mining and metal-working interests. The most novel of his experiments, the shop tax, was also highly unpopular and was eventually brought to an end in 1789. Pitt also had regular recourse to lotteries, in particular to provide funds to satisfy the claims of the American loyalists.

Slower to yield results, but extensive and ultimately of more importance were Pitt's innovations in financial management. It is hardly exaggerating to say that his tenure of the financial departments signified the watershed between medieval and modern financial administration. When he took office in 1783, the officials' best guide to the system of the exchequer was still the twelfth-century *Dialogus de Scaccario*. Wooden tally sticks were still used in public accounting, as in Angevin times. The machinery of administration was extremely cumbersome, cluttered with ancient survivals of practices and of offices, the original purpose of which was almost forgotten.

As so often, war was the stimulus to administrative improvement. The old machinery had managed to carry the burden of the Seven Years War, but the struggle over American independence was another matter entirely. The strain of this conflict had driven home the need for speedy, efficient, and economical collection and use of public funds, and criticism of the system had grown more bitter as the war gradually moved on to humiliating defeat. North had set on foot one or two departmental inquiries as preliminaries to reform. More important, in 1780 he had secured Parliament's agreement to the appointment of an independent commission to examine the public accounts. By December 1783 the commission was about half way through its labours of investigation and the production of its 15 exhaustive reports. The detailed descriptions of departmental structure and practice and the recommendations contained in these reports provided an indispensable basis for any reform. Pitt's contribution lay chiefly in his willingness to apply these ideas.

Accordingly after entering office Pitt immediately adopted the practice of putting government contracts out to public tender. He made permanent a system of raising government loans by limited competition through sealed tender between competing reliable syndicates of financiers — a method first adopted by North in 1782. He created in 1785 a treasury commission of audit, through which the auditing of government accounts was considerably improved. He undertook a gradual rationalization of the revenue services, reshuffling the responsibilities between the various boards with a larger degree of treasury control. In 1785 the tax office took over responsibilities for duties on coaches, carriages, and wagons, which at various past dates had been somewhat illogically placed on the commissioners of excise. He shrank however from the examining commission's proposals to amalgamate with it the various minor commissions and boards responsible for the salt tax, stamp duties, and the licensing of hawkers and pedlars and hackney carriages. In the interests of efficiency and economy he gradually eliminated custom house sinecures by declining to fill offices as they fell vacant: some 50 were eventually abolished by statute in 1798: in all the revenue services were cut by some 440 places between 1784 and 1793.

In line with Burke's reform of the paymaster's office in 1782 Pitt ended the practice of treasurers of the navy holding their balances in accounts under their own management and control, requiring that any moneys issued for the service of the navy should be kept in account in the Bank of England and withdrawn only as required; henceforth the accounts were to be closed and balanced each year. Creation of the stationery office under treasury control in 1787 secured economies in the supply of stationery to the departments. In the same year Pitt attacked the abuses arising from the parliamentary privilege of franking mail. There was little he could do about civil list expenditure. The traditional quasi-independence of the various government departments severely limited the influence of the treasury. But when the civil list once again ran into debt and the king had to make a fresh appeal to Parliament for help to discharge his debts in 1786, Pitt seized the opportunity to obtain detailed returns of the various classes of payment. One more step was taken along the road towards regarding civil list expenditure as not the sovereign's sole responsibility but a matter with which Parliament and the treasury were also concerned.

The creation of the consolidated fund was a major step forward in efficient administration. Existing imposts were consolidated from the point of collection through to their entry into a single consolidated fund account at the treasury. The gain in economy of labour and avoidance of confusion was enormous. Hitherto there had been no less than 103 different exchequer revenue accounts, all of which had had to be kept completely separate. Revenue collectors had had to forward funds under 68 different accounts. The reckoning of the fractional sums thus involved had created particular occasions for confusion and loss. However this reform was not at that time carried through to its logical conclusion. Certain accounts still remained outside the consolidated fund, particularly the civil list annuity and the land and malt taxes on which specific blocks of funded exchequer bills were secured. Moreover the Consolidated Fund Act of 1787 required that new taxes should be accounted for separately, a flaw only put right in 1797.

One reform Pitt found it impossible to effect in accordance with the recommendations of the commissioners on the public accounts was the substitution of salaries for fees and gratuities in the public offices. He appointed a commission of inquiry into fees in 1785, but although the administrative desirability of such a system was apparent, it would have transferred to the taxpayer unacceptably large financial liabilities then met by individuals doing business with the offices.

Pitt's reformed sinking fund of 1786 was perhaps more important as a step towards recreating national confidence than producing financial improvement. The basic principle of such a fund remained as before. Each year a fixed sum, drawn from surplus revenue, was to be set aside for the redemption of government bonds. But two features of the scheme were distinctly new. One was the elaborate precaution taken to prevent heads of the treasury from raiding the fund for other purposes. It was now placed under the control of a statutory board of six commissioners, where the chancellor of the exchequer was flanked by the speaker, the master of the rolls, the accountant general of the court of chancery, and the governor and deputy governor of the Bank of England. By statute the continuance of the board's operations was to be inviolable. The other novelty was the decision that stock bought by the commissioners should not be cancelled, but should remain in the hands of the commission, which would receive the interest on it and apply this to swell the fund available for further

operations. Given peace and prosperity, and parliamentary willingness to grant the necessary taxation to meet the debt interest owing on
stock in the hands of the commissioners, there was nothing basically
wrong with the scheme, and in the seven peacetime years that
followed they cleared nearly 11 millions worth of stock off the market.
In wartime, however, it was to prove a liability, partly because the
statutory entrenchment made a simple administrative suspension
impossible and partly because too many people were deceived by the
will-o'-the-wisp of compound interest which seemed to offer ultimate
limitless possibilities of debt redemption.

III

Financial solvency rested partly on buoyant trade and a prosperous
populace, and from the start Pitt's ministry was concerned with both
these matters. Somehow the ruins of the old empire and commercial
system had to be drawn together and made serviceable to the state.

If in 1782 Pitt had sympathized with Shelburne's desire for special
commercial relations with the United States, by the end of 1783 he
seems to have accepted the fact that this was not practical politics,
and that the nation approved the exclusionist stand taken up by the
coalition ministry during 1783. There was a general assumption that
if Great Britain were to have any chance of economic recovery, then
the continuance of the old monopolistic system in the West Indies was
essential. The Navigation Acts must therefore be maintained in all
their rigour. In 1783 by order in council American shipping had been
excluded from the islands. Despite the pleas of the sugar planters
their communities were required to obtain their meat and other
supplies from Ireland and fish from Newfoundland, instead of from
the cheaper sources in the United States. In face of extensive illegal
traffic with North America in these commodities via the French and
Spanish islands, imports from these sources were made illegal in 1787.
In 1788 the order in council was replaced by statute, and authorities
were enjoined to strict enforcement. The free port system of 1766 was
re-established with some restrictions in 1787, in order to foster the
important trade with the Spanish colonies, but United States shipping
remained excluded. The British Indies were to remain a prized
commercial reserve. If this brought some penalties for the islands it
also entailed such advantages as a bounty for the production of

indigo, previously obtained from the Carolinas, and active support for the production of cotton wool to feed the rapidly expanding British textile industry.

By contrast with the West Indies the surviving British territories in North America remained an area of remote future promise rather than immediate advantage in the 1780s. Their populations were small and their export surpluses negligible. For the moment the ministry had chiefly to reckon with the fact that they had become a refuge for large numbers of loyalists from the now independent states to the southward. Some 25,000 settled in the area of Nova Scotia, and in 1784 that portion of it lying north of the Bay of Fundy was erected into the separate province of New Brunswick. Perhaps another 20,000 including overland migrants from Pennsylvania and upper New York, found new homes in upper Quebec.

After 1784 the government handled potential constitutional conflicts in this area with care. The loyalists were regarded as deserving of generous treatment, and it was also evident that in matters of rights and privileges they could not be placed in distinct disadvantage in comparison with the citizens of the United States. And so, the home country continued to defray the major part of the civil expenses in both Quebec and Nova Scotia, and assumed a similar responsibility in New Brunswick. In Quebec the authoritarian regime set up in 1774 was continued, but in time the pressures for change became irresistible. Not only did the loyalist settlers in the western districts begin to press for representative government of the traditional kind, but before long the financial burden of administering Quebec was becoming insupportable. By 1790 the total costs to the British treasury were some £100,000 *per annum*. A local revenue had been granted by Parliament in 1774 by the Quebec Revenues Act, but the sums collected defrayed only a small part of the expense. Owing to the Renunciation Act of 1778 no further taxation could be imposed by Parliament, and the establishment of a local legislature to authorize it became essential.

In 1791 the Canada Act, largely shaped by Pitt's cousin, William Lord Grenville, radically recast the government of the province. The problem of the two nationalities was dealt with by dividing Quebec into the two provinces of Upper and Lower Canada. A governor-general acted as supreme executive over both, with a deputy in each. Each province acquired a representative assembly and an upper house of legislature recruited on the basis of nomination with life tenure. Separate executive councils were established to support administration, their members being appointed at pleasure. Some features of this new regime reflected a ministerial intention already evinced in other ways to try to preserve British forms of society and polity in the remaining colonies, with a view to resisting the penetration of American republican influence. An early step was the appointment in 1787 of a loyalist, Charles Inglis, as Anglican bishop of Nova Scotia with a general jurisdiction over the North American provinces. This move reduced the likelihood that aspirants to orders might seek ordination from the American bishops who began to be appointed after 1785. Windsor, Nova Scotia, became the home of a collegiate school in 1788 and of a theological college in 1789. At the political level Lord Grenville's introduction of the legislative councils in the Canadas in 1791 was intended to provide an institution having some parallels with the House of Lords, and he was anxious also that the new executive councils might provide a means whereby members of both Houses of the Canadian legislatures could assist the governors in carrying on the administration, thus avoiding the gulf which had existed between representative assemblies and royal executives under the old colonial system.

No considerations of imperial dominion entered into the establishment in 1788 of the convict settlement of New South Wales. This was purely an *ad hoc* move to deal with the problem of convicted criminals, for whom there was no prison accommodation in the British Isles. The settlement was run as a military outpost, and years were to pass before it developed either as a colony or as a centre for commercial penetration of the South Pacific.

Ship-building and shipping enjoyed a boom in the years after 1783 as British entrepreneurs moved in to fill the gap created by the exclusion of American-based shipping from imperial trade. Their advantage received further legislative sanction by the Navigation Act of 1786, which tightened up the regulations regarding vessels defined as British and instituted the new system of a register of British shipping, a further move aimed against the Americans. Since a politically independent New England could not be allowed to resume the role of main supplier of whale products thrust upon it by George Grenville in the 1760s, the government turned to subsidizing new whaling ventures in Greenland waters and in the South Atlantic and Pacific, welcoming skilled whalers from Nantucket who were prepared to change their domicile. In the Pacific during the 1780s the whalers pioneered the routes for a commercial system linking the Pacific coast of North America with the South Sea islands and Canton, and the government negotiated on their behalf successive inroads on the East India Company's charter monopoly of navigation in these areas. Acknowledgement of their rights was one of the terms successfully exacted from Spain at the end of the Nootka crisis of 1790.[1]

[1] See p. 196 below.

Revenue from tea was but one aspect, though an important one, of Pitt's concern with India and the Far East. Since it was on the question of control over the East India Company that he had overturned the coalition, this matter had a high priority and was quickly dealt with by the East India Act of 1784. This measure suffered to some extent from the limitations imposed by past political conflicts. Having allied with a faction in East India House, Pitt was bound to pay attention to their susceptibilities and could not force upon the company the loss of authority which Fox and Burke had contemplated. Nor could Pitt assimilate the government of India to the crown in face of the charges and counter-charges about executive influence which both sides had thrown at each other during the previous months. The creation of a strong executive at Calcutta was also blocked by prevailing prejudices. The best he could do was to establish an instrument of ministerial control which might gradually extend its power as opportunity offered and occasion compelled. Such was the board of control set up by the Act, composed of six members of the privy council, on which the head of the treasury and the secretary of state for home and colonial affairs were to sit *ex-officio*. In practice the presence among its members of Henry Dundas and of Pitt's cousin, William Grenville, made certain that its operations would be directed by an inner group within the ministry closely connected with the prime minister. Government intervention operated indirectly. The Company continued to conduct the Indian correspondence, but this was now put in the hands of a secret committee of three of the directors, an arrangement which facilitated liaison and the exercise of influence by members of the government. All business of a political nature could be withdrawn from the general body of the direction, and this power was used systematically to secure ministerial control over diplomatic relations and military affairs, and also the finances of the Carnatic which was linked with both. The Act also paved the way to economies and a limitation of the patronage in the directors' hands by forbidding any fresh appointments to the civil or the military service in India until reductions considered sufficient by the board of control had taken place.

For the position of governor-general in Bengal the ministry sought a strong personality independent of the Company and therefore more likely to pay attention to principles of national policy. After an initial failure they persuaded Cornwallis to accept the position. His price was an enlargement of the discretionary authority vested in the post and power if necessary to override his council, and a statute of 1786 put through the necessary amendments to the India Act of 1784, in addition enabling him to hold also the post of commander in chief. With this appointment the effort to bring good order to the provinces now under the Company's rule at last began to take effect. Cornwallis consulted constantly with the ministry through a private correspondence with Dundas, and policy was often shaped with little reference to the directors. Economies in the civil service were achieved by a rigorous paring of sinecures and a new standard of efficiency in administration, and a better order, were imposed in the revenue system by Cornwallis's 'permanent settlement' which fixed for all time the tax charges payable to the Company by the *zamindars*. A rational approach to the defence problem in India would have involved the assimilation of the Company's military force into the regular army, but this was unacceptable to the directors and would probably have been strongly opposed at home on political grounds. In 1788 the government strengthened its hand by a statute enabling the board of control to authorize and charge to the Company's account in India the upkeep of a military force of up to 8,000 royal troops and another 12,000 on the Company's establishment.

On this firm basis government and Company pursued a policy of trade expansion in the east. Purchases of Chinese tea at least doubled between 1783 and 1791. Increasingly credits for payment were obtained from the private export trade from India to China and the Malaysian area, which the government took active steps to promote. In 1785 the personal initiative of Francis Light led to the establishment of a valuable entrepôt at Penang, which served as a centre for the interchange of goods from India, China, and the Malay lands. By the end of the '80s cargoes of Cornish tin, English woollens, Indian cotton wool, sandalwood, pearls, ivory, sharks' fins and spices, entering Canton in increasing quantities, were relieving the Company from the need to make large payments in silver bullion for the tea it brought back to Europe. But not all the ministry's hopes were realized. The Dutch successfully warded off attempts to establish a British entrepôt in eastern Malaya, and the Chinese, preferring to keep the West at arm's length, continued to confine foreign traders to Canton: to no effect the government planned an abortive mission to Peking in 1787–8 under Cathcart and launched a second headed by Lord Macartney in 1791.

IV

In 1783 Britain's diplomatic position was weaker than at almost any

period of the eighteenth century. The ascendancy won for her by
Chatham 20 years before had left her without friends and an object of
jealousy and fear among the other powers. French diplomatic caution
after 1763 ensured that no other nation would be pushed into seeking
a British alliance to safeguard itself, and on the morrow of the peace
of 1783 Britain was generally regarded as finished, reduced to the
rank of a second- or third-class power by the loss of her American
empire. The Battle of the Saints and the successful defence of
Gibraltar showed that these judgments might be wide of the mark.
Nevertheless immediately after the war a defeated Britain seemed to
have little attraction as an ally, and the diplomatic dispositions in
Europe were unfavourable. France was allied with Spain and Austria,
held the ascendancy in Sweden, and was to secure a defensive pact
with the Dutch in 1785. Austria was secretly committed to Russia in a
combination directed against the Turks. Frederick of Prussia saw his
safety to lie in the preservation of peace in eastern Europe, relied on
his good relations with St Petersburg, and was wholly determined
not again to become embroiled on Britain's behalf. When Lord
Carmarthen took over the seals of the foreign office, the opportunities
for a successful diplomatic initiative seemed remote indeed.

In 1783 Charles Fox had naïvely hoped for the restoration of the
Anglo-Prussian alliance. Carmarthen at first preferred to seek a
counterpoise against France at Vienna, and he and Pitt were on the
alert for any chance to weaken the Austro-French alliance. In 1785 it
looked as if the opportunity had come. Joseph of Austria quarrelled
with the Dutch over their military presence in the 'barrier fortresses'
and also demanded cession of the territory of Maastricht. However,
the French mediated with great skill to avert a breach between their
Dutch friends and their imperial ally. During the same year
Carmarthen was deeply embarrassed in his attempts to open overtures for an understanding with Vienna by the action of George III
as Elector of Hanover in joining Frederick of Prussia's League of
German Princes, the Furstenbund, to help defeat Joseph's plan of
consolidating the Habsburg territory in south Germany by exchanging the southern Netherlands for Bavaria. Neither Elector George
nor Frederick regarded their co-operation as opening the way to an
Anglo-Prussian combination, and at the beginning of 1786 British
diplomatic isolation appeared as complete as ever. In the United Provinces British agents intrigued with the pro-British partisans of the
House of Orange, but this activity seemed to offer little prospect of
significant gain.

Pitt was thus in no situation to hold out against increasing French
pressure for a commercial agreement which came to a head in 1785. It
had been a constant principle of British policy to keep trade with

France to a minimum on the grounds that it would minister to the financial and economic strength of the nation's greatest rival. Probably on the grounds that the British contention was correct, the French statesman Vergennes was determined to break down this barrier, and a commitment to commercial negotiations had been written into the peace treaty of 1783. When the British dragged their feet Vergennes threatened commercial reprisals, and in face of this the cabinet agreed to treat. The Anglo-French commercial agreement which eventuated in 1786 is generally hailed as one of Pitt's great successes, and indeed it was. Information was carefully assembled, the ground prepared, and in William Eden, assisted at times by William Grenville, the British had two negotiators of great skill. British rather than French businessmen gained the lion's share of advantage out of the general lowering of tariffs on both sides of the Channel which the treaty secured.[2] It was ironic that this triumph should result from British diplomatic weakness and from a French economic miscalculation in exploiting it.

On the death of Frederick the Great in August 1786 the British government approached his successor, Frederick William II, with new feelers for an alliance to counter French influence in the United Provinces. Any hope of a rapprochement with Austria had now been abandoned. This overture was rebuffed. The Prussian king was still in the hands of francophil advisers. He feared attack from Austria or Russia, and he declined to consider French intrusion into the affairs of the Dutch as dangerous to his interests. For the time being the fact that his sister was the wife of the Prince of Orange, whose position had been eclipsed as a result of French influence did not seem a compelling reason to act. Accordingly at the end of the year the cabinet decided upon a cautious policy, of subsidizing the Orangist party, hoping thus gradually to undermine French influence.

Despite this intervention, during the first half of 1787 the pro-French party in the United Provinces, the 'Patriots', increased their hold upon the machinery of government and deprived the Prince of Orange of still more of his powers. But in July an incident occurred which led to a rapid resolution of the situation in favour of the British. The Princess of Orange attempted a secret journey from Guelderland into Holland to rally her husband's party. Intercepted by a party of Patriots, she was arrested, detained for some days, and then sent back to her starting point. Stung by this insult to his sister the King of Prussia demanded that she be given satisfaction by the Estates of Holland and that her husband be reinstated in his constitutional rights. At this point Pitt and his colleagues boldly urged more decisive

---

[2] For the provisions of the treaty see pp. 167–8 above.

action. By this time the French approach to national bankruptcy was evident. French military intervention was hardly to be expected, and was most unlikely in face of a threat of war. The cabinet agreed to put a small naval force in commission and arrangements were made to hire Hessian mercenaries. Frederick William was persuaded to move with the promise of active British support in case of hostilities, and was suddenly free to do so when the outbreak of the Russo-Turkish war in August 1787 engrossed the attention of his eastern neighbours. In September Prussian troops entered the United Provinces, the Patriot regimes were overthrown, the Orangist ascendancy was restored, and for the time being French influence was eradicated. There followed a series of agreements in late 1787 and early 1788 by which the three states entered into a close diplomatic combination. The British and the Prussians each signed treaties with the United Provinces guaranteeing the Orangist government and a further pact between themselves binding themselves to act in defence of it. A triple alliance signed in August 1788 completed the edifice.

The diplomatic isolation of Great Britain was thus brought to an end, the French were shouldered out of Holland, and an alliance system had been created to bar their return. It remained true, however, that this diplomatic combination had inherent weaknesses. It had developed at a moment when French power was in eclipse through internal disorder and when the great powers of eastern Europe were committed elsewhere. Its durability when these conditions ceased to operate might well be in doubt. Prussian interests in the east of Europe might lead her to ignore her obligations in the west, or put her in such a situation that she could not fulfil them. The Dutch element in the combination was unstable, because a large Patriot party still existed in the United Provinces, ready to overthrow the pro-British government at the first favourable opportunity. It was problematic how far the British would be able to go in meeting obligations towards Prussia. In 1788 the Prussians had pulled British chestnuts out of the fire. The Triple Alliance primarily served the British design of countering French ambition and influence. But the Prussian government also had to show that the treaty brought them advantage. To do this they had to involve Britain in quarrels in eastern Europe, in which the British Parliament and people had no interest. At first they had some success in this, because Pitt was convinced of the value of the alliance and was willing to shoulder obligations in order to keep it alive. But in the end Pitt was obliged to scrape out of eastern entanglements, and then the alliance ceased to be of any interest to Prussia.

Despite these inherent weaknesses, the alliance at first worked fairly successfully from the British point of view. Pitt's ministry was able to get its way in two crises during 1790 — the Belgian revolution and the Nootka Sound dispute — as a result of firm Prussian support.

When Joseph of Austria provoked widespread disaffection in the southern Netherlands by his attempts to rationalize and centralize the local administration, the British government exerted all efforts to restore the status quo. Pitt and his colleagues were concerned above all to maintain the position of the provinces as a barrier to French expansion. They could only serve as such if they remained a part of a great military empire, on terms which guarded against any recurrence of revolutionary discontent. Independent, or seething with revolt they would be liable to fall into the hands of France. The provinces therefore must submit to the emperor; but the emperor for his part must abandon the reforms which had provoked rebellion. Pitt was able to secure Prussian diplomatic aid in enforcing his policy both at Brussels and at Vienna. But in doing so he gained more than the Prussians, who had wanted to exploit the rebellion as a lever in their anti-Austrian policy in eastern Europe and toyed at different times both with the recognition of Belgian independence and with an unconditional restoration of Austrian authority in return for concessions elsewhere — proposals which were both incompatible with British interests.

Prussian support also served Pitt in the dispute which broke out with Spain in 1790 over Nootka Sound. During the previous few years several enterprising British merchants had sought profits in the carriage of sea otter furs from the North American coast to Canton, and a base for this purpose had been set up on Vancouver Island. This was in an area not occupied but claimed by Spain, and Spanish patrols proceeded to arrest ships and break up the settlement. When the news reached London, Pitt was faced with an issue he could not neglect. All the precedents showed that public opinion would turn and rend any ministry which did not stand up against the Spanish on behalf of freedom of navigation. Moreover a general election was in the offing. In the spring of 1790 the cabinet resolved to threaten Spain with war if she did not renounce her claims to ownership of the American Pacific coast round Vancouver Island. As the Spanish had no hope of finding an ally — France being by this time in the throes of revolution — the government gained its point.

These benefits from the association with Prussia involved obligations, and the British cabinet inevitably found itself involved in Prussian designs intended to maintain a balance of power in eastern Europe. Berlin preferred that neither Russia nor Austria should emerge with additional territories from the war they were waging against the Turks; or if they did then Prussia should have equivalents.

When in 1788 the Swedes launched an attack on Russia, this seemed likely to assist the Prussian plan; and when Russia stirred up Denmark to attack Sweden in the rear, Pitt in pursuance of the Prussian alliance, threatened the Danes with British intervention and forced them to withdraw.

Two years later, in 1790, the cabinet again came to the support of the Prussians in putting pressure upon the Austrian emperor to withdraw from the Turkish war and make a peace upon the basis of returning all conquests. With this achieved the Prussians wished to turn the alliance against St Petersburg and oblige the Russians either to return all conquests likewise or else make equivalent surrenders of territory to Poland which would enable Prussia by further exchanges to increase its resources. In this case Anglo-Prussian policy foundered on the determination of the Russians to keep the strategically important fortress and district of Ochakov on the north-west coast of the Black Sea. Pitt believed that the Russians should be coerced by force if necessary into returning Ochakov, and there is no doubt that this was partly in order to re-affirm and honour the alliance with Prussia. But there is also evidence that for the first time British ministers were beginning to regard as desirable the Turkish presence as a barrier to Russian access to the Mediterranean. In March 1791 Pitt carried the cabinet with him and preparations for war began. But the political nation at large saw no reason for such a conflict, strong opposition was shown in the Commons and there was an alarming falling-off of ministerial votes. Foreseeing defeat Pitt abandoned his policy. Prussian schemes were thwarted, and Russia kept its conquests from Turkey.

Throughout the decade after the Peace of Versailles relations with the United States remained correct but distant. While normal trade was rapidly resumed, and much private British capital began to flow into the newly independent states, ministers were not inclined to concede commercial special favours. They believed rigorous adherence to the system of the Navigation Acts to be essential to national prosperity, and this was the main reason for the rejection in 1785–6 of American proposals for a comprehensive commercial treaty which would have granted Americans some of the privileges of British subjects. Other considerations also kept them aloof, especially resentment at breaches of the Versailles agreement relating to the loyalists and to payment of debts due to British merchants. The state governments' refusals to honour obligations undertaken in the name of the confederation by its representatives seemed to offer no basis for any further agreement. Indeed it was understood in London that the power to make commercial treaties still remained with the various states, and negotiations on this local basis were of little interest. Nor did ministers apprehend any serious retaliation against British commercial pressure while political power remained so fragmented in the new nation. Even the continuance of its precarious unity was doubted.

By the late 1780s the premises of British policy began to change. The establishment of the federal constitution of the United States, followed by congressional enactments requiring state implementation of the terms of the peace treaty, provided a fundamentally new basis for Anglo-American diplomatic relations. The federal government was capable of imposing a national policy and making its subjects conform to it. It could also inflict retaliation, and was much more effectual in bringing pressure to bear on London for a British withdrawal from frontier posts still maintained in territory south of the Great Lakes which had formally been ceded to the United States. From 1790 onwards both sides were beginning to edge slightly towards agreement. But until the outbreak of war with France in early 1793 the British government still felt under no urgent pressure to respond to American overtures.

V

Much of this work of national reconstruction was politically non-controversial and created few or no parliamentary problems for Pitt and his colleagues. Furthermore, the general election of 1784 had produced a substantial majority for the king's ministers. Nevertheless, Pitt had to learn that the Commons must be handled with care, and the decade 1784–93 was not without its political strains. Although the coalition forces had gone down in defeat in 1784, nearly 200 members of the Commons were committed on the side of Charles Fox. While this number, even at full strength, fell far short of a majority, its presence meant that casual opposition from other parts of the House could be expected to outvote the ministry on occasion, and the hope of the Foxites after 1784 was that this would happen sufficiently often seriously to shake confidence in the administration.

Charles Fox and the titular leader of the party, the Duke of Portland, had more success in holding their following together than might have been expected. The few conspicuous defections, as for example that of William Eden in 1786, were not typical, and former supporters of North remained as committed in opposition as the members of the old Rockingham connection. Through the efforts of the Scottish MP William Adam, an embryonic organization for electoral purposes began to develop, and the Whig Club, founded in May 1784, provided a combined social centre and a political society of considerable value for fostering party coherence and loyalty. The former Rockinghamite and the Foxite sections of the party were held together by strong ideological ties. After 1784 it was an article of faith among them that Pitt had established himself in power by unconstitutional means, that he represented the presence of a secret influence at work, which was dangerous to the principles of 1689. This belief provided the rationale for the existence of a regular sustained opposition to the king's ministers, for which the generally recognized forms of the eighteenth-century constitution made no provision; but the conventional dislike of such an opposition among the greater part of the political nation placed a distinct curb upon its aspirations, as had been the case with the Rockinghamites a decade or so earlier. What Fox and his friends denounced as secret influence other people accepted as the natural exercise of the king's role as head of the executive to pick the men who were to conduct the nation's affairs.

Since an outright, seemingly factious opposition by a minority could serve no useful purpose, Foxite tactics followed the line of selective attacks on vulnerable aspects of the ministry's activities which might attract the support of public opinion and of the independent members in the Commons. In 1785 Pitt found himself thrice exposed to embarrassment — on the Westminister scrutiny, on parliamentary reform, and on his proposed Irish settlement.

In 1784 Charles Fox's return as MP for Westminister was challenged on the ground that numbers of votes cast for him were spurious, offered by individuals who had no legal qualification as electors. His defeated opponent, a Pittite, demanded a scrutiny, and when the parliament met Pitt used his majority to block opposition motions to instruct the returning officer to return Fox and bring the examination of questioned votes to an end. Since Fox had also been returned for a Scottish pocket constituency there was no question of keeping him out of the House, but it would have been a severe blow to the morale of a party which prided itself on its concern for public opinion if Fox had been denied a seat for one of the three or four most populous and prestigious English constituencies. By early 1785 many of Pitt's supporters had become convinced of what was true, that a scrutiny was a completely impracticable way of dealing with a disputed election in so large a constituency, and in face of desertions Pitt let an opposition motion for the return of Fox go through.

In April 1785, for the third and last time, Pitt put proposals for constitutional reform before the House of Commons. He himself still believed in the necessity, hoping for advantage from reform both in Britain and in Ireland. His idealism clearly weighed more with him on this question than the obligation under which he lay towards Christopher Wyvill for decisive support against the coalition in the general election in Yorkshire the previous year. On Pitt's initiative Wyvill undertook yet one more publicity campaign in the hope of stirring up public demand, but on this occasion the response outside Yorkshire was derisory, and prospects that added weight would come from a Scottish movement for reform in burgh government proved equally illusory.

Pitt's proposals were deliberately couched in moderate terms. Provision was to be made for the gradual extinction of 36 insignificant parliamentary boroughs on the basis of financial compensation to their electors. By the offer of compensation electoral venality was to be turned to service in eliminating the venal boroughs, a proposal which, if it had elements of realism, was nevertheless most distasteful to many reformers on moral grounds. Moreover, it was unlikely that the scheme would work against boroughs under aristocratic influence, which many reformers earnestly desired to see extinguished. As and when boroughs disappeared, their seats were to be transferred to the English counties and the metropolitan area: this approach avoided the consequence of Wyvill's scheme, that a considerable number of new seats would be added to the House of Commons. In an additional appeal to country opinion Pitt suggested an extension of the county electorates by the enfranchisement of copyholders and some categories of leaseholders and a system of local polling centres which would reduce the cost of elections.

Even these limited reforms were opposed by most of the cabinet ministers. The king's dislike of any tampering with the constitution was notorious. Fox and other members of the opposition previously sympathetic towards reform were not prepared to give Pitt any countenance that would raise his reputation. But the decisive circumstances were that the country had failed to demand reform and that more than half the MPs on either side of the House were firmly opposed to it. In the debate which finally took place after many delays on 18 April, the conservative forces in the Commons threw out the measure by 248 votes to 174.

Pitt was faced with an Irish problem in a new guise in 1784, because the emancipation of the Irish parliament in 1782 rendered hazardous the British ministry's control of Irish tariff policies. Co-ordination of customs charges on both sides of St George's channel had been an explicit part of the commercial concessions of 1779. In 1783 popular demands in Dublin for a protective tariff to support a nascent sugar-refining industry based on the now permissible direct imports of

British West Indian sugar cut across that settlement and threatened the interests of the British sugar refiners. The extension of these aspirations might give rise to a general tariff war between the two kingdoms. Although the superior economic strength of Great Britain would be bound to prevail in such a conflict, the prospect of the commercial dislocation it would cause was intolerable. Popular Irish pressure for tariff reform was unacceptable in London, but in early 1784 that pressure took a particularly ugly form at Dublin. The city was convulsed with riot and outrage, there were calls for boycotts of British goods, and merchants trading in them were tarred and feathered. Irish political leaders concluded that to continue opposing a blank negative in the Irish parliament to these popular demands was politically impracticable and would provoke a still more dangerous situation. They accordingly approached London with a request for concessions.

During 1783 and 1784 these dangers in the Irish situation appeared to be compounded by the spill-over of a radical movement, which found expression among some elements of the Volunteers, and which drew its inspiration from a compound of factors — the debates of the previous decade on representation in the light of American example, the incipient Irish nationalism which saw the Irish Commons as corruptly controlled in British interests, and the oppositionist concern to set effective curbs on executive power. The Dublin MP Sir Edward Newenham called for a reform bill in the spring of 1782, and during the following 18 months the subject underwent further discussion among the Volunteers, one of whose leaders, Colonel Sharman, conducted an extensive correspondence with Christopher Wyvill, the Duke of Richmond and other sympathetic figures in England. In September 1783 500 delegates representing 276 corps of Volunteers in Ulster met at Dungannon, called for a grand national convention to prepare an extensive plan of reform, and put forward their own radical proposals for a redistribution of seats, a wider franchise, annual parliaments, secret ballot, and the exclusion of placemen from the Commons. Although by this time the question of Catholic emancipation was beginning to prove itself strongly divisive, the delegates also advocated a limited enfranchisement of Catholics. The convention duly assembled at Dublin on 16 November, elected Lord Charlemont as its chairman, and drafted a reform bill which Flood sought unsuccessfully to have discussed in parliament towards the end of the month. In the aftermath of this defeat, the Volunteers organized a petitioning movement, and after 22 counties and towns had called for reform, Flood tried again in March 1784 only to have his Bill thrown out by a decisive majority. Although there was some further agitation in Dublin in June, the issue of Catholic emancipation caused increasing disagreement, and faced with the immovable obstacle of the Irish Commons, the reform movement collapsed.

When Pitt turned his attention to these Irish questions he immediately saw possibilities for a comprehensive bargain, but one far transcending Irish aspirations. He was prepared to concede an almost unlimited communication of commercial advantages, provided the Irish parliament would bind itself to make a contribution to imperial defence which would increase in proportion with the country's wealth and revenue. His schemes provided for an equalization of the duties on imports entering the two countries, free traffic between them in foreign and colonial goods, and the abandonment of further duties or of bounties in respect of produce of one country being moved to the other. For good measure he threw in proposals for a parliamentary reform which would strengthen the Irish Commons, though only as an instrument of the Protestant Ascendancy whose interest was closely tied to the British connection. This last was not an integral part of the package and it rapidly sank from sight when Pitt's proposals for parliamentary reform in England were defeated at Westminister. Even without it, however, Pitt had gone too far for either British or Irish critics. The scale of commercial concession to the Irish which he contemplated aroused the fear and the hysterical fury of British manufacturing and commercial interests. The potter Josiah Wedgwood became the leading spirit in a chamber of manufacturers formed to co-ordinate the business opposition to the scheme. West Indian interests were brought into line against the ministry by the argument that theoretically the Irish would be able to evade the Navigation Acts. The Foxite opposition took an unscrupulous lead in organizing a nation-wide agitation based on misrepresentation and prejudice against Pitt's proposals.

In Irish eyes the stipulation for a defence contribution echoed the policies of Grenville and North towards the American colonies and involved additional taxation which Irish parliamentary leaders could only contemplate if very substantial trade concessions were received in return. Furthermore, Pitt's offer to the Irish of a virtual customs union was not what they wanted. It traversed the Irish demand for local tariff protection even against British competition and would have nullified a new and highly successful Irish policy of subsidizing the manufacture of linens, silks, cottons, drapery, glassware, gloves and hats which had been pushed forward with vigour since 1782. In addition to these good reasons for rejecting Pitt's scheme, the Irish parliamentary leaders were still, in 1784–5, on the defensive against a radical, populist, middle-class political movement seeking sweeping constitutional change aimed against aristocratic government, organized through the armed Volunteer movement — a movement which still seemed formidable, although in fact it was becoming acutely divided over the question of political emancipation for Roman Catholics and was on the verge of collapse.

During the crucial proceedings in London and Dublin in the early months of 1785 Pitt was caught in a vice from which it proved impossible to escape. Hope of overcoming British commercial opposition to his proposals rested upon securing cast-iron guarantees of the Irish defence contribution. But the guarantees sought so traversed the constitutional claims of the Irish parliament as to be unacceptable in Dublin and the opposition there was strengthened by Fox's championship of Irish constitutional rights. It gained also from Pitt's attempt to build into the arrangement a guarantee that the Irish would be fully bound by the Navigation Acts. When Pitt proposed that the Irish parliament should undertake to re-enact any British legislation on shipping and colonial trade that affected the subjects of both kingdoms, Grattan and others treated this as an encroachment on Irish legislative independence. Under British pressure, to which the Foxite opposition materially contributed, Pitt had been obliged so to amend his proposals that the lord lieutenant found there was no hope of getting them through the Irish parliament, and after an opening debate and a close division in the Irish Commons they were tacitly abandoned.

Anglo-Irish commercial co-operation thus remained dependent on *ad hoc* agreement between the two parliaments. This in fact did prove capable of achievement. In 1786 the Dublin legislature adjusted Irish tariffs to conform with the Anglo-French commercial treaty. In 1787 it passed an Irish Navigation Act, in line with the British Act of 1786. What was totally lost by the defeat of Pitt's Irish plan was the proposed Irish contribution to imperial defence. What was further revealed was the fact that the Irish parliament might at any time run out of control and could not be relied on to conform to policies put before it by the imperial government through the lord lieutenant.

After the parliamentary session of 1785 Pitt began to display a greater degree of political realism and caution. He had outgrown the over-confidence of 1784, and his care henceforth not to expose himself over unpopular issues greatly strengthened his hand, for the opposition found it difficult to launch damaging attacks. To Fox he seemed a minister 'who thrives by defeat and flourishes by disappointment', and Fox's increasing withdrawal into domestic bliss at St Anne's Hill bore witness to his political disillusionment. The opposition's attempt in 1786 to create further embarrassment for Pitt by the impeachment of Warren Hastings on the grounds of sundry crimes and misdemeanours committed during his governor-generalship in India merely recoiled on its makers. Fox undoubtedly believed that to prove Hastings' misrule would be a retrospective justification of his and Burke's India Bill and would prove the unwisdom of Pitt's Act in leaving wide powers in the governor-general's hands. Burke saw the chance to make a moral case against ministers who, in his view, had come into office in a manner identifying themselves with the corrupt system of which Hastings was a part, who had thrown out the proposed legislation which would have righted the situation in India, and who, it seemed, were bound to uphold Hastings and so tar themselves with the brush of his ill-doing. Whether deliberately or not, Pitt sidestepped this challenge by associating himself to a limited extent with the prosecution of Hastings, and thus prevented Fox from converting it into a party issue which might be used to blacken ministers' reputations. Within two years the impeachment was beginning to create increasing strain within the ranks of the opposition. Fox realized that it was an incumbrance that could bring no political profit, and found himself more and more out of step with Burke, who believed the moral case against corruption both in London and in India must be pressed through at whatever cost in time and reputation. At the centre of the affair Hastings, if not wholly innocent, became a victimized martyr to the violent political animosities in Westminister.

By 1786 the traditional eighteenth-century pattern of politics polarized between a stable administration on the one hand and an impotent minority on the other had become clearly re-established.[3] Fox and his friends acting as a party could make no impression on Pitt's position. Setbacks suffered by the government on particular issues in no way reflected a withdrawal of parliamentary confidence. The Westminister scrutiny was perforce abandoned because a majority in the Commons, while accepting the scrutiny to be lawful, had reached the justifiable conclusion that it was inexpedient. Parliamentary reform and the Duke of Richmond's defence proposals were both thrown out on their merits. The Irish treaty stirred up a hornet's nest of vested interests which the opposition exploited to the full, but at least one scholar has judged that Pitt's defeat was due to a failure of nerve and that by firmness he could have secured his aims. After March 1784 straight party issues were exceptional rather than a regular feature of parliamentary business. Much of the work of the Commons lay outside the sphere of party politics, and a good deal of it, such as the main stream of financial business, appealed to the traditional feeling that the king's government must be carried on and so tended to blunt the impact of party. While the attention given by historians to the 'Whig' opposition of this period has tended to over-

[3] For this analysis see Paul Kelly, 'British Parliamentary Politics, 1784–1786', *Historical Journal* 17 (1974), pp. 733–53.

emphasize the significance of party, uncommitted contemporaries saw the situation very differently, in terms of the rivalry of two great political contenders, one of them secure in power not because he headed a party but because he had been chosen by the sovereign to head the administration. An Independents' analysis of the Commons in 1788 distinguished first of all 185 members of the 'Party of the Crown . . . all those who would probably support his Majesty's government under any minister, not peculiarly unpopular', second, 52 members of Pitt's party, third, four supporting squadrons of between 9 and 15 members each, then the 'Opposition to the present Administration', composed of 138 Foxites and 17 friends of Lord North, and finally 108 'unconnected' Members. No party based on ideology confronted the opposition: to the compilers of this analysis and the audience of Independents to whom they appealed the terms 'Whig' and 'Tory', party principle and ideology, clearly had no relevance.

VI

The relative calm into which domestic politics had fallen was shaken towards the end of 1788, and opposition hopes revived, when George III was stricken by his first major attack of porphyria, his mind became disordered, and he ceased to be able to discharge his kingly role. At the outset the Foxites anticipated their return to power at the nomination of the Prince of Wales on his succeeding as king; then, as George III to their disappointment seemed long a-dying, they hoped for office under the prince as regent. By 1787 the Fox–Portland group had been connected for over five years with the reversionary interest. Fox's magnetic personality had captivated the prince as it had charmed other political associates, and the prince, like heirs to power in all times and circumstances, clutched at levers with which to assert himself against his father. In some ways, however, the association was beginning to become an embarrassment to the party. Its leaders felt obliged to take the unpopular course of supporting applications for a grant to clear the prince's debts. On this occasion Fox's denial of any marriage between the prince and Maria Fitzherbert, despite the illegal solemnization of their vows in 1785 – a denial virtually rebutted in the Commons by Sheridan a few days later – created such a scandal that Portland and other aristocratic leaders of the party were deeply alienated from the prince, and Mrs Fitzherbert's rancour against Fox brought Sheridan's star into the ascendant at Carlton House.

It was unfortunate for the Foxite party that these stresses should have developed shortly before the king's illness brought on a crisis emphasizing in a marked manner its dependence on the prince for its future prospects. Since George III was adamantly hostile to Fox his son's favour seemed the only road to office. The party's aspiration to power by this route cruelly underlined the illogicality of Fox's denunciations of Pitt, who had owed his advancement particularly to the will and favour of George III.

This difficulty was compounded by the disarray, confusion, and lack of foresight among the party's leaders. Fox was on holiday in Italy when the regency crisis began, and this circumstance enabled Sheridan, secure in the favour of both the prince and his mistress, to take initiatives which predictably ignored any question of principle. Sheridan's sole concern was to secure powers of regency for the prince on any terms as soon as possible and then to consolidate the party's hold on office as occasion served. To ease matters he intrigued with Thurlow, the lord chancellor, the one cabinet minister who had no loyalty towards Pitt and was ready to desert him in return for continuation in his office, and this move threatened the pretensions of the Foxites' leading lawyer, Lord Loughborough. Thus Pitt and his colleagues faced no testing challenge when they decided to block an unconditional regency in order to safeguard the possible future situation of George III.

To Pitt's good fortune the opposition never recovered from this weak start. Returning exhausted and ill, Fox played straight into Pitt's hands by demanding an immediate unconditional regency for the prince as a matter of right, and on top of this strange reversal of his role as champion of parliamentary authority showed himself incapable of combating Pitt's professional and controlled expert handling of questions of historical precedent and constitutional principle. As in 1784, ministry, press and public made the most of Fox's inconsistencies. Within the opposition only Burke sought to attack the government's policy from the basis of a reasoned, coherent constitutional argument, alleging that it would overturn the hereditary principle of the monarchy. Burke argued that the prince should have immediately assumed the royal functions as soon as his father became incapacitated, and he condemned Pitt's proposals for a regency with limitations as unconstitutional, as destructive of the independence of one of the three elements on which rested the balance of the constitution. Burke's colleagues missed the immediate opportunity to follow this course and afterwards neglected the logic of his plea: possibly some of them felt there was once again inconsistency in a *soi-disant* 'Whig' upholding the powers of the crown.

Despite a few desertions Pitt's majority held. During December 1788 he and his colleagues carried through both Houses a resolution that it was the right and duty of the Lords and Commons 'to provide the means of supplying the defect arising from the King's incapacity'. During January and February they pushed through their Regency Bill, imposing for a period of 12 months important restrictions on the powers to be exercised by the prince as regent. To safeguard the king personally from the ambitions of his son the care of his person and the direction of his household was to be entrusted to the queen. The regent might not grant any office in reversion, or any office or pension save those which had by law to be filled for life or on good behaviour, other than on the term of the king's pleasure. He might not create peers, save in the case of a brother reaching the age of 21. Should the king recover in a few months his son would be powerless to block his return to activity, and a Foxite ministry could have made no use of crown patronage to consolidate its position which he could not reverse.

In the event the prolonged proceedings on the regency caused them to be unnecessary. By mid February the Bill was reaching its final stage in the Lords, but then dramatically the king's recovery became apparent and the process ended. On the eve of tasting the sweets of office the Foxites found the cup suddenly dashed from their lips. Bitter disappointment added to the tension and recrimination within the party, and Pitt's position was stronger than ever. Not until after another 10 years was his hold on power to be finally shaken, and then as one consequence of sweeping changes in the character and context of politics quite unforeseen in 1789.

The regency question revealed once again the fragile nature of executive control over the Irish parliament. At Dublin both Houses declined to model their proceedings on those in London and passed addresses inviting the Prince of Wales to assume the royal functions without conditions. This action seems to have been due to an admixture of prejudice against a servile imitation of London, dislike of a Bill of this nature being approved under the British great seal, and concern to greet the new powers which seemed about to be in the ascendant. Had not George III been on the road to recovery by the time the addresses from the two Houses reached London, an anomalous and embarrassing situation would have arisen. The crisis caused a permanent breach between the Irish administration and some of the deserters, the Duke of Leinster, the Earl of Shannon and Lord Ponsonby moving into the ranks of the opposition; and the resultant weakening of the position of the Dublin executive in relation to both parliament and people promised further difficulty as the British isles and western Europe moved into the decade of revolution.

VII

In 1776 Jeremy Bentham began his *Fragment on Government* with the remark: 'The age we live in is a busy age, in which knowledge is rapidly advancing towards perfection. In the natural world in particular, everything teams with discovery and improvement.' This spirit of challenge to accepted knowledge and ways of doing things, gathering pace from decade to decade, had no natural bounds, and as the eighteenth century drew towards its close, forms of government and social structure came under scrutiny. The old world-picture of stasis was being abandoned. The belief was growing that men had the capacity to change things for the better, and this critical activity involved questions which impinged directly on politics because they seemed to demand legislative solutions. The nature of politics was changing, and the quiet days of the old eighteenth-century system drew to a close before the century itself was sped.

Religious dissent contributed an important strand to this development. Protestant nonconformists, old and new, conscious of their growing social strength and importance, increasingly resented the formal Anglican political exclusiveness of the English state, and they were encouraged in their aspirations after 1783 by observing in North America the dissolution of old religious establishments and the existence of various Christian churches side by side on equal terms. Hence in 1787 leaders of the nonconformist community launched a campaign for the repeal of the Test and Corporation Acts. Even if the accepted practice of passing annual Indemnity Acts relieved dissenters from the penalties of taking public offices, nevertheless the Acts were a stigma and gave legal colour to the exclusion of nonconformists from borough corporations by the narrow Anglican oligarchies which controlled most of them. Fox declared himself sympathetic, and numbers of MPs representing towns, not themselves dissenters, bowed to formidable pressure from groups of their constituents and gave it support. Pitt, having consulted the bishops, who were uniformly adverse, felt obliged to throw in his voice with the forces of the establishment which opposed any such alteration in church or state. Motions were made annually in the Commons from

1787 to 1790 and the ayes rose gradually from 87 to 105, but by 1790 an overwhelming opposition evinced itself in the House. Threats from the pen of Joseph Priestley of an ultimate disestablishment of the Church of England probably did no good to the cause and events in France were increasing the fear of innovation.

American example – more specifically that of the Quakers – also triggered off another 'liberal' meliorist campaign in the late 1780s, the demand for an ending of the slave trade. The main impetus was religious and humanitarian. The growing emphasis in eighteenth-century thought on the concepts of liberty, benevolence and happiness inclined educated men to regard slavery as anomalous and illegitimate. But it was a minority of passionate Christian believers, like William Wilberforce, Thomas Clarkson, Granville Sharp, and the members and associates of the Thornton family who constituted the core of what became known as the 'Clapham Sect', who provided the driving force for the movement. In 1787 the English Quakers formed a London Abolition Committee to fight the slave trade and soon found in Wilberforce an able parliamentary spokesman who could even command the ear and sympathy of the Prime Minister. But the House of Commons as a whole was unsympathetic. Even men who disliked the trade were persuaded that it was a crucial factor in the prosperity of the West Indies and in the maintenance of the nursery of seamen on which the country's naval strength depended. In 1788 Sir William Dolben, MP for Oxford University, horrified by his personal inspection of a slave ship, carried a regulating Act to check overcrowding and promote attention to the health of negroes on the passage across the Atlantic, but further progress was blocked. After 1790 the pleas of the anti-slave-trade campaigners, like those of the dissenters, faltered in face of conservative reaction provoked by developments in France.

From mid 1789 the progress of the revolution in France deeply affected the course of British politics. Its coincidence with the centenary of the 'Glorious Revolution' renewed the enthusiasm of speculative thinkers and of urban radicals, and rekindled demands for reforms along the lines of those sought in the early 1780s. In March 1790 Henry Flood ably put the case in the Commons for an addition to the House of a hundred members to be chosen by an electorate of resident householders, 'responsible citizens from the middle ranks of the people to fortify the constitution and render it impregnable'. But the wilder speculations of a host of radical pamphleteers were already raising fears in the minds of the politicians. The writings of Mary Wollstonecraft, Thomas Paine, James Mackintosh, and John Thelwall laid stress upon the political and social rights of the individual, the injustices which seemed to stem from social inequality, the iniquities of the criminal code, the clogs upon the free expression of opinion, the need to relieve poverty. From Thomas Spence came calls for the nationalization of land, from William Frend a blast against the political role and the religious monopoly of the established church. In 1790 John Cartwright and other former members revived the Society for Constitutional Information and began a new campaign of disseminating reformist literature which scored its greatest success with the widespread distribution during 1791−2 of Thomas Paine's *Rights of Man*. The publication in November 1790 of Edmund Burke's *Reflections on the Revolution in France*, to which Paine's work was a reply, ensured that the issues of reform and reaction would be widely read and discussed.

Paine's appeal for wide public support for a call for reform, which obtained exceptionally wide circulation in cheap editions and in excerpts in various forms of publication, threw down the clearest challenge to the old order. Unlike the last generation of reformers, the men of the 1790s saw that historical precedent would not serve their turn, and turned away from history to the appeal of reason. To Paine the authority of the past was meaningless or rather could be made to stand for whatever men wished it to mean. Reason had long led Paine to denounce both monarchy and aristocracy, and since 1776 he had been able to observe the development in America of polities which had dispensed with both. This extreme republican view by no means commanded universal support among the radical publicists of the 1790s. Nor did they all give an unqualified acceptance to Paine's view that the ideal constitution was one in which all men enjoyed a full and constant participation in the election of representatives, by the adoption of the practices of universal male suffrage, equal electoral districts, annual elections, secret ballot, payment of representatives and the abolition of any property qualification for them. Mackintosh, Godwin, and Thelwall, to name but three of the more prominent radicals of the 1790s, all had reservations about the extent to which the ignorant masses should participate in government, and tended to think in terms of a polity in which the men of property, education and enlightenment took charge of affairs on behalf of the people. All these men were concerned in a general way with the need to ameliorate the hard lot of the poor, but scarcely any of them had a social programme as such. Their assumption was that the destruction of royal and aristocratic power and the creation of a popular democratic system would of itself automatically give rise to improvement in the condition of the people, and this belief was in turn based on the naïve assumption that the miseries of the poor were simply due to heavy taxation levied to provide the perquisites of the governing class. Paine was unique in presenting definite proposals for discharging society's responsibility towards the poor by the institution of old-age pensions, child allowances, maternity and marriage grants, assistance with the cost of funerals, and the allocation of funds to assist in the provision of employment. Thomas Spence was the only radical to advocate the confiscation and reallocation of land: Paine, Thelwall and others all accepted as inevitable the existing inequalities in the distribution of property and preached the dangers of any attempt to interfere with it.

The last thing these men contemplated was violent revolution. They hoped to achieve change by peaceful means. They seem to have believed optimistically, but as events proved, totally without justification, that a massive propaganda campaign and the mounting of a great petitioning movement would persuade the politicians in Parliament to accept the necessity for change. At most they thought in terms of a great demonstration by a national convention, which by its mere moral example would overwhelm the conservative forces in Parliament. Most significant in the wake of their propaganda efforts was the consequent generation of political activity at levels low down the social scale, where social protest had hitherto usually taken apolitical forms. At the end of 1791 tradesmen and artificers in Sheffield began to enroll in hundreds in the Sheffield Society for Constitutional Information, adopting an organization of local divisions as their swelling numbers made meetings of the whole impossible. Within the next few months constitutional societies and corresponding societies were springing up in urban centres all over the country, and approaching the Society for Constitutional Information for advice and supplies of radical literature. In London early in 1792 the shoe-maker Thomas Hardy and a group of personal friends founded the London Corresponding Society. Before long both the Sheffield and the London societies were claiming memberships of about 2,000. To the poor and underprivileged who flocked to the meetings of these groups to read or hear read excerpts from the works of Paine and other radical thinkers, sweeping constitutional reform appeared a panacea for all ills. 'Soon then', declared the London Corresponding Society, 'we should see our liberties restored, the press free, the laws simplified, judges unbiased, juries independent, needless places and pensions retrenched, immoderate salaries reduced, the public better served, taxes diminished, and the necessaries of life more within the reach of the poor, youth better educated, prisons less crowded, old age better provided for, and sumptuous feasts at the expense of the starving poor less frequent.'

By contrast with the reform movement of the previous decade, this time Scotland was as widely involved as England. Since 1788 the citizens of the Scottish burghs had been pressing for a reform of municipal administration, and their continued frustration laid a foundation for a more ambitious agitation. By 1792 radical societies had come into being all over Scotland, demanding parliamentary reform. In Glasgow, in July 1792, the lord provost presided over a meeting at which resolutions were adopted in favour of equal representation, frequent elections, and universal suffrage, and a group of 'friends of the Constitution and of the people' called for annual parliaments. In Edinburgh the cause was taken up by a Society of the Friends of the People, whose leading spirit was a prosperous young advocate, Thomas Muir. Other centres of active agitation developed in Perth, Stirling, Paisley, Dalkeith, and other places. The agitation also spread to Ireland, where initially it found firmest root among the Ulster Presbyterians. In 1792 Theobald Wolfe Tone took the lead in promoting the Society of United Irishmen, with a programme of manhood suffrage, equal electoral districts and annual parliaments which, if achieved, would have destroyed the oligarchical regime at Dublin, through which the harmonious relations between the British and the Irish legislatures were maintained.

The political reactions of the ruling class to this phenomenon were varied and to an important extent influenced by the growing tide of anarchy and conflict across the Channel.

In 1789 and 1790 it had been possible for British politicians on all sides to hail the French revolution with patronizing detachment, as a step towards the ideals of constitutional government which the British had already achieved in 1689. In the meantime the power of the French state had dissolved, and the British need no longer fear their ancient rival. In one of the most inept forecasts ever made by a statesman of the first rank Pitt accompanied the introduction of his budget early in 1792 with the remark that 'unquestionably there never was a time in the history of this country when from the situation of Europe we might more reasonably expect 15 years of peace than we may at the present moment.'

While the more conservatively-minded reviewed the situation with complacency, a minority of the younger politicians associated with Charles Fox felt that the right course was, on the one hand, to forestall extremism by promoting a moderate constitutional reform and on the other to exploit the popular ferment in order to obtain it. This sentiment provided support for the motion for reform by Flood in 1790, and early in 1792 Charles Grey, Sheridan, Thomas Erskine, Lambton, Whitbread, Tierney and other young Foxites launched a new, exclusive reform association, the Society of the Friends of the People. In April 1792 Grey gave notice in the Commons that he would move for reform in the following session. Grey and his friends were anxious to maintain the traditional dominance of the propertied class in politics, and committed themselves to only limited extensions of the franchise: in 1793 Grey was to suggest the addition of copyholders and rate-paying householders. The main thrust of their proposals was aimed at the destruction of the various anomalous features of the old representative system which to them appeared to support what they believed to be the excessive influence of the crown. To eliminate the channels by which this influence was exerted they sought sweeping changes in the constituencies, increasing the number of seats for counties and the new great unrepresented towns at the expense of the rotten and pocket boroughs. They had no sympathy with such wilder radical demands as universal male suffrage and annual parliaments, and set themselves to act as a brake on the popular societies.

Fox himself wisely evaded invitations to join the society, a step which would have fatally prejudiced his efforts to keep his parliamentary forces united. As it was, the wedge thus thrust among his political associates was a considerable embarrassment. The aristocratic wing of the party led by former associates of Rockingham like Portland and Fitzwilliam deplored any involvement in discussion of reform which might encourage the wilder notions circulating in pamphlets and in reports of proceedings of the popular societies. During 1791 and early 1792 the party was exposed to growing strain. In November 1790, on the publication of the *Reflections on the Revolution in France*, scarcely anyone had shared Burke's deeply felt instinctive revulsion against the approach of democratic anarchy in France and its threat to the stability of society in Britain. Six months later, although Burke had won few converts, apprehensions were rising. On the occasion of the famous debate on the Quebec Bill of 6 May 1791, when Burke took the opportunity to denounce Fox's admiration for the revolution and its principles and to declare his personal breach with Fox, Fox's insistence that the French revolutionaries were simply good Whigs pursuing the same conflict against royal power and royal encroachments on rights and liberties that he and his friends were conducting in Britain seemed to some to ring hollow. Fox's publicly stated belief that the British constitution was more in danger from the encroaching power of the crown than from an increase in the power of the people, deepened the rift between himself and men like Burke, Windham, and Loughborough, who disagreed violently with his premise, and who believed that the rising agitation for parliamentary reform must be resisted. Still, for the time being, the main centre group of the party avoided any break with Fox. The personal attachment of its members to him, and a strong commitment against what they persisted in regarding as Pitt's unconstitutional regime, led them to hope that Fox would be wooed away from radical extremes. Burke's further call for a conservative reaction in August, in the *Appeal from the New to the Old Whigs*, had for the moment no greater success in drawing the magnates of the party to his side, though it posed squarely the dangers implicit in the principle of the sovereignty of the people which Fox persisted in upholding. But a great wave of popular revulsion from radicalism, which erupted in spectacular fashion in the 'church and king' riots of July 1791 in Birmingham, when dissenting chapels were wrecked and Joseph Priestley's home and laboratory were destroyed, showed that public opinion was moving in this direction.

By early 1792 the split within the opposition was becoming more evident, and the tensions produced by the formation of the Society of the Friends of the People gave Pitt ground to think a large part of the Foxite group might be drawn to his side in support of law and the established order. In May the first overt ministerial step was taken against extreme radicalism, with the issue of a royal proclamation against seditious practices, and the following month Thomas Paine was indicted, in his absence, on a charge of seditious libel. Portland's agreement to join in consultations over these moves was a first significant step along the road towards the transformation of the British political scene and a consolidation of the forces of reaction, which was completed two years later under the continuing impact of the French Revolution.

9   War Against Revolution 1793 – 1796

I

By the end of 1792 British ministers were finding it no longer possible to continue their role of detached, disinterested observers of affairs on the Continent. The dynamic of revolution in France was producing a basic clash of national interests between the two countries, and the resulting conflict was to bring about fundamental shifts in the conduct of domestic policy and politics.

During the opening stages of the revolution Pitt and his colleagues had been determined to stand aloof. They had ignored the Austrian emperor's Padua circular calling for support for the monarchy in France and the Austro-Prussian declaration of Pillnitz. The French declaration of war on Austria in April 1792 followed by the invasion of the southern Netherlands was not regarded with alarm in London, for it was the general belief that a country so disorganized by its own internal disruptions would not be able to resist the German powers. Ministers made clear repeatedly during the following months their desire to remain neutral in the struggle.

But by the autumn matters wore a different aspect. The rapid progress of revolution at Paris, involving the overthrow of the monarchy, the September massacres, and the development of French ambitions, as the armies recovered their ground, and first one and then another more extremist group gained control of the revolutionary government, began to create threats both to the balance of power in general and to British interests in the Low Countries in particular. By early November the French were across the Rhine at Mainz and in the wake of their victory at Jemappes were in control of most of the Austrian Netherlands. On 16 November, on the basis of the 'imprescriptible laws of universal justice', the French decreed the freedom of navigation of the Scheldt, repudiating a series of international agreements which ran back to the treaties of Westphalia of 1648, and prepared to send vessels up the river through Dutch territorial waters to take Antwerp from the rear. On the 19th the French assembly resolved to grant fraternity and assistance to all peoples desirous of recovering their liberty. This implied a challenge to the sovereignty of the emperor in the Belgian provinces, to the dominance of the pro-British Orangist regime in the United Provinces, which Britain was bound by treaty to defend, and ultimately to the monarchical system in Britain itself: at the end of November there was sufficient rumour and report afloat in London to make the ministry momentarily fearful that the French intended to foment an insurrection. The collapse of the British cordon against French expansion in the Low Countries appeared imminent, and French control of the naval bases at the mouths of the Scheldt and Rhine was not to be contemplated. A further French decree of 15 December, involving the suppression of existing authorities in all occupied districts and inviting popular revolution, appeared to indicate a determination to exclude the Emperor permanently from his Belgian provinces. At the same time the incorporation of Savoy into France, though less of a direct threat, betokened aggressive intent and disregard for international law and the balance of power.

From November onwards Pitt and his cousin William, Lord Grenville, who had taken over the foreign office, were agreed in demanding the cancellation of the decrees, the promise of a withdrawal of French troops from foreign territory, and a French renunciation of any interference with the internal government of other states – particularly of the United Provinces and Great Britain. The Dutch received assurances of support if a French attack led them to invoke the Anglo-Dutch treaty of guarantee. Meanwhile ministers made clear that they would not concern themselves with French decisions about their own form of government, and on French acceptance of their terms would be ready to attempt a mediation between France and the German powers with a view to securing recognition of the Republic.

However, the French leaders felt themselves on the crest of the wave. They refused to rescind the decrees. They indulged in chauvinistic propaganda. In an act of defiance against all monarchical regimes they decapitated Louis XVI in Paris on 21 January 1793. On 1 February, in anticipation of British action, they declared war on Great Britain and appealed to British republicans to help them. The fraternal messages passing between the two sides of the channel had quite misled them and they anticipated massive revolutionary support within the British Isles. Pitt was suddenly faced with problems of internal security as well as of war.

His position was eased by a closing of ranks in all cases of society once the war had begun.

In Parliament this development produced a widening split within the ranks of the opposition. Charles Fox persisted in regarding the threat from the crown as a greater danger to the British constitution than the threat from the French. Pitt's issue of a proclamation on 1 December embodying the militia, as a precaution against insurrection, provoked in him a rage that knew no bounds, and at the opening of the parliamentary session, when Portland and his aristocratic friends had agreed not to put down motions suggesting disapproval of Pitt's action, Fox 'with an oath declared *that there was no address at this moment Pitt could frame, he would not propose an amendment to, and divide the House upon'*. In the debate on the address on 13 December his isolation from the Portland group was painfully clear, and less than 40 committed Foxites divided with him.

Former friends of North were among the first to defect, and were gradually tempted by ministerial offers. Lord Loughborough's position was particularly vulnerable, for Pitt, having quarrelled with Thurlow and secured his dismissal from the chancellorship, put that office into commission until such time as Loughborough might be ready to accept it, which he did in January 1793. After the outbreak of war on 1 February, Windham, Burke, and a group of their friends made it clear that they would act as a body in support of a war policy and in opposition to Fox, despite the refusal of Portland and Fitzwilliam to break with him. They held out the prospect that Portland, when ready, would find them a hard core round which to rally a conservative 'Whig' party. For the time being, however, Portland shunned this step. The magic of Fox's personality still ensnared him. He still valued the unity of the party on the ground that it stood against Pitt for the purity of constitutional government and the principles of 1689. He hoped that the disagreements between its two wings would prove merely temporary, and that a return of moderation in France, or the collapse of the revolution, or some other favourable circumstance would enable its unity to be restored. Only the prolongation of the war and the increasing violence of the revolution were ultimately to destroy his hopes. But like Windham he made it clear that he would join in no step likely to embarrass Pitt's conduct of the war or his efforts to ensure order and social stability.

One circumstance after another made this stand increasingly difficult to maintain. On 6 May, despite the onset of the war, Grey introduced his promised motion for parliamentary reform. Fox's decision to support it caused Portland and his friends to emphasize the ground they held in common with Burke and Windham, and Portland's drift in their direction was signalled by the resumption of cordial social relationships which had been suspended during the previous months. In the debate of 6 May the two wings of the party were in outright opposition to each other, and many of Portland's followers sided with supporters of the ministry in the crushing majority of 282 which confronted the 41 votes mustered by Fox and Grey. Fox's motion on 17 June for peace with France further sharpened the conflict within the party, and as champion of the established order Pitt exerted a growing, irresistible attraction. He renewed his efforts to draw rebels to his side, and the failures of his government in the conduct of a war which many of the opposition regarded as just and necessary drove them to believe that rather than criticize they should co-operate. In September this feeling led the hitherto staunch Sir Gilbert Elliot to take up a post as civil commissioner at Toulon, and in November Fox's friend Lord Malmesbury accepted a diplomatic mission to Berlin. In December the French recovery of Toulon made it impossible for Portland and his friends any longer to hope that a quick collapse of revolution in France would resolve their difficulties, and Pitt's successes at detaching individuals began to convince Portland that if he did not break with Fox and carry his party as a whole into the government camp, it would be destroyed in driblets. For a time, he still hesitated, torn between his sense of obligation to serve the country at a time of crisis, his belief in existence of the 'Whig' party as vital to the preservation of the constitution, his distrust of Pitt's constitutional principles, and his resentment at Pitt's efforts to steal his followers. But in January 1794 he committed his friends to general support of the ministry and made clear that they would now act separately from Fox. Fox, unrepentant, taking up a stance in some ways similar to that of the Rockinghamites during the American war, opposed the ministry on the grounds, not only that the allied Powers intended to destroy the French republic and restore the monarchy, but also that the power of the crown in Britain would know no bounds if the cause of monarchy triumphed on the Continent.

In the early months of 1794 Pitt sedulously cultivated the Portland group. The help of the local magnates in organizing the Volunteers as a further line of defence against insurrection furnished opportunities for co-operation. There was consultation over policy, and a flow of suggestions from Portland began to reach the ministry. Pitt consulted Portland's friends over the legislation to permit the formation of a corps of French royalist troops in Britain. The connections drew closer in May, when the government decided to act against the popular radical societies. Prominent members of the Portland and Windham groups were chosen members of the committees of secrecy set up by both Houses of Parliament to advise on future measures against possible insurrection. Thus by the summer Portland's identification with Pitt's policy of repression was virtually complete, and the idea of coalition developed a logic which became gradually more compelling. By July the time was ripe. Pitt was anxious to bring new talent into the ministry. Portland's friends were ready to come in on terms which made it clear that they took office as a party with a voice on policy and were not merely absorbed into a Pittite administration. In policy terms this entailed a commitment to a restoration of the Bourbons and to a liberal religious and political settlement in Ireland. In terms of office key positions were yielded by Pitt to his new allies. Portland himself took the home office with the colonies. Earl Fitzwilliam became lord president of the council with a promise of the Irish lord lieutenancy as soon as its present holder could be accommodated. Lord Spencer took the privy seal and soon succeeded Pitt's brother as first lord of the Admiralty. Windham accepted the post of secretary-at-war. Lord Mansfield (the former Viscount Stormont) entered the cabinet without portfolio but soon succeeded Fitzwilliam as lord president. However, the direction of the war was kept in the hands of Pitt's confidential inner circle, consisting of himself, Grenville and Henry Dundas.

Whatever jarring elements it might contain, this new combination of men proved effective in administration. Ten years in office had given its leader, Pitt, a remarkable political ascendancy. Less than two years before he had outfaced the king's favourite, lord chancellor Thurlow, and forced his dismissal. Prodigal of energy, fertile in source, uniquely formidable in debate in the Commons by virtue of the extreme tenacity and lucidity of his mind, so long as he had the king's confidence there seemed no possibility of his hold on office being successfully challenged. However extreme his alternations of mood — his spirits 'either in a garret or a cellar', said his intimate, Henry Dundas — he showed an unflagging grasp of essentials, and although restrained by a keen sense of what was politically practicable, he was capable of bold initiatives.[1] His cousin, Lord Grenville, brought very similar qualities, an unwearying industry and an adamantine determination, to his handling of the business of the foreign office. Henry Dundas, bluff, popular, hail-fellow-well-met, whose ascendancy in Scottish politics won him the nickname of 'Harry the ninth', and whose rise to the top at Westminster personified the triumph of the Scottish union of 1707, showed energy and administrative talent, and sometimes a flair for strategy, at the war department created in 1794. Scottish through and through in personality, and proud of it, he was guided by a keen vision and a sharp sense of responsibility as one of the rulers and defenders of a great empire, part of which — India — had for years been his especial responsibility at the board of control; and with the viewpoint of a member of

---

[1] For example, on Pitt's foray into state trading to relieve the grain shortage of 1795–6, see Walter M. Stern, 'The Bread Crisis in Britain, 1795–1796', *Economica* 31 (1974), pp. 168–87.

a minority group he tended to react to both the political and the religious aspects of the Irish problem from a more elevated and liberal stance than some of his colleagues. Portland, a newcomer to this ministerial circle, perhaps lacked something of the robust vitality displayed by these fellow ministers, but his correspondence shows that he could devote himself with energy to public affairs. Like his former party chief, Lord Rockingham, he displayed an evenness of temper and a high degree of political probity, which made him a judicious administrator and a scrupulous colleague. Both qualities passed a supreme test the following year in the crisis over Fitzwilliam's lord lieutenancy of Ireland.[2] Of Portland's two chief political associates whom he brought with him into the cabinet, Fitzwilliam was to prove himself impetuous and devoid of political judgment to the point of wrecking his career within a few months. Earl Spencer, on the other hand, though inexperienced and overbearing, infused a new energy and order into the Admiralty, was to prove a vigorous and successful minister, and showed outstanding determination, adroitness and humanity in his handling of the naval mutinies of 1797.

Within a few months of its formation the new coalition survived near shipwreck on the Irish question. Here a combination of religious and political factors was creating a dangerous tension which the Portlanders felt it their mission to resolve.

In Ireland the religious animosities temporarily buried in the early days of the Volunteer movement had rekindled anew in the mid 1780s. The threat of radicalism at home and of revolution abroad made this situation highly dangerous, and Pitt's ministry was drawn to turn against the Protestant Ascendancy at Dublin in an effort to damp down Catholic discontent and win the loyalty of the Catholic gentry. In 1792 an Irish Catholic Relief Act freed Catholics from remaining disabilities relating to mixed marriages, education and the profession of the law. In 1793, in face of further pressure from the Catholic Committee, another Relief Act conceded to Catholics the same municipal and parliamentary franchises as the Protestants enjoyed and opened most civil and military posts to them. However, they remained debarred from membership of the Irish parliament and from holding military rank above that of colonel, and in practice they remained excluded from borough guilds and corporations. Their leaders continued to press for the removal of these disabilities, much to the dismay not only of the members of the Protestant Ascendancy led by Fitzgibbon and the Beresfords, who saw the last pledges of their dominance of Irish politics thus threatened, but also of some of the politicians connected with the Portland—Devonshire set. Fox's

[2] See p. 221 below.

friends in Ireland were thus themselves divided on the issue, and this was to have a bearing on the crisis of 1795. In an attempt to make the dominance of the Beresford group at Dublin less unpalatable Pitt obliged the lord lieutenant to push through various administrative reforms, notably a reduction in the number of pensions, the disfranchisement of revenue officers, and the disqualification of some place-holders from sitting in the Irish Commons, including the holders of offices created after 1793.

The formation of the Pitt—Portland coalition raised a further Irish problem, namely how far Pitt could uphold the interest of the 'Protestant' politicians in Dublin who had staunchly supported his administration for the past 10 years, or how far concessions would have to be made in terms of displacements and new appointments for Irish supporters of the Portland connection. In the search for compromise at the outset of the coalition, both sides seem to have been at fault in blurring over this issue. Fitzwilliam retained the impression that when he succeeded as lord lieutenant he would have the general management of Ireland, and that this might mean the wholesale replacement of the officials in post. Once he reached Dublin the pressure from the party followers there for a speedy share of the loaves and fishes became more than he could resist. Not only did he come to believe that peace and loyalty in Ireland depended upon a purge of the Beresford party from the administration, but he was also convinced of the necessity of conceding the remaining Catholic claims for equality of political rights. He anticipated as one result the raising of largely Catholic yeomanry divisions for local defence.

In the crisis of the next few weeks much blame was due to Pitt, who had failed to make absolutely clear his stand on these two issues, and a further share fell upon Portland, the departmental minister concerned, who was dilatory in his conduct of the Dublin correspondence and failed to warn Fitzwilliam against making unacceptable commitments. In the end Fitzwilliam fell sacrifice to Portland's conviction that the coalition must be held together. Pitt insisted that there must be no proscription of the Beresfords and no concession on the Catholic question. In London there was great doubt whether Catholics could safely be admitted to the yeomanry or militia, or whether the inflated Irish Episcopal Church establishment would be tolerated by a Catholic-dominated legislature, and there appeared to be a serious threat of political disruption from the magnates of the Protestant Ascendancy. In March Pitt's friend, the second Earl Camden, succeeded Fitzwilliam with instructions to reverse his policies. Dismissed officials were reinstated and an Irish Catholic emancipation Bill was strangled at second reading. Probably whichever way events in Ireland had gone in 1795 the result would have been divisive. As it was, bitterness was kindled between the Catholics and the

Protestant Ascendancy, and a grievance remained to provide a pretext for extremists.

II

Outside parliamentary circles the same tendency to close ranks in support of the established order was evident. During 1792 the rapid spread of the Association for the Preservation of Liberty and Property against Republicans and Levellers drew a wide response from magistracy, clergy, and the propertied classes. Initiated by the minor place-holder and police official, John Reeves, with encouragement and unobtrusive collaboration from the government, this movement emerged immediately after the publication in France of the November decrees. Its members engaged actively in the suppression of 'seditious' activity, preparing the ground for prosecutions of printers and publishers, amassing information about radical groups and their proceedings, and urging magistrates to dissuade by threats owners of assembly rooms from allowing them to be used for reform meetings. They also organized counter-reform propaganda. Anglican feeling against dissent readily lent itself to this work. In Manchester and Birmingham the old church and king clubs quickly transformed themselves into local Reeves associations. Members of cathedral chapters promoted the formation of branches in their districts. Often prominent members of the local gentry took the lead, and in Yorkshire numbers of Wyvill's former associates were busy in promoting the movement. In Westminster every parish had its society linked by delegates to a 'Westminster Committee' very different in character from that over which Charles Fox had presided little over a decade before. Not all the societies were wholly reactionary, and on numbers of occasions meetings pledging themselves to uphold law and order also claimed that there might be scope for the promotion by constitutional means of necessary moderate reforms; but these signs of moderation do not obscure the general repressive nature of the movement and its widespread success. Often anti-radical feeling went over the line. Mock executions and burnings of Paine and his works were commonplace. Pressure was brought on local radical leaders, sometimes by threat of economic boycott, sometimes by direct intimidation and riot. Magistrates in Manchester remained inactive when the office of the *Manchester Herald* and meeting place of the local

Reformation Society were totally wrecked. Local Reeves associations raised funds by subscription to purchase and distribute anti-radical tracts, including Hannah More's *Village Politics* and Paley's *Reasons for Contentment*. In some towns the local leaders entered into direct consultations with the treasury solicitor over the mounting of prosecutions for sedition. Their enmity extended widely to dissenting congregations and to trade clubs, which were suspected of harbouring revolutionary and republican agitators. Shortlived as the Association proved to be, within a year it had done its work, and with the war fever which gripped the public after February 1793 its activities proved the less necessary. A nation-wide wave of anti-radical feeling had been whipped up, which both incited and strengthened the ministry in the repressive action it took against the reform societies.

The deeply-rooted nature of this reaction has in general not attracted attention; but the view has been recently expressed that the radicals of the 1790s were outfaced by the force of their opponents' arguments and by the pervasive conservative opinion among the politically conscious section of the community, and not defeated merely by the *force majeure* at the disposal of the government.[3]

Many men had a firm commitment to the established political system which rested upon an intellectual conviction of its superiority to anything which reformers might offer in its room. Much credit on its record might be claimed for the form of government in operation since 1689. It had been a successful barrier against absolutism and an instrument for the protection of liberty and property rights and a government of laws, and it was to the intricate and delicate system of checks and balances that admirers attributed its success. George III was not alone in considering it the most perfect system of government that had ever been framed. As it came increasingly under challenge an able band of publicists, including Edmund Burke and William Paley, built up an intellectual defence which had considerable appeal. These and other conservative thinkers compared it favourably with the concept of a popularly mandated democratic House of Commons advocated by radical reformers, which they maintained would destroy this balance; to just such a development in the American colonies did some attribute the onset of the American Revolution and the partial destruction of the Empire which had resulted. Further back in the nation's history the Long Parliament of Charles I presented one more grim example of what might happen if one section of the institutions of the country asserted an inadmissible supremacy. If any one institution or group seized absolute power the

[3] See H. T. Dickinson, *Liberty and Property. Political Ideology in eighteenth-century Britain* (1977), chapter 8.

restraints of justice and morality inherent in the divine creation would be overthrown by the unchecked passions of men.

Conservatives thus argued that the anomalies of the electoral system and the influences exercised by the crown and the peerage through nomination boroughs, patronage, connections, and the lengthy duration of Parliament, were essential elements in maintaining the 'mixed system' of government and preserving the balance within it. 'Influence' exerted by the holders of office charged with the interests and affairs of the nation as a whole was also defended on the ground that it would overbalance the partial, self-interested and corrupt tendencies at work among unconnected men thrown together in a political assembly. Contemporary emphasis on the preservation of property rights as a primary function of society led to concern that only property owners should have the parliamentary franchise. Those without property could, it was believed, have no interest in maintaining it, and their ignorance, passions, and state of dependence would make them ripe for manipulation by demagogues.

Conservative defenders of the constitution frequently stressed the manner in which the House of Commons represented the great variety of important interests throughout the country and the duty of its members to act not as delegates but as representatives of the country as a whole. The theory of 'virtual representation', however inapposite it may have been in relation to the American colonies, was not entirely without force in considering the nation's internal polity: as the proceedings of the House of Commons on commercial questions constantly revealed, the interests of Manchester, Leeds, or Birmingham, for instance, received attentive consideration and found their champions among the local elements of the political class, despite the fact that these places did not have their own Members of Parliament. In 1797 James Mackintosh re-stated the Burkean position: 'The best security which human wisdom can devise seems to be the distribution of political authority among different individuals and bodies, with separate interests and separate characters, corresponding to the variety of classes [of] which civil society is composed, each interested to guard his own order from oppression by the rest.'[4]

Conservatives credited such a system with the merit that it harmonized with social and economic realities. Its destruction would be the harbinger of social revolution. And as the threads of the intellectual defence were drawn together during the 1790s, there developed a deliberate attack upon current radical doctrines of the natural equality of man and the virtues of human reason. The great virtue of existing institutions was held to lie in the way they had evolved over time, in a process of development and adaptation over

[4] Quoted, Dickinson, *Liberty and Property*, p. 283.

many human generations, distilling the wisdom of the ages. Such evolution would always outperform conscious human contrivance or systematic design. It was, Burke wrote, 'a presumption in favour of any settled government against any untried project, that a nation has long existed and flourished under it.'[5] While Burke and others who shared this vision of the prescriptive constitution did not deny that changes must occur, they were anxious that these should proceed in a gradual, evolutionary manner, which would inhibit the release of destructive forces. On such reiterated and familiar intellectual foundations the defenders of the existing constitution rested their case against French revolutionaries and domestic radical reformers. As conservatism closed its ranks in the 1790s it rallied to it forces acting out of conviction not merely interest, and gathered an inestimable addition to its strength in consequence.

III

Before February 1793 the reform societies had already been falling under suspicion. During 1792 they had engaged in extensive exchanges of fraternal greetings with the French assembly, and several of the English radical leaders had paid visits to Paris. These courtesies were purely innocent, but in the context of events in France and of some of the more extreme doctrines circulating in pamphlet form, especially Paine's *Rights of Man*, they appeared in a suspicious light in the eyes of authority, and at the beginning of 1793 the French appeal for help from British republicans made them look downright sinister. Save for one or two rash individuals the leaders of the London Corresponding society and other groups about the country cut short their contacts with France immediately upon the outbreak of war, and strongly protested their loyalty and attachment to the monarchy and the constitution, but at the same time they insisted on their right peacefully to promote the cause of reform and their desire to secure it. Despite harassment by the authorities and the constant pressure on owners of public houses and assembly rooms to refuse access to their premises, the divisions of the London Corresponding Society continued to grow. At the end of 1792 Hardy claimed a membership of 20,000. The considered view is that it was probably about half this figure, but that in itself marked a considerable expansion since the

[5] Dickinson, *Liberty and Property*, p. 300.

society's formation. Meanwhile the sale of Paine's *Rights of Man* shocked the authorities. During 1793 it was estimated to have reached 200,000 copies.

To those in authority, whatever the disclaimers of the societies, their demands for universal male suffrage and annual parliaments were clearly incompatible with continuance of the established social and political order. They were therefore a menace to the state. In November 1792 the government circulated instructions to lords lieutenant to enforce the proclamation of May against sedition. On 1 December a second proclamation reinforced the first, and also ordered the embodiment of the militia as a safeguard against seditious activity fomented from abroad. At the beginning of 1793 the ministry began to launch a series of prosecutions for sedition against individuals in Scotland, where officialdom from Henry Dundas downwards was excessively nervous about the implications of radical activity. In particular the lord advocate picked on a prominent agitator, Thomas Muir, who had prolonged a visit to France after the declaration of war. In August he was brought to trial. In a court case of unexampled unfairness, where in the prejudiced minds of judge and jury even the advocacy of reform had become a criminal offence, Muir was convicted and sentenced to 14 years' transportation. On similar grounds the Revd Fyshe Palmer, Unitarian minister from Dundee, received a seven years' sentence. Further fears were kindled when, in October 1793, the Scottish reformers convened a British Convention in Edinburgh to campaign for universal suffrage and annual parliaments, and delegates from several English societies made their appearance. French example suggested the most sinister overtones in the description 'convention'. Was this intended as a body which might challenge the authority of Parliament? After a fortnight the authorities broke up the proceedings, the leaders were subsequently prosecuted for sedition, and a number were convicted and sentenced to transportation.

The events in Scotland provoked the London Corresponding Society to outright defiance of the government. At a full meeting in January 1794 it was resolved, 'that upon the first introduction of any Bill or Motion inimical to the liberties of the people, such as for landing foreign troops in Great Britain or Ireland, for suspending the Habeas Corpus Act, for proclaiming martial law, or for preventing the people from meeting in societies for constitutional information', a general convention of the people should be summoned. In April the society held an open air meeting at Chalk Farm, at which government policy was denounced and the proceedings of the British Convention in Edinburgh approved, and shortly afterwards the plans for a convention began to be discussed. Indiscreet toasts at the annual dinner of the Society for Constitutional Information on 2 May added to ministerial convictions that revolutionary designs were afoot, and 10 days later action was taken. Thomas Hardy, John Horne Tooke, and 11 other leading members of the two radical societies were arrested and put on trial for high treason. Here the government overreached itself. Possibly the lesser charge of sedition might have been accepted by English juries in the apprehensive days of late 1794, but treason could not be proved. Hardy, Tooke, and Thelwall were discharged, and the charges against the remaining suspects were dropped.

Nevertheless the government's action was sufficient to cause a general suspension of the activities of the reform societies. Briefly the London Corresponding Society rallied. In May 1795 it had a regular membership of about 2,000 organized in 70 divisions. It has been suggested that it may have had as many as 5,000 subscribers and a nominal role nearly double this in the later months of that year. Active political discussion was carried on in the divisional meetings, and open air rallies to publicize the cause took place in suitable open areas — in St George's Fields on 29 June 1795 and at Copenhagen Fields the following October and November. On the evidence of such members as Francis Place these meetings have usually been described as vast public rallies in favour of reform with numbers of up to 100,000 attending. The facts seem to be otherwise, and those present mere shifting groups of the public wandering past and drawn by curiosity to linger listening to stump orators, in a scene since familiar to Londoners at Hyde Park Corner, with the added attraction of refreshment booths and vendors peddling radical broadsheets and pamphlets. One contemporary thus described the November meeting:

> You may have seen in the papers of prodigious numbers being at the meeting. This is not true in the sense such accounts would be understood. In the course of the day many thousands were doubtless in the field, but never at one time. I was there between two and three and I don't believe there were 500 in the field, and I saw it at the fullest time so far as I can understand.[6]

These meetings thus are no evidence that there was any widespread support for programmes of radical reform. On the contrary, Place later testified that the mass of shopkeepers and craftsmen in the metropolis tended without much understanding of the issues to approve the government's actions. The Society itself was soon rent by dissension between moderates and extremists. The former, like Place, believed that its role should be that of quiet firm support for reforms acceptable to and sought by aristocratic and middle-class champions

---

[6] Quoted in A. D. Harvey, *Britain in the early nineteenth century* (1978), p. 82.

of the cause, while on the other hand, John Gale Jones and John Binns wanted to force reform through by the weight of mass popular opinion. The Irish connections of Binns, and his close involvement in the United Irishmen, and his personal commitment to the ideal of a republican system of government, were gradually to draw the remnants of the London Corresponding Society in the direction of underground organization and insurrection.

In 1794 the ministry secured the suspension of *Habeas Corpus*, enabling it to detain political dissidents on suspicion; and having failed to destroy the corresponding societies by prosecutions, in the autumn of 1795 it gave statutory reinforcement to its policy. The Treasonable Practices Act made spoken or written words calculated to bring the king, the government or the constitution into contempt a treasonable practice which entailed seven years transportation for a second offence. A Seditious Meetings Act required resident house-holders to give magistrates prior notice before the holding of meetings of more than 50 people, and empowered the magistrates to attend and to close the proceedings if seditious language were used. The suspension of the Habeas Corpus Act was continued year by year, and the government made ample use of its powers to hold suspects without trial. In face of growing difficulties the London Corresponding Society reorganized its divisions in small groups and adopted the new technique of sending members on missionary tours. But by 1797 it had become a spent and exhausted force manipulated by a small minority, among whom were certainly men of treasonable intent.

Although the authorities' reaction included inexcusable excesses, not least in the Scottish trials, its virulence and its deeprootedness can nevertheless be understood. From February 1793 the country was at war with an enemy nation which had committed itself to the extensive destruction of the old European social order, had promised to give help to other peoples to do the same wherever its power might reach, and whose leaders were convinced that a formidable revolutionary and republican potential existed in Britain which could be used to overthrow the government and take the country out of the war. The Belgian and Dutch provinces afforded examples of the danger of this pro-French subversion from within. The causes of anxiety had not lessened by 1795, when bad harvests and high food prices created widespread popular discontent. The existence at that time of at least a small core of revolutionary republicanism in Britain is evident, though it was very much less extensive than the French believed and impotent in face of ministerial determination and of the tremendous opposing swell of loyal and anti-revolutionary sentiment manifest throughout the country from the end of 1792. The government's conviction that the whole social order was in jeopardy made it unwilling or unable to distinguish between speculative opinion and downright conspiracy. The landed class believed that the expropriation of property would follow inevitably on the grant of universal suffrage, and there were sufficient hints in the radical literature of the time to give them good cause. Aristocracy had not had a good press in Paine's *Rights of Man* in 1792, and in 1795 its role was further reprobated in John Baxter's *Resistance to Oppression* and Thomas Spence's *The end of Oppression*, the latter a writer who advocated expropriation of the land.

IV

The outbreak of war with France in February 1793 confronted the ministers with difficult and complex problems, for which none of them was prepared by any previous experience.

After two years of withdrawal and virtual isolation, since the Ochakov fiasco, they now faced the necessity of establishing a firm diplomatic system directed against France. In particular, Grenville as foreign secretary sought assurances of military support and agreements to uphold the old 'rule of 1756' which would preclude French commerce from gaining protection under neutral flags. This second point was secured in treaties successively made with Russia, Spain, Prussia, Austria and Portugal between the months of March and September 1793. With the Dutch Britain was already allied by the treaties of 1788 and Prussia was likewise committed to the protection of the Dutch. By an Anglo-Prussian treaty of July 1793 Grenville offered subsidies in return for military support under these agreements, and during the summer he also entered into subsidy treaties with France's victim, Sardinia-Piedmont, and with the kingdom of Naples. The primary British concern was the defence of the Austrian and Dutch Netherlands against French aggression, but this ran into both strategic and diplomatic difficulties. Almost from the start the cabinet found it exceedingly difficult to be single-minded in the choice of objectives, and its troubles were compounded by the determination of both Prussia and Russia to become involved in the west as little as possible while seeking gains in Poland at Austria's expense.

The state of the armed forces exerted their influence on strategy. The royal navy had been carefully nursed for the past nine years after the shocks of 1779−83. Over 30 ships of the line had been built. Sir

Charles Middleton's reforms of dockyard administration during the 1780s had made sure that ample reserves of stores were available for the speedy fitting out of ships lying in ordinary for active service. Once the men had been found to man them, if necessary by the crude but time-honoured press, the means existed to cut France off from overseas supplies and markets, to squeeze her into financial ruin, and to assume control of her colonies. The French fleet was hardly in a state to resist, for discipline in the ships and yards had disintegrated under the levelling effects of the Revolution. To Pitt, who saw the war as one more effort to re-establish the balance of power, overthrown by French aggression, an oceanic war had much to commend it.

On the other hand, the call of a traditional 'blue-water' strategy was muted by the obligations to allies near at hand and by the situation created by French arms. In April 1793 the treachery of Dumouriez seemed to open the Belgian provinces and Paris itself to the armies of Austria. Accordingly the cabinet agreed to concentrate its available military force in Flanders. As usual at the beginning of a war, however, the British army was too defective both in numbers and in training to provide an effective force for continental warfare. Half the force of 50,000 men was needed for police and garrison duties at home, and most of the rest was scattered abroad. As in 1775 the government turned to German allies for mercenaries. Fourteen thousand Hanoverians and 8,000 Hessians were taken into pay. Less than 7,000 native British infantry and cavalry were available under the Duke of York's command in Flanders at the end of April, and part of this force was described as 'totally unfit for service.' Its mobility was gravely impaired by lack of an established wagon train.

This combined Anglo-German force assisted the Austrian advance leading to the capture of Valenciennes, but was then withdrawn north for an attack on Dunkirk, on the ground that this base for French privateers must be eliminated. A quick success might have justified this division of forces, but skilfully though York conducted the operation, he was fatally hampered by lack of a battering train and the failure of the navy to give gunnery support. His little force was powerless to resist the new armies raised by the *levée en masse*, which the French poured into the Low Countries during the summer. Early in September he was obliged to break off the siege of Dunkirk and retreat.

By the late summer the ministry was hesitating between conflicting war commitments. Was it to reinforce the corps in the Netherlands? Should it aid counter-revolutionary forces in arms in France, as Windham and Burke were never tired of urging, and if so, should its aid go to the royalists of the Vendée or to those who in August called in the British blockading force at Toulon to take charge in the name of

Louis XVII? Or should the main thrust be against the French empire in the West Indies? In London there was confusion over both policy and strategy. A war fought for the balance of power called for choice of the first or last of these courses. If peace and security required a Bourbon restoration, then the second or third should be chosen. In either case sound strategy was to concentrate force on one object only, and yet the political pressures prevented this. To Henry Dundas, the secretary of state in charge of war operations, keeping the Netherlands independent was one of the 'uncontrovertible maxims of British policy'; but at the same time he could not forgo humbling the power of France in the West Indies and thereby 'enlarging our national wealth and security.'[7] The cabinet was not clear for which object it was fighting, and the Portland group whose political support Pitt was wooing were clamouring for a monarchical crusade. As a result the army operated in ineffective driblets. York was left unaided. Only a weak force was sent to the West Indies. Support for the Vendée was delayed until too late. At Toulon the ministry was obliged to depend on an international force composed of troops from Spain, Piedmont, Naples and Austria, a polyglot army which could not be properly co-ordinated and which crumpled immediately before the determined attack which the French launched in December. By the end of the year the French were everywhere secure within their frontiers, but seapower had cut them off from the overseas world, their factories in India at Pondichery and Chandernagore had been occupied, and in the West Indies they had lost Tobago to the British while much of Santo Domingo was in rebellion with support from the British Jamaica command.

The continuance of war into 1794 made more pressing a diplomatic settlement with the United States, over which ministers had been hesitating for the past two years. They were concerned lest the Americans should become involved under their treaty with the French of 1778, and there was potential ground for conflict in the British determination to treat foodstuffs as contraband and prevent importation by France in neutral bottoms. However, American leaders were firmly committed to neutrality. Washington and his colleagues thought a breach with Britain would be ruinous and bitterly resented the clumsy attempts of the French envoy to involve them in the war. Despite resentment caused by British enforcement of their rules of contraband, Washington sought a settlement by negotiation. Out of this resolve and British anxiety came the Jay mission and the Anglo-American commercial treaty of 1794.

In these negotiations the British ministers conceded two crucial

---

[7] Cyril Matheson, *The Life of Denry Dundas, first Viscount Melville* (1933), p. 182.

American requirements. They at last fulfilled the terms of the treaty of 1783 by withdrawing garrisons from Detroit and other outposts in the wilderness between the Ohio and the Great Lakes which had been ceded to the United States. They also gave limited commercial access to the British West Indies, by agreeing to admit United States vessels of up to 70 tons burthen. This concession was restricted by a veto on the re-export of British West Indian products shipped to the United States. In consequence this clause was rejected by the American Senate and did not form part of the final treaty, but nevertheless the two nations continued to operate it in practice.

For their part the Americans met a major British grievance hanging over from 1783 by their agreement to appoint a commission to handle claims for compensation still pending from British creditors, and they accepted a great part of the British position on belligerent rights regarding contraband and enemy trade, in particular abandoning the principle 'free ships, free goods'. By a series of mutually convenient clauses relating to trade, the two governments agreed to most-favoured-nation treatment in matters of customs, tonnage, and harbour dues, to free intercourse on the intra-continental frontier between the United States and British North American possessions, and to rights of free navigation on rivers in North America. American vessels were given free access to British possessions in Europe and in the East Indies.

Although the British government by this agreement accepted a qualified breach of the Navigation Acts in the West Indies and the Americans obtained the special fraternal commercial relationship which they had been seeking in one form or another since 1785, the main outlines of the British trade and navigation system remained intact. A small price was paid in order to avert the dangers of a Franco-American war alliance, and the government in substance safeguarded the advantages in war which it expected to reap from naval superiority in the conflict with France — advantages which were to become increasingly crucial in the years ahead.

This was as well, for during 1794 British forces continued to be overstretched and there were ominous cracks in the grand European alliance which had seemed to emerge during the previous years. General Grey's little army of 7,000 men in the West Indies extended its hold over the French islands of Martinique, St Lucia and Guadeloupe, but when the wet season arrived yellow fever decimated its ranks and it had to abandon Guadeloupe before the end of the year. British forces withdrawn from Toulon were thrown into Corsica, and established a precarious foothold, which for a time gave useful facilities to the navy in the western Mediterranean. The Atlantic fleet failed to stop the exit of a French fleet from Brest and permitted the French to convoy in a vital grain fleet from the United States, a failure only partly offset by Howe's subsequent defeat of the squadron with the capture of about a third of the French ships of the line engaged. York's army played its part in the battles in the southern Netherlands, but in the summer it had become clear that both Austria and Prussia were more concerned with the affairs of Poland than with the west. Without subsidies the Prussians would send no help under the terms of the Triple Alliance of 1793, and Pitt's Prussian subsidy treaty of 1794, under which 60,000 men were to be supplied, failed to operate owing to British delays in producing the cash. The Austrians abandoned the Netherlands after their defeat at Fleurus, and York began the long retreat across Holland which ended with the evacuation of most of his force from Bremen in April 1795, his cavalry being detached to support the defence of Hanover.

The first coalition against France was now in a state of collapse. In April 1795 Prussia signed a peace with the French at Basle. In May the republican government of the United Provinces entered into an alliance with France. In July the Spanish threw in their hand and bought peace at the price of ceding Hispaniola to France. Since the Prussian agreement with France bound the court of Berlin to guarantee the neutrality of north-west Germany, the British were obliged to release the Hanoverian and Hessian troops they had in pay or risk a Prussian attack on Hanover. Of the continental allies only Austria remained in the war. In the spring of 1795 a convention was finally settled with Vienna whereby the British government underwrote a loan to be raised by the Austrians on the London money market in return for an undertaking to maintain 170,000 troops in Germany. This was followed by an Anglo-Austrian defensive treaty. Grenville also tried hard to obtain an effective Russian alliance, but the defensive treaty which he managed to negotiate in February 1795 did not apply to the French war apart from a Russian undertaking to furnish 12 ships of the line and six frigates for Atlantic service. In September 1795 the Russians agreed that their treaties with Britain and with Austria should be merged into a single three-power alliance, but this arrangement still did not oblige them to produce troops for service against France.

The Dutch defection dictated an important part of British strategy in 1795 and early 1796, for it became imperative to deny the French the use of Dutch overseas bases. In the spring of 1795 the government risked a substantial reduction of the regular military force available for home defence in order to send out an expedition which seized the Cape of Good Hope and secured the route to India from French interference there. An East India Company force detached from Madras, with help from the navy, took control of the Dutch bases in Ceylon,

Colombo and Trincomalee. A further West Indian expedition launched at the end of the year reinforced the British islands, largely denuded of their former defender by the ravages of yellow fever, put down local negro rebellions, and took possession of the Dutch possessions of Demarara, Berbice, and Essequibo, areas of major importance for their yields of cotton, cocoa and sugar. This West Indian commitment was vital, but it was also ruinous for the army, since few troops survived more than one campaign in face of tropical diseases, and the continued drain − 40,000 men in two years − helps to explain the slowness with which the regular army was raised to a strength effective for intervention on the European continent.

By early 1796, from the British viewpoint, the war was reaching a position of stalemate. British trade and the overseas empire rested secure behind the shield of sea power, though the French *guerre de course* was by no means checked and shipping losses were considerable. On the other hand, French mastery of western Europe appeared complete, and the prospects of Austria effectively shaking this by success either on the German or Italian battlefields seemed unlikely. After the West Indian campaign had confirmed the safety of the Empire in the west, the cabinet moved to the view that in face of frustration on the Continent and growing fears of bankruptcy at home, peace should be sought. In October the veteran diplomat, Lord Malmesbury, set off for Paris. But even before he left England the train of events was beginning to suggest to the French Directory that the fortunes of war were moving in their direction, peace became unlikely, and before long the British were to be plunged into the deepest crisis of the war.

10 Fight for Survival
1796 – 1801

I

From the middle of 1796 until mid 1797 the course of events grew increasingly unfavourable for Great Britain and put out of possibility the achievement of peace terms which would safeguard her vital interests. In early October the Spanish, putting their grievances against Britain before their dislike of republicanism, joined the French and declared war, creating new pressures in the Mediterranean, in Portugal, and in the West Indies. A British withdrawal from Corsica became necessary, and British naval confrontation of French forces in Toulon more difficult to sustain. A limited number of troops had to be detached to support Portugal in the event of a Spanish attack. These events followed hard upon a Franco-Prussian agreement of August, which implicitly threatened British traffic with the Baltic states.

Nearer at hand lay the threat of disaffection in Ireland. In Ireland as in Britain, the French Revolution encouraged a new wave of political radicalism, but this movement soon took on more menacing overtones. In 1792 the lead was taken by the Dublin Society of United Irishmen, a group limited in numbers and middle-class in social composition. The political programme which it eventually published early in 1794 was almost Painite in its proposals for adult male suffrage, equal constituencies, annual parliaments and the exclusion of placeholders from the Commons. In the Irish context adult male suffrage inevitably became linked with Catholic emancipation, for the one demand made no sense without the other.

The Irish administration's concession of the franchise to Catholics in 1793 did something to counter the appeal of the United Irishmen. It also let through some further concessions: a limited Placeholders' Act, a Civil List Act providing for regulation of issues of public money and a reduction of the pension list, and a Libel Act similar to that passed at Westminster on Fox's initiative in 1791. By its Militia Act of 1793 it undercut the intention of the radicals to recreate the

Volunteer movement, and a Convention Act of the same year put an end to the calling of any assembly of delegates which might be construed as a rival or challenge to the Irish parliament.

What the administration could not do was to combat effectively the appeal which the United Irishmen made to Irish nationalism, to their exploitation of every grievance, commercial or otherwise, which might be attributed to the British connection, and to their fostering of a sense of Irish identity based on geographical separateness. The major objective of the United Irishmen was the reduction or elimination of British influence or control over Irish affairs. From an early date a minority among the leaders was prepared to exploit for this purpose the hostility between Britain and France. After the movement was officially suppressed in 1794, they worked to build up an underground organization. This came to include very diverse and to some extent mutually hostile elements, the Presbyterian middle class in Ulster and the discontented Catholic peasantry in parts of the south. In part the organization took the form of military cadres and caches of arms began to be prepared. Many of those enrolled knew little about the ultimate objects and sought no more than a measure of parliamentary reform and full Catholic emancipation; but by 1796 the leaders were prepared to go further, and so the Irish question increasingly meshed into the general war situation. Theobald Wolfe Tone and his immediate circle were prepared to accept French help to achieve a revolution in Ireland with an independent republic as the ultimate aim, and by November plans for a French descent were well advanced. Paris now controlled three European fleets, its own, the Dutch, and that of Spain, and it was by no means clear that British naval superiority was sufficient to ward off this threat. The land defence of Ireland was pinning down at least 40,000 men and was soon to demand even more. The administration in Dublin, well aware of the dangers in which it stood, strengthened its police powers during 1796 by a partial suspension of *Habeas Corpus*, the enactment of an Insurrection Act, and from 1797 onwards protected officials who overstepped the law in combating disaffection by a series of Indemnity Acts.

In 1796 British ministers had these and many other good reasons to seek peace if acceptable terms could be secured. Although the Duke of York had begun his distinguished career as commander-in-chief at the Horse Guards in 1795 and was to prove exceptionally capable in this role, the administrative reforms which under his guidance were to improve the quality of the British army were as yet only at their beginning. The military security of Britain itself left much to be desired. Many of the best trained troops had been swallowed up in the West Indies. Others were dispersed to Gibraltar and the Cape of Good

Hope. Regiments on which home defence depended were relatively untrained and at a low pitch of efficiency. Supporting them were the militia and the volunteers, whose ability to fight against professionals was even more dubious.

The domestic front also gave cause for concern. Although Pitt encountered no difficulty up to 1797 in financing the war, and money always seemed available, the cost was high. In December 1796 a 'loyalty loan' of £18,000,000, on terms relatively favourable to the government, was subscribed in less than 16 hours. The will to support the war was still strong, but the fiscal difficulties began to multiply. Up to this point Pitt had hesitated to screw up taxes, and had relied heavily on borrowing to meet war expenditure. Owing to the pressures on the money market he had been forced to float government loans at high discount, rather than borrow money near par at high rates of interest which might at some future time be commuted for lower rates. The ultimate effect of his loan policy was to add nearly twice as great a sum to the national debt (£200,000,000) as he received in loans (£108,000,000). The effect was high inflationary. Obstinate adherence to his sinking fund added to his commitment: he would have been better advised to close down that operation for the duration of the war. As a result, by the beginning of 1797, the delicate mechanism of a gold-backed currency fell out of balance, and news of the landing of a small French raiding expedition at Fishguard in February provoked a run on the banks, the bullion holdings of which were not large enough to meet their commitments. At the end of February the government had to hurry through legislation authorizing the Bank of England to suspend cash payments and to issue notes in small denominations (£1 and £2) as legal tender. The abandonment of the gold standard opened the way to still further inflation: between 1797 and 1800 the Bank's note circulation was to rise from £8,500,000 to some £16,000,000. But the result was not wholly unfortunate. Almost inadvertently, and in conflict with classical monetary theory, the administration had stumbled upon one facet of a successful wartime fiscal policy. Not until the end of the year was Pitt to pursue other aspects of it by the adoption of taxation of a stringency never hitherto contemplated.

Between 1795 and 1797 the combined effects of enemy commercial pressure, inflation, and unseasonable weather were creating a wave of discontent at home sufficient to damp ardent ministerial spirits. A wet summer and a bad harvest in 1795 sent bread prices soaring. The poor felt the pinch in both town and countryside, and in that autumn the poor law authorities began increasingly to adopt the expedient of making up wages with reference to bread prices and the number of

children in a labourer's family.[1] Early the following year, in an astonishing initiative, Pitt suggested the adoption of this system as a
national policy. In November he laid the heads of a comprehensive
measure before the House of Commons. His plan provided that a
father unable to support his children should be paid for each child a
shilling a week till it became self-supporting. The industrious poor
were to be entitled to have wages below a certain level supplemented
from the rates. Still more revolutionary was his proposal for the establishment of parochial funds, to be raised partly from subscriptions,
partly from rates, which might provide a form of contributory
pension for the aged poor, a parish fund from which support might be
given to men requiring only a beast and tools to establish their families
as self-supporting, and money for the setting up in parishes or groups
of parishes of schools of industry to ensure children grew up with a
craft or trade. The administration was to be placed in the hands of the
clergy and magistrates.[2] The purpose was to extinguish social discontent at its source. By such means, Pitt told the House, 'you disarm
the Jacobins of their most dangerous weapon.' However, the gentry
proved reluctant to take on such commitments, especially the extra
burdens which would fall on the rates. A better harvest in 1796
lessened the urgency, and the financial crisis of the following
February made the further pursuit of it politically impracticable,
even although another bad harvest that autumn renewed the conditions of dearth which had initially inspired it.

Before high prices and inflation produced their most dangerous
reaction, French ambitions had received a check, and the worst
consequences for the British of the remaining sea-power in French
hands had been averted.

The French expedition to Ireland finally got to sea in mid
December 1796 and evaded the British forces on watch round Brest
which easterly winds had driven far out into the Atlantic. The danger
it created was extreme, for even if the whole of Ireland did not fall like
a ripe fruit as the French hoped, the possession of bases at Cork and
Waterford could give privateers a near-stranglehold on British traffic
proceeding between the Channel and the Atlantic. By the 22nd the
French had reached Bantry Bay without interception with a force of
15,000 troops, but then the gales which had enabled them to escape
unscathed from Brest parted the French general and admiral from
their command and thwarted the army's attempt to land. After
three days trying to beat up the Bay the expedition was perforce

---

[1] See p. 176 above.
[2] For fuller details of this interesting scheme see J. Holland Rose, *Pitt and Napoleon. Essays and Letters* (1912), pp. 79–92.

abandoned. Weather, not British arms, had saved Pitt's ministry in one of the great crises of the war.

Two months later the second French attempt to prepare the ground for a blow at Ireland led to the blasting of their hopes at the hands of one of the most competent of British admirals. The attempt to bring the Spanish fleet based at Cartagena in the Mediterranean round to Brest, so that a combined allied force might contest the naval supremacy of the Channel, delivered it into the hands of Sir John Jervis. At the battle of Cape St Vincent, Jervis with 15 ships of the line routed the Spanish force of 27, captured four, and drove the rest into refuge at Cadiz.

Ministry and public scarcely had time to absorb the significance of this success before facing another shock — the outbreak of naval mutiny. The seamen's grievance was genuine. The pay scales for other ranks in the navy had not been altered for over a century. On top of a hundred years of creeping inflation the high prices of food-stuffs and other necessities from 1795 onwards created the greatest hardship for seamen's families, a grievance all the harsher since naval service in most cases was involuntary and many of the men snatched by the press had been earning up to four times their naval pay, while they were in the merchant marine. Furthermore, by 1797 a consid-erable percentage of the lower deck was drawn from other civilian occupations, from the criminal ranks, and from impressed followers of the United Irishmen.

Early in March the crews of the Channel fleet sent to the Admiralty a respectful representation of their case, but in the immediate after-math of the financial crisis of February, no one in Whitehall was pre-pared to pay attention. Accordingly, when the fleet was ordered out again in mid April the men refused to obey orders. There was little sign at this stage of any taint of a revolutionary movement. The men insisted upon discipline and on respect towards officers, declared they would sail if the French actually appeared, and refused to involve frigate crews in their protest, so that merchant vessels should continue to have naval protection. However, as the affair developed, there appears to have been at least some element of hostility to the war, possibly linked with the activities of the rump of the London Corresponding Society.

The Admiralty showed sense in its response. It agreed to discussions and accepted the substance of the men's demands, including a royal pardon for their mutiny. The fleet began to prepare for sea; but on 7 May the men struck again owing to fear that the government would not honour the Admiralty's undertaking. To make the position clear ministers were obliged to hasten through Parliament a supplemen-tary estimate providing for the promised increases in pay.

On 17 May the Channel fleet finally put to sea. But on the 12th a further mutiny had broken out at the Nore, which for a time crippled the navy's endeavours to blockade the Dutch fleet in the Texel. This demonstration ignored the general settlement reached at Spithead in mid May. Its leaders were moved by resentment of authority and among their demands included the right of seamen to dismiss their officers. It is possible that more sinister motives were at work. The government certainly suspected treason linked with the London Corresponding Society and the United Irishmen: this explanation is at least plausible although direct proof was never forthcoming. Before long the activities of the leaders had degenerated into rebellion for the sake of rebellion, and when the crews proceeded to the extremes of blocking the Thames to commercial traffic, public as well as ministerial opinion swung firmly against them. Their provisions and other contacts with the shore were cut off, and on 6 June they were proclaimed to be rebels, with an offer of pardon to those who submitted, save for the ringleaders. Any dangers of a show of sympathy among the soldiers who were brought in to enforce this policy were fended off by a comparable rise in army pay. In face of this pressure one ship's crew after another at the Nore surrendered themselves, and by the end of June the mutinies were finally ended.

II

The war situation still seemed to offer so little hope of real success that the cabinet agreed once more to attempt peace negotiations, and in July 1797 Lord Malmesbury was sent to meet French plenipotentiaries at Lille. Orangist anti-Catholic outbreaks in Ulster kindled the fires of Catholic resentment over the rest of Ireland, and provoked growing support for the United Irishmen. From the lord lieutenant came a string of warnings of the dangers of rebellion. The naval mutinies left a legacy of disquiet, sharpened by the ministry's knowledge of the numbers of Irish serving with the fleets — but for good luck a Franco-Dutch invasion force might have got out of the Texel during the insurgency at the Nore. Any hopes that France would break down commercially and financially as a result of the chaos of revolution or the pressure of British blockade now seemed vain. Austrian resistance was virtually at an end. Portugal, the source of supplies for the British fleet blockading Cadiz, was threatened with attack by Spain. The

ministry agreed they could no longer continue to resist French occupation of the southern Netherlands and its control over the Batavian
republic, and were prepared to give up all conquests overseas, except
the Spanish colony of Trinidad, and the two keys to their Indian
empire, Ceylon and the Cape of Good Hope. But members of the
French Directory were not ready for peace unless it meant a complete
British surrender, and the *coup d'état* of Fructidor marked the ascendancy of extremists backed by Bonaparte, whose ultimate objects
included British surrender of India, Canada, Gibraltar and the
Channel Islands. When the French demanded the immediate return
of all British-occupied Dutch and Spanish colonies as well as their
own, as a preliminary to continuing negotiations, Malmesbury was
recalled and the government prepared to continue the war. The
terms it had offered would have left France master of Europe; but no
British cabinet could contemplate voluntarily also making France
master of the world.

This decision came at a time when the last major ally against
France on the Continent was about to be lost. In October the
Austrians signed the Peace of Campo Formio, abandoning the
Belgian Netherlands to France, and also the left bank of the Rhine,
and conceding French primacy in Italy exercised through her puppet
regimes in the Ligurian and Cisalpine republics. Venetian territory
was partitioned between the two powers, and France acquired the
Dodecanese as a naval base in the eastern Mediterranean. French
power might now be thrown against the British Isles without thought
of diversion, and it was no coincidence that side by side with the
peace-making at Campo Formio came a French decision once more to
challenge British control of the narrow seas. But the outcome justified
British trust in the naval screen. When in mid October the Dutch fleet
emerged from the Texel with orders to disable the British North Sea
squadron and prepare the way for coastal raids, it was virtually
destroyed. Only seven Dutch vessels escaped.

In the winter of 1797—8 Pitt's fiscal proposals were an earnest that
the war would be carried on with all available resources as a struggle
for survival. Although he included a further loan of £15,000,000
among his proposals, a new emphasis was placed on taxation. Calcu-
lating the taxable income of the country at just over a hundred
millions, he aimed to take a quarter of it for the nation's service, and
the assessed taxes were raised to three or sometimes four times their
former level. In addition, a further two and a half millions was raised
by a new voluntary contribution, to which the Foxite Duke of
Bedford, hitherto a strong opponent of the war, contributed
£100,000. In face of the massing of a further French army of invasion,
vast numbers of volunteers were enrolled, and the government

accepted the necessity for a widespread arming of the people. 'I am well aware', declared the secretary of state for war, 'of the danger of entrusting arms to the whole population without distinction; but serious as is the danger, it is nothing to the risk we should run if, when invaded by the enemy, we were unprepared with any adequate means of defence.'[3] Fortunately these amateur defence forces were never put to the test. Bonaparte rated the risks of a Channel crossing too high, and persuaded the Directory of the merits of his proposal for an attack on British power in India, to be supported from bases in the Near East. Early in 1798 French agents began to intrigue with the East India Company's great foe in southern India, Tipu of Mysore, the military camps on the Channel coast were broken up, and the efforts of the French war machine began to be directed to the south and east.

While British ministers did not at first take the rumours of an enterprise of India seriously, in the spring of 1798 they did contemplate a new effort in the Mediterranean, as part of an attempt to resuscitate a European coalition against France. Without some such combination, which would divert French pressure, the adherence of Portugal to her alliance with Britain was problematical and without the friendly port of Lisbon the blockade of Cadiz could not be sustained for long. By mid April the government was also aware of embarkation preparations at Toulon and other French Mediterranean ports and jumped to the conclusion that these were preparations for yet another expedition to Ireland. If they could be interrupted near their starting point, so much the better. So it came about that Horatio Nelson at the head of a small British fleet was already approaching Toulon when Bonaparte's invasion force, with 40,000 troops and numerous technicians on board, slipped out on its way to seize Malta as a staging post on the road to the Nile delta. Not until August did the cabinet finally believe that India was the chosen French objective, and then forces in Portugal, Gibraltar and the Cape were stripped of over 40,000 men to provide reinforcements for the Company which were to play their part in the final overthrow of Mysore in 1799.

Lacking frigates, misled by incorrect intelligence, and anticipating a French descent on Naples or Sicily, Nelson missed the French expedition before it had reached Malta, and then, believing it had already sailed eastwards, made for Alexandria. In fact the French were just behind him, and the two fleets actually crossed paths in the dark south of Crete. Nelson, finding an empty roadstead, beat back to Sicily, missing Bonaparte by a few hours. The French were able to land and seize the city, and by 22 July were also in possession of Cairo. On the 25th, after revictualling in Sicily, Nelson, sure that the French

---

[3] H. F. B. Wheeler and A. M. Broadley, *Napoleon and the Invasion of England* (2 vols., 1908) I, p. 126.

were not to the west of him, resumed his search in the eastern Mediterranean. On 1 August he found the French fleet at anchor in Aboukir Bay, and in a daring night attack, penetrating the shoal waters between the French line and the shore, annihilated it.

His victory had far-reaching military and political consequences. French naval control of the Mediterranean was destroyed. French bases in Egypt, Malta, and the Dodecanese were isolated, fruit ripe for the plucking. British sea-power could act effectively as a shield to Sicily. A major French army was cut off from its base and from reinforcements and unable to return to France. Its hopes of intervening effectively in India were doomed — doubly doomed when its advance guards pushing south to Suez found a small British naval detachment from the East Indies command lying off shore. European states nursing resentments against the French were encouraged to show their hand. The Turks declared war on the invaders of their Egyptian province. The Russian tsar, incensed by Bonaparte's rape of the island base of the Knights of St John, gave a welcome to British overtures, the Austrians began to veer, and that autumn, overoptimistically, Nelson encouraged the Neapolitan government to enter the war, hoping that this move would bring in the Austrians and lead to a general collapse of the French in Italy.

The Austrians were not yet ready, and the French soon occupied Naples. The British and Neapolitans fell back on Sicily and secured it, and a new base, Minorca, was seized from the Spanish. But by the end of 1798 British hopes of a new coalition against France were beginning to brighten. Furthermore, the position in the British Isles had become more secure. During the spring the government uncovered the plans for a major Irish rising, the leaders of which had felt encouraged to bring matters to a head by the general belief that the French were planning a major expedition to their shores. The French for their own ends did nothing to disabuse the Irish leaders from this false impression, and the latter were also drawn into overconfidence by returns of numbers on paper which suggested well over 100,000 enrolments in the United Irishmen in Ulster, some 60,000 in Dublin and the eastern counties, and up to 90,000 in the county and city of Cork. The administration at Dublin was well informed and it reacted vigorously. Dozens of arrests deprived the military cadres of most of their leadership. On 19 May, the day that Bonaparte, betraying Irish hopes, left Toulon for Malta and the Levant, the Irish leader, Lord Edward Fitzgerald, was arrested in Dublin, and the forces preparing for rebellion lost their chief co-ordinator. In the following days outbreaks in Kildare and Wicklow and on the outskirts of Dublin were quickly suppressed. More serious trouble occurred to the southward, where armed peasantry of Wexford to the number of some 30,000 rose and prepared to hold out till the expected French aid arrived, and were crushed only after nearly a mouth of insurrection at the battle of Vinegar Hill. A small French detachment under General Humbert finally reached Killala in western Ireland late in August, but by that time all hope of Irish co-operation was over, and after a fortnight's raiding it was rounded up at Ballinamuck. In October a further small French expedition was intercepted at sea and most of it taken, the prisoners including the exiled Theobald Wolfe Tone.

III

During the last months of 1798 and the early part of 1799 the foreign secretary, Lord Grenville, worked strenuously to re-assemble a great European coalition against France, and fought his way through serious obstacles. Having good grounds to believe that the Dutch and Belgian provinces were riddled with disaffection against the French, he tried to mount a major offensive which would first achieve the liberation of this area and then sustain the momentum with a march on Paris. Only the overthrow of the republican government in France, he thought, would make possible a durable peace.

Prussian support appeared essential for any offensive on France across the lower Rhine, and Grenville dangled the prospects of subsidy payments in return for armies in the field. However, the Prussian court clung tenaciously to its policy of neutrality. The Austrians were also hesitant, and relations with them were embittered by what Grenville regarded as a breach of faith. After receiving loans amounting to one and a half million pounds during 1796−7 the Austrian government had refused to ratify an undertaking to repay it. Anticipating formidable parliamentary criticism Grenville was adamant that no subsidy should be offered to Vienna until the ratification had taken place. For their own reasons − perhaps partly in order to maintain their freedom of political manœuvre − the Austrians refused to comply.

At St Petersburg the British government had better fortune. In December the tsar entered into a treaty of alliance under which he promised in return for a subsidy to make 45,000 troops available to operate alongside the Prussians if they could be persuaded to enter the war. As Russia already had a defensive treaty with Austria, under which troops were to be supplied at need, this treaty marked a step towards a three-power combination, and the final stage in effecting it was precipitated by the French themselves by an ultimatum to Vienna in January 1799, demanding the exclusion from Austrian territory of Russian troops moving in to give support to the emperor. When it was ignored, on 1 March the French resumed hostilities. Austrian and Russian armies engaged them on a long front extending through north Italy, Switzerland, and south Germany, and by a further treaty the Russians agreed to co-operate with Britain despite continued Prussian neutrality. The British government for its part conceded that the 45,000 troops for which it had stipulated and for which it would pay should be sent to support the Austrians. However, Grenville, cheated by Prussian policy of his hopes of an invasion aimed at Paris from the north-east, insisted that this force should operate in the area of northern Switzerland, with a view to an offensive into Franche Comté as part of a conjoint effort to overthrow the republican regime at Paris. As a further contribution to this scheme he agreed to take 30,000 Swiss into British pay as soon as their country was liberated. Swiss independence now became a key theme in his policy – an essential prerequisite for the security against France of both Austria and of northern Italy.

At the beginning of March the French lost Corfu to a joint Russo-Turkish naval force. A week or two later Bonaparte found his drive north from Egypt towards Syria blocked by a Turkish garrison sustained by British naval support at Acre. The seizure of his siege train by the British as it crept up the Palestinian coast on board a group of gunboats put it out of his power to storm the fortress. Before long he was forced to withdraw, his forces suffering heavily from disease.

Simultaneously the other element of Bonaparte's eastern design collapsed in ruins. The French had placed high hopes on the inveterate hostility to the British of Tipu Sultan, ruler of the south Indian principality of Mysore. Tipu, finding his ambitions everywhere thwarted by the British and their connections and resentful of losses of territory exacted from him by Cornwallis after his defeat in the brief war of 1791–2, in early 1798 opened negotiations with the French at Mauritius and recruited a number of French agents and military volunteers. News of Bonaparte's landing in Egypt further encouraged him, but at the same time this convinced both the British cabinet and the new governor-general in India, the Earl of Mornington, of the need either to bully him into a decisive break with the French or to overwhelm him with a pre-emptive strike. Mornington received substantial reinforcements from Europe,[4] and having secured the

[4] See p. 242 above.

alliance of the Nizam of Hyderabad, he opened hostilities early in 1799. A brief campaign conducted in overwhelming force from both east and west ended in the death of Tipu during the successful British storming of Seringapatam. The territory of Mysore was partitioned between the British, the Nizam, and the former ruling Hindu dynasty, whose representative became a client under the protection of the East India Company. By extensive annexations, including the remainder of the coastal strip under the Western Ghats, the British cut off Mysore completely from the sea and established virtually complete control over the shoreline of southern India. The disclosure in documents found after the capture of Seringapatam that the ruler of the Carnatic had been deeply involved with Tipu cleared the way for Mornington's annexation of this principality to the Madras presidency in 1801. Two years earlier the Company had also taken over the administration of the south Indian principality of Tanjore. Furthermore, to the north, in face of a vague threat from Afghanistan which might plausibly be linked, however tenuously, with French designs, Mornington established a virtual protectorate over Oudh by a settlement dictated to its ruler in 1801. Extensive frontier areas to the south and west of the principality, Doab and Rohilkand, were ceded to the Company, to provide revenues for the upkeep of its forces henceforth to be stationed there, and the Company's jurisdiction was carried far up the valleys of the Ganges and Jumna.

Bonaparte's schemes had thus indirectly resulted in embroiling the East India Company even more deeply in the sub-continent and led to enormous increases in its power and influence. In the future these were to involved still further commitments. For the present, some indirect gain had been achieved by the French elsewhere. The offensive potential of the Company's forces and of the naval force assigned to support it had been diverted. The launching of an expedition from Madras against Manila had been abandoned in 1797 and could not be resumed. During the following years the need to hold the Malabar coast and detach patrols to the Red Sea precluded the possibility of an attack upon the French privateer base at Mauritius or the strengthening of the British hold on the Dutch East Indies.

By the spring of 1799 the French appeared everywhere to be on the defensive, and the British cabinet took up again its most urgent project, the expulsion of French forces from the Low Countries. Grenville still found it impossible to tempt Prussia into action, but in June the Russians entered into a further agreement under which a joint Russo-British force would invade Holland. The British were to pay for up to 45,000 Russian troops and would themselves contribute an army of 12,000—15,000 men. It was confidently expected that the Dutch would rise as a body as soon as landings were effected.

This ambitious project marked a limited step forward in the development of British military power. A reserve was beginning to come into being, for at last some check had been placed — through the enrolment of negro troops in the West Indies — upon the ruinous practice of exposing British forces to the ravages of tropical disease as soon as they had been brought to an effective pitch of training. The Duke of York had become chief military administrator at the Horse Guards in 1795, and after four years the reforms he had done much to foster were bearing fruit. Improvements in clothing, pay, and rations made the army more attractive to recruits and reduced grievances in the ranks. In the year of naval mutinies in 1797 there had been no sign of disaffection in the land force. The deficiency in light infantry was being rectified. The idiosyncracies of regimental drill had been suppressed and an improved, uniform system based on De Rottenburg's training manual was being applied. But there was still no systematic attack upon the problem of forcing sufficient of the available manpower into the army. In 1798 militia regiments had had to be drafted for service across St George's Channel to put down the rebellion in Ireland, and in the spring of 1799 the regular army was still below the strength considered necessary for home defence. This circumstance itself dictated that in 1799 the only foreign theatre to which troops might be sent could be nearby Holland, from which they could be quickly withdrawn to the home base. A British military reinforcement for the Mediterranean to support the Austrians in northern Italy was out of the question.

The plan of the Anglo-Russian campaign underwent several modifications before it was finally launched in August 1799, partly as hopes of Prussian participation rose or fell. Initially Grenville proposed an attack through Emden into the north-eastern United Provinces. In the early summer much thought was given to an assault upon south Holland in the expectation of triggering off widespread revolt against the French. Grenville also projected an attack into the Belgian provinces where further risings were expected, hoping thereby to forestall any Austrian design to switch troops northwards to the detriment of his scheme for an Austro-Russian advance on Lyons from northern Switzerland. Till the last, Grenville hoped for joint offensives in north and south which would smash through French positions and penetrate French territory. In terms of the forces which could be mobilized his scheme was unrealistic, and it involved a desperate diplomatic gamble: 'He knew he could not rely on Austria, but proceeded as though he could.'[5] None of these plans was based on adequate naval and military appreciation or

[5] Piers Mackesy, *Statesmen at War. The Strategy of Overthrow, 1798–1799* (1974), p. 317.

intelligence. Although the government hastily passed an Act to enable militia to volunteer for the regular service and quickly obtained another 10,000 men, no time was allowed for these to shake down in the regiments to which they had been drafted. The British commander, Abercromby, showed a sound appreciation of the limitations and the possibilities open to the force under his command when he chose to make his landing in the relatively isolated district of the Helder, capturing a useful port and naval base at the start of the operations, and the whole Dutch battlefleet to boot.

Planned in confusion and launched hastily for political reasons, the Helder expedition, even when joined by the Russian contingent, disposed of only half the force Grenville had hoped — some 22,000 British and 11,000 Russians. The revolt which was expected to bring over Dutch troops and immobilize the French garrisons did not occur, and the government had grossly underestimated the French military forces in the Low Countries and the resourcefulness of their commander. From the start the equinoctial weather severely hampered operations. In mid October the Anglo-Russian force of over 30,000 men was still bogged down in north Holland, the chances of a disaster were plainly looming ahead, and the decision was taken to withdraw. Meanwhile, Austrian refusal to co-operate torpedoed Grenville's hopes of an invasion of southern France. Moving off to the middle Rhine the Austrians deliberately left the British-paid Russian army in Switzerland exposed to attack by superior forces, and it was soundly trounced at the battle of Zurich. Mutual recriminations presaged the collapse of the second coalition.

British war policy was scarcely more effective during 1800. The ministry was torn between proposals to give support to the Chouan rebels in western France or to the Austrians in Italy, and substantial bodies of troops spent weeks and months moving round Europe on transports, seeking to attempt blows first at one place and then another, arriving only after the possibility of success was extinguished. At the beginning of June the chance of supporting the Austrians on the Ligurian coast was let slip and a few days later Bonaparte, returned to France, destroyed the Austrian hold on northern Italy at the battle of Marengo. An Anglo-Austrian accord was reached too late. During June, in order to keep the Austrians in the ring, the British government decided not to insist any longer upon the loan convention of 1797, to finance 30,000 German mercenaries in Austrian service, and to make an interest-free loan of two million pounds to the Austrians in return for their undertaking not to make a separate peace. In earnest of this agreement ministers conceded that British colonial conquests might be offset against French territorial demands upon the Austrians in Europe. But after Marengo and a

French victory in southern Germany at Moesskirch, an armistice suspended Austro-French hostilities, and the Austrians were virtually out of the war. The only noteworthy British success was the reduction in September of the French garrison at Valetta. Strokes were planned against Ferrol and Cadiz but both proved impracticable; and in the autumn the cabinet's decision to round up the French army in Egypt, successfully begun early in 1801, precluded sending adequate support to stiffen Portuguese defences against a threatened attack to which the Spanish were committed by their treaty of San Ildefonso with France.

By the end of the year the war prospects were gloomy. At the end of November the Austrians were finally knocked out of the war at Hohenlinden, and their submission to French peace terms was thereafter only a matter of time. During the autumn, with a view to opening French trade with northern Europe and closing that area to the British, Bonaparte cultivated good relations with Russia, Prussia and Denmark, and encouraged action by them to break the British commercial blockade of France. Since English harvests had failed once more, and there was an urgent demand for Baltic grain, these moves threatened serious consequences. At the end of 1800 a French peace settlement with Russia seemed to have laid the foundations for a new 'Armed Neutrality of the North' which might mobilize a formidable naval force in support of economic warfare against Great Britain. In aid of French policy, and to enforce the demands of the Armed Neutrality for an end to British blockade measures against the members' trade with France, Prussian and Danish forces invaded Hanover.

Ruthless British naval action overcame this menace. In March a fleet under the command of Hyde Parker and Nelson smashed the Danish fleet at its anchorage and dictated terms with a threat of the immediate bombardment of the Danish capital. The effect at Berlin and St Petersburg was immediate, and it coincided with the death of Tsar Paul and the accession of Alexander I who had no wish to pursue vendettas against Britain. Prussian and Danish troops were withdrawn from Hanover. In May the Russian government ended the embargo it had placed on British ships, and in June the two powers signed a convention affirming the two essential British points: the full legality of the right of search and of the seizure of hostile goods on neutral vessels. Meanwhile the British forces in the Levant defeated and outmanœuvred the army deserted by Bonaparte and step by step made themselves masters of Egypt. In this campaign, more clearly than in Holland, the army had at last proved its capacity to stand up against the formidable fighting qualities of the French. However, this success was won at the cost of a serious reverse on France's western flank. With only a minimum of British support the Portuguese were unable to hold back a Spanish invasion. By the treaty of Badajos in June 1801 the Portuguese government was obliged to agree to the exclusion of the British from the port of Lisbon. Four months earlier the Austrians had finally bowed to French demands and signed a peace at Lunéville, confirming the terms agreed at Campio Formio four years before. The second coalition was dead, and Britain stood isolated in face of French power.

IV

Meanwhile, six years after the establishment of the war coalition of 1794, Pitt's ministry had come to an end. Its downfall owed nothing to the work of the opposition. After the break with the Portland circle, Fox and his friends remained an impotent minority, isolated by their doctrinaire adherence to their view that militarism and monarchy were greater dangers than the French.

The breach within the ranks of the opposition in 1794 was not wholly a split between left wing and right wing, and thereafter Fox found himself still having to play a balancing role between opponents and proponents of reform, much as he had done since 1790. The survival, and even the gradual growth of the Foxite party – it gained in numbers by at least eight at the general election of 1796 and the 74 members then returned had been augmented to 80 by 1801 – did not therefore depend entirely upon its adherence to progressive policies. Nor can it be attributed to any party organization. Little trace remained after 1794 of the organizing activities carried on by William Adam in the preceding decade: the wealthy subscribers to party funds who had made it possible had left the party. In salient respects Foxite 'Whiggism' remained old-fashioned. This was the case not merely in regard to its ideas. In terms of constituencies represented, the Foxites were not untypical of the House of Commons as a whole, though there were fewer men among them proportionately who found their way into the House by way of small, open but easily bribable borough electorates. They did rely considerably upon pocket boroughs, but a fair number were also returned from constituencies – both urban and rural – with large electorates. It appears that the electoral base of the party rested partly upon the interest and influence of certain great landed families – the

Cavendishes, Russells, Petty-Fitzmaurices and others — but partly also on the intensely local nature of electoral politics. Such a party, without any clear ideological commitment beyond the traditional oppositionist hostility to the influence of the crown, and drawn together by a combination of such factors as personal influence, local allegiance, and personal loyalty to Fox, belonged in style to the eighteenth rather than to the nineteenth century, was closer to the party of Lord Rockingham than to the party of Earl Grey, Melbourne, and Lord John Russell. Because of this its capacity to influence events was limited, and unlikely to grow unless through some drastic transformation of the political scene.

There was little prospect of this during the 1790s. For members of the party to challenge the purpose of the war, which more and more appeared to be one for national survival, was soon shown to be beating their heads against a brick wall. Fox and his colleagues, in their advocacy of negotiation rather than war, showed, in a different way, no more appreciation than did Pitt of the ruthless dynamic aggressiveness of the revolution in France, and did not, as did Pitt in office, have the opportunity to learn and come to terms with it. By their calls to end the war, they left themselves open to charges of pro-French sentiment and defeatism. Rather better ground might be found for attacks on the ministry's effectiveness in conducting the war; but since the Foxites had ruled themselves out as an alternative war administration, and the public was convinced that the nation's safety depended upon pursuing and winning it, there was no possibility of shaking the ministry's majority in the Commons on this issue. Indeed, despite defeats, and the failure of the continental allies on whom Pitt relied, his position in the House became stronger rather than weaker. In these discouraging circumstances Fox lacked the tenacity and steadiness of purpose to keep his party up to the mark and did not in these years distinguish himself as an effective party leader. The futility of opposition led him and many of his friends to secede from Parliament in the spring of 1797.

After 1794 the appeal to constitutional reform, as a means of redressing the balance of the constitution and permitting the formation of a peace-seeking Foxite ministry, had no chance of acceptance in Parliament, and it was equally clear that the notion commanded little support out of doors. Christopher Wyvill's attempt to raise an agitation in Yorkshire in 1797 and 1798 showed plainly that the issue was dead in this northern former centre of reforming enthusiasm. When Grey brought the subject forward again in the Commons in 1797, his proposal was thrown out by 256 votes to 91. Grey's scheme — more radical than the Act he was to carry in 1832 — was well calculated to destroy the bases on which, it was believed, the influence of the crown consolidated a majority for the ministry of the king's choice. He suggested household suffrage, triennial parliaments, an addition of 21 county seats, the division of the English counties into single-member constituencies to end the compromises between proponents of ministry and of opposition, under which the county representation was commonly shared between the two sides, and a reformed borough representation constituted with attention to proportions of population, which would have wiped out many of the rotten and pocket boroughs. Inevitably Grey faced the charge that even if his proposals did not fully embrace the extremes of revolutionary democracy, nevertheless they led in that direction and were therefore a threat to social and political stability.

Firmly entrenched against the opposition in Parliament, Pitt — save for Ireland — had even less to fear from popular movements. The suspension of *Habeas Corpus* and the two statutes against treasonable and seditious practices passed in 1795 gave the government ample powers to suppress any agitation suspected to be dangerous to national security. There was in fact little to fear. The negative result of the careful investigation made by ministerial agents into the question whether the London Corresponding Society had been involved in the naval mutinies of 1797 makes clear that all but a few of its members then were innocent of any subversive intent. Very soon afterwards the Society collapsed, after running into debt trying to keep going its own radical journal. However, the ministry strengthened its hand by securing the passage of two more Acts, one imposing severe penalties for inciting the armed forces to mutiny, the other proscribing the administration of unlawful oaths. During 1797 ministers used their new powers to break up a secret society of United Scotsmen by the prosecution of its leaders. They also kept a close watch upon a small surviving group of extremist members of the London Corresponding Society, who were tempted by Irish example and Irish contacts to form a revolutionary society of United Englishmen. In April 1798, with the arrest of the leaders, who were held in goal until 1801 under the government's emergency powers, the remnant of the Corresponding Society came to an abrupt end. In 1799 a further general Act (the Corresponding Societies Act), aimed against treasonable and seditious organizations, proscribed by name the London Corresponding Society, and the societies of United Irishmen, United Scotsmen and United Englishmen.

It was neither failure in war, nor pressures within Britain, but a train of events in Ireland, which eventually led to the downfall of the Pitt administration.

If in 1795 Pitt and his colleagues, and his nominee as lord lieutenant, Lord Camden, nursed the illusion that a standstill policy based on the power of the Protestant Ascendancy would keep Ireland secure, they were soon disabused. Every crisis — a near bankruptcy at Dublin in November 1796, the French appearance in Bantry Bay in December, the uncovering of further French designs concerted with the leaders of the United Irishmen, and finally the Irish insurrection of May—June 1798 — spelled out the lesson that the Ascendancy could not keep Ireland loyal. Nor was the regime any longer financially solvent. In 1797 and again in 1798 the British Parliament had to raise credits which were to be spent on the Irish account. But if Irish loyalty could only be gained by a full political emancipation of Roman Catholics, which it was believed would be followed by an irresistible demand for parliamentary reform, then an Irish legislature might emerge which was totally beyond the powers of the British government to control. In these circumstances the idea of a constitutional union of the two kingdoms became increasingly attractive to ministerial circles in London. By June 1798 it was beginning to emerge as the only safe solution, and Pitt and many of his colleagues had become convinced that in the policy they had adopted since 1795 of supporting the Protestant Ascendancy they had backed the wrong horse. In June 1798 Camden was replaced by Lord Cornwallis who received full powers as both lord lieutenant and commander-in-chief. Cornwallis was favourably disposed towards the Catholics and he pursued a policy of clemency towards rebels, contrary to the wishes of the Ascendancy, refusing to be stampeded by their clamour that popery, not French principles, had been responsible for the rising.

In the plans which began to be canvassed in earnest at Westminster during the autumn, a clear intent to give satisfaction to a Catholic political nation in Ireland was evident. Pitt, Grenville and other liberal-minded ministers considered as essential the removal of all remaining disqualifications of Catholics from parliament and from tenure of office. In their view the sacramental test should be abandoned, and replaced by an oath of allegiance and a declaration against Jacobin principles, to be taken by all those holding public positions, all teachers, and all clergymen of any description. Although the question of Catholics sitting in the projected united Parliament was temporarily shelved, it was proposed that they should be eligible for all offices, and that a state provision should be made for the Catholic clergy along the lines of the *regium donum* enjoyed by the Presbyterian clergy of Ulster. But the path ahead was anything but smooth. The opposition of most of the Ascendancy was inevitable, and they could command the sympathy of many leading politicians at Westminster, including the two previous lords lieutenant, Westmorland and Camden. A still more serious obstacle was the attitude of the king; for George III, with a purblind disregard of the religious dualism already in existence in the united realm of England and Scotland, persisted in believing that, 'no country can be governed where there is more than one established religion.'[6] To admit Catholics to office or to Parliament was anathema to him.

In consequence, as finally enacted the Union with Ireland, duly passed in both parliaments, made no concession on either point. In deference to pressures coming from various groups, it was agreed that the 32 Irish counties should retain their two representatives, that two each should be given to Dublin and Cork, one to Dublin University, and that 31 should go to single-member Irish borough constituencies roughly on the basis of population. Indeed, inadvertently the statute of Union operated as a Reform Act, for it eliminated the great mass of petty rotten and pocket boroughs which had characterized the old representation in Ireland. Irish peers were to have a representation of 28 in the House of Lords, election as a representative peer being for life, and one archbishop and three bishops, chosen on a principle of rotation, would speak in the Lords for the Established Church. Irish peers who did not become representative peers of the United Kingdom remained entitled as formerly to sit in the Commons for English or Scottish constituencies. The right of the crown to confer Irish peerages was not extinguished, but the number was gradually to be reduced to 100 and not to exceed this thereafter. Not more than 20 placeholders in Ireland were to sit in the Commons. The two Established Churches were declared to be indissolubly united, and the continuance of the united establishment was declared to be an 'essential and fundamental part' of the Union; however, no institutional link between the two parts of the united Church was provided. The Act conferred full equality of commercial rights and privileges. All prohibitions and bounties on exports of native products of one country passing to the other were ended, and various goods on which specific duties were charged were to be subject only to counter-vailing duties on importation into the other country. For the next 20 years Ireland was to contribute two seventeenths of the national expenditure of the United Kingdom, but the charges on the national debts of the two countries were to be defrayed separately. Legal administration was largely unified, saving certain areas of Irish private and civil law jurisdiction.

At Westminster the Act of Union was approved almost without any difficulty. In Ireland a preliminary adverse vote was recorded in January 1799, but in the winter session of 1799–1800 the lord lieutenant and his able chief secretary, Lord Castlereagh, obtained safe majorities for it in both Houses. Recent investigation has shown that

[6] Cited in G. C. Bolton, *The Passing of the Irish Act of Union* (Oxford, 1966), p. 56.

this success was not merely the squalid triumph of bribery that its critics denounced. The swing of Irish parliamentary opinion between 1799 and 1800 was not due to purchase of votes in the house of commons. Very few of those who had initially committed themselves against Union in January 1799 changed their views. The Irish administration picked up the votes it required from among the substantial proportion of politicians who had not initially committed themselves, and from men who replaced opponents of Union who had been required to resign their seats by patrons who had themselves changed sides on the question: over 60 seats changed hands between the preliminary discussions of 1799 and the debates on the Bill early in 1800. Some potentially very dangerous opposition was bought off by a decision to give financial compensation to proprietors who were to lose the political benefits of pocket boroughs – Lord Downshire, who had opposed Union to the end, pocketed over £50,000, and Lord Ely, who had supported it, £45,000: in all one and a quarter millions were expended in this way. But at least as decisive was the fact that the idea of union appealed to important sections of informed Irish public opinion. If the Dubliners were rabidly hostile to the prospect of losing some of the trappings of a capital city, on the other hand Cork merchants were in favour of Union in the hopes that it would bring important commercial gains, especially in the American and colonial trades. The strongly Presbyterian counties of Ulster were hostile, but to a considerable extent Catholic opinion in the south and west, especially in Connaught, came down in favour of Union on the grounds that a government at Westminster would be less hostile to them than the Protestant Ascendancy at Dublin, and this flow of opinion had its effect on their parliamentary representatives.

Pitt and his colleagues hoped that the Irish Union would bring an end to the tensions which put Irish loyalty at hazard. In fact it did very little to resolve either of the two great issues causing alienation – land tenure and religion. The confrontation between a predominantly Protestant landowning class and a Catholic peasantry remained and grew increasingly bitter as the expanding peasant population pressed harder on the means of subsistence, and the identification in the popular mind of landlord interests with the Union was a guarantee of continued disaffection. This issue was perhaps even more fundamental a source of discontent than the religious one, though the latter also ran deep and gave it bite and direction, and was fuelled by disappointment of an outcome thwarted by forces which not only frustrated the objects of the policy of Union but also led directly to the downfall of Pitt's government.

Catholic hopes of a favourable treatment of their aspirations after Union were not based merely on supposition, for during 1799 Pitt and his colleagues authorized Cornwallis to spread the news that they were well-disposed, although they foresaw some difficulties, even from the *'highest'* quarter. Pitt, Grenville and Dundas were undoubtedly committed to the idea of full emancipation, and it seems probable that they believed they could win over the king, as they had done over such previous issues as the opening of negotiations with the French Directory. If so, they under-estimated George III's obduracy on this point, and under-estimated also the extent of the support he would command among the politicians. In the autumn of 1800 Lord Loughborough, the lord chancellor, stirred up the king to reject concession; Westmorland and Camden threw their weight on the same side; and in the government ranks Portland and Pitt's brother, Chatham, wavered when the crisis was reached.

After the assurances that had been given, vague as they were, Pitt could do no less than offer his resignation if the king rejected the policy he believed to be necessary. George III, correctly advised that an alternative 'Protestant' administration could be found, took him at his word and in February 1801 commissioned the speaker, Henry Addington, to form a new ministry. Pitt agreed to remain for a few weeks, to see the financial business of the session through and give Addington time to complete his arrangements. The interministerium was prolonged when George III fell dangerously ill with an attack of porphyria, became mentally disturbed, and at one moment seemed likely to die. On his recover he attributed his attack to the stress caused by the Catholic question, and this led Pitt to give verbal assurances that he would not again bring the matter forward during the king's lifetime. Pitt was then 41, George III 62 and not in good health, and it could hardly have been foreseen that the king would outlive his retiring prime minister by nearly 15 years.

For once George III had intervened to dictate government policy on a capital issue and did so with success because, in his outlook, he reflected the general attitudes and prejudices of his British subjects. In consequence higher statecraft was sacrificed, and a crucial opportunity to rally the Irish Catholic gentry and commercial classes to the Union was lost. Before long it was to be shown that political stability was also a victim of George III's intervention. Although Addington was to remain prime minister far longer than such outright critics as Canning expected, the monolithic force of government following, so long sustained by Pitt, as in the past by Walpole and by North, was for the time being shattered, politics entered upon a state of flux and change, and some years were to elapse before the re-establishment of firm and stable administration.

11 Britain Faces Napoleon 1801 – 1807

I

From its commencement Addington's ministry suffered from a general widespread sense that it was second-best and a poor one at that. When Pitt declared he must resign, George III turned to Addington to fill the gap. Pitt himself urged him to accept, and but for his insistence and assurance of support, it is likely that Addington would have declined. A former back-bencher supporting Pitt's ministry, son of Chatham's physician and a friend of the family, Addington had acted successfully for the past 10 years as speaker of the House of Commons, but his hesitation about shouldering supreme responsibility under the king was not unjustified.

The new prime minister's position was highly vulnerable, for on the one hand such senior leading cabinet ministers as Dundas, Grenville, and Spencer were too committed on the Catholic question to support a ministry set up to block a pro-Catholic policy, and on the other Canning, Rose, Long, and other able junior politicians were too devoted to Pitt personally to give loyalty to the man who had supplanted him, even at his own urging. Addington retained Portland, Chatham and Eldon – all leading 'anti-Catholics' – from the upper ranks of the former ministry, prevailed on St Vincent to take the Admiralty, found a few respectable second-raters and one able House of Commons man, Spencer Perceval, to fill other important posts, and supplied a number of minor offices from among his own friends and relations. The administration included three future prime ministers, and did not lack men of executive ability, but it was weak in debating talent, and its leader's inarticulateness and unreadiness at repartee was a serious embarrassment. Furthermore, although Addington sought, so long as was possible, to work with Pitt and retain his patronage of the administration, he was inevitably overshadowed by this great figure and unable to survive politically without his assistance, and by November 1802 this essential co-operation was becoming fragile. Pitt grew critical of Addington's financial measures, and by the spring of 1803 had arrived at the stage of declining any junction with Addington under a nominal premier in the House of Lords. Only as a principal minister was he willing to return, and for the time being neither Addington nor George III was prepared to make this concession to his pretensions.

Any help from the Foxites was ruled out by the price demanded. Foxite politics were still dominated by the old paranoic fear, that a corrupt ministry and an ill-intentioned court were threatening the destruction of British constitutional liberties. Their condition for support was a dominant position in the administration, plus passage of legislation that would set a seal upon it. Back-benchers were even more insistent than the leaders on these two conditions for an acceptable merger. In view of George III's known attitude to Fox, which had not changed since 1783, such demands were totally unrealistic. Moreover, Addington barred the way in 1801, when he refused to consider repealing the Treason and Sedition Acts of 1795.

Not the least of the government's difficulties was the war situation which it inherited. The defeat of Austria, which concluded with France the Peace of Lunéville early in 1801, left Britain once more without an ally, and with no prospects of victory. Sea power and land power had fought each other to a standstill, each dominant in its own sphere, and the need for a breathing-space was recognized on both sides. Bonaparte, having made himself first consul and virtual dictator of France at the end of 1799, took the initiative in opening negotiations, and discussions proceeded in desultory fashion until the late summer, when the French, feeling themselves in a dominant position, forced the pace. Deprived of any leverage on the Continent by the surrender of Austria, the government accepted terms tantamount to a recognition of French predominance in Europe and an abandonment of virtually all counterbalancing overseas advantages. All British conquests were restored to France, Spain, and the Dutch, except Spanish Trinidad and the Dutch settlements in Ceylon. These terms included the abandonment of the important strategic base of Tobago in the Windward group of the Lesser Antilles, and the Cape of Good Hope, the southern gateway to the Indian Ocean. The undertaking to withdraw from Malta and return it − under certain conditions − to the Knights of St John, meant surrender of the barrier to a northern approach to India via the Near East. While making these large concessions Addington and his foreign secretary, Lord Hawkesbury, accepted French annexation of Savoy, control of the Cisalpine Republic, and a French military presence in the United Provinces, and secured no confirmation of those elements of the Treaty of Lunéville by which the French had given undertakings to Austria to recognize the independence of the Dutch, the Swiss, and the Ligurian Republic. The final terms signed at Amiens early in 1802 were in some respects even more adverse than the preliminaries: in particular, whereas the latter laid down that Cape Town should be a free port open to both French and British commerce, the final terms retroceded the Cape in full sovereignty, leaving the British no legal pretext for protest in the event of a French annexation. The government also decided not to negotiate over the renewal of a trade agreement with France, thus leaving Bonaparte free to close all French colonies to British commerce as soon as he had recovered control of them.

No good peace could have been obtained in the circumstances, but critics had good ground for complaints that too much had been conceded. In particular, Lord Grenville, the ex-foreign secretary, regarded the treaty as an outright disgrace and declined any longer to give the ministry his countenance. Grenville and also Windham attacked the terms vehemently in Parliament, moving permanently into opposition and opening a split between themselves and Pitt, who was not yet ready to abandon Addington.

However, whatever the failings of Addington and his colleagues as negotiators, it was a measure of their clear-sighted concern for the national interest that from the start they treated the Peace of Amiens as no more than a truce, and were quick to react to what appeared to be mounting French threats to what remained of the balance of power. This concern was to bring on a British declaration of war within 12 months.

It was natural that, once the treaty was signed, Bonaparte would seek to re-establish French power in conquered or revolted French islands (which thus once more became pawns for Britain's taking) and to reap the benefits of the renewed freedom to trade across the oceans without British interference. This was accepted in London as a natural outcome of the peace. What was not acceptable in the long run was the French dominance of the coastline of the Low Countries. What was not acceptable even in the short run was the exclusion of British commerce from French-controlled territories, the aggressive advance of French supremacy on the Continent, and the development of further threats against British power. While it was not known in London that Bonaparte contemplated the probable resumption of war in 1804, his measures to bring the resources of Europe more firmly under his own control were evident, and his own impatience was mainly responsible for the early breakdown of the peace. In the months that followed, he assumed the presidency of the Cisalpine Republic, declined to withdraw his troops from Holland, annexed Piedmont to France, and shortly afterwards Parma also, revealed that the nominal independence of the Swiss cantons was a mere façade for French control, and above all continued to bar British commerce from all those parts of Europe which were under his sway. Some of these steps were violations of the letter of the peace treaty; others violated its spirit, at least so far as the British interpretation was concerned. Bonaparte's remodelling of Switzerland and northern Italy strengthened the French strategic position as against Austria and increased the likelihood of a take-over of the whole Italian peninsula whenever he might wish. British ministers were shaken by the hints in the Sebastiani memorandum of Bonaparte's continued interest in a possible French conquest of Egypt, the strategic gateway to the Indian Ocean and the possessions of the East India Company. In October 1802, in anticipation of an early resumption of hostilities, they sent instructions to the governor-general at Calcutta to delay the formal restitution of Pondichery to France.

These developments rapidly swung against the treaty wide sections of British opinion which at first had welcomed it, and the ministers soon decided to deny Bonaparte the further advantages of peace upon such terms. By the beginning of April 1803 their own terms hardened into a speedy withdrawal of French troops from the Dutch provinces, and a modification of the treaty of Amiens which would leave Malta in British hands as an equivalent for the strengthening of the French position in Switzerland and northern Italy. Ministers indicated that these terms were to some extent negotiable, but they encountered an outright rebuff with the drafting of further French troops into strategic points in Holland and a formal objection to the installation of the British in any possession in the Mediterranean. To the British Malta was a naval base from which southern Italy might be succoured and a French drive into the Near East intercepted. To Bonaparte it was a stepping stone to Egypt and India. In mid April the British terms became an ultimatum: French withdrawal from the Dutch Republic and a lease to Britain of Malta for at least 10 years. By remaining in actual occupation of the island the British were technically within their rights, for two treaty conditions of their withdrawal had not been fulfilled. No new Grand Master of the Order of St John had been elected, and no steps had been taken to bring into being a projected six-power guarantee of the island's independence. After four further weeks of diplomatic exchanges had made clear that the French would not give way on either point, the British government declared war on 18 May. It was thus able to cut off parts of the fleets which Bonaparte had sent to restore French rule in the West Indies, blockade French ports before the full fruits of renewed peacetime commerce had been realized, and force war upon Bonaparte before his plans for military recovery were far advanced and when the British position was still relatively favourable.

For British strength had not been run down after the Peace of Amiens. For this Addington deserved well of his country. Although the unwise economies of Lord St Vincent temporarily created some shortages of naval stores and timber in the royal dockyards, the remobilization of the fleet proceeded steadily during 1803, and the peacetime military establishment was greater than it had ever been. Addington had retained a regular army of over 130,000 men. About 50,000 were on overseas stations: in the West Indies a sufficient force was available to permit the prompt re-occupation of St Lucia, Tobago, Demarara and Essequibo. The 81,000 or so men left in Britain, with the addition of 50,000 militia, provided a garrison far larger than any invading force Bonaparte could hope to land with the shipping at his disposal in 1803. Furthermore, various military reforms sponsored by the Duke of York were now bearing fruit. Control over the quality of young officers was tightened; a small staff college had been set up in 1801; the Royal Military College came into being in 1802. Light infantry units armed with marksmen's rifles were being developed, which provided an answer to the formidable French *voltigeurs*. For the moment Addington's strategy was simple: to sit tight at home, blockade the French fleets, sweep French commerce from the seas, reoccupy the colonies recently returned to France and her clients, thereby re-acquiring useful commercial resources and denying them to the enemy; and finally, to stir up the Continent once more to resist the onward advance of French ascendancy. Along these general lines the duel between Britain and France was to be waged for the next 12 years.

As the breach over Malta indicated, war in the Mediterranean involved particular preoccupations. The over-riding object was to thwart French expansion eastward. With this went the provision of a counter to the French and Spanish fleets of Toulon and Cartagena, the protection of Turkey, the Levant and Egypt, the exclusion of the French from Sicily, and the safeguarding of trade with the Ottoman Empire and southern Europe. War policy in this theatre was also affected by the prospect of an accord with Russia which might lay the seeds of a great European coalition against France. The tsar was no more anxious than the British to see the French in Turkey. Eventually, to prevent this, he flung a shield of troops and naval forces into the Dodecanese. Common interest now rapidly drew the two powers closer together.

II

Although Addington was not to remain in charge of the war for long, he made notable contributions to the successful conduct of it. His Army of Reserve Act of 1803 produced an additional 30,000 men, more than half of whom soon accepted the option of transferring to the regular army. His revival of the Volunteers, backed by an Act giving the government powers to raise a levy en masse, brought forward so large a force — ultimately 380,000 men in Britain and another 70,000 in Ireland — that it took months to provide many of the units with arms. By 1804, however, some of them were becoming effective fighting formations. Under the Duke of York's guidance the war office took care to ensure the mobility of these auxiliaries, often by fixing concentration points near to canals, or by the provision of horse buses to reduce the fatigue of marching. A system of well-supervised training was kept under constant review, with admirable results.

Nor was this all; for Addington far outdistanced Pitt in his success in providing a fiscal underpinning for the enormous war effort circumstances demanded. His 'property tax', a form of income tax, levied at the rate of a shilling in the pound on all incomes of over £150, derived its great effectiveness from adoption of the principle of deduction at source. To a large extent this scheme overcame the weakness of Pitt's income tax — the unchecked temptation for taxpayers to understate their incomes — and it would have been even more effective in this respect had not Pitt forced Addington to accept his own scruples about applying the method to income in the form of interest on government stock. This concession lost the treasury about half the revenue that should have been derived from this source. Even so, unlike Pitt in 1798, Addington was able to forecast revenue with extraordinary precision. Another forward-looking step (which Pitt forced Addington to drop) was his proposal to discriminate in favour of earned as against unearned income. Despite this, Addington's budgets of 1803 and 1804 laid sound foundations for war finance during the next 12 years.

Nevertheless, by the spring of 1804, Addington's position in relation to the House of Commons had become untenable. The members of the Foxite opposition were once more in full cry. Throughout the months of peace their hands had been tied, for by making the treaty of Amiens Addington had fulfilled one of their major aims, an end to war with France. When the conflict was renewed their condemnation knew no bounds, and the desertion of those few of their number, led by Sheridan, who constituted a party round the Prince of Wales, brought little effective addition of parliamentary strength to the administration.

At the end of 1803 Fox began working actively for an understanding with Grenville, who for his part regarded the Addington ministry as even less competent to run a war than to negotiate peace. The moment was propitious, for whatever the merits of Addington's war preparations, there was a widespread feeling in the country that he was not a fit leader for such a crisis. After the outbreak of war Grenville had become firmly convinced of the need for a broadly-based administration with Pitt at its head; and as Pitt continued during 1803 to show reluctance to turn against Addington, so Grenville was driven closer to Fox in his search for the basis of a comprehensive ministry. It was, however, an association which provoked a good deal of cynical comment, for in some respects it seemed almost as grotesque as that between Fox and North in 1783.

Be that as it may, the new alignment created a powerful force in opposition, and when Pitt, early in 1804, also turned against Addington, the administration, faced by a perfect galaxy of hostile talent in the Commons, was inevitably doomed. Yet its successor was even less strong. The logical culmination of the joint assault upon it should have been a national coalition, and all the leading critics of Addington were prepared to sink their differences to form it. The stumbling-block was the king. George III put an absolute veto on the employment of Fox in a cabinet office. Fox's friends refused to join in a coalition without him, and Grenville, by this time totally convinced of the need for a ministry of all the available talents, also felt in honour too deeply committed to Fox to accept office without him. Called upon as the obvious successor to Addington, Pitt could not, in 1804, commit the breach of contemporary constitutional conventions which he himself had stood forward to defend in 1783, by forcing the king to accept an unwanted minister or by leaving him to be coerced by the factious pressure of others. The difficulties of his situation were compounded when the king succumbed to another attack of porphyria, which made the politicians anxious not to put too much strain on him for fear of causing his death or a complete mental breakdown. The events of the past few months ruled out Pitt's forming a coalition with Addington. Accordingly, he resumed the premiership at the head of a ministry no broader based than Addington's, almost devoid of senior talent save for Melville (formerly Henry Dundas) as first lord of admiralty, and relying in the Commons mainly on the support of young disciples, several of whom, like Castlereagh and Canning, were of excellent calibre, but as yet lacking in weight and experience.

The threefold division of the old Pittite governing connection between followers of Pitt, of Grenville, and of Addington, was now virtually complete. Not only did Pitt suffer in consequence, but he took office in circumstances damaging to his personal credit, since it appeared that Addington had been victimized not to make way for a great coalition but merely to serve Pitt's ambition. Although at the end of 1804 Pitt managed to patch up an alliance of sorts with Addington, who became lord president of the council with a peerage as Lord Sidmouth, their understanding did not long survive the strains placed upon it by recent events. New tensions soon arose. The inquiries into naval administration which Sidmouth had launched unearthed financial irregularities reflecting upon Melville from the days when he had been treasurer of the navy. This disclosure forced Melville's resignation, itself a serious blow to the ministry. The choice of his successor led to a rebuff for Sidmouth, and the vehemence with which one or two of Sidmouth's supporters pushed on an impeachment of Melville added to the friction. In July 1805 Sidmouth resigned, a move which might have been a good deal more damaging to Pitt's administration had it not been postponed almost till the end of the parliamentary session.

It fell to this weakly administration to prepare to meet the blows which the ruler of France planned for the destruction of his major enemy in 1805. In May 1804 Bonaparte confirmed his position as dictator in France by his elevation as Napoleon, Emperor of the French. During the early months of 1805 his preparations along the Channel coast for an invasion of England rose to formidable proportions. He believed that temporary command of the narrow seas would give him sufficient time to land an army of over 150,000 men in eastern Kent and that a swift French occupation of London would end the war before any threat to his line of communication could have a serious effect. His invasion plan was daring and by no means without promise of success, though he possibly underestimated the tenacity and resilience of the resistance which his troops would have encountered. His scheme depended upon a concerted breakout of the French fleets at Toulon and Brest, which were to make for the West Indies, the former picking up Spanish squadrons from Cartagena and Cadiz on its way. Having, so he hoped, diverted a large British pursuing force to the Caribbean, the combined fleet was to slip back, pick up still other detachments from Ferrol and Rochefort, take the northern route round Scotland into the North Sea, add the reconstituted Dutch fleet at the Texel to its force of 40 to 50 ships of the line, and then enter the Channel from the North Sea in overwhelming force. It was to brush aside the dozen or so ships of the British North Sea Squadron and hold the narrow straits while the army crossed into Kent. Napoleon calculated that most of the British fleet would be caught seeking to intercept the French in the Bay of Biscay and the Western Approaches, and that by the time it was recalled and pushed its way up Channel, the war would be over.

Part of this scheme was foiled at the outset, for the close British blockade prevented Admiral Ganteaume from leaving Brest. Admiral Villeneuve successfully escaped from Toulon. His fears of interception drove him to pass Cartagena without picking up the Spanish warships there, but he was able to add the force at Cadiz to his own before heading across the Atlantic. As soon as he knew that Nelson had arrived in the West Indies in pursuit, he doubled back in order to complete the naval concentration Napoleon had planned.

A situation of great danger for Britain began to unfold, but the qualities of the navy and the skills of the Admiralty proved adequate to the test. The blockade on Brest was never relaxed. Owing to superior ships and seamanship, Nelson had reached the West Indies in three weeks, whereas Villeneuve had taken five. He himself was back in Spanish waters three days before Villeneuve, and his dispatches sent by fast frigate warning of Villeneuve's probable return were in London almost a fortnight ahead of the French arrival back in European waters. Villeneuve sailed straight into the net carefully spread for him by the Admiralty. He was intercepted by Sir Robert Calder with a force inferior in number of ships but nearly equal in guns and far superior in fighting quality. Owing to Calder's hesitation to risk a battle of destruction, the engagement was indecisive, and Villeneuve successfully got through to Ferrol where, despite losses, he brought the main armament of his combined fleet to 29 ships of the line. Could this considerable force have reached the Texel unexpectedly, the danger of an invasion of England would have been considerable; but the element of surprise was now lost; and knowing that British forces were ranging against him to the northward, Villeneuve threw in his hand. In mid August he took refuge in Cadiz. A week later, and before Napoleon knew that his naval schemes had come to ruin, events on the Continent put an end to the invasion plan.

For during 1805, though with much hesitation, both Russia and Austria began to move against France. London had been putting out feelers for an alliance with Russia ever since the Peace of Amiens. Now in April an Anglo-Russian accord bound the two powers to face Napoleon with a demand for a French withdrawal from Germany, Holland, Switzerland and Italy. Napoleon's assumption of the crown of Italy at the end of May, and his seizure of Genoa a week later to strengthen his naval resources against Britain, proved the last straw for the Austrians, who acceded to the alliance on 9 August. Having raised the income tax by a further 3*d*. in the pound, Pitt was making lavish promises to support the military efforts of the European nations. Help was offered to Naples, and Sweden was drawn into the alliance. He hoped also to draw Prussia into the anti-French combination. With the arrival at Malta of 6,000 British troops and the massing of Russian forces in the Dodecanese, the Neapolitans were encouraged to declare their hostility towards the French, and this move precipitated the beginning of the war of the third coalition. From July onwards Castlereagh at the war office began to prepare for effective military intervention on the Continent, planning a 'disposable force' of 45,000 men, with transports for 10,000 troops permanently on call.

On 24 August the destruction of the Austrian army became Napoleon's first priority, and for the time being the threat of an invasion of England was over. His need to counter British pressure in the Mediterranean led almost immediately to the undoing of Villeneuve. Ordered to proceed to the Italian war theatre, and acting under the threat of immediate supersession, in October Villeneuve exposed his fleet to almost complete destruction at Nelson's hands at the battle of Trafalgar. In the short term this British victory had decisive consequences. French naval pressure on Sicily was ruled out, nor was there any immediate danger of a French descent upon Egypt. An early resumption of the invasion plans was now out of the question. The heavy strain on the British navy was eased. Secure at sea in the Mediterranean the government felt able to bow to Russian insistence and sent a small force into southern Naples alongside a Russian force detached from Corfu. In face of the numbers the French eventually poured down the peninsula the position of this allied army was anything but safe, and both detachments were withdrawn early in January, but the campaign had not been without effect. It pinned down considerable French forces in northern Italy which might otherwise have joined the offensive against Austria, prolonged the war in Italy into 1806, enticed a substantial French army into southern Naples where it became the target of peasant guerillas, and ended in the firm establishment of the British in Sicily. For the time being British and Russian naval forces closed the mouth of the Adriatic and disrupted French communications with the former Venetian territories on the Dalmatian coast.

Meanwhile, in India the governor-general, Lord Mornington, had continued his policy of eliminating possible spring-boards for French intrigue and intervention against the East India Company, and the impetus already built up during the last years of the revolutionary war spilled over through the months of peace into the opening stages of the struggle against Napoleon. After the conquest of Mysore Mornington still saw dangers ahead. Both the Nizam of Hyderabad and the leaders of the Maratha confederacy feared the looming power of the Company. French military adventurers were helping to train Maratha armies in European military methods and took part in the internecine power-struggles of their chieftains. Living by and for plunder, the Marathas posed a direct threat to the territories of the Company and of its clients. Regardless of any complications with the French a confrontation with them appeared inevitable.

This was the background to the governor-general's decision to enter into a treaty for mutual defence with the fugitive Peshwa, Baji Rao, putative leader of the confederacy, and to reinstate him in Poona, a step taken early in 1803. The wisdom of a policy which would draw the Marathas into a clientage relationship with the Company seemed to be confirmed, first when the British cabinet's warning not to hand over Pondichery reached Mornington, and still more when the French expedition sent to reoccupy it began to open up relations with the Marathas and other native potentates. But the policy was not without its embarrassments. Mornington had hoped that the prestige of the Company would ensure voluntary subjection to its ascendancy. Events turned out far otherwise, and from 1803 to 1805 the Company's forces were involved in campaigns against the dissident Maratha princes, Scindia and Holkar, over extensive areas of central and western India as far north as the valley of the Jumna. The great expense alarmed both East India House and the cabinet. Subsequently there was diplomatic failure to press home the advantages won by force of arms, and the compromise peace completed by Mornington's successors left in being a latent threat to the British position in India; but the prestige of the Company was now such that the peace in India was not disturbed again during the period of the Napoleonic war.

Nearer home, Pitt's main offensive design in the autumn of 1805 was a campaign in north Germany in support of the eastern powers and aimed particularly at the liberation of Holland. Once the threat of French invasion was lifted, a force of over 60,000 men was prepared, and advance parties were sent to the Elbe. But this scheme depended upon Prussian co-operation. Perhaps in a determination not to be involved, the court of Berlin set an impossible price on its intervention – no less than the cession of Hanover, a temptation which Napoleon's diplomats were already dangling before it. No effective British move was possible before Napoleon, at the beginning of December, smashed the Austro-Russian armies at Austerlitz. A fortnight later the Austrian government signed a peace. Russia was left alone facing Napoleon's forces on the plains of northern Europe.

One effective contribution Pitt made to the future waging of the war: he approved, and the Duke of York ably executed, the establishment of a formidable coastal defence along the narrows of the

Channel. The vulnerable landing beaches on either side of Dungeness were isolated by the Royal Military Canal. A total of 73 martello towers were built along the Kent and Sussex coast, impregnable to an enemy without proper siege equipment, and so placed that there was no area which could not be swept by grape or case shot from one tower or another. Substantially completed by the end of 1806 this barrier put out of all possibility a descent of the kind planned by Napoleon in 1805. Guarded by this defensive screen the British government could release substantial military forces for overseas expeditions. Henceforth Napoleon's only hope of a decisive blow at Great Britain depended upon outbuilding and outgunning the British at sea to the point where full naval supremacy could be established. Given time his empire's shipyard resources were fully capable of this undertaking. Right till the end of the war this ultimate threat existed, and the destruction of French naval power by sea or by land attack remained a major preoccupation of the British.

Pitt's other legacy to his successors who were to carry the war against France to a successful conclusion was a comprehensive reassessment of British war aims, drawn up in the context of the Anglo-Russian diplomatic exchanges of 1804. There is some justice in the view recently expressed, that the proposals put to Tsar Alexander in January 1805 contained little that was strikingly original, and that in the main they derived from the general prevailing trend of British eighteenth-century opinions about the establishment and preservation of a European balance of power. France was to be restored to her old limits, the countries she had conquered were to be liberated, and adequate systems for their future security against French aggression established.[1] Even so, a number of Pitt's specific suggestions were novel and suggested lines of approach which his young associate, Castlereagh, was later to follow.

On the lower Rhine Pitt proposed the addition of territory to the Dutch state to make it a stronger barrier against France: part at least of the southern Netherlands with the city of Antwerp was to be allotted to it. A further restraint was to be imposed on the French in this area by allocating German territory west of the Rhine, and perhaps a share of the southern Netherlands, to Prussia. This suggestion was also intended to satisfy demands from Prussia for compensation for her losses at the hands of Napoleon, and to head her away from her schemes of annexing George III's electorate of Hanover.

In order to overcome the rivalries between Austria and Prussia, and

[1] S. R. Graubard, 'Castlereagh and the Peace of Europe', *Journal of British Studies* 3 (1963), pp. 79–87.

secure their indispensable co-operation in a common front against
the French, Pitt proposed that many of the small pre-revolution states
in Germany and Italy should be allotted to the satisfaction of their
ambitions, Austria being encouraged to expand in the south of
Europe, especially in Italy. He considered that, both in Italy and in
Germany, an attempt might be made to set up some sort of regional
organization, to strengthen these areas against any future threat from
France. To the south-east of France, the kingdom of Piedmont was to
be built up as a strong buffer state with additions of Italian territory,
including Genoa.

As for France, once she was restored to her ancient bounds, Pitt saw
no objection to concluding a peace with Napoleon and to accepting
the Napoleonic regime provided the emperor gave up his schemes of
conquest. True to his attitude ever since 1792, he thought no change
should be made in the internal government of France, unless the
French people themselves repudiated Napoleon, and if they did this
the choice of another form of government should be left to them. He
did not commit himself to a Bourbon restoration.

Assuming a European alliance was able to re-establish peace in
Europe on some such terms, Pitt suggested there should be a general
territorial guarantee of boundaries and possessions signed by all the
powers of Europe; and in this context, he considered that Britain and
Russia, the two powers which, in a sense, stood outside Europe but
were vitally concerned about its affairs, might conclude a further
treaty between themselves guaranteeing the whole settlement. In
general the whole scheme was a shrewd exercise in *realpolitik*, in the
distribution and balance of power. In essentials it looked not forward,
but back to the eighteenth century. Pitt, no more than Castlereagh
after him, had any awareness of the forces of nationalism which the
age of revolution had begun to conjure forth, in Italy, in the
Netherlands, in due course elsewhere also. He had nothing to
say − and in the context of *pourparlers* with the Russians could have
nothing to say − about the problems of nationality in Poland.
Austria, to which most British politicians looked as the main preserver
of the balance in Europe against France, was not a national state, and
would be made even less so by the projected gains in Italy. But within
the framework of European politics as these existed at the turn of the
century, the plan was a realistic one (provided only that the French
could be defeated), and the true measure of its realism lies in the
extent to which it was to be implemented 10 years later.

III

From the end of 1805 Pitt's health rapidly failed: it has been surmized that, as with his rival Charles Fox, the breakdown was due to cancer. With his death in January 1806, the fragmentation of political groupings which had begun in 1800 reached its culmination. Four major parties faced each other, any one of which could be defeated in Parliament and forced out of office by a combination among the others once the ministry had lost its main asset, the charismatic appeal of its deceased head. Pitt's friends felt unable to govern without him, and Sidmouth's resentments against them burned too strongly for him to rejoin them. George III was obliged to have recourse to the opposition. Wiser than in 1783 — and working against the background of a much more menacing international situation — he wasted no time in trying to shake the alliance between Fox and Grenville, and conceded that Fox, however much he still felt him to be his personal opponent in politics, must be admitted to high office. However, it was Grenville, not Fox, who was offered the treasury and commissioned to form a government. It is possible that the king may have hoped that he might eventually play against Fox the role of Shelburne against Rockingham in 1782. But if so, the king was mistaken. Grenville's object now, as for the past three years, was to unite all the leading parties in a war coalition and end dissension, and he gained assurances from Fox that there would be no confrontations over policy, assurances which meant the dropping of demands for constitutional reform. Thus came into being the administration to which, ironically in view of its inept performance, contemporaries and later historians attached the label 'Ministry of all the Talents'.

In many respects this ministry was a fortuitous concourse of atoms. At least four competing interests entered into it. A lion's share of posts fell almost equally to the followers of Grenville and Fox, but some were conceded to the Carlton House set attached to the Prince of Wales, led by Lord Moira and R.B. Sheridan, and others, partly due to pressure from the prince, to the Addingtonians. The compromises of principle involved amused some and bruised the feelings of other back-benchers. To Fox the king's capitulation struck a blow for constitutional purity. Opposing the Commons' address for a public funeral for Pitt, Fox, with Rockinghamite dogmatism, reiterated the charge that Pitt 'had countenanced and supported a system of government which had unfortunately prevailed through the whole of the present reign, that of invisible influence, more powerful than the public servants of the crown.' He did not explain by what distinction his new ally, Grenville, 'was exempt from the same imputation.'[2] Constitutional purity sat ill with Fox's zealous support for a legislative dispensation to enable Grenville to continue to enjoy the fruits of his sinecure of auditor of the exchequer at the same time as he took the office of first commissioner of the treasury, the expedient adopted of a parliamentary trustee being suggested by the leading spokesman of the Pittites in the Commons, Spencer Perceval. Nor did past professions seem consonant with Fox's bowing to the insistence of Sidmouth that one of his associates must join him in the cabinet, to the extent of accepting there Lord Ellenborough, a lord chief justice — an overlapping of executive and judiciary, and an expedient last associated with the Rockinghamites' *bête noire* Lord Chief Justice Mansfield in the years 1757−63, and described in 1806 by one young Foxite as 'a foul stain upon the new system of government.'[3]

Politically the various strands of the administration were more united by their recent common disparagement of Pitt's ministry than by anything else. Maintenance of unity depended greatly upon their sinking issues on which they had formerly been at odds. This meant in particular that the Foxite leadership was bound seriously to disappoint the expectations of its back-benchers long fed on a diet of irresponsible opposition rhetoric. Grenville and, still more self-consciously, Sidmouth represented conservative influences likely to conflict with the more reformist instincts of Fox's friends. On the Catholic question Sidmouth was a die-hard, and on the subject of negotiations with France he was more inflexible even than Grenville who, under the impact of defeat, was moving resignedly to the view that Britain might have to seek terms. Moreover, both these questions were issues on which there was likely to be conflict with the king. George III's relations with the new ministry were correct but hardly cordial — it is noticeable how often he used the tepid commendation 'does not disapprove' in response to cabinet minutes. At various times ministerial proposals caused him concern. The formal courtesy shown by the ministers scarcely masked a determination to go their own way, which was to end in a confrontation rather in the manner of December 1783, and if Lord Eldon's report can be trusted, an underlying tension seems to be indicated by the unprecedented lengths to which they went to screen attendance at the levees.[4] Their veiled demand for full confidence on questions of defence and military administration, aimed against the Duke of York, implied an unprecedented invasion of an area of government hitherto traditionally

---

[2] *The Diary and Correspondence of Charles Abbot, Lord Colchester*, ed. Charles, Lord Colchester (3 vols, 1861) II, p. 31.
[3] Spencer Walpole, *The Life of . . . Spencer Perceval . . .* (2 vols., 1876) II, pp. 180, 189n.
[4] *Diary and Correspondence of . . . Lord Colchester* II, pp. 126−7.

sovereign's responsibility.[5] Whole-hearted backing from the crown was hardly to be expected if they fell out among themselves or if they came under serious pressure from the Commons.

In 1806 this last seemed most unlikely. Pitt's friends were leaderless and there was no clearly acceptable successor. In terms of parliamentary and administrative performance, Perceval, Castlereagh, Canning and Hawkesbury all had respectable pretensions, but none could command the rest. Their resignation from office signalled a belief in their inability to govern, and they saw little better to do than limit the power of the Foxites by trying to strengthen Grenville's hand. Their recent role as the party of government inhibited them from going into systematic opposition, which might be considered unpatriotic, if not disloyal. Initially there were no issues on which to rally. Parliamentary reform was dead. The Catholic question cut across party lines. All parties accepted the war, although they differed over the means. There was no evidence of a constitutional issue — of the king needing to be rescued from ministerial 'toils'. In these circumstances the Pittite opposition was bound to confine itself to the tactical harassment of ministers, highlighting inconsistencies between their actions and their professed principles, denouncing instances of jobbery and corruption, and arguing over the merits of their proposals. In the spring of 1806, only on the question of Windham's army reforms were they able to create serious embarrassment for the ministers. In any case their power to do damage was limited, as they could muster a party vote of barely 100 in the Commons. During the next 12 months there were periodic ministerial attempts, usually through Canning, to recruit their leaders, and Grenville's hopes of reuniting all the disparate Pittite groups under his leadership were not ruled out right up to the moment of the ministry's collapse.

How to increase the military strength of the country effectively but also economically was a problem which coalition politicians insisted, against much of the evidence, that neither Addington nor Pitt had been able to solve. To the incoming ministers it had the highest priority. Windham as secretary of state for war worked out a plan which, on the one hand, was intended to cut down what he believed to be wasteful expenditure on the Volunteer force, and on the other would make the army more attractive to both officers and other ranks by financial inducements, and would provide a pool of men with elementary military training by requiring some 200,000 a year chosen by ballot to undergo instruction. Much of this was acceptable to

---

[5] Historical Manuscripts Commission, *Report on the Manuscripts of J. B. Fortescue, esq., preserved at Dropmore* VIII (1912), p. 2.

George III, but as head of the army he dissented sharply from the introduction of what Windham regarded as the core of his proposals, enlistment on seven-year engagements instead of for life, with the possibility of re-engagements after seven and 14 years' service at higher rates of pay. Windham was obliged to concede that there must be limitations on the right of a soldier to demand his discharge during a period of war. His proposal to cut expenditure on the Volunteers offended the Addingtonians, aroused considerable odium out of doors, gave the opposition the opportunity to make considerable mischief at the ministry's expense, and was disastrous in its effect on this important section of the country's defence forces. By abandoning the militia ballot and hoping that a limited bounty would be a sufficient stimulus to recruitment, he removed the one sanction which had been invaluable in keeping up numbers. By docking training allowances and abolishing the Inspecting Field Officers, he removed any incentive and any check on the Volunteers' efficiency. The mass training of men which he projected was useless, for nothing beyond elementary military instruction by a training sergeant was provided, there were to be no uniforms, and training would extend only to 24 days. His whole policy had to be jettisoned as soon as the Talents ministry fell.

Foxites had for so long criticized the policy of war against France as one of political reaction, that some at least of their ranks may have assumed that a virtuous ministry of their own party would be able to arrange a peace. It is doubtful if Charles Fox himself nursed these illusions when he took over the foreign office, and if he did, it was not for long. From the start he saw that gains in French power in Europe must be counter-balanced on the British side, and although he was disposed to see if negotiations were practicable, in early March the cabinet resolved that they would hold on to Sicily come what may and deny this vital Mediterranean base to Napoleon. Arms were hastily shipped out for the Sicilians and a reinforcement of four battalions embarked early in May.

Militarily the situation was kept well under control by the local commanders. Thanks to Trafalgar the French were powerless to intervene effectively at sea, and the major menace to Sicily was a crossing by the narrows from Calabria, which the garrisoning of Messina, together with British sea power, made highly risky. Local naval forces maintained steady pressure against the French all along the Neapolitan coasts, prolonging the defence of the Neapolitan fortress of Gaeta, and capturing French war *matériel* in coastal raids. In July a small British army inflicted a decisive defeat at Maida on the French detachment operating in Calabria, and although no serious military challenge could be offered to the greatly superior French armies in Naples, this campaign opened the way for widespread insurgency which added to their difficulties. The British presence tied down considerable French occupation forces in southern Italy, and light naval forces operating the length of the Adriatic harassed French communications with the Dalmatian coast. On the political level, the Russian willingness to discuss with France the abandonment of Sicily created some difficulties, and at times Fox was led to concede this as a possibility, provided alternative naval bases were yielded to Britain in Minorca or Sardinia — but nothing came of these discussions.

When the discovery of a plot to assassinate Napoleon gave Fox a chance to make a gesture to Paris, it was within the context of these decisions that he prepared to listen to overtures from the French on the basis of *uti-possidetis*, but it became clear before long, as the king warned from the beginning, that the French object was merely to keep the British in play and if possible destroy the alliance with Russia which was the last remaining vestige of the third coalition. Recourse to the services of professional diplomats might have brought earlier enlightenment to the foreign office, but Fox's employment in this crucial business of the amateur and unreliable young Earl of Yarmouth was a last instance of the erratic judgments which flawed his performance in public life.

In other areas the 'Talents' found French pressure dictating events. Soon after Pitt's death the Prussians, at Napoleon's instigation, took possession of Hanover. In April the British retaliated with a blockade of Prussian ports and action against Prussian shipping, and a state of war existed for most of the year. The ministry has been blamed for not seizing early opportunities for a reconciliation when the Prussians began to become disillusioned with the French, but after the bad faith shown by the court of Berlin perhaps they could hardly be expected to do so. There was less excuse for failure to give support with arms and money to Russia when the tide of French military advance rolled towards the Vistula. Russian appeals for raids on the French coast which might tie down some of Napoleon's reserves were ignored on the ground that troops could not be spared. Even a request to under-write a Russian loan to be raised in London was refused. For the next few years Russian goodwill was lost. A bungled attempt to put pressure on the Turks, once again at war with their Russian neighbours over the Danubian principalities, was not in Russian eyes an equivalent for the support they had requested, and the countering of a non-existent French threat by the occupation of Alexandria in March 1807 merely dispersed military force which would have been better held as a threat to Napoleon's southern flank. Nothing was done to counter the emperor's growing mastery of central Europe, which culminated in the ruthless destruction of Prussian opposition at the battles of Jena and Auerstadt in mid October 1806.

More to the taste of some at least of the ministers was a blue-water war to exploit the advantages offered by naval supremacy. When news came in June that an unauthorized expedition from the Cape of Good Hope had occupied Buenos Aires, Windham and some of his colleagues began to build castles in the air about political and economic penetration of Latin America. But with the loss of Buenos Aires before the end of 1806 it began to become clear that a policy of conquest in that area was beyond British resources on the spot, and the launching of a further expedition against the River Plate settlements did more than anything else to convince Tsar Alexander that the British were faithless allies playing for their own hand. All in all, the war policy of the 'Talents' displayed an incoherence and an incapacity to marshall armed force to effective purposes. In a parting shot after they had been expelled from office, the *Morning Post* of 28 April 1807 declared that all they had done to help potential allies in Europe was to advance £80,000 to Prussia − 'a sum not equal to the yearly emoluments enjoyed by the Grenvilles when they were in office.'

The South American designs appeared to the government to promise commercial compensation for growing difficulties in Europe. On 21 November 1806, a few weeks after making himself master of Prussia, Napoleon issued the Berlin Decree, the commencement of his efforts to exclude British trade from the Continent. In the event this produced only temporary uneasiness, for with hostilities still pending against Russia, Napoleon could not make good his threat to control the ports of the Baltic coast and the North Sea. Both the negligence and corruption of French officials, and the ill will of the local populations forcibly incorporated into Napoleon's system, defeated the effects of the decree during the spring and summer of 1807. For much of that time Tonningen in Denmark acted as an entrepôt for the Hamburg trade. There was still much direct trade with Holland and with Spain, and in face of French agricultural interests the emperor refrained from banning the export trade to Britain in wines, brandy and cereals. British arrangements for the licencing of commerce in British or Spanish ships between Spain and the Spanish colonies, allowing the latter to receive among other goods the quicksilver essential for the refining of silver, ensured that three quarters of the cargo of each outgoing vessel was made up of British goods. Up till the time the 'Talents' left office, Napoleon's plans for economic warfare had scarcely begun to ruffle the smooth waters of British commercial prosperity.

Friendship with the United States was a cardinal point in Fox's policy, and negotiations were in progress for much of the year. Here the government had little fortune, for on the crucial issue of neutral trade it could not give way without both destroying the most effective weapon in its armoury against Napoleon and raising a storm in Parliament and among the public. The British negotiators produced a draft of a treaty which sidestepped both the points of prime importance to the Americans — impressment of seamen, and neutral trade — and which was so unsatisfactory to American interests that the administration at Washington declined to present it to the Senate for ratification. Indirectly linked with this issue was the problem of the British response to the Berlin decree. In retaliation the 'Talents' ministry issued the Order in Council of 7 January 1807, which prohibited any sea-borne trade between ports under the control of France from which British vessels were excluded. In an attempt to avoid unduly antagonizing the United States, the Order put no ban on neutral vessels carrying produce from the New World to a French or French-controlled port in Europe; and to some extent this arrangement actually favoured the merchant marine of the United States at the expense of the British.

IV

Although its association in the public mind with French revolutionary principles had killed parliamentary reform for the time being, the Foxites as a party remained pledged to attack corruption and extravagance, and were bound to do so if they wished in any way to cultivate the favour of popular opinion out of doors. This fact in part explained the virulence with which some of the ministers countenanced the impeachment of Lord Melville, whose acquittal on charges of malversation was considered a major setback by some of their followers. From a different viewpoint Grenville also interested himself in administrative improvement. Here the government's record was speckled. Various reforms in the procedures in the financial departments were put into effect, though these followed up investigations instituted before the 'Talents' had taken office. On the other hand, the creation of nine commissionerships for West Indian accounts and a number of auditorships of public accounts hardly accorded with principles of economy. The handling of the nation's finances by Grenville and his chancellor of the exchequer, Lord

Henry Petty, involved some unpopular and not wholly sound expedients. Fox, who in 1805 had bitterly denounced Pitt's 25 per cent increase of the property tax, now in 1806 had to help defend a further increase of some 60 per cent, coupled with a cumbersome and oppressive scheme which required those entitled to exemption to pay first and make good their claims to reimbursement afterwards. Further embarrassment arose from Petty's proposals for taxes on iron and on private brewing, which raised such a storm that they had to be dropped. Addington's property tax was improved by abandoning the exemption of holders of government stock from liability to deduction of tax at source. An ominous financial nightmare was dreamed up by Grenville at the beginning of 1807. In order to avoid increasing taxes further, he planned to raise larger loans backed by additional sinking fund commitments, which would have loaded the country with an enormously inflated debt and years of peacetime taxation at wartime rates to bring it down. Fortunately the ministry did not last long enough to launch this scheme.

During 1806–7 Grenville, Fox, and Howick – rather than the ministry as a whole – could claim an important triumph for humanitarian principles with the final abolition of the British slave trade. Although Sidmouth and Windham were adverse, ministers could represent to indifferent followers the need to secure the support of the abolitionist group in the Commons, and the cause could also command many votes among the Pittites. In 1806 ministers secured the passage of legislation confirming the policy of an Order in Council of 1805 issued by Pitt's government, prohibiting the import of slaves into conquered Dutch Guiana, and extending it to other captured territories. This measure could be represented as a self-interested denial of future economic advantage to commercial rivals whose colonies were likely to be returned when war ended, and so as beneficial to the West India planter interests, whose opposition was thus disarmed. In fact, interest was exploited as a disguise for altruism. At a blow the slave trade was reduced to a quarter of its former extent. Slaving interests thus had little left to fight for, and the trade fell a ready victim to the *coup-de-grâce* early in 1807, when the final statute for abolition was avowedly presented, and accepted, by Parliament on grounds of humanitarian and religious duty.

As the year 1806 passed by, various circumstances undermined the position of the administration. Fox's death in September deprived it of a speaker of supereminent ability in the Commons. Grenville's decision to reinforce the reorganized ministry by a dissolution of Parliament did indeed give an impression to the outside world that the government's position with regard to the king was more secure, and it produced a gain of about 20 seats; but this was achieved at the cost of a net loss in Sidmouth's following, which left that minister resentful and more vulnerable, a vulnerability increasingly felt as Grenville, worried about his Commons front bench if Howick succeeded his ailing father in the Lords, made clear his wish to recruit Sidmouth's enemy, Canning, in his place. The 'delicate investigation' carried out by a commission consisting of Grenville and some of his colleagues, into the charge that the Princess of Wales had given birth to an illegitimate child four years previously, loosened the links between the ministry and Carlton House, for the prince was bitterly disappointed that the commission did not emerge with findings which would justify him in seeking a divorce. Opposition was still weak and divided, and the ministry's parliamentary strength was still sufficient to carry it through political calms; but a crisis blowing up from Ireland suddenly threatened its unity and swept it away.

Far from eliminating the problems arising out of the Irish connection, the Act of Union of 1800 merely projected them more directly on to the British political arena. In particular, the Catholic question, which George III had attempted to brush aside by a display of royal obstinacy, refused to disappear. By 1805 the Catholic demand for political emancipation was falling under the leadership of a wealthy young Catholic merchant, James Ryan, and that year, largely as a result of his efforts, the first of many petitions on the subject was presented to Parliament. This development created serious embarrassment for Fox when the 'Talents' ministry took office early in 1806. His rebuff of Ryan led to the formation in Ireland of a more broadly based Catholic Association to co-ordinate and intensify the agitation, and the movement gained further impetus from the circumstance that the new ministry left most of the Ascendancy politicians in the Castle administration undisturbed.

It was thus continued Catholic pressure during 1806–7 that led the 'Talents' into a politically fatal confrontation with George III. Fearing the growth of a formidable nationalist agitation underpinned by a sectarian cause, both the lord lieutenant and the cabinet concluded at the beginning of 1807 that some significant concession must be made. Directed to submit suggestions, the lord lieutenant advised London that Roman Catholic gentry should be admitted to the commissions of the peace, and that the extension to the rest of the British Isles of the liberty of Catholics to serve in the army, established in Ireland by the Irish statute of 1793, should be made explicit at law. This last point seemed desirable owing to official abuse: Catholics in both the regular forces and the militia had been required by military authorities to attend Anglican services.

These recommendations came nowhere near to resolving the

problem. They evaded such really crucial issues as the right of Catholics to enter Parliament and their ability, as distinct from their formal right, to become members of borough corporations. But even the first of them seemed to ministers in London to go beyond what was politically practicable. They decided to limit their concessions to the army, a move which would dovetail with their general policy of making the military service more attractive and improving recruitment. To the Irish Catholics this issue was wholly marginal and in no way likely to reduce popular agitation in Ireland, as the government hoped.

George III agreed to the extension to the whole United Kingdom of the rights regarding military service conceded in Ireland by the Irish Act of 1793; but in the meantime, as clauses were drafted for incorporation into the Mutiny Act, the ministers moved further on two points. The formula which they adopted would admit Catholics to rank of general on the staff, which had been excluded in the Act of 1793. It would also make clear that there was no discrimination against any Protestant nonconformist either. This scheme was brought forward in the Commons as a separate Bill only a fortnight after the king had seen a draft dispatch assuring Dublin that staff appointments were still to be reserved to Anglicans. To compound their error the ministers decided to extend their concession to the navy also, including the ranks of admiral. Without directly consulting or advising the king they had thus gone far beyond what he was prepared to accept. Their move was pointed out to the king by Sidmouth, who opposed Catholic relief, who was critical of Windham's military administration and of Grenville's fiscal policy, and who resented Grenville's attempts to bid for Canning's support. George III now informed the cabinet of his refusal to agree with its policy, and at this point the Duke of Portland, from the side of opposition, also intervened to stiffen the king's resistance – by one of the ironies of politics, the man who had been chief victim of George III's intervention in the Lords' proceedings in 1783 now urged him to brief the Lords against the Bill and even to use his legislative veto against it.

In face of royal resistance, Grenville and his colleagues resolved to abandon the Bill, but they insisted upon their right in the future to advise any measure of Catholic relief they might think expedient in the light of circumstances. On the point of constitutional propriety the ministers had a good case, but on the main question the king was more representative of public opinion. As in 1800 George III stood by his coronation oath and the Protestant constitution: when Lord Eldon resumed office as lord chancellor on 1 April, the king told him he considered the struggle as one for his throne – 'He must be the

Protestant King of a Protestant country, or no King.'[6] When the
ministers refused in writing a promise not to bring the question of
Catholic relief forward again, he immediately turned to the opposition. His demand for this pledge is clearly to be explained by the fact
that the ministers had deliberately misled him over the extent of the
concessions they were bringing before Parliament, and his decision to
turn them out arose not simply over a major disagreement on policy
but over ministerial sharp practice which made it impossible for him
to feel he could trust them. By the end of March the main corps of
Pitt's friends were once again installed in office, under the nominal
leadership of Portland at the treasury, with Spencer Perceval as chancellor of the exchequer and leader in the House of Commons.

[6] Horace Twiss, *The public and private life of Lord Chancellor Eldon, with selections from his correspondence* (3 vols., 1844) II, p. 34.

12 Politics after Pitt and Fox 1807 – 1815

I

The government which replaced the Talents was largely a resurrection of Pitt's second administration. Its members regarded themselves as the heirs of Pitt, though there were branches of the main trunk, led by Sidmouth and by Grenville, which remained outside the ministry, or in opposition. The new prime minister, Portland, was aged, ill, and ineffective, scarcely ever attending either the treasury board or the cabinet: his major service was to lend the prestige of his name to a ministry the pretensions of whose various members might otherwise soon have dissolved it into discordant fragments.

Nearly half the cabinet were amiable nonentities. In the Lords the main defence of the administration fell upon the two practised debaters, Lord Eldon, the lord chancellor, and Lord Hawkesbury, soon to succeed as second Earl of Liverpool, who took the home office. The front bench in the Commons included one brilliant debater in Canning, who now moved into the foreign office. Neither of his chief associates carried his weight. Castlereagh at the war office was pedestrian in delivery though respected in the House for his cool common sense. Perceval at the exchequer up till this time had made his way as a professional lawyer, and in opposition had proved his great ability to speak from a brief, but now and for some time to come was disappointing in impromptu argument. A figure of eminence whom the ministers would have liked to recruit was Lord Wellesley, recently returned from his tour of duty as governor-general in India. For a variety of motives Wellesley hesitated and then declined. Old ties of friendship linked him to Grenville. On the issue of Catholic emancipation he sympathized with the Talents. But the crucial factor was that in March 1807 his conduct in India was about to come under attack from the nabob, James Paull, who saw himself as another Francis hunting down a second Warren Hastings. While Wellesley's three brothers accepted junior offices — Arthur, the future Duke of Wellington, in the role of chief secretary in Ireland — he himself stayed in the sidelines until finally accepting the post of envoy to the Spanish junta in the spring of 1809.

The main issues uniting the administration were the vigorous prosecution of the war and the protection of the king against pressure from the 'pro-Catholics'. Both Perceval, a narrow Evangelical, and Eldon, who in early life had trained for the ministry, were oppressed by a sense of the Protestant Church in danger and on principle were as adamant as George III himself in opposition to any concession to the Irish Catholics. Hawkesbury, Castlereagh and Canning, though accepting the expediency of this policy for the moment, were open to persuasion otherwise. Indeed Castlereagh had favoured Pitt's plans in 1800. Here were seeds of possible future dispute; but the chief potential source of disruption was the ambition of Canning, an eager and impatient politician, whose loyalties to his colleagues sat lightly upon him, and whose aspirations to leadership threatened conflict with Castlereagh and perhaps with Perceval. Meanwhile Canning's recruitment of a personal following in the Commons, eventually numbering about 17, portended further divisions among the friends of Pitt.

Although there was an unexpected upsurge of votes in favour of the new administration when it first faced the Commons, the ex-ministers could still deploy a powerful phalanx of over 200, and Portland and his colleagues wisely determined on a dissolution of the Parliament their opponents had managed at the elections of 1806. The general election of May 1807 in the popular constituencies turned largely on the Catholic issue and reflected popular prejudices dating back to Elizabeth I and to 1689. As a result several of Grey's supporters were ousted. More important, largely as a result of the ministry's dispositions in treasury and nomination boroughs, nearly 50 new party recruits of the Talents brought into Parliament for the first time in 1806 now lost their seats. Altogether the opposition strength in the House may have been cut by between 50 and 60. In the new Parliament the government carried the Address by 350 votes to 155.

Even so, Portland and his colleagues were in the vulnerable position of relying on independent support for decisive majorities in parliamentary divisions. For the fragmentation which had been overtaking British politics ever since Pitt's resignation in 1801 now reached its culminating phase, and the House of Commons presented a bewildering diversity of parties, groups, factions, and unattached members, comparable in many respects to the situations obtaining in the 1760s or the 1780s. To many contemporary observers the terms 'Whig' and 'Tory' seemed no more meaningful as political labels after 1807 than they had been earlier in George III's reign. Lines of cleavage over royal prerogative, Catholic emancipation, and parliamentary reform all cut at different angles across the spectrum of the House. No clear distinction between two sides was apparent save with respect to the rivalry for ministerial office. If the reconsolidation of the Foxite party after 1801 with some clear ideological basis justifies the description of the opposition after 1807 as a'Whig' party, then reservations have to be made about its newly engrafted Grenvillite component; and no such solidarity or intellectual bonding appears among the groups of politicians among whom the former followers of Pitt and Portland were now divided. These were professional politicians who saw their métier as government of the realm at the king's command and their duty as defence of the safety, integrity and prosperity of the state. Ministers in the Portland government referred to themselves not as Tories but as the 'Friends of Mr Pitt'. Portland's successor as prime minister, Spencer Perceval, never throughout his career accepted the label of Tory. Shortly after Perceval's death the members of the next administration firmly repudiated it. In a comment on opposition propaganda they pointed out to the Prince Regent:

> It is almost unnecessary to observe that the British Government had for more than a century been and could only be a Whig Government; and that the present administration is, as every administration in this country must necessarily be, a Whig administration. For a Whig Government means now, as it has all along meant, nothing else than a Government established by laws equally binding upon the King and the subject.[1]

Not all county members eschewed partisan loyalty, but the addition in 1801 of 64 Irish county representatives to the 80 sitting for English shires somewhat increased the proportion of men in the House of Commons who professed no party allegiance, and about 150 were genuine independents, who tended to avoid involvement in the in-fighting of the political factions and abstained from the divisions in which they clashed: it is noticeable that in the divisions on the highly partisan regency proposals of 1810−11, at least a third and often more of the House was absent. It seems probable that on a number of occasions after 1807 men in this group, though often helping to defeat the government on particular issues, nevertheless supported it in those crucial divisions in which its existence was at stake rather than let into office the Foxites and Grenvillites, whose political and constitutional positions they mistrusted or disliked.

Perhaps another 150 or so members constituted the increasingly amorphous party of court and administration, the 'floating trans-

---

[1] Ministerial memorandum, *The Letters of King George IV 1812−30*, ed. Arthur Aspinall (3 vols., Cambridge, 1938) I, p. 143.

ferable body' as one contemporary described it, which would form the core of any majority for an administration of the king's choice. Purgings of places and sinecures and the increasingly professional character of some of the under-secretaryships had reduced the place-holding element in this body since 1760. Apart from a few office-holders and courtiers it included a motley array of military officers, commercial men whose business interests led them to cultivate a connection with the government, country gentlemen interested in commanding the local resources of patronage which the treasury and other departments might make available, and relatives of peers whose courtly inclination drew them in this political direction. On all sides the real nature, and the advantage of this phalanx was recognized. To the more conservative-minded it guaranteed to the king 'the free and effectual use of his prerogative of appointing his own ministers' and (as in 1783–4) preserved that prerogative from the peremptory negative of a particular House of Commons.[2]

On the other hand the head of the opposition acknowledged in 1811 that the combination of the court votes with those of his party would provide a firm basis for governing if he were called to office.[3] Even so, the reliability of this element in the House was not what it had been. More of its members than at earlier times gave support through goodwill rather than a sense of obligation. And given the extent of independence claimed by many members, an administration could not presume too much on the support of the House. At the outset of Perceval's ministry the new premier found that while he could beat off an opposition motion of censure by 263 votes to 167, he could not prevent a vote for an inquiry into the Scheldt expedition from being carried against him by 195 votes to 186, nor block motions upon it making inevitable the resignation of a cabinet colleague, Lord Chatham, from the board of ordnance; nor was he able to get all his nominees elected to the House's investigatory committee on public expenditure.

After 1807 fragmentation seemed to have proceeded furthest among the 150 or so former friends of Pitt in the Commons. Apart from a main corps of about 100 rallied behind Perceval, Castlereagh, Canning, Hawkesbury and Eldon, which had turned out regularly to vote against the Talents, and which included some 15 who were to break away as a separate faction under Canning in October 1809, there were small groups led by Lord Melville, by Lord Wellesley — who was attributed a following of some 10 or 11 up until 1812 — and by Sidmouth, who commanded a well-drilled formation of

[2] John Ranby, *An Inquiry into the Supposed Increase of the Influence of the Crown* (1811), p. 39.
[3] Michael Roberts, *The Whig Party, 1807–1812* (1939), p. 226.

about 12 in the Commons and six or seven in the Lords. On the fringe of these groups stood on one hand the great independent borough mongers, Lord Lonsdale and the Duke of Rutland, each with seven or eight votes at command; and on the other the coherent but equally independent party of the 'Saints' led by William Wilberforce, whose six or seven votes and, still more, whose moral weight in the House no ministry dared ignore. The importance of the 'Saints' was such that when in 1812 a speaker's all-party conference was convened to consider a provision for Perceval's family they were allotted two of the 10 places on it.

The reunion of Pitt's party was periodically the preoccupation of various of its leading members; but there was no one commanding individual who could secure the loyalty of all its scattered bands, although Wellesley tried to cast himself in this role between 1810 and 1812. Canning was responsible for much of the difficulty. His sharp wit had bitten too deep into the nerves of the Sidmouth group after 1801, and their reconciliation in the same ministry proved impossible until after 1815. In 1808 Canning was at loggerheads with most of his colleagues in wanting to throw the generals to the wolves after the Convention of Cintra, and his disapproval of Castlereagh's management of the war in 1808 and 1809 involved him in intrigues for Castlereagh's removal which rent the cabinet and ended in turning its members decisively against him. It was not until after Perceval's death in 1812 that Lord Liverpool, with the quietly persistent support of the Prince Regent, was able to bring most of these divided fragments together, at the not excessive price of Wellesley's virtual retirement from active politics. With Canning out after 1809 the way was clear for the recruitment of Sidmouth in the spring of 1812, and Canning and his friends were reabsorbed into the old Pittite phalanx between 1814 and 1816.

One former Pittite section remained aloof up to and after 1815 — the family party led by Lord Grenville. After 1801 Grenville had driven the lines of cleavage too deep for conciliation, opposing Addington while Pitt still supported him in 1802—4, opposing Pitt himself in 1804—6, and coalescing with the Foxite opposition to form the Ministry of the Talents in 1806. Furthermore his stand upon Catholic emancipation made him *persona non grata* at court and thrust a barrier between him and such Pittites of 'Protestant' persuasion as Perceval and Eldon. Above all, Grenville's 'Catholic' policy and his co-operation in office with Fox's friends bound him in honour in a political alliance which he could not abandon, although in many respects it was satisfactory neither to his own group nor to his Whig allies.

Lord Grey as the political heir of Fox headed a party which, at first sight at least, seemed to have weathered with relative success the political strains of the early 1800s. It numbered over 150, comprising nearly a quarter of the House of Commons, and moreover prided itself on its social eminence — as the party newspaper, the *Morning Chronicle*, described it, 'a minority of 157 persons of the first consideration in point of landed property, as well as of political talents.' So large a party depended for its political cement upon intellectual convictions rather than personal and family connections; and a certain element of ideology gave it strengths but also weaknesses. It is easy to be cynical about 'Whig' party beliefs. Fox's colleague Robert Adair, in a memoir of one of the party's magnates a few years later, wrote:

> In his political principles, the Duke of Devonshire was a thorough Whig. With all due respect for the crown, he felt that the foundation of the Whig character is laid in a love for the liberties of the people. To support the crown in its lawful authority, he considered at all times to be proper and decorous, but he felt that his more immediate duty was to defend the people, and the popular part of the constitution . . . . He saw, therefore, the necessity of keeping the prerogative strictly within its limitations. Against the system of favouritism and exclusion with which the present reign commenced, and with little exception, has been continued, he uniformly set his face.[4]

This sounds little more than a claim that, despite lip-service to the role of the sovereign as head of the executive, he was not performing this role properly unless he chose and kept the Foxites in power. There were one or two more positive elements in party thinking, but its inherited ideas still led it disastrously in this direction in the 1800s, as had been the case ever since 1766.

The commitment to Catholic emancipation was a principal plank of policy on which the whole party was united, though this lost it support both at court and among the people at large. Economical reform remained a shibboleth of the party, but the more sober leaders realized little remained to be done in this field, and at the back of the agitation carried on by their less knowledgeable back-benchers lay irrational and unreal fears about 'the influence of the crown'. Should these fears drive the party to deny the participation of the crown in the political process, it would fly in the face of prevailing orthodox theory about the working of the constitution and was likely to line up a conservative majority of the politicians with the crown — as had happened in 1784 and to some extent in 1807. In theory the party was also committed to parliamentary reform, but here Grey was caught in the trap of his own past, rather as Fox had been in the 1790s. Faced with the enthusiasm of Samuel Whitbread and other Young Turks of the

---

[4] Quoted in A. D. Harvey, *Britain in the Early Nineteenth Century* (1978), p. 118.

party, who sought to catch in their sails the favourable breeze of popular agitation and deny it to such latter-day exponents of Painite radicalism as Sir Francis Burdett, Grey could not in honour and consistency entirely forswear the cause he had himself once embraced with youthful zeal. But the fire had long burnt out in him, and he had to consider the aristocratic stalwarts like Lansdowne on the right wing of the party, who would have been alienated by any threat of the destruction of their borough interests. The excesses of left-wing denunciation of governmental corruption, fuelling ignorant popular cynicism about the politicians as a class, alarmed the Foxite grandees who feared for the stability of the political system of which in general they approved. These strains weakened the unity of the party. Moreover, on this subject Grey was held in thrall by the events of the immediate past, for like Grenville he too was bound in honour by their recent ministerial alliance, which he valued for the additional strength which it brought to his party; and to countenance parliamentary reform would have disconcerted these ex-Pittite associates. The view has been put forward that the party might have gained ideological unity and consolidated itself had the Grenville connection been sloughed off, but in view of its internal differences on the reform question this seems unlikely. In any case neither Grey nor Grenville was prepared to contemplate such a step.

The opposition thus presented anything but a monolithic front and its parliamentary performance was often ineffectual. After Grey's succession to his father's peerage in November 1807 no charismatic or dynamic leader could be found in the Commons to draw together men of such divergent opinions. Grey's brother-in-law, Samuel Whitbread, had energy and drive but his radical sympathies made him unacceptable to both Grey and Grenville. The man selected, George Ponsonby, was an ineffectual compromise candidate, who found himself at the head of a team he could not drive. At the beginning of 1809 the party was in such disarray that it could not even produce an agreed amendment to the Address. Later that year Samuel Whitbread, increasingly impatient on the subject of parliamentary reform, virtually seceded, the main body declining to capitalize on the popular interest in reform which was beginning to show itself. Opposition weakness during this session was particularly advantageous to the Portland ministry, then vulnerable to attack over the Cintra Convention and itself falling into increasing disarray as a result of Canning's demands for the removal of Castlereagh from the war department.

If in these ways the opposition proved to be less effective than a first impression derived from its numerical strength would suggest, it suffered also from the weaknesses of its leaders and from its attitude towards the French war. Neither Grey nor Grenville felt that urgency of ambition to serve either their country or their own careers that would keep them in constant touch with events and ready to intervene. Too often they sought their country pleasures in the remoter provinces, Grey in Northumberland and Grenville in Cornwall. Neither was available, for instance, when the Convention of Cintra created a favourable chance to mount a very damaging attack upon the government.

More generally, the opposition's difficulty in dealing with the war was that they had an abject record themselves in 1806–7, and subsequently could produce no effective suggestions for war policy. Although temporarily swept up in the universal enthusiasm for the cause of national liberty in Spain and Portugal in 1808, they regarded defeat in the Peninsular theatre as inevitable. Relying overmuch on information from disgruntled army officers who had no grasp of Wellington's strategic appreciations or the solid grounds for his optimism, they gained no credit from annual prophecies of doom which were invariably disproved by events and which they continued to indulge right up to the triumph of Vitoria. Their criticism of the government's conduct of the war tended throughout to be sterile and defeatist, and the party suffered both internal disunity and public disapprobation from the circumstance that the left wing led by Whitbread still clung to the idealist view formerly urged by Fox, that the war was quite unjustified and that satisfactory terms of peace could easily be arranged. In February 1808 Whitbread insisted on proposing motions for peace in the Commons. He attracted 58 and 70 votes in divisions, figures which merely emphasized that a large proportion of the right wing of the opposition declined to support him, and its disarray was evident during the debate. The main body of the party, including its leaders, did accept that a continuation of the war was inevitable, but were wholly pessimistic about any effective British military intervention on the Continent. Grey and Grenville consequently destroyed their own credibility as leaders of an alternative war administration. This had two major effects. It led independent members in the Commons to withhold support for opposition motions even when the government was open to most damaging attack for fear of putting Grey and Grenville into office, enabling ministries which were often weak and embarrassed by failure to survive parliamentary criticism. And it lost Grey and Grenville the confidence of the Prince of Wales. Prince George led his own small political party which included one or two peers fairly closely in sympathy with the Foxites, but his leading crony in the Commons, Sheridan, was no longer favoured by them, and the prince's reliance on Sheridan for advice was a source of damaging jealousy.

Both the ideological and the personal cargo the opposition carried on board go far to explain the failure of its leaders to return to office under conditions which on the surface appeared far more favourable than those Fox had faced at any time between 1784 and 1801. Up to 1810, indeed, Grey and Grenville were targets of the king's dislike, but this obstacle disappeared with the start of the regency. And unlike Fox they confronted weak administrations rent by internal squabbles and deprived through various circumstances of important sections of former Pittite strength. It is therefore not surprising that on more than one occasion after 1807 the rank and file were not only disappointed but confused and puzzled at the failure to recover power.

II

Administration faced its first crisis in September 1809. The Duke of Portland fell mortally ill and was obliged to resign. Meanwhile he had failed to contain the intrigue Canning had been carrying on against Castlereagh and created a situation which terminated in their duel and the resignation of both. Canning's rivalry with Perceval for the leadership, his bad relations with Castlereagh, and the degree of prejudice against him engendered generally among the ministers by his recent intrigue, ruled out the possibility of a ministry headed either by himself or by a neutral peer, and yet without him the rump of the administration led by Perceval and Liverpool seemed hardly capable of survival.

In this situation these two ministers obtained the king's leave to approach Grey and Grenville with proposals for a broad-based coalition to carry on the war. They hoped that the legacy of tension over Catholic emancipation dating from 1807 might be brushed under the carpet in such a way as to avoid offending the susceptibilities of either George III or the opposition leaders. Grey however rejected this plan from the outset. His refusal may in part have reflected the traditional dislike of his party for coalitions and the desire to have complete control of administration; but it also seems likely that in 1809 he shrank from assuming responsibility for a war which he had no idea how to win. George III who had agreed to the offer of a coalition only with great reluctance, wishing to avoid receiving into office any men who would not give a firm commitment against emancipation, now relied on the remaining ministers to continue in office, and with the general consent of the cabinet Perceval became first lord of the treasury. The decision was a tribute to the strength of character, the determination, and the industry that Perceval had displayed during the years at the exchequer and as a leading spokesman for the administration in the Commons. At the exchequer and later at the treasury Perceval rose to his new responsibilities. He does not rank as a great prime minister, though he might have grown in stature had his fate allowed him a longer career, and he was no innovator. But he was a capable conductor of the nation's financial business and he showed a clear-sighted determination to support the war against Napoleonic hegemony. The king thought him 'the most straightforward man he had almost ever known.'[5] Though not a great orator he matured greatly as a debater and had the capacity to command the respect of the Commons, where, during his term as premier he had no superiors and few equals in debate. To the tasks of politics and statecraft he brought qualities of toughness, tenacity and integrity.

Canning's place at the foreign office was filled by Lord Wellesley. Over the past months Canning had cultivated a connection with Wellesley whom he had intended as Castlereagh's successor at the war office. But in the autumn of 1809 Wellesley's attachment did not extend to standing by the attempt of Canning to force himself into the office of prime minister on the ground that this post must be held in the House of Commons − a pretension that would have extinguished Wellesley's own. Wellesley's acceptance guaranteed a resolute pursuit of the war and the fullest possible backing for his younger brother, Wellington, in the Peninsula, but it soon created new tensions in the cabinet. On first taking office he assumed that he would be accepted as the dominating figure in the administration. As governor-general in India he had enjoyed autocratic power, and he did not bow willingly to the political exigencies of government by committee. He longed for great sweeping decisions: the details of administration were beneath his notice. His attendance at cabinet meetings was erratic, and at the foreign office he set an example of idleness and incompetence which shocked colleagues and subordinates alike. Lacking any appreciation of the problems of political and parliamentary management he resented as disloyalty to his brother the government's failure to pour unlimited resources into the Peninsular campaign. With similar obtuseness he resented the fact that it proved impossible during 1810 to draw in Canning, Castlereagh and Sidmouth together to strengthen the administration, and a contemptuous dislike of Perceval tempted him to seek any opportunity to replace him, in some grand design of reuniting all the dispersed forces

[5] Cited Denis Gray, *Spencer Perceval. The Evangelical Prime Minister* (Manchester, 1963) p. 463.

of Pitt's friends under his own leadership. These were castles in the air. With far greater realism Perceval analysed the precarious standing of the government towards the end of 1809: 'We are no longer the sole representatives of Mr. Pitt. The magic of that name is in a great degree dissolved, and the principle, on which we must rely to keep us together, and give us the assistance of floating strength, is the public sentiment of loyalty and attachment to the King. Amongst the independent part of the House, the country gentlemen, the representatives of popular boroughs, *we must find our saving strength or our destruction.*'[6]

The illness of George III at the end of 1810 created a situation which the opposition initially thought highly favourable to their pretensions. It was soon apparent there would have to be a regency. The Prince of Wales had old ties of personal friendship and political connection with Grey and his followers, and some of the prince's own personal political following had close links with them. The prince held Perceval in great dislike owing to the leading role the latter had taken in defending the Princess of Wales during the 'delicate investigation' of 1805–7. As regent he might well be expected to turn out the administration and bring in his friends. The prospects of office drew the party together. In particular Whitbread, who had been sedulously cultivating the leaders of the radical movement in Westminster, broke off his contacts with them and abandoned leadership of the crusade for parliamentary reform to his colleague Thomas Brand.

Between December 1810 and February 1811 the debates on the regency enabled the opposition to pose as champions of the prince's right to be regent without conditions. Perceval approached the question along exactly the lines set by Pitt in 1788–9, commencing with the passage of three resolutions in the Commons. The first declared that the king was incapacitated, the second that it was the duty of Parliament to provide a means of supplying the defect of the personal exercise of the royal authority. Both of these the opposition were prepared to accept. The third resolution stated that Parliament should establish a means for giving the royal assent to a Bill defining the manner in which the powers of the crown would be discharged during the king's illness. The Prince of Wales summoned his brothers to issue a joint protest against this procedure. The opposition argued that a Bill was unnecessary, and that the Prince of Wales should simply be invited to assume the regency by Addresses of the two Houses. But these views ran counter to those of many MPs regarding the august role of the legislature and Perceval had no difficulty in

---

[6] Cited, Gray, *Spencer Perceval*, p. 258.

securing approval for his policy by a crushing majority of 269 votes to 157. The subsequent Bill laid down that for a period of about 12 months the regent would be restrained from creating peerages, save in reward for military or naval services, and from granting offices in reversion or bestowing pensions. The queen assisted by a council was to have custody of the sick monarch. Only on a proposal that the queen should have the power of appointment over the whole royal household did Perceval overstep the mark. Castlereagh, Canning and others all condemned this proposal as an excessive reduction of the powers of the executive, and the transfer of about 20 votes to the other side together with abstentions by independents left the administration in a minority. Eventually the queen's powers of appointment were limited to those officers in immediate attendance upon the king.

Perceval's policy intensified the prince's hostility. Nevertheless as the Regency Bill approached its final stage at the end of January 1811, the opposition's prospects grew dim. In order to preserve the unity of his party Grey felt obliged to re-attach Whitbread with the offer of a cabinet post. Grenville deplored this yielding to the radical spirit, and would have preferred to leave Whitbread in the wings and recruit Canning. On this point Grenville's view chimed with that of the prince, but on another they did not — the prince was seriously offended by Grenville's opposition to the immediate reinstatement of the Duke of York as commander-in-chief. Towards the end of January Grey and Grenville fell out with the prince when the latter referred a draft of a speech to Sheridan for his advice. These frictions may have been factors contributing to the decision by the prince a few days later not to make any immediate change of administration, but his main reason was the news that his father seemed to be on the road to recovery. To jeopardize this return to health by placing in office a ministry the king disliked was a risk the prince clearly decided should not be taken and the leaders of the opposition fully concurred. But the position of Perceval and his colleagues was not a happy one, for they were generally regarded as a caretaker administration which would be removed whenever the prince and his friends thought it expedient. As the king's condition deteriorated sharply from May onwards and his death was more than once feared, they felt their situation increasingly insecure.

The decision which had thus been postponed came up for review early in 1812. The restrictions imposed by the Regency Act lapsed on 18 February and the possibility of George III's recovery now appeared remote. The ministry itself was rent with dissension, for Wellesley would not work with Perceval, and the rest of the cabinet, thoroughly disillusioned with Wellesley's performance at the foreign office, had no mind to accept him in the premiership at which he was now openly aiming. At the beginning of the year, in a plain bid for the regent's favour, Wellesley openly dissociated himself from his colleagues' opposition to the expensive financial proposals for the royal household on which the prince tried to insist. Perceval's demand for a more economic settlement of the household came on top of a series of wrangles during the past year over matters of patronage, which had periodically strained his relations with the regent.

Nevertheless by early 1812 the inclinations of the prince, which would be decisive in determining the continuance or the change of ministry, were less clear-cut than they had been at the end of 1810. To some extent he had grown accustomed to dealing with Perceval and understood the importance of his command of the House of Commons. His attitude towards another of his father's ministers, Lord Chancellor Eldon, whom he had regarded as an outright enemy, had undergone a complete reversal as a result of his perusal of his father's ministerial correspondence. Ministers had also given satisfaction early in 1811 by reinstating the Duke of York as commander-in-chief.[7] Moreover continued discussions throughout 1811 threw up difficulties in the way of switching power into the hands of the opposition and the prince's natural inertia disinclined him to grapple with them. The prince had a sentimental feeling for his old friends of the Foxite party, but he had none for Grenville, and he was out of sympathy with Grenville's extreme pessimism regarding the outcome of the Peninsular war. Then, although Grey had raised no objection to the Duke of York's reinstatement, Grenville had been unsympathetic, and some 40 of the wilder spirits in the party had cast their votes for a motion of protest. Nor by this time was the prince so inclined to concede to the Catholic claims over which both wings of the opposition were firmly committed. Twelve months of royal responsibility had wrought a change in his views.

It can be deduced that, throughout the second half of 1811, the prince hankered after a broadened and strengthened ministry, excluding Perceval and including his old Foxite friends and his personal followers, which would be as firmly committed to the war as the existing administration, and willing to postpone action on the Catholic question; and it gradually became clearer that neither Grey nor Grenville fitted well into such a scheme. In the spring of 1811 the prince had approved action taken by the Dublin administration to suppress the Irish Catholic Convention and he was angered and embarrassed when, early in 1812, the opposition pushed motions on the Irish question to a division in both Houses. A further ground of dissension had emerged during the summer of 1811, when the regent

[7] See p. 302 below.

supported the ministers in their resistance to opposition demands for an early resumption of cash payments.[8] By the beginning of January 1812 the regent was giving Perceval the most positive assurances that he would be retained in office, and it seems clear that the approach to the opposition leaders through the Duke of York which he launched early in February, in the form of an invitation to discuss broadening the administration, was in effect part of an elaborate charade, designed to save the face of the prince in his dealings with them but at the same time to create a situation in which the existing government would be strengthened by their refusal to serve. The prince's offer stressed his commitment to the Peninsular war, his wish for a coalition and, implicitly, his desire to have Grey but not Grenville. The opposition leaders resented the attempt to divide them. They declined these terms, and their declaration that they felt committed to the immediate introduction of a Catholic Relief Bill if they took office widened still further the gap between their position and that of the regent. In this situation the regent persuaded Perceval and his colleagues to broaden the possible basis of their 'Pittite' support by making Catholic emancipation an 'open question'. This cleared the way for the return to office of both the 'anti-Catholic' Sidmouth and his group on the one hand, and on the other of the 'pro-Catholic' Castlereagh, who took the foreign office when Wellesley resigned, finally thwarted in his hopes of heading a grand coalition.

The assassination of Perceval only three months later threw these arrangements into disarray. Initial plans for Liverpool to assume the premiership with the Sidmouthite Vansittart as his chancellor of the exchequer foundered when a back-bench sympathizer of Canning carried against the ministers an Address requesting the regent to establish a strong administration. The ministers had no option but to resign. During the next fortnight negotiations for the formation of a broad-based administration took place in the hands first of Wellesley and then of the prince's personal follower, Lord Moira. Once again, by setting reasonable but unacceptable conditions the regent manœuvred to ensure that Grey and Grenville excluded themselves from any new arrangement. Wellesley's unacceptability to the old ministers made it impossible for him to recruit a ministry from either side, and the way was clear within less than three weeks for Liverpool to reconstitute the government much as before, retaining the combination of Sidmouth and Castlereagh on the basis of *laissez-faire* as regards Catholic emancipation, and establishing an administration which Canning, the outstanding dissident, had no political grounds for opposing. Wellesley with very little personal following

[8] See pp. 296–7 below.

passed into ineffectual retirement. Canning, recognizing he no longer had any effective leverage to use for his faction's advantage disbanded it early in 1813, and the absorption of this group piecemeal into the administration during 1814 signalled the virtual reunification behind Liverpool of all the former Pittites except for Grenville's group. In September 1812 Liverpool took advantage of the military successes in the Peninsula, an excellent harvest, the dying down of violence in the industrial areas, and of a spell of quiet in Ireland, to strengthen his position by the election of a new parliament. His gains in the Commons were reckoned at nearly 60 — if this was an overestimate, still they were decisive enough — and some of the administration's most pertinacious critics — Brougham, Tierney, Curwen and Horner — lost their seats. During the next three years the collapse of the Napoleonic system and the triumph of the final European coalition against France ensured that his ministry would not face the parliamentary tribulations of its immediate predecessors and enabled it to become impregnably entrenched in power.

The story of the political manoeuvres of 1811 and 1812 makes plain the still essentially eighteenth-century character of the political system at the outset of the regency. The importance of the sovereign's will (or that of his deputy) in determining the choice of ministers was clearly recognized. No simple two-party confrontation as yet dominated the politics of Parliament. There was a general assumption that any combination of one or more of a number of different political factions or parties with the court group and a modicum of independent support would provide a majority for the government in the House of Commons. The exact nature of the successful combination would depend partly on the willingness of various politicians to work with each other and partly (within these constraints) upon royal decision. In the end, by a careful exploitation of stipulations and persons and policies, and perhaps with more dexterity than George III had ever displayed, the Prince Regent kept intact the royal prerogative of selecting ministers, and obtained what he wanted: a ministry committed to outright prosecution of the war and prepared to avoid raising the troublesome issues of Catholic emancipation or parliamentary reform.

III

An underlying factor in the survival of the fragile administrations of

1807 to 1812 and the impotence of the opposition was the relative inability of the latter to exploit popular feeling against the ministers.

The war occasioned Grey and Grenville embarrassment rather than opportunity. Although, as the Napoleonic continental system and American non-intercourse bit deep into the bases of British prosperity, stirring up a movement of petitioning for peace in the industrial districts among businessmen and craftsmen who had no capacity to weigh up the consequences for them of a Napoleonic world hegemony, the opposition leaders remained pessimistic about continental operations, nevertheless they knew that the war could not easily be abandoned and could only deplore the disunity created in their party ranks by the activities of its pacifist wing. In 1810 they seem to have misjudged the growing agitation in the industrial areas and assumed it was a protest against taxation which they might be able to exploit, whereas in reality it derived much more from the grinding effects of dislocation of trade. In fact they grossly underestimated the country's financial resources. After 1807 war expenditure began to soar into a new dimension, to which the more restricted operations of 1803–6 had not given rise, and which Grenville as head of the Talents ministry would not have contemplated as practicable. In 1807 on leaving office he believed a major continental campaign to be beyond the country's financial capacity, and this conviction continued to dictate his dismal forecasts up to 1812. In terms of strict orthodox financial principles he may have been correct. In practice he was proved utterly wrong. Although there was nothing very novel about Perceval's fiscal policy, he found it possible to raise hitherto unexampled proportions of war expenditure by taxation without damaging credit to the point at which he could not also float the loans he required. The country's capacity to pay had greatly increased. Whether Perceval, any more than anyone else, really understood the reason for this is doubtful, but in part it may be traced back to the forced abandonment of the gold standard in 1797. With the Bank of England no longer obliged to make 'cash payments' in gold on request, its bank notes had become in effect though not at law full legal tender. In that situation the effect of heavy war expenditure was to expand credit without the constraints imposed by an obligation to pay gold and to produce, more especially after 1807, a steady inflation which by 1811 had depreciated the paper pound by something like 20 per cent. Inflation on this scale was not so violent as to be damaging and it fostered economic development of every kind, aiding the economy to bear increased burdens of taxation.

By 1810 the opposition believed it had an issue to exploit. It secured a packed House of Commons bullion committee under the chairmanship of Francis Horner, which brought forward in the Commons in

1811 resolutions aimed at a resumption of cash payments by the Bank of England within two years. The economic repercussions of the committee's work were unfortunate: the mere rumour of its intentions may have contributed to commercial recession owing to the threat that a deflationary policy carried for future dealings. The implications for the conduct of the war were far more serious. Any gold and silver specie that came into the country was immediately required for the payment of forces abroad. Only by the continuance of the existing monetary policy could the government not merely maintain garrisons at numerous points overseas but also subsidize Austria, Portugal, Sicily, Sweden, and ultimately Russia and Prussia, finance such expeditions as those to Copenhagen and Walcheren, and support Wellington's lengthy and expensive campaigns in the Peninsula. When Horner and his colleagues demanded an early return to cash payments Perceval pointed out that such a policy would destroy the capacity of the country to fund the war. He recognized clearly that it was the large-scale foreign expenditure which had drained the country of specie and forced the Bank of England 'to supply the domestic deficiency in circulation' thus occasioned 'by a paper currency'.[9] In the House of Commons the force of his logic turned the scale. While accepting the theoretical soundness of the bullion report, the House agreed with the ministers that resumption of cash payments must be postponed until the end of the war. When a leading landowner, Lord King, threatened to torpedo this policy by demanding payment of rents in gold or in paper estimated at the value of gold and not at its face value, the government rapidly pushed through an Act which made banknotes a legal tender. The occasion was marked by a sharp clash between the opposition and the prince's party, the former opposing, the latter supporting the Act.

On the issue of Catholic emancipation, the opposition was wholly out of sympathy with popular feeling. Deplorable though the fact was for the development of the role of Ireland within the Union created in 1801, popular sentiment in England and Scotland showed itself overwhelmingly anti-Catholic at the general election of 1807; and though there was a deceptive slackening of the tension in the years that followed, the anti-Catholic outburst of 1829 revealed again the undercurrents of which the politicians had to be aware. The periodic re-emergence of the Catholic question at Westminster thus tended to strengthen the position of the administration. At the same time Grenville's tactical approach to it weakened the support given to the opposition in Ireland.

Seen from London Ireland presented two main issues: law and

---

[9] Gray, *Spencer Perceval* pp. 382–3.

order, and the Catholic question. As regards law and order, the Portland ministry took over a firm policy already outlined by the Talents and implemented it by pushing through Parliament the Insurrection Bill and Arms Bill which their predecessors had introduced. No points could be scored by the opposition against the government over this question. On the second issue Grenville and Grey were bound to the treadmill by their past conduct and by their statesmanlike appreciation of the Irish situation. In face of government hostility — of which the reduction of the Maynooth grant by £4,000 was a token symbol — the Irish Catholics gathered their forces to press more strongly for concession. They did so against an Irish background of swelling agitation for the abolition of church tithes and for repeal of the Union.

During 1808 the aristocratic element in the leadership of the Catholic Association sought Grenville's help in promoting a scheme of emancipation which might be made palatable to the British government by the inclusion of guarantees of the loyalty of the Irish Catholic clergy. They brought forward once again proposals which had been aired in 1800 for a form of royal veto on episcopal appointments. A petition drawn up on this basis was presented in the Commons by Grattan on 25 May. Perhaps predictably the results were unfortunate. Although the petition attracted substantial opposition support, as well as that of 40 of the Irish MPs, the government rallied an overwhelming vote of 281 against it. Meanwhile the Irish Catholics themselves fell into disarray over the veto and irresistible pressure from the laity against this proposal was brought to bear on the moderates among the Irish bishops. Since Grey and Grenville stood for the next three years unyieldingly by the policy of the veto, a wedge was driven between them and the Catholic Association. At the same time dissension grew among their followers as the more liberal elements, Whitbread, the Russells, and the Holland House circle, sought to free party policy from this constraint. At meetings held during 1810 to promote a further petition, the Irish Catholic laity again firmly rejected the veto, and the Irish bishops reaffirmed their sole right to ecclesiastical authority, although they did make the significant gesture of undertaking not to acknowledge the validity of any papal bulls so long as Pope Paul VII remained a captive of the French.

The establishment of the regency aroused new hopes in Ireland. The Prince of Wales was assumed still to hold the views of his old Foxite friends and he had indeed given innumerable past assurances of his sympathy for the Catholic claims. His close friends, Lord Moira, Lord Donoughmore, and Donoughmore's brother Lord Hutchinson, were all enthusiastic champions of emancipation:

Hutchinson regarded the prince as committed, 'over and over again'. The time seemed ripe for a new petition, and the leaders of the Catholic Association called for the election of delegates from the counties to a convention to prepare it. But this action fell foul of the Irish Convention Act of 1793. In a circular letter to magistrates the chief secretary prohibited the elections and ordered the arrest of anyone attempting to organize them. At Westminster his action was subsequently criticized on the technical ground that it should have been taken by proclamation, but in substance it was upheld, for by 1811 government circles were increasingly concerned about the way in which the Catholic Committee had been assuming something of the role of an Irish Catholic parliament.

Various consequences flowed from this crisis. Hostile feeling grew between the Catholic Committee and the Dublin administration, and at an aggregate meeting the young Irish barrister Daniel O'Connell carried a resolution for an address to the regent calling for the dismissal of both the chief secretary and the lord lieutenant. The Prince of Wales for his part took the administration's view about the need to maintain law and order in Ireland and was estranged both from his personal followers and from the opposition. On the other hand the crisis persuaded a number of open-minded ministerialists, notably Castlereagh and Canning (both then out of office), that emancipation would be preferable to a policy of repression likely to create a dangerous revolutionary situation in Ireland. The opposition was thus deprived of a distinguishing party characteristic: emancipation was no longer an opposition monopoly clearly demarcating them from their ministerial rivals. Although the full consequences of this development took some years to come to fruition, its significance was almost immediately apparent. When, on 22 June 1812, following the presentation of a further Catholic petition, Canning introduced a motion pledging the House of Commons to take the Catholic claims into consideration the following session, he triumphed easily, and Wellesley's parallel motion was lost by only one vote in the House of Lords. However deceptive the impression, the mood of the country seemed to be changing. In September 1812 the lord chancellor declared that, 'unless the country [would] express its sentiments on the Roman Catholic claim, and that tolerably strongly, between Dissenters, Methodists and Papists, the Church [was] gone.'[10]

Had Eldon been correct in his assessment of the situation the course of Anglo-Irish relations within the Union might have flowed more smoothly. His pessimism was matched by overweaning optimism on the part of the Catholics. On 30 April 1813 Grattan introduced a Bill

[10] Twiss, *Life of . . . Eldon* II, p. 225.

for removing all remaining civil and military disabilities from Roman
Catholic subjects and there were great hopes in Ireland that it would
be enacted. Canning struck the first discordant note, one highly
embarrassing to Grenville and also offensive to the Irish, by proposing
an amendment which would permit the crown, through the agency of
a commission, to exercise a veto on the appointment of bishops. But
the Bill suffered the *coup de grace* from a hostile motion for the exclusion of Catholics from Parliament which was carried by four votes in a
crowded chamber. 'Anti-Catholic' backwoodsmen had rallied in
sufficient numbers to tear the heart out of the Bill, and it was therefore abandoned. In face of this setback the very limited Catholic
Relief Act which ministry and opposition concurred in passing during
this session had little significance. This statute provided that a
Roman Catholic who held any civil or military office in Ireland under
the Irish Act of 1793, and who had taken the oaths required by that
Act, would not be liable in England, the Channel Islands, or on board
H.M. ships of war to any penalties under the Test Act of 1673 or any
other enactment imposing a test; and also that any Roman Catholic
holding a military commission within the terms of the 1793 Act would
not be liable to any penalties on receiving a higher commission in
Great Britain. These were substantially the proposals to which
George III had agreed during the first discussions of the Catholic
question by the Talents in 1807. The Act made no concession to Irish
Catholic claims to full emancipation: it did no more than eliminate
minor inconsistencies in the laws of the two constituent parts of the
United Kingdom. Up to, and after, 1815 Irish Catholicism remained
an unsatisfied and potentially revolutionary force.

Proposals for constitutional reform in one guise or another presented more difficult ground for the administrations of 1807–14 to
defend themselves in Parliament against opposition attack, and
afforded the opposition more hope to attract popular support; but
these issues also presented pitfalls for the opposition leaders.

Before the dismissal of the Talents the Foxite party had been drawn
by the initiative of a private member into action on 'economical
reform'. This was a touchy issue from the viewpoint of the
Grenvillites, the extent of whose sinecures was deplored by their
Foxite allies. Otherwise it provided relatively safe and acceptable
ground, and the prospect that financial waste in government could
somehow be eliminated and taxation thus eased had an irresistible
popular appeal. A House of Commons committee on public expenditure, packed with Foxite supporters, had been set up with a carefully
defined remit to look into the elimination of waste and corruption
provided action could be taken without detriment to the public
service. Popular concern made it impossible for the Portland ministry

to wind up this committee after it took office and in any case the ministers inherited the Pittite tradition of administrative reform. Inquiries continued but in a committee reconstituted to give roughly equal representation to government and opposition, and under the chairmanship of the highly respected independent Henry Bankes.

But, as the Talents' chancellor of the exchequer, Lord Henry Petty, had admitted on the first setting up of the committee, after the administrative reforms of the past 25 years little remained to be done, and this view appeared to be borne out by the committee's report of 1809 on places and sinecures held by members of parliament. This revealed that 76 MPs, from ministers downwards, held offices of some sort of the total annual value of £150,000. Many of these were efficient posts. Offices held at pleasure accounted for over £100,000. Twenty-eight members held sinecures or received pensions totalling £42,000. Since sinecures might sometimes be used to upgrade otherwise inadequate emoluments they were by no means indefensible. Little support was given to the desultory opposition campaign for their abolition, which dragged on until a Bill was thrown out by the Lords in 1812 and the small numbers voting in divisions reveal the indifference that prevailed on this issue in the House of Commons. When Whitbread in June 1809 raised the question of abolishing such offices still tenable with a seat in the Commons as the junior lordships of the various boards and the Welsh judgeships, his opposition colleague Petty declared there was no object to be served since the influence of the crown in the Commons had rather diminished than increased over recent years; and from the other side of the House Canning was able to make an effective defence for the survival of what remained.

The opposition were indeed impaled on the horns of a dilemma. Accepting, as they could hardly avoid doing, the truth of these arguments, they were forced to rest their traditional alarms about the dangerous growth of the influence of the crown upon a hostility to the growth of public establishments in general, especially of the armed forces and the increased revenue services which the war had generated for their upkeep. Some of them genuinely agonized over this issue. But on the other hand the leaders of opposition while in office during 1806–7 had cheerfully dispensed the patronage of the inflated establishments and they were clear-sighted enough to see that a reduction of these establishments was not compatible with a continuation of the war which, on the whole, they, though not all their followers, accepted as necessary and inevitable. Grey and Grenville seem also to have feared after 1807, that the sovereign was gaining control over patronage at the expense of the administration; but in this they were very wide of the mark, as the relations of Perceval and still more of Liverpool with the Prince Regent were in due course to show.

The former practice of granting offices in reversion came under much more unanimous criticism in Parliament after 1807 and the very readiness of ministers to abandon it deprived the opposition of any advantage from a crusade on the subject. Except in Ireland the practice had already largely been abandoned. Only two considerable British offices were held in reversion in 1807, and the annual sum involved, £35,000, was negligible in relation to the total annual expenditure. The Commons proved ready to pass a Bill abolishing the system in almost every session between 1807 and 1812, but these invariably fell in the House of Lords, where the voting revealed a clear distinction between the ministers, who supported the measure, and the members of the court party who were able to block it in defiance of the party politicians on both sides of the House. The most that reformers were able to achieve was a temporary enactment in March 1808 suspending grants in reversion until the beginning of 1810, followed by another similar Act in 1812. For much of the intervening period grants in reversion were halted by the provisions of the Regency Act of 1811.

Attacks upon corruption brought the opposition little political mileage, for either the cause was such that the administration would give cordial support, or else it produced confusion and division. Early in 1809 the political adventurer Colonel Wardle, MP, raked up against the Duke of York charges of conniving at the receipt of money by his mistress, Mrs Clarke, for her supposed influence in procuring commissions and forwarding claims to military promotion. Grey viewed the whole affair with distaste, and in the outcome his judgment was vindicated; but the back-benchers threw themselves hotly into the chase. The opposition had the initial mixed satisfaction of forcing the Duke to resign his office of commander-in-chief although seeing him cleared of charges of corruption by the House of Commons sitting as an investigating committee; but a subsequent squalid dispute between Wardle and Mrs Clarke brought to light that she had received considerable financial inducements from him and added to the impression that her testimony was not worth the breath with which it was uttered. The Duke's serious mistake was to have become entangled with her, and for that he paid with two years out of office. The chancellor of the exchequer himself took the initiative in dealing with the point of principle by steering through Parliament a Sales of Offices Prevention Act, which made it a penal offence to solicit money for procuring offices.

In the same session the independent country gentleman J.C. Curwen brought in a Bill for preventing the sale of parliamentary seats, which in substance merely carried further the principle of Perceval's Sales of Offices Act. Once Curwen had raised this matter legislation became unavoidable; for as the speaker trenchantly observed, to reject the Bill would have been virtually equivalent to legitimizing the evil it was intended to prevent. Again the ministers co-operated, and indeed so far took charge of the Bill by reshaping it with amendments that in its enacted form it was virtually a government measure. While Curwen himself and many Foxites regarded this Act as a foretaste of further essential reforms, the rift in the opposition was revealed when the Grenvillite Lord Temple supported it on the ground that it would make a general parliamentary reform less necessary. A further Foxite attempt to discredit Perceval and Castlereagh for insisting that an MP elected on the treasury interest should resign the seat if he intended to go into opposition backfired on its authors, and displayed the party in the worst possible state of disarray. The allegations were in fact untrue: the MP concerned had insisted upon following the prevailing convention. All the former members save one of the Talents administration voted against the motion of censure and were deserted in the division by 85 of their back-benchers.

The opposition were anything but united over parliamentary reform, but this question could not be ignored after the recrudescence of popular middle-class radicalism in the metropolis after 1806. This movement scored its first decisive success in Westminster at the general election of 1807 when the politics of the city underwent a veritable revolution. The dominance of the court and a few great ground landlords was overthrown, and the independent electors led by Francis Place and other members of the former London Corresponding Society secured the return of the independent radical politicians Sir Francis Burdett and Thomas Cochrane, RN. The Mrs Clarke scandal two years later propelled the movement into more positive action. There was such widespread belief in the Duke of York's guilt that his exoneration by the House of Commons was widely accepted as plain proof of its unrepresentative nature. When in March 1809 the members of the Westminster Committee led by Place and his friends held a meeting to vote thanks to Wardle for pressing his accusations against the Duke, they were supported both by Burdett and by Whitbread, who made a forthright declaration in favour of parliamentary reform. Over the same period a radical party led by Robert Waithman had gradually been acquiring power in the Common Council of the City of London, which on 6 April voted Wardle the freedom of the City in a gold box. A fortnight later, at a dinner meeting of the 'independent livery', Waithman called for a speedy and radical reform of the representation, and on 1 May the veteran reformer Major John Cartwright held the first of a series of dinner meetings at the Crown and Anchor tavern which attracted radical reformers from all over the metropolis and marked the return of parliamentary reform to the surface of popular politics. Cartwright was now acting in close collaboration with Sir Francis Burdett, and in June the latter outlined a plan of reform in the Commons, involving shorter (by which he meant annual) parliaments, equal constituencies, and a franchise embracing all freeholders, householders, and tax-payers, with polling in local centres to be completed within a single day. In a thin House at the end of the session the division, 15 for, 74 against, made plain Foxite distaste for such radical panaceas and the unlikelihood of any co-operation between them and the popular movement out of doors.

In February 1810 Burdett attacked the action of the House of Commons in imprisoning the radical agitator John Gale Jones for contempt of the House, and suffered the same penalty for his pains. This event provoked widespread rioting in the capital followed by an outbreak of agitation for reform. A deluge of petitions demanded the release of Burdett, and a number including those sent in from Middlesex, London, Westminster, Southwark, Worcester, Nottingham, Liverpool, Sheffield and Hull, demanded a reform of the representation. The opposition could no longer ignore the issue, but the leaders were hostile or apathetic, and it was left to one of Whitbread's close associates, Thomas Brand, to introduce in the Commons the first comprehensive Foxite plan of reform since 1797. A major object of Whitbread, Brand, and their friends was to seize the initiative from Burdett and the Westminster Committee and pre-empt the field against Painite demands for annual parliaments, equal constituencies and the delegacy of members of parliament. Brand outlined a scheme which was moderate and conservative in general intention. Rotten and pocket boroughs were to be eliminated and Brand, like Pitt in 1785, was prepared to consider schemes of compensation. He thought triennial parliaments should be restored. But he rejected the idea of equal electoral districts as throwing too much weight of representation to the great towns. His franchise proposals were distinctly modest, involving an extension of voting rights merely to a rather wider range of the propertied class — the county franchise to copyholders, who were not very numerous, the borough franchise to householders paying parochial and other taxes. A system of district polling centres was to be established — this was not a radical proposal but one that had actually briefly gone on to the statute book in the 1780s.

A hundred and fifteen MPs representing the main body of the old Foxite party voted for this scheme, but some of the Grenvillites opposed it — their group was hopelessly split in the division — and it was known that Grey refused to give his approval. Thereafter the reform cause languished. The mutual distrust between the Foxite reformers in Parliament and the democrats of Westminster was complete and attempts to salvage some sort of alliance merely emphasized their differences. When Brand sought to recruit a delegation from his party to join the Burdettites at a general conference on reform he encountered almost universal refusals and was threatened with desertion by his parliamentary colleagues. During 1811 and 1812 the extra-parliamentary reformers sought to open up a general public agitation through the Society of Friends to Parliamentary Reform, the Hampden Club, and the more extreme Union of Parliamentary Reform, and Cartwright set out on a proselytizing mission through the provinces. These developments coming on top of disorders in the industrial districts of the north and the east Midlands increased the fears of the Foxite grandees about the dangers of constitutional innovation. In 1812 Brand introduced in the Commons a second, much more moderate proposal for extending the vote to copyholders and transferring seats from nomination boroughs to counties, but on this occasion he could attract only 88 votes and was defeated by an overwhelming majority vote of over 200. Thereafter, as the popular movement gradually spread under the influence of Cartwright, Cobbett and other reformers, the members of the opposition in Parliament were too divided among themselves and too concerned with the last triumphant dramatic stages of the Napoleonic war to give further attention to the subject of reform.

13 Britain and Napoleon: The Final Phase 1807 – 1815

I

When the Portland ministry took office in the spring of 1807 its first concerns were the winding up of the 'Talents', two disastrous undertakings in Egypt and in the River Plate, and the improvement of the manning situation in the army, for Windham's idealistic schemes had done nothing to strengthen the military forces. The 'disposable force' which Castlereagh had formerly raised was down to 12,000 men and the pool of transports he had held ready had been dispersed. To get quick results, Castlereagh, on his return to the war office, secured the passage of a Militia Transfer Bill, under which militiamen were induced by a bounty of £10 to volunteer for the line. This measure temporarily wrecked the militia, though this was less serious in view of the strong coastal defences which now barred a renewal of any threat of invasion on the lines planned by the French in 1805. But it immediately added nearly 30,000 men to the regular army, making possible the raising of a striking force for overseas operations. In August Sir John Moore was ordered to Gibraltar with 7,000 troops as a mobile reserve, and reinforcements were sent to Sicily where, by early 1808, a force of 16,000 men was established. Castlereagh strengthened the home defences by reconstituting the Volunteers, later reorganizing them into a form of local militia nearly 200,000 strong, and the militia itself was recruited to 120,000.

This reorganization came too late to enable Britain to intervene in northern Europe before Napoleon had overwhelmed the Prussian and Russian armies at Friedland, but it provided resources to deal with the consequences of Napoleon's bargain with Tsar Alexander at Tilsit, which swung the Russians into the enemy camp. Napoleon immediately set in motion plans to gather up Russian, Swedish, Danish and Portuguese warships in pursuit of his designs against Britain. If the three Baltic fleets were added to the Dutch squadron at the Texel they could muster about 60 ships of the line, and the pressure on the British navy would become extreme. By late July the cabinet could see clearly that a resolution of the difficulty depended upon whether Britain or France struck first at Copenhagen. A combined expedition with 25,000 troops was launched across the North Sea, which forced a Danish surrender by bombarding the city and carried away most of the Danish ships of the line to the number of about 15, together with some 90 transports loaded with naval stores. This stroke encouraged the Swedes to stand out and ended the chance of a dangerous hostile naval combination in the Baltic. The tsar's declaration of war which followed in November was thus taken lightly and seen in London as coerced.

Be that as it might, the breach with Russia seemed to place the coping stone on the edifice of continental blockade which Napoleon had attempted to institute in November 1806 and which he proceeded to draw tight during the second half of 1807. The break with Denmark in July closed one important means of commercial access to north-west Germany. Further to the east, after September the Prussian authorities could no longer connive at the use of Memel by British vessels masquerading under foreign flags. To some extent Sweden remained open, and Gothenburg became a vital entrepôt for British exports, which continued their journey into the Baltic in the guise of neutral goods on neutral ships. However, by the latter part of 1807 the ever-tightening blockade was having two serious effects: causing a loss of freight to neutrals, and cutting British exports to Europe, especially the re-export trade in West India produce.

These circumstances led to a new departure in British maritime policy. Hitherto this had been aimed simply at cutting off contraband trade with enemy ports and all coastal traffic between enemy ports, including any entrusted to neutral ships. But by orders in council of November and December 1807 far more draconic sanctions were decreed. All harbours from which British ships were excluded were declared to be in a state of blockade. Any trade which was not carried on with Britain was interdicted. Neutral traffic with these harbours must pass through specific British ports, paying transit duties in the process. A prohibition was set on any French or French-allied trade direct with colonial or American destinations. A major purpose of the orders in council, and one which before long they had achieved, was to create general European discontent with the Napoleonic regime by the dislocation of European commerce. Shortages of sugar and other colonial products began to force up prices on the continental markets, whilst a glut of European commodities seeking overseas outlets soon developed. The economic incentive to sabotage French prohibitions on traffic with Britain steadily increased. At the same time neutrals were debarred from capturing the British carrying trade, and the new tariff system was intended to preserve a favourable cost margin for goods of British or British colonial origin forced on to the European markets. For much of 1808 Sweden provided a major path of entry for this traffic.

One particular consequence of this policy was denial to the merchant marine of the United States of direct access to the European Continent. The cabinet gambled on the assumption that, much as the government of the United States would resent this action, nevertheless on the principle of accepting half a loaf American commercial interests would insist on keeping open the commercial links with Britain, and through Britain with Europe. In the short run this assumption proved correct, although in the longer term, after 1810, it was to be defeated by the adroit diplomacy of Napoleon.

As the trade war intensified, the British government had to face the loss, though only temporarily, of access to the friendly anchorage of Lisbon. In the autumn of 1807 Napoleon's plans extended to a take-over of the Iberian Peninsula and the closure of its ports to British trade. On the last day of November a French army under Junot reached Lisbon and placed Portugal under the emperor's heel. However, one prize, the Portuguese fleet, eluded him, for on the urgent insistence of the local British resident and the naval commander, the Regent of Portugal betook himself and the fleet to Brazil. The émigré government granted the British naval facilities in Madeira, and during the same period British command at sea was further strengthened by the seizure of Danish Heligoland and the Danish West Indies.

In the spring of 1808 the ministry saw support for Sweden against Russia as its first priority, but an expedition of 12,000 men under Sir John Moore proved not to be welcome at Stockholm, and just as it sailed new, more favourable opportunities began to offer in the Peninsula. Napoleon's plan to set his brother on the throne of Spain provoked a nationalist rising, and in May Spanish envoys arrived in London appealing for support in money and weapons. Within weeks much of Portugal was also aflame.

Faced with these new developments, and concerned about the fate of the Spanish fleet, the cabinet's first option was direct military intervention in Spain, but when the Spanish suspiciously refused help of this kind, a military expedition under Arthur Wellesley landed at Mondego Bay south of Oporto and began an advance on Lisbon. Wellesley won a skirmish at Roliça and then a decisive defensive battle against the main French army of Portugal at Vimeiro, but his supersession by a senior commander on the morning of the battle prevented any exploitation of the victory. Nevertheless, Junot decided that his position was untenable. On 30 August the Convention of Cintra confirmed an armistice, the French troops were repatriated, and Portugal set free. By a separate agreement between the British naval commander off Lisbon and the Russian admiral Sinyavin, who had taken refuge there with nine ships of the line after withdrawing from the Mediterranean in the aftermath of the Tilsit agreement, the Russian force passed into British custody for the duration of hostilities. Meanwhile, the Spanish revolt carried over from the French to the British side the Spanish fleets at Cartagena and Cadiz and immobilized several French warships in the latter port. The change in the balance of forces was significant: had Napoleon during 1807 and 1808 been able to add the Russian, Portuguese and Spanish ships of the line to the vessels building in French and Dutch dockyards and at Antwerp, he could soon have mounted a formidable challenge to the British at sea within a few years of the battle of Trafalgar.

II

Thus opened a new theatre of the war, in which British troops, assisting Spanish and Portuguese allies, were directly to face and eventually to outfight Napoleon's armies and after five years to invade French soil. But the road to the crossing of the Bidassoa was tortuous both in military and political terms. Although the main British force in this theatre was eventually built up to a strength of nearly 60,000 men, it was never adequately equipped. The British government, harassed by financial stringencies, never came to terms with the need to match the generous French supply of light mobile field guns. Lack of artillery often forced Wellesley to offer battle from defensive positions, using reverse slopes which French guns could not command, and this weakened his offensive capacity. The lack of a properly trained engineering corps with siege equipment added greatly to the cost in manpower of reducing enemy fortresses. Transport had to be improvized, and until the last year of the campaigns in the Peninsula the army lacked sufficient pontoon bridging equipment. On a different level, relations with the allied governments were never easy. Portuguese politicians soon developed resentment against the commanding position that British leaders, and especially Wellesley, came to assume in their country, and the British for their part deplored the administrative mismanagement and corruption which undermined the fighting strength of the Portuguese army, part of which was taken into British pay. Spanish jealousies and suspicion were even more difficult to combat. Provincial commanders and juntas constantly squabbled between themselves and with the central junta at Seville (later at Cadiz), and their co-operation in providing supplies was almost worthless. Much of the resources the British poured in in the form of weapons and silver coin was wasted or lay unused. Nevertheless guerillas and provincial armies, which dispersed in face of French attacks only to rally again beyond the next mountain range, and which constantly harassed French communications, pinned down large French forces in northern, eastern, and later in southern Spain, and the interplay of British action in the west with that of the nationalist forces everywhere reduced French opportunities for a decisive military stroke.

In November 1808 the new commander in Portugal, Sir John Moore, moved into Spain with 20,000 men, intending to give support to the Spanish defences in the Ebro valley. Before he could reach Salamanca Napoleon, personally in command, had burst through the Spanish lines and rapidly marched upon Madrid. Moore's mission was thus ended before it had well begun, but he nevertheless hoped by rapid movement either to cut off and destroy a small French force advancing across northern Castile or at least to divert Napoleon's attention from southern Spain. He failed in the first object but achieved the second, and then successfully withdrew his army through mountainous Galicia to Coruna, whence it embarked for England. For the loss of about 8,000 men and of Moore himself a year had been gained for Spain, and a setback given to any French timetable for an attack on Portugal.

The year 1809 opened with British successes at sea and in the West Indies. Cayenne and French Guiana were occupied, and in February Martinique, one of the two most important French Caribbean islands, was taken. There followed in the summer a successful Anglo-Spanish invasion of San Domingo. The French privateering base in Senegal was captured. In April a daring raid on Aix Roads near Rochefort destroyed four French ships of the line and severely damaged another seven. In September the British hold on the eastern Mediterranean was extended by the occupation of four of the Dodecanese islands, with the object of denying them to the French and of establishing a defensive cordon to safeguard Turkey from French attack. This was virtually the last major action in the area east of Spain. Both France and Britain thereafter treated the Balkans and southern Italy as merely a side-show. British efforts were increasingly concentrated on the Peninsula and cuts were made in the resources allotted to the central Mediterranean command.

In April 1809 Arthur Wellesley returned as British commander-in-chief in Portugal. In May, after a brilliant engagement at Oporto, he bustled a French invading force under Soult back across the Galician

frontier less all its guns, ammunition and stores. Lured by the promise
of a series of converging attacks on the French forces round Madrid,
weakened by Napoleon in anticipation of the war soon to break out
between France and Austria, Wellesley then struck up the valley of
the Tagus well inside Spain. Bringing his 20,000 troops into a
junction with a Spanish army of over 30,000, he fought a successful
defensive action at Talavera, but was then forced to fall back in face
of superior numbers upon Badajos and the Portuguese frontier. For
the rest of the year he covered Portugal, and from his position at
Badajos checked any French move into southern Spain. For both sides
attention now temporarily swung eastwards to central Europe.
Austria's renewed defiance of Napoleon led to another campaign in
Germany, but the British government was not poised to give effective
help. It was therefore too late to aid Austria, when an improvised
force of some 40,000 men was launched on an expedition to
Walcheren, in the hope of diverting French troops northwards, destroying Napoleon's naval base at Antwerp, and perhaps raising a
Dutch revolt. None of these objectives was achieved, and the army's
losses by disease were compounded by the government's failure to
insist upon a prompt withdrawal. This mismanagement may have
been partly due to the disintegration during those weeks of Portland's
ministry.

III

Up until 1810, despite some measure of economic strain, the campaign of economic warfare unleashed by Napoleon by the Berlin
decrees and subsequent measures was far from causing the damage to
British commerce which he had expected. This was largely due to his
failure to sustain his policy. During 1807 there had been some
encouraging results, and British trade with Europe had been reduced
substantially. The quantity of goods that could be pushed into
northern Europe through Gothenburg and into a hostile Spain by way
of Gibraltar was strictly limited, and the French had a firm hold on
the ports of mainland Italy. Heligoland, seized from the Danes to be a
base for smuggling into north-west Germany was of little use so long as
the coasts between the Dutch and the Danish borders swarmed with
French customs officers and supporting troops. Although the route
into Russia by way of Archangel was beyond the reach of French

interference and Russian officials there did little to interfere with traffic, the difficult long land transit southwards from this port placed strict limitations on the extent of the trade it could handle. French action almost completely closed Portugal from December 1807 until the following autumn and strangled the British intercourse with northern Spain during the early months of 1808. An increase of trade with the Turkish empire by way of Malta, and the opening of commerce with Brazil by the émigré Portuguese government, did not provide any adequate compensation for the loss of trade with Europe.

In the first half of 1808 total British exports fell by about a quarter; but while this was sufficient to produce an incipient industrial depression, it could not alone be crippling. Traffic with Europe in any case formed only two fifths of Britain's overseas trade. No serious economic crisis could be induced by Napoleon's policy of continental blockade so long as the British could continue to trade with the overseas empire and the Far East, with Latin America and with the United States. Although relations with the United States were strained over the orders in council, and the government at Washington sought to put pressure on both Britain and France by non-importation and embargo, intended to hit their export trade and starve them of American produce, the American people had too great an appetite for English cheap woollens, cottons, metalwares, pottery, and salt, for this policy to be firmly applied at least for a time. In practice American policy tended to reinforce the effects of British policy against France.

But even such gains as French economic warfare had made up until mid 1808 were wiped out by the nationalist revolt in Spain and its consequences elsewhere in Europe. As Spain became a main theatre of war, the continental blockade, no longer the major object of Napoleon's unremitting personal attention, virtually collapsed. As French veterans were drawn towards Spain the subject peoples of Europe, hungry for British manufactures and tropical produce, and anxious to export their own, sought to sabotage the blockade in any way possible. The profits to be won offered an ample margin of inducement to local French officials who were often but too ready to be bribed. At Danzig the French consul was bought by a levy of 10 per cent *ad valorem* on imported cargoes. The growing defiance and eventual renewed military challenge to Napoleon from Austria prolonged this situation through 1809, and by the end of that year British trade was enjoying a modest boom. Heligoland became the centre of feverish activity as the French grip on the north-west German coast relaxed. The Duchy of Oldenburg came to be described as almost an English province. Substantial traffic entered the Prussian Baltic ports and, despite rather greater difficulties, the ports of Russia also,

British goods entering under various flags of convenience. In order to get essential supplies of grain into Norway, which was not self-sufficient, the Danish government was obliged to connive in a traffic under British licences involving imports of colonial produce in return for British purchases of timber. Commercial pressures in Holland, a French client kingdom under Napoleon's brother, Louis, forced open a traffic in which British manufactures were exchanged for Continental produce, including the Italian raw silk essential to sustain the British silk manufacture. Much of this commerce was brought to an end by the invasion of Walcheren, but so long as British forces held that island every endeavour was used to employ it as a base for a smuggling trade with adjacent Dutch territories. From the spring of 1809 Napoleon was even forced by the pressures of agricultural interests in western France to permit a substantial Anglo-French commerce operated under licences granted by the two governments. This opened a source of considerable grain imports which were badly needed in Britain owing to the poor harvest of 1809, and large quantities of wines and brandies were also accepted. In return the French admitted large consignments of drugs, chemicals, dyewoods, hides, codliver oil, and various metals, much of this being British re-exports of foreign or colonial produce. About one million pounds' worth of exports were sent to French and Belgian ports during the first half of 1810. Commerce with Spain and Portugal, although fluctuating with the course of the military campaigns, added significantly to British trade and economic resources. The Portuguese and Spanish empires in the New World remained a lucrative area for traffic. In February 1810 the conquest of Guadeloupe destroyed the last French privateering base in the West Indies and materially strengthened the British strategic and commercial position in that area.

Napoleon's policy, foiled in Spain, was also undermined by the resumption of Anglo-American trade early in 1809, as internal American pressures broke down the policy of embargo and non-importation. American ships bent the rules in every possible way. For a time much of the traffic was carried on by way of the Azores and Madeira, in order to evade the regulations prohibiting United States ships from touching at British (or French) ports, but Lisbon soon became a centre for their reception. Through these channels British merchants built up very substantial reserves of the cotton wool essential to the Lancashire spinning and weaving industry, and a large export trade in manufactured goods sustained the industrial boom until the opening weeks of 1811. But by that time the emperor's bid to throw the United States into conflict with Britain had begun to succeed. In 1810, in response to American pressure, he agreed to abrogate the Berlin and Milan decrees, on the understanding that the

British government would both revoke the orders in council and renounce its policy of blockade. While the first of these points was negotiable in London, the second was not, and in American eyes Britain thus appeared to blame for the continuance of the barriers to neutral trading which the United States government was anxious to remove. American economic sanctions began to be applied with renewed vigour, foreshadowing the actual clash of arms which was to occur in 1812.

Well before the end of 1810 Napoleon's efforts to reimpose the Continental blockade were beginning to take effect, and partly as a consequence 1811 and 1812 were bad years for the British economy. Once Austria had been crushed substantial French occupying forces were redeployed along the German coastline. The Dutch territories, hitherto nominally an independent state, were annexed to France in July 1810; so also, a little later, was the Duchy of Oldenburg. In October Napoleon decreed the destruction of British-owned goods found anywhere in territories under his control. In the Baltic ports that autumn some 240 ships with British cargoes were seized and their contents condemned. Trade with northern Europe virtually ground to a halt. Although there were some slight favourable portents, no one in early 1811 might have gauged their importance. Sweden was forced to declare war on Britain: nevertheless the Swedish authorities still connived at a small trickle of trade. Tensions between Napoleon and Alexander of Russia were still largely concealed, though sufficient rumours were afloat late in 1810 to encourage the cabinet in its determination to pursue the war. Napoleon's attempt to veto a Russian seizure of the Danubian principalities was not well received at St Petersburg. The French annexation of Oldenburg, ruled by the tsar's uncle, deeply irritated Alexander. Furthermore, his country's dependence on trade with the west, from which it acquired essential credit balances, led him in October to refuse to take more steps against British commerce in the Baltic. A year later, in December 1811, Russian economic difficulties led the tsar to impose heavy preferential tariffs directed against French goods reaching Russia overland – tax burdens not inflicted on goods arriving from foreign sources by sea. This was virtually a declaration of economic war upon France.

Meanwhile, repulsed in northern Europe, British merchants exercised all their ingenuity to penetrate the European trading area by other routes. Malta developed enormously as an entrepôt not merely for the Turkish trade, but for a traffic carried on by way of the Balkans and the Adriatic coast, through which British goods reached the Danube valley and Germany. Largely as a consequence of this enterprise, British trade with Europe as a whole was greater in 1811 than in the years 1806—8 and little less than in the years of uninterrupted traffic, 1803—5. In 1812 the trade rose above the much higher level which had been achieved in 1810. By this measure Napoleon's Continental blockade had clearly failed. Unless he could dictate to the whole of Europe this was inevitable.

IV

In the Iberian Peninsula during 1810 the British government had to face one of Napoleon's most formidable attempts to win such control. At the end of 1809 the collapse of Spanish resistance west of Madrid forced Wellesley (now Viscount Wellington) to fall back into Portugal and seriously to consider the possibility of evacuation. Manpower was a major problem. From the end of 1809 a British force was needed to help hold the French out of Cadiz, and there was only a limited pool of men on which to draw. But the difficulty was partially overcome. The thorough training of the Portuguese army, stiffened with a strong sprinkling of British officers, produced by mid 1810 an effective ancillary force of over 50,000 men. Local militia amounted to perhaps another 50,000. To these forces was entrusted the defence of the difficult mountainous northern approaches leading to Oporto. French difficulties in eastern Spain limited the power of the thrust they were able to mount against Portugal. That spring and summer partisans and local armies in Catalonia and Aragon, supported by units of the British Mediterranean fleet, were tying down nearly 90,000 French troops. Seventy thousand were bogged down in Andalusia, and others in the Galician mountains. Over 100,000 troops were required to maintain communications with France in the face of constant harassment by guerillas.

Less than 90,000 men therefore were available for the invading army led by Marshal Masséna, which broke through the frontier defences at Almeida at the end of August, and forced its way into central Portugal. Nevertheless, this was too superior a force for Wellington to hold back near the frontier. Masséna suffered a check when he attempted to smash through the Anglo-Portuguese army at Busaco — an action which showed the British-trained Portuguese troops that they could stand up to French veterans on level terms — but he was able by flanking actions to force a series of further withdrawals on Wellington, until at last the allied army reached positions on the impregnable defence lines of Torres Vedras thrown across the peninsula from the sea to the Tagus estuary north of Lisbon. Behind these defences, with the benefit of short supply lines, Wellington rested and reinforced his troops. In front of them Masséna maintained his army as well as he could off a land which had been partly laid waste, while disease and starvation took toll of his numbers. The Portuguese ancillaries in the north and Spanish guerillas operating east of the southern Portuguese frontier cut him off completely from communication with other French commanders, and in particular thwarted the attempt of Marshal Soult to mount a converging attack from Spain upon the lower Tagus. By March 1811 lack of supplies made Masséna's position no longer tenable, and he withdrew harassed by flanking movements by an Anglo-Portuguese force now more numerous than his own.

For the British in the Peninsula, the rest of 1811 was the year of battles for the control of the frontier fortresses, and although no decisive advance was made, the Portuguese frontier was safeguarded, and the war thus prolonged for another year. By this time the shadows of Napoleon's impending breach with Russia were already influencing operations, checking the flow of experienced reinforcements to the French armies in Spain. Spanish regular forces and partisans still posed a threat to the French in various provinces and tied down large numbers of troops in defence of the lines of communication leading west from the Bidassoa. As Napier described it, the war, spreading throughout the Peninsula, quivered 'like a spider's web to the most distant extremities if a drag was made at any point.' British warships helped the country people along the Catalan coast to evade French requisitioning parties, and in March 1811 a British force under Graham operating from Cadiz gave a smart check at Barossa to the French army operating in Estramadura. Along the north coast and especially in Galicia British supply vessels sustained guerilla forces on the flank of the major French supply line, while Wellington's operations between the Douro and the Tagus gave cover to the Galician partisans.

In March 1811 Spanish-held Badajos on the Guadiana was betrayed to the French, and an Anglo-Portuguese siege of it was begun, for while it remained in French hands Portugal was not secure, nor could Wellington safely engage upon any offensive movement into Spain. In April Wellington himself, entrenched at Fuentes de Onoro on the central front, undertook the siege of Almeida, the last enclave of Portuguese territory held by the French, and beat off Masséna's attempt to relieve it. In May Soult's efforts to relieve Badajos were beaten off by the Anglo-Portuguese army under the command of Beresford with heavy casualties on both sides at the battle of Albuera, but the following month the arrival of a greatly superior French force obliged Beresford and Wellington to abandon the siege.

In August Wellington took up a central position in the area between the rivers Coa and Agueda, south of the Douro. The build-up of British forces had continued steadily, and he now commanded a total of 80,000 men, 56,000 of them British. From this position, and with this force, on one hand he threatened the communications of French troops trying to subdue Galicia, on the other he put a curb upon the reinforcement of French armies trying to control southern Spain. But his immediate object was to stand poised for a quick attack at a favourable moment upon the Spanish frontier fortress of Ciudad Rodrigo. At the beginning of 1812 he seized his opportunity and within a fortnight the place was breached and taken by storm. At the end of March Badajos was similarly reduced. Both triumphs were bought at heavy cost, for his army was still deficient in siege equipment. But the two keys to Spain were now in his hands — the second won only weeks before Napoleon set out for Moscow on his fatal attempt to bring the tsar to heel.

Wellington's plan for the 1812 campaign was to strike east through northern Castile for Burgos and the Pyrennes, leaving French detachments in the south of Spain cut off from their base. By mid June he was in Salamanca with over 40,000 British and Portuguese troops and a supporting Spanish force of nearly equal strength. Four weeks later, after intricate and dangerous manœuvres, he caught the French relief force under Marmont off balance and destroyed it. The ripples of this first decisive allied victory in open battle spread wide. In Britain criticism of the war was stilled. Everywhere in Spain partisans took new heart. Secret negotiations between Joseph Bonaparte and the national cortes at Cadiz were abruptly ended. The road to Madrid was open, and in August Wellington cleared Joseph out of the Spanish capital. Although in the following months he found it impossible to corner the French army in the north of Spain or, for lack of proper siege equipment, to capture Burgos, he had imposed upon the French a general movement of withdrawal northwards which freed much of southern Spain from occupation. As the French armies drew together in the north their concentration proved too strong for him to face, and at the end of the year he was forced to fall back on his Portuguese supply lines at Ciudad Rodrigo. But the French could not both face him and hold Madrid, and although Joseph temporarily reoccupied his capital, Spanish nationalist forces pushing up from the south reclaimed it towards the end of the year.

For 1813, brushing aside suggestions that he should leave the Peninsula in order to lead a campaign in Holland or Germany,

Wellington planned a further campaign to clear the French out of Spain. The circumstances were now far more favourable. Thousands of Napoleon's veterans had been lost in Russia during the retreat from Moscow, any major reinforcement of the French forces in Spain was unlikely, the resources of large areas of the south were now at the disposal of the Spanish national government, and, not least, the confidence his achievements had inspired in the ministers and in Parliament meant that his demands for equipment at last received attention. Negotiations with the Spanish cortes led to an arrangement whereby 50,000 Spanish troops to be paid out of the British subsidies were to be placed under his full control; and the Spanish provincial commands were reorganized with the object of securing greater co-ordination of operations. New steps were taken to improve the effectiveness of his own forces. Tents and prefabricated hospitals were ordered out from England, to sustain the health of the troops and improve the treatment of the wounded, and he at last obtained a pontoon train.

As the allied preparations went forward, the French, weakened by the withdrawal of veterans to Russia the previous year and starved of reinforcements owing to Napoleon's commitment in Germany, were increasingly hampered by the actions of partisans. By April 40,000 guerillas were disrupting the main line of communication from Bayonne to Valladolid, and the north Spanish ports were becoming available to support British operations. That spring Wellington was co-ordinating the activities of some 200,000 allied troops, extending from Catalonia through central Spain to the Portuguese border, and thence arching round through the mountainous country to the northward, supported on both flanks by British sea power, and inclosing as it were in a loose sack the French armies, no longer superior in numbers, which still held the area of Old Castile.

His own main campaign started in May with a feint to mislead the French, one contingent of 30,000 men advancing north-east along the obvious route from Ciudad Rodrigo to Salamanca, while the main body, 60,000 strong, plunged into the difficult mountainous country further north, to emerge on the French flank north of the Douro. Outnumbered and outflanked the French fell back across Castile and over the Ebro until at last, late in June, they were cornered at Vitoria. From the battle which followed most of the French troops managed to make their escape to the border, but an enormous booty in money and military stores fell to the allies. About 5,000,000 dollars, all the pay for the French army, which had just arrived, passed into the hands of the allied forces, and for the most part was distributed 'unofficially'; only about 100,000 dollars reached Wellington's military chest. In Europe the effect of the French catastrophe was electric. The

Austrians who had been hesitating as to whether to engage once more in war to defeat Napoleonic hegemony at last abandoned their hedging policy, and in St Petersburg cathedral, for the first time in history, a *Te Deum* was sung for the triumph of a foreign army. The groundwork was laid for the grand European alliance for which British statesmen had long hoped, and for the last phase of the Napoleonic war.

V

Twelve months before the battle of Vitoria Great Britain had become the recipient of a declaration of war by the United States. Napoleon's policy towards the United States had thus succeeded, although the event came too late to restore the balance in his favour. His rescinding of the Berlin and Milan decrees contingent upon the British government abandoning the orders in council of 1807 swung the full weight of American diplomatic pressure against Britain, which now appeared to be solely responsible for the continued damaging interruption of American trade with Europe. By the spring of 1812 the patience of the statesmen in Washington reached breaking-point. Other counts were totted up against the British. For years there had been friction over the practice of British naval commanders pressing suspected British sailors out of American merchantmen. The outbreak of an Indian war in the area south of Lake Michigan was attributed to British influence operating from Montreal, and a strong western lobby called for the expulsion of the British from Canada. However, as the government was well aware, important sections of American opinion deplored an outbreak of hostilities. The New England states in particular opposed it, declined to mobilize their militia, and for some time after war was declared continued a substantial trade with Nova Scotia and New Brunswick. In the spring of 1812 the British government put too much faith in the influence of these more pacific forces in America, and not until too late did it decide to abandon the orders in council. Even a commitment to do so would not have cleared the air completely, since it continued to demand compliance with the 'rule of 1756', a point Napoleon had insisted must be given up during his negotiations with the Americans in 1810.

Once war began much of British North America remained neither molested nor threatened owing to the neutrality operated in practice by the New England states. Upper Canada was the area most exposed and was the prize that American 'hawks' had promised themselves, but the vigorous defence put up by General Isaac Brock in 1812 and the arrival of veterans from the war in Europe in 1814 ensured its safety. At sea American privateers inflicted considerable damage on British trade, but the overwhelming naval pressure the British were able to exert along the whole length of the American Atlantic coast wiped out American seaborne traffic and communications and gradually inclined the government in Washington to become more disposed to peace. A destructive raid on Washington in August 1814 underlined the British capacity to do serious damage.

During the war and through the negotiations leading up to the Treaty of Ghent of December 1814, eventually ratified by the American senate in 1815, Castlereagh and his colleagues remained determined not to give way over the 'rule of 1756'. For this reason they declined a Russian offer to mediate in 1813. In addition, at the beginning of the negotiations, the British cabinet bid high for the future protection of Upper Canada, demanding American agreement to an Indian reserve in the area south of the Great Lakes and various other boundary rectifications. It also sought abrogation of special rights conceded to the United States in the Newfoundland fisheries by the peace treaty of 1783. But these were bargaining points which the government was not in a sufficiently strong military position to sustain, and in the end the peace treaty registered a compromise. Existing boundaries were accepted, possible modifications being referred to discussion by special commissioners. The fisheries question was likewise postponed for further discussion in relation to British claims to access to the Mississippi from the Great Lakes. American claims for war damages were abandoned. Nothing was said about maritime rights: the British were content with a treaty which did not commit them to forego these in future, and since the war in Europe had ended they no longer constituted an immediate American grievance. Nor was there any reference to impressment. In fact, not a single one of the original causes of the war received any mention in the treaty of peace.

VI

In the spring of 1813 the all-absorbing concern of British diplomacy was the creation of a further great European coalition against Napoleon. In the first place Russia must, if possible, be kept in the ring; and when the Prussians threw in their lot with the Russians against France by the treaty of Kalisch in February, approaches were immediately also made to Berlin. Well in advance of any treaty commitments quantities of muskets began to be shipped for the armies of both powers. In March the government entered into an alliance with Sweden, offering a subsidy of one million pounds and recognizing Sweden's pretensions to Norway in return for a promise of 70,000 men. The two eastern monarchies were finally drawn into alliance in June by the treaties of Reichenbach. The British made credits of two millions sterling available, the tsar and the king of Prussia agreed to keep large armies in the field, and all the contracting powers undertook not to make a separate peace. Yet even as the treaties were signed, it appeared they might be dishonoured. Napoleon still remained in Germany in formidable force. Metternich, director of Austrian policy, appeared bent on avoiding war, and on his initiative a six-weeks' truce signed between Napoleon and the eastern powers was prolonged into August. Castlereagh's struggles to abort a compromise peace in eastern Europe were aided though by no means clinched by the news of Wellington's triumph at Vitoria. In despatch after despatch he reiterated the dangers of such a course. In a message to the tsar he pointed out, as a general warning to the continental powers:

Fatal would it be for them, and for the world, if they could for the moment think of seeking their safety in what is called a continental peace. . . . We may sink before the undivided power of France, and, if we do, Germany, and even Russia, will soon resume their fetters. We are protected against this evil by the obligations of good faith; but we are also protected against it by the plainest dictates of common sense. We have now got the bull close pinioned between us, and if either of us lets go our hold till we render him harmless, we shall deserve to suffer for it.[1]

Napoleon's intransigence defeated Metternich's hopes, and by August the Austrians also were committed to war against him. Castlereagh immediately guaranteed a subsidy of a million pounds, part of it in the form of arms, and an Anglo-Austrian alliance signed early in October bound the Austrians to maintain 150,000 men in the field and not to make a separate peace. Less than two weeks later, the great three-day engagement at Leipzig — the 'battle of the nations' — destroyed Napoleon's hold on Germany. Almost simultaneously Wellington's army on the Pyrenean frontier crossed the Bidassoa, captured Pampluna and forced its way into French territory.

[1] Quoted in C. K. Webster, *The Foreign Policy of Castlereagh, 1812–1815* (1931), p. 152.

In London there was now great anxiety lest the Continental powers should patch up a peace with Napoleon which would leave vital British interests in the Low Countries, the Peninsula, and elsewhere unsecured. In mid December, to ward off this possibility, the cabinet agreed to send Castlereagh to allied headquarters in Germany armed with full powers to negotiate. He was provided with firm guidelines on policy. The surrender by France of the southern Netherlands and of as much as possible of the German territories on the west bank of the Rhine annexed since 1790 was specified as the primary British objective. The independence of Portugal and Spain was essential, and the British commitments in the Peninsular war made any compromise on either impossible. In return the British would restore conquered French colonies, but only if an alliance were concluded between the four allied powers, which would guarantee post-war Europe from further attack by France. Castlereagh was thus committed to working for long-term harmony among the three eastern powers. This was to lead to a meeting of minds with Metternich, for the concern they shared about the intrusion of Russian power into western Europe helped to cement an understanding between these two statesmen which contributed powerfully to the ultimate establishment of a stable European settlement.

Between January and March 1814 Castlereagh was primarily engaged with the negotiations with the eastern powers which led up to the Treaty of Chaumont of March 1814. He got less by this treaty than he had hoped. Before it was concluded, he had to bargain away Britain's colonial assets against the undertaking of the other allied powers to reduce France to her ancient limits: to secure this conquered French colonies would have to be restored to France. Nothing was said at first about post-war guarantees of the settlement, and Castlereagh faced the question, whether he could use the bait of the British subsidies required for the forthcoming military campaign to make the allies guarantee the future settlement not only against France, but against one another. In the end, by the Treaty of Chaumont he obtained the first requirement but not the second. The treaty was in the first place a war alliance: all the signatories bound themselves each to maintain 150,000 men in the field till the war was won. Secondly, it guaranteed Europe against French aggression for a period of 20 years. This guarantee was worthless if the eastern powers were to fall out among themselves, but on this point Castlereagh could gain no more than undertakings to enter into future consultation.

Military operations on the eastern frontier of France continued during the period of these negotiations, and the brilliant defensive campaign fought by Napoleon during February helped Castlereagh to win agreement to the terms accepted at Chaumont. He insisted, strongly against the wishes of the tsar, that the allies should not undertake to impose a new regime on France. A channel of negotiation was kept open with Napoleon, but his stubbornness prevented any satisfactory agreement, and by the beginning of April the overwhelming military pressure of the eastern allies had resolved the question what was to happen to the existing government. Allied troops occupied Paris, Napoleon abdicated, and the Bourbons, in whose favour royalist movements had begun at Bordeaux and in Paris, were brought back with the very cordial support of the British ministry.

Castlereagh thus faced the prospect of shaping the details of a peace with Bourbon France before completing the wider European settlement on which the guarantee of it would turn. In general he favoured a generous policy towards France, not least in order not to associate the restored monarchy with national humiliation and so weaken its precarious hold. Therefore he did not object to the French keeping minor accessions of territory, but he insisted upon a retirement to the frontier of 1792, which meant the complete surrender of the southern Netherlands. Moreover, he also insisted, that the French should agree in the peace treaty to the union of these Belgian provinces with the kingdom of Holland, although this matter had not yet been settled with the other allied powers. In return the British restored all the French colonies except the strategically important West Indian islands of Tobago and St Lucia, and Mauritius, from which the French navy had been able to harass the supply routes of the East India Company. Castlereagh successfully fought off Prussian proposals for the exaction of a monetary indemnity from France, and for the sake of giving the restored Bourbon government a good start, it was even agreed that the French should keep the plundered art treasures which Napoleon had brought to Paris from all over Europe. On these terms the first Peace of Paris gave peace to France.

Would the powers stand together to enforce it? From May, when the peace was signed, and through the visit of the allied leaders to London in June, this remained Castlereagh's chief preoccupation. The shadows on the horizon derived partly from the fact that all three eastern powers had rival ambitions in Poland; and partly from the circumstance that Prussia coveted more territory in eastern Germany, and Austria, apprehensive about Prussian influence and military strength, was resolutely hostile to Prussian expansion in that quarter. Castlereagh, proceeding to Vienna in September on his second prolonged diplomatic assignment on the Continent, deplored the advance of Russian power into Poland. He wished to combine Austria and Prussia to resist it, but could not do so because of their conflicting ambitions in Germany and the tsar's assurances that he would back

Prussian claims. During the autumn this intractable problem was postponed in favour of less contentious issues. In Italy Castlereagh supported an arrangement, accepted by all the powers, that Austria should become the dominant and superintending power, with the object of putting a curb on the liberal ferment left behind by 18 years of French predominance. Ensconced in the Milanese and Venetia the Austrians provided a barrier against further French aggression, and the kingdom of Sardinia-Piedmont was strengthened in its role as a forward buffer state by the acquisition of Genoa. Meanwhile the British had made their own peace with the enlarged Netherlands state, withdrawing from the Dutch East Indies, and retaining only Ceylon, trading centres in Guiana, and the staging post to India at the Cape of Good Hope. In return the Dutch received a payment of two million pounds, to be spent on fortifying their new frontier with France.

By November 1814 the diplomatic exchanges at Vienna had made it clear that Russia blocked the satisfaction of Prussian aspirations to territory in Poland, and that Prussian demands for the whole of Saxony as 'compensation' threatened a complete breach between the German powers. Castlereagh faced the extinction of his plan for a common European front against future French aggression. He was also afraid that, as he put it, 'through the contentions of Austria and Prussia, the supremacy of Russia would be established in all directions and upon every question',[2] and he feared that this would react unfavourably on the completion of the settlement about the United Netherlands, the eastern frontier of which had not yet been fixed. Despite the extreme reluctance of the cabinet in London, he began to move towards the idea of a combination with France in support of Austria. Indeed, the French now had the opportunity to resume a position of equality among the great powers, and Talleyrand, in charge of French foreign affairs, seized it at once. In mid December he proposed to Castlereagh a triple alliance with Austria. The latter held off till the last moment, but after a Prussian hint of war over Saxony on 31 December, he accepted the proposal, and on 3 January he signed the agreement, justifying it to his colleagues in London on the ground that it was the most likely step to prevent a war over Saxony. The weight he carried at Vienna in making this move was greatly increased by the conclusion in December of the Treaty of Ghent ending the war with the United States, and his argument proved absolutely correct. The triple alliance opened the way to a very complete and rapid settlement of all outstanding questions in central Europe during the early weeks of 1815. Prussia received a

[2] Webster, *Foreign Policy of Castlereagh*, p. 350.

minor concession from the tsar in northern Poland. More important, a large block of German territory on the lower Rhine was allotted to the Prussians, and in return they agreed to be content with a portion only of Saxony. This arrangement implemented the ideas of Pitt in 1805, refurbished by Castlereagh, that Prussia should be established in western Germany as part of the cordon against any future threat from France. Britain's client state, Hanover, received various minor accessions of territory, and its status as a kingdom was recognized. British possession of Malta and of the Ionian islands was accepted. The whole vast rearrangement of boundaries involved in these and other agreements was embodied in one bulky diplomatic instrument, the Treaty of Vienna, which was signed in June 1815 by all the interested powers.

Before this European settlement was completed, or the permanent alliance sought by Castlereagh in guarantee of it had been achieved, Napoleon made his bid to recover power, and the forces of the nations associated in the Treaty of Chaumont had to be mobilized once again. The main shock was taken in Belgium by the polyglot army of British, Dutch and west German troops hastily collected under the command of Wellington and the Prussian army under Blucher, which held and destroyed Napoleon's last army in the Waterloo campaign; and the fact that neither the Austrians nor the Russians had been involved greatly strengthened the hands of Castlereagh and the British government in shaping the peace which followed. Castlereagh exerted his influence to secure a second moderate peace with France. He and Wellington intervened to check the plundering and depredations of the Prussian and other German forces, and all demands by the German states for cessions of territory on the eastern frontier of France were strongly resisted. In the end the French losses were confined to the Saar, Savoy, Landau, and one or two small rectifications on the Belgian frontier, but they were now required to pay a heavy indemnity, return all plundered art treasures, and accept an army of occupation in the north-eastern districts for a limited period. This last course was adopted on the prompting of Castlereagh as a measure for solving the immediate problem of security without dismembering France on an extensive scale — the last thing he wanted, as it would have laid the seeds of future wars and also have made it much more difficult for the legitimist Bourbon government to establish itself. On these terms the second Treaty of Paris ended the state of war with France in November 1815.

On the same day Austria, Britain, Prussia and Russia signed the Quadruple Alliance of 1815. This completed the edifice of international security which Castlereagh had sought to create for the past two years. The signatories bound themselves for 20 years to maintain the peace settlement against any attempt on the part of France to overthrow it and to exclude the Napoleonic dynasty from the French throne. Principally on Castlereagh's insistence, and contrary to the wishes of the tsar, the four powers did not undertake to perpetuate the restored Bourbon monarchy. If the French should wish hereafter to change their system of government, so be it, so long as such a revolution did not threaten the general peace – this the powers would watch. The Quadruple Alliance did not only guarantee the general European territorial settlement agreed in June as the final act of the Vienna Congress; it included – here once again the hand of Castlereagh was seen – the famous clause six, which bound the contracting parties to meet periodically in conference to consult on measures for achieving their common interests and the maintenance of European peace. Despite the considerable isolationist sentiment in Britain, the logic of 22 years' struggle against French ascendancy dictated the assumption of a binding commitment and of engagements for future consultation to safeguard the preservation of the post-war order.

Bibliography

Abbreviations

AHR   *American Historical Review*
BIHR   *Bulletin of the Institute of Historical Research*
EHR   *English Historical Review*
EconHR *Economic History Review*, 2nd series
HJ   *Historical Journal*
J   *Journal*
SHR   *Scottish Historical Review*
TRHS   *Transactions of the Royal Historical Society*
Place of publication is London unless otherwise stated.

Bibliographies

The fullest guides are S. Pargellis and D.J. Medley, *Bibliography of British History. The Eighteenth Century, 1714–1789* (Oxford, 1951) and Lucy M. Brown and Ian R. Christie, *Bibliography of British History, 1789–1851* (Oxford, 1977). The former gives little listing of literature published after 1939: it can best be supplemented up to 1964 from the series *Writings on British History* – two vols. on 1940–5, compiled by A.T. Milne (1960), and further volumes by D.J. Munro, J.M. Sims, Heather D. Creaton, and others (1973–7); thereafter from the *Annual Bulletin of Historical Literature* published by the Historical Association, and for 1975 onwards from the *Annual Bibliography of British and Irish History*, edited by G.R. Elton for the Royal Historical Society (1976, in progress). There is a copious guide to the literature on the American Revolution in Lawrence Henry Gipson, *The British Empire before the American Revolution*, volume XIV: *A Bibliographical Guide to the History of the British Empire, 1748–1776* (New York, 1969). W.H. Chaloner and R.C. Richardson, *British Economic and Social History. A Bibliographical Guide* (Manchester, 1976), is excellent.

Documentary Collections

English Historical Documents, 1714–1783, edited by D.B. Horn and Mary Ransome (1957) and *English Historical Documents, 1783–1832*, edited by A. Aspinall and E.A. Smith (1959), provide general selections of documents and good bibliographies. Best on the constitution is E. Neville Williams, *The Eighteenth-Century Constitution, 1688–1815. Documents and Commentary* (Cambridge, 1960), which can be usefully supplemented from W.C. Costin and J. Steven Watson, *The Law and Working of the Constitution* (2 vols., 1952).

General Histories and Biographies

J. Steven Watson, *The Reign of George III, 1760–1815* (1960), in the Oxford History of England, gives full treatment from slightly different perspectives. Other recommended histories include, John B. Owen, *The Eighteenth Century, 1714–1815* (1974), Dorothy Marshall, *Eighteenth Century England* [1714–1784] (1962) and Asa Briggs, *The Age of Improvement* [1784–1867] (1959). The period is well served with biographies of major political figures, which should be consulted as appropriate in supplementation of the chapter bibliographies below: John Brooke, *King George III* (1972), S. Ayling, *George the Third* (1972); Reed Browning, *The Duke of Newcastle* (1975); A.F. Basil Williams, *The Life of William Pitt, Earl of Chatham* (2 vols., 1915), Brian Tunstall, *William Pitt, Earl of Chatham* (1938); Ross J.S. Hoffman, *The Marquis. A Study of Lord Rockingham, 1730–1782* (New York, 1973); P.D.G. Thomas, *Lord North* (1976); John Norris, *Shelburne and Reform* (1963); John Holland Rose, *William Pitt and National Revival* [to 1791] and *William Pitt and the Great War* (1911); John Ehrman, *The Younger Pitt. The Years of Acclaim* [to 1789] (1969) – two more volumes of this study are in progress; Cyril Matheson, *The Life of Henry Dundas, first Viscount Melville* (1933); John W. Derry, *Charles James Fox* (1972); G.M. Trevelyan, *Lord Grey of the Reform Bill* (1920); Leslie Mitchell, *Holland House* (1980), on the 3rd Lord Holland and his circle; Philip Ziegler, *Addington. A life of Henry Addington, first Viscount Sidmouth* (1965); Denis Gray, *Spencer Perceval, 1762–1812, the Evangelical Prime Minister* (Manchester, 1963); C.J. Bartlett, *Castlereagh* (1966); W. Hinde, *George Canning* (1973). Lord Liverpool, the prime minister, lacks a good modern biography, and there is none for either George Grenville or his son William, Lord Grenville: in both cases work is now in progress. For the political careers of minor figures who were in the House of Commons, see Namier and Brooke (below, 2).

1   The Nation and its Wealth 1760–1780

The discussion about population growth is summarized in M.W. Flinn, *British Population Growth, 1700–1850* (1970). The most recent highly technical, detailed treatment is E.A. Wrigley and R.S. Schofield, *The Population History of England 1541–1871: a Reconstruction* (1981). See also the essays collected in *Population in Industrialization*, edited by Michael Drake (1969), and *Land, Labour and Population in the Industrial Revolution: Essays Presented to J.D. Chambers*, edited by E.L. Jones and G.E. Mingay (1967). J.D. Chambers and G.E. Mingay, *The Agricultural Revolution, 1750–1880* (1966) provides an excellent summary, and its brief treatment of Scotland is supplemented by J.E. Handley, *Scottish Farming in the eighteenth century* (1953) and *The Agricultural Revolution in Scotland* (1963). For the role of the landowners in improvement in England, see also G.E. Mingay, *English Landed Society in the eighteenth century* (1963). The development of communications is treated in William Albert, *The Turnpike Road System* (Cambridge, 1972), J.R. Ward, *The Financing of Canal Building in eighteenth-century England* (1974), the various works on canals by C. Hadfield, and Ralph Davis, *The Rise of the British Shipping Industry in the seventeenth and eighteenth centuries* (1962). T.S. Ashton, *The Industrial Revolution* (1948) is an admirable introduction to its subject. P. Mantoux, *The Industrial Revolution in the eighteenth century* (English translation by Marjorie Vernon, 1928) remains a classic. There is also a good general account in Peter Mathias, *The First Industrial Nation: an Economic History of Britain, 1700–1914* (1969). Literature on the causes of industrialization is discussed in M.W. Flinn, *The Origins of the Industrial Revolution* (1966), and other contributions of particular interest are: Phyllis Deane, *The First Industrial Revolution* (1965); Ralph Davis, *The Industrial Revolution and British Overseas Trade* (Leicester, 1979), and D.E.C. Eversley, 'The Home Market and Economic Growth in England, 1750–1780', in E.L. Jones and G.E. Mingay, *Land, Labour and Population*, cited above. There is excellent treatment of industrialization in Scotland in Henry Hamilton, *The Industrial Revolution in Scotland* (Oxford, 1932), and *An Economic History of Scotland in the eighteenth century* (Oxford, 1963). The subject also requires to be followed through the histories of particular industries, notably: T.S. Ashton, *Iron and Steel in the Industrial Revolution* (Manchester, 1924); A.P. Wadsworth and Julia De Lacy Mann, *The Cotton Trade and Industrial Lancashire, 1600–1780* (Manchester, 1931); N.B. Harte, 'The Rise of Protection and the English Linen Trade, 1690–1790', in *Textile History and Economic History: Essays in honour of Miss Julia De Lacy Mann*, edited by N.B. Harte and K.G. Ponting (Manchester, 1973); R.G. Wilson, 'The Supremacy of the Yorkshire Cloth Industry in the eighteenth century', *ibid*. Information about the silk industry is available in the rather antiquarian work, *The Silk Industry of the United Kingdom. Its Origin and Development*, by Sir Frank Warner (1921). On the Potteries see N. McKendrick, 'Josiah Wedgwood, an eighteenth-century entrepreneur in salesmanship and marketing techniques', *EconHR* XII (1959–60). The general role of science and technology is discussed in A.E. Musson and E. Robinson, *Science and Technology in the Industrial Revolution* (Manchester, 1969), and the beginnings of the chemical industry in A. and N.D. Clow, *The Chemical Revolution* (1952).

2 State and Church

The best treatment of the concept of 'mixed monarchy' in this period is to be found in chapters III and IV of Corinne C. Weston, *English Constitutional Theory and the House of Lords, 1556–1832* (1965), and suggestive points are made in Betty Kemp, *King and Commons, 1660–1832* (1957). For George III's ideas and performance of his role the biography by John Brooke (above) is indispensable, and there is much useful material in Richard Pares, *King George III and the Politicians* (1953). On the king's relations with ministers see Ian R. Christie, 'The Cabinet in the reign of George III to 1790', in his *Myth and Reality in late eighteenth-century British Politics and other papers* (1970), and A. Aspinall, 'The Cabinet Council, 1783–1835', *Proceedings of the British Academy* XXXVIII (1952). The general character of the administration is treated in the early chapters of Emmeline W. Cohen, *The Growth of the British Civil Service, 1780–1939* (1941), and there are valuable studies of various departments: Henry Roseveare, *The Treasury. The Evolution of a British Institution* (1969); R.R. Nelson, *The Home Office, 1782–1801* (Durham, N.C., 1977); C.R. Middleton, *The Administration of British Foreign Policy, 1782–1846* (Durham, N.C., 1977); Margaret M. Spector, *The American Department of the British Government, 1768–1782* (New York, 1940); D.M. Young, *The Colonial Office in the early nineteenth century* (1961). The series *Office-Holders in Modern Britain*, compiled by J.C. Sainty and J.M. Collinge (1972, in progress), includes material on office organization, and information about reforms will be found in J.E.D. Binney, *British Public Finance and Administration, 1774–1792* (1958). The role of senior officials is discussed in Franklin B. Wickwire, 'King's Friends, Civil Servants or Politicians', *AHR* XXI (1965).

The standard work on the House of Lords is by A.S. Turberville – *The House of Lords in the eighteenth century* (Oxford, 1927) and *The House of Lords in the Age of Reform, 1784–1837* (1958). Michael McCahill, *Order and Equipoise. The Peerage and the House of Lords, 1783–1806* (1978) provides some important revisions. See also J.C. Sainty, 'The origin of the leadership in the House of Lords', *BIHR* XLVII (1974), and his *The Origin of the Office of Chairman of Committees in the House of Lords* (House of Lords Record Office Memorandum no. 52, 1974). At present the History of Parliament has only completed part of its survey of the House of Commons for this period: Sir Lewis Namier and John Brooke, *The History of Parliament. The House of Commons, 1754–1790* (3 vols., 1964), provides detail on constituencies, short political biographies of MPs, and some general analysis of the representative system and the membership. Jerrit P. Judd IV, *Members of Parliament, 1734–1832* (1972) provides some materials for analysis over a longer period. E. and A.G. Porritt, *The Unreformed House of Commons* (2 vols., Cambridge, 1903–9) is still standard, though supplemented at many points by recent research: for the position about 1760 Sir Lewis Namier, *The Structure of Politics at the accession of George III* (rev. edn., 1957) remains indispensable. For the working of the House see P.D.G. Thomas, *The House of Commons in the eighteenth century* (Oxford, 1971), and Sheila Lambert, *Bills and Acts. Legislative Procedure in eighteenth-century England* (Cambridge, 1971). A.S. Foord, *His Majesty's Opposition, 1714–1830* (Oxford, 1964) is a stimulating presentation of materials, which provokes further reflections. Oppositions have been discussed as 'Whigs' in Frank O'Gorman, *The Rise of Party in England. The Rockingham Whigs, 1760–1782* (1975), L.G. Mitchell, *Charles James Fox and the Disintegration of the Whig Party, 1782–1794* (1971), D.E. Ginter (ed.), *Whig Organization in the General Election of 1790* (Berkeley, 1967), and Michael Roberts, *The Whig Party, 1807–1812* (1939). A more sceptical opinion about party descriptions is introduced in Ian R. Christie, 'Was there a "New Toryism" in the earlier part of George III's reign?' in his *Myth and Reality* (above), and the present treatment is in broad terms a projection of this view. See also the slightly different analysis by J.C.D. Clark, 'A General Theory of Party, Opposition and Government, 1688–1832', *HJ* XXIII (1980).

On the Church of England Norman Sykes, *Church and State in England in the eighteenth century* (Cambridge, 1934) is standard, and can be supplemented for the later years covered by this chapter from E.R. Norman, *Church and Society in England, 1770–1970* (Oxford, 1976), and R.A. Soloway, *Prelates and People; ecclesiastical social thought in England, 1783–1852* (1969). For the rewarding nature of local studies in this field, see Diana McClatchey, *Oxfordshire Clergy, 1777–1869. A study of the Established Church and the Role of its Clergy in local Society* (Oxford, 1960), and Arthur Warne, *Church and Society in eighteenth-century Devon* (Newton Abbot, 1969). J.H. Overton, *The Evangelical Revival in the eighteenth century* (1886) is a classic, but needs supplementation: see Leonard Elliot-Binns, *The Evangelical Movement in the English Church* (1928); John Venn, *Annals of a Clerical Family* (1904), and E.M. Howse, *Saints in*

Politics (1952). There is considerable discussion of religious attitudes, from a sceptic's viewpoint, in Leslie Stephen, *English Thought in the eighteenth century* (Harbinger edn., 2 vols., 1962): evangelicalism, especially but not exclusively in connection with John Wesley, is given a sympathetic and penetrating treatment in R.A. Knox, *Enthusiasm. A chapter in the history of religion with special reference to the seventeenth and eighteenth centuries* (Oxford, 1950).

Two recent works, both dense but worth close examination, deal with the general questions of interaction between the Church of England, Methodism and dissent: A.D. Gilbert, *Religion and Society in Industrial England. Church, Chapel and Social Change, 1740–1914* (1976), and W.R. Ward, *Religion and Society in England, 1790–1850* (1972). An older work, E.D. Bebb, *Nonconformity and Social and Economic Life, 1660–1800* (1935) is also worth consulting. There is excellent treatment of the character and growth of Methodism in *A History of the Methodist Church in Great Britain*, edited by Rupert E. Davies and E.G. Rupp (2 vols., 1965–78). F. Baker, *John Wesley and the Church of England* (1970) is an important treatment of its theme; and for various aspects of the Methodist movement see M.L. Edwards, *After Wesley. A study of the social and political influence of Methodism in the middle period, 1791–1849* (1935); E.R. Taylor, *Methodism and Politics, 1791–1851* (Cambridge, 1935); R.F. Wearmouth, *Methodism and the working-class movements of England, 1800–1850* (1937); and Bernard Semmel, *The Methodist Revolution* (1974).

Although slightly old-fashioned, H.W. Clark, *History of English Nonconformity* (2 vols., 1911–13), volume II, provides an admirable survey. The history of particular denominations may be followed in A.C. Underwood, *A history of the English Baptists* (1947), R. Tudur Jones, *Congregationalism in England, 1662–1962* (1962), and C.G. Bolam and others, *The English Presbyterians* (1968). The revival of Roman Catholicism in England is traced in exhaustive detail in B.N. Ward, *The Dawn of the Catholic Revival in England, 1781–1803* (2 vols., 1909), and *The Eve of Catholic Emancipation* (3 vols., 1911–12). The slightly romantic tone requires correction from the excellent modern study by John Bossy, *The English Catholic Community, 1750–1850* (Cambridge, 1975). E.I. Watkin, *Roman Catholicism in England from the Reformation to 1950* (1957) provides a general introduction.

Andrew L. Drummond and James Bulloch, *The Scottish Church, 1688–1843: The Age of the Moderates* (1973) provides a valuable survey with attention to the social background. A fuller though in some respects old-fashioned narrative is provided by volume 4 of George Grub, *An Ecclesiastical History of Scotland from the Introduction of Christianity to the present time* (4 vols., 1861), which includes an account of the fortunes of the Episcopal Church. Additional material for the Highlands may be found in John MacInnes, *The Evangelical Movements in the Highlands of Scotland, 1688–1800* (Aberdeen, 1951). For further consideration of the role of the Moderates, see Ian D.L. Clark, 'From Protest to Reaction: The Moderate Regime in the Church of Scotland, 1752–1805', in *Scotland in the Age of Improvement: Essays in Scottish History in the eighteenth century*, edited by N.T. Phillipson and Rosalind Mitchison (Edinburgh, 1970); and J.J. Cater, 'The Making of Principal Robertson in 1762. Politics and the University of Edinburgh in the second half of the eighteenth century', *SHR* XLIX (1970). Scottish Catholic history is traced in volume 4 of

Alphons Bellesheim, *History of the Catholic Church of Scotland*, transl. by
D.O. Hunter Blair (4 vols., Edinburgh, 1887–90).

3   From Bute to North: Safety Abroad and Order at Home

Z.E. Rashed, *The Peace of Paris, 1763* (Liverpool, 1951) is a meticulous
account of the negotiations and their outcome. The introduction and
documents in *The Fourth Earl of Sandwich: Diplomatic Correspondence,
1763–1765*, edited by Frank Spencer (Manchester, 1961), throw light on
diplomacy during the Grenville ministry, especially in relation to the
northern courts, a subject also treated in Michael F. Metcalf, *Russia,
England and Swedish Party Politics, 1762–1766* (Stockholm, 1977). The
northern theme is also traced in Michael Roberts, *Splendid Isolation,
1763–1770* (Reading, 1970), and 'Great Britain, Denmark and Russia,
1763–1770', in *Studies in Diplomatic History: Essays in memory of David
Bayne Horn*, edited by Ragnhild Hatton and M.S. Anderson (1970); H.M.
Scott, 'Great Britain, Poland and the Russian Alliance', *HJ* XIX (1976). See
also Michael Roberts, *Macartney in Russia*, supplement 7 to *EHR* (1974).
British relations with France after 1763 have been treated from the French
side in J.F. Ramsey, *Anglo-French Relations, 1763–1770: a study of
Choiseul's foreign policy* (Berkeley, Calif., 1939). Nicholas Tracy has
examined the British angle on a number of issues: 'The gunboat diplomacy
of the government of George Grenville, 1764–5', *HJ* XVII (1974); 'The
administration of the Duke of Grafton and the French invasion of Corsica',
Eighteenth Century Studies VIII (1974–5); 'The Falkland Islands crisis of
1770: Use of Naval Force', *EHR* XC (1975). The Falkland Islands crisis is
examined in detail in J.L. Goebel, *The Struggle for the Falkland Islands: a
study in legal and diplomatic history* (New Haven, 1927).

George III's role in the domestic politics of the 1760s is detailed in the biography by Brooke (above), and his own statements of his attitudes to men
and affairs appear *in extenso* in *Letters from George III to the Earl of Bute*,
edited by Romney Sedgwick (1939). Leading studies of politics include Sir
Lewis Namier, *England in the Age of the American Revolution* (revd. edn.,
1961); John Brewer, *Party Ideology and Popular Politics at the Accession of
George III* (Cambridge, 1976); Paul Langford, *The First Rockingham
Administration, 1765–1766* (1973); John Brooke, *The Chatham Adminis-
tration, 1766–1768* (1956). Some aspects of the domestic politics of the
Grenville ministry are treated in the introduction to *Additional Grenville
Papers*, edited by John Tomlinson (Manchester, 1962). John Brewer's inter-
pretations are further developed in two articles: 'The Misfortunes of Lord
Bute: A Case-Study in Eighteenth-century Political Argument and Public
Opinion', and 'Rockingham, Burke and Whig Political Argument', *HJ* XVI
(1973) and XVIII (1975). The Duke of Grafton's own account in *Auto-
biography and Political Correspondence of Augustus Henry, third Duke of
Grafton*, edited by Sir William R. Anson (1898), is selective but still of value.
The Letters of Junius, edited by John Cannon (Oxford, 1978), makes these
political polemics readily available.

Horace Bleackley, *Life of John Wilkes* (1917) still remains the best biography. The issue of general warrants is best followed in M.A. Thomson,
The Secretaries of State (Oxford, 1932). The best general account of the
Wilkite movement is G.F.E. Rudé, *Wilkes and Liberty: a Social Study of
1763 to 1774* (1962), which should be read together with the important
reassessment in John Brewer, 'The Wilkites and the Law, 1763–74', in *An*

Ungovernable People, edited by John Brewer and John Styles (1980). The Wilkites' championing of freedom of parliamentary reporting is discussed in two papers by P.D.G. Thomas: 'The Beginning of Parliamentary Reporting in Newspapers, 1768–1774', *EHR* LXXIV (1955), and 'John Wilkes and the Freedom of the Press (1771)', *BIHR* XXXIII (1960). There are good accounts of radical thought in Caroline Robbins, *The Eighteenth-Century Commonwealthman* (Cambridge, Mass., 1959), and Colin Bonwick, *English Radicals and the American Revolution* (Chapel Hill,· N.C., 1977).

4 Imperial Problems in British Politics 1760–1773

P.J. Marshall, *Problems of Empire: Britain and India, 1757–1813* (1968) contains a valuable introductory survey and a collection of documents. British enterprise in south and south-east Asia receives stimulating treatment in V.T. Harlow, *The Founding of the Second British Empire, 1763–1793* (2 vols., 1952–64). *The Cambridge History of India*, volume 5: *British India, 1497–1858*, edited by H.H. Dodwell (Cambridge, 1929), is a standard outline account. The career of Clive is best followed in Sir George William Forrest, *The Life of Lord Clive* (2 vols., 1918), and modern scholarship on the career of Warren Hastings is well summarized in the biography by Keith Feiling (1954). Lucy S. Sutherland, *The East India Company in eighteenth-century Politics* (Oxford, 1952) is indispensable, with full detail on the years 1760–83.

There is a vast literature on the American colonies on the eve of the American Revolution, and it is not possible to give more than limited guidance. Lawrence Henry Gipson, *The British Empire before the American Revolution* (15 vols., New York, 1936–70), volumes X to XII, gives a valuable survey, and provides a full bibliography in volume XIV. Ian R. Christie and Benjamin W. Labaree, *Empire or Independence, 1760–1776* (New York, 1976), is an attempt to pull together some of the more recent scholarship. More detailed studies dealing with British policy include T.C. Barrow, *Trade and Empire: The British Customs Service in Colonial America, 1660–1775* (Camb., Mass., 1967); O.M. Dickerson, *The Navigation Acts and the American Revolution* (Philadelphia, 1951); M.G. Kammen, *A Rope of Sand: The Colonial Agents, British Politics, and the American Revolution* (Ithaca, New York, 1968); Langford, *First Rockingham Administration* (above); John Shy, *Toward Lexington: The role of the British Army in the Coming of the American Revolution* (Princeton, N.J., 1965); J.M. Sosin, *Agents and Merchants: British Colonial Policy and the Origins of the American Revolution, 1763–1775* (Lincoln, Neb., 1965), and *Whitehall and the Wilderness: The Middle West in British Colonial Politics, 1760–1775* (Lincoln, Neb., 1961); P.D.G. Thomas, *British Politics and the Stamp Act Crisis* (Oxford, 1975). Among leading works on reactions in the colonies are Bernard Bailyn, *The Ideological Origins of the American Revolution* (Camb., Mass., 1967); Joseph A. Ernst, *Money and Politics in America, 1755–1775* (Chapel Hill, N.C., 1973); Jack P. Greene, *The Quest for Power: The Lower Houses of Assembly in the Southern Royal Colonies, 1689–1776* (Chapel Hill, N.C., 1963); Pauline Maier, *From Resistance to Revolution: Colonial Radicals and the Development of American Opposition to Great Britain, 1765–1776* (New York, 1972); Edmund S. and Helen M. Morgan, *The Stamp Act Crisis: Prologue to Revolution* (Chapel Hill, N.C., 1953); A.M. Schlesinger, *The Colonial Merchants and the American Revolution, 1763–1776* (New York, 1918), and *Prelude to Independence: The Newspaper War on Britain, 1764—1776* (New York, 1958).

R.B. McDowell, *Ireland in the Age of Imperialism and Revolution, 1760—1801* (Oxford, 1979) is a first-class standard account. Edith M. Johnston, *Great Britain and Ireland, 1760—1800* (Edinburgh, 1963) is particularly strong for constitutional and administrative relationships. M.R. O'Connell, *Irish Politics and Social Conflict in the age of the American Revolution* (Philadelphia, 1965) brings important issues into focus. F.G. James, *Ireland in the Empire, 1688—1770* (Camb., Mass., 1973) provides useful perspectives. For views of the Irish economy, see G. O'Brien, *The Economic History of Ireland in the eighteenth century* (1918), and L.M. Cullen, *Anglo-Irish Trade, 1660—1800* (Manchester, 1968). W.E.H. Lecky's classic, *A History of Ireland in the eighteenth century* (5 vols., 1892) can still be consulted with profit.

5   The Loss of America

Bernard Donoughue, *British Politics and the American Revolution: The Path to War, 1773—1775* (1964) provides a detailed account of British reactions to the Boston Tea Party. The course of the war is traced from the British viewpoint in Piers Mackesy, *The War for America, 1775—1783* (1964), and there is good material on policy and direction during the first three years in Gerald Saxon Brown, *The American Secretary: The Colonial Policy of Lord George Germain, 1775—1778* (Ann Arbor, Mich., 1963). The activities of the British commanders have been considered in, Troyer Steele Anderson, *The Command of the Howe Brothers during the American Revolution* (New York, 1936); W.B. Willcox, *Portrait of a General: Sir Henry Clinton in the War of Independence* (New York, 1964); Franklin and Mary Wickwire, *Cornwallis: The American Adventure* (Boston, Mass., 1970). For the administrative and logistical difficulties of the British forces see David Syrett, *Shipping and the American War, 1775—1783* (1970); Norman Baker, *Government and Contractors: The British Treasury and War Supplies, 1775—1783* (1971); R.A. Bowler, *Logistics and the Failure of the British Army in America, 1775—1783* (Princeton, 1975). Military affairs are well treated from the American viewpoint in J.R. Alden, *The American Revolution, 1775—1783* (1954), and Don Higginbotham *The War of American Independence: Military Attitudes, Policies and Practice, 1763—1789* (1971). Eric Robson, *The American Revolution* (1955), and John Shy, *A People Numerous and Armed: Reflections on the Military Struggle for American Independence* (New York, 1976), raise important points of interpretation. The problem of the role of the Loyalists is treated in Paul H. Smith, *Loyalists and Redcoats: A Study in British Revolutionary Policy* (1965). There has been less specialized examination of naval operations since the publication of A.T. Mahan, *Major Operations of the Navies in the American War of Independence* (Boston, Mass., 1913). More recent writings include William Bell Clark, *George Washington's Navy* (Baton Rouge, Louisiana, 1960), A Temple Patterson, *The Other Armada: The Franco-Spanish Attempt to Invade Britain in 1779* (Manchester, 1960), and two articles by David Syrett: 'Lord George Germain and the Protection of Military Storeships, 1775—1778' and 'The Organization of British Trade Convoys during the American War', in *Mariner's Mirror* 60 (1974) and 62 (1976). Samuel Flagg Bemis, *The Diplomacy of the American Revolution* (2nd edn., 1957) is indispensable for background on this subject, though not orientated to a close examination of British policy. Isabel de Madariaga, *Britain, Russia and the Armed Neutrality: Sir James Harris's mission to St. Petersburg during the American Revolution* (1962), covering the years 1778–82, is an excellent contribution to a largely neglected field.

On the affairs of India during the American War see bibliography to chapter 4.

6 The Years of Crisis

Sir Herbert Butterfield, *George III, Lord North and the People, 1779–1780* (1949) is a detailed study, and parliamentary politics from the general election of 1780 to the fall of North are traced in Ian R. Christie, *The End of North's Ministry, 1780–1782* (1958); several of the same author's papers in his *Myth and Reality in late eighteenth-century British Politics* (above, 2) bear on points of detail. Also of interest is N.C. Phillips, 'The British General Election of 1780. A Vortex of Politics', *Political Science* (Wellington, New Zealand) XI (1959). Events of the next two years are discussed in John Cannon, *The Fox – North Coalition. Crisis of the Constitution, 1782–4* (Cambridge, 1969), and in the opening chapters of L.G. Mitchell, *Fox and the Whig Party* (above, 2). Reference should also be made to biographies of leading politicians listed above.

The county association movement is fully discussed in Ian R. Christie, *Wilkes, Wyvill and Reform. The Parliamentary Reform Movement in British Politics, 1760–1785* (1962); and see also: Sir Herbert Butterfield, 'The Yorkshire Association and the Crisis of 1779–80', *TRHS*, 4th series XXIX (1947); N.C. Phillips, 'Burke and the County Movement', *EHR* LXXVI (1961) and 'County against Court: Christopher Wyvill, a Yorkshire Champion', *Yorkshire Archaeological J* XL (1959–60) and *Yorkshire and English National Politics, 1783–1784* (Christchurch, New Zealand, 1961). Radical associations are also examined in chapters 2 and 3 of E.C. Black, *The Association. British Extra-parliamentary Political Organization, 1769–1793* (Cambridge, Mass., 1963). Paul Kelly, 'Radicalism and Public Opinion in the General Election of 1784', and 'British Politics, 1783–4: The Emergence and Triumph of the Younger Pitt's Administration', *BIHR* XLV (1972) and LIV (1981) add some detail on the downfall of the Fox – North coalition.

For the course of Irish affairs see the works by McDowell, Johnson and O'Connell (above, 4).

R.B. Morris, *The Peacemakers. The Great Powers and American Independence* (New York, 1965) is detailed but one-sided. There is no full study from the British side, but V.T. Harlow gives good treatment of Shelburne's diplomacy in volume I of *The Founding of the Second British Empire* (above, 4).

7 The Sinews of Recovery

Most of the works listed in the bibliography to chapter 1 are relevant, but need supplementing from the following:

F. Crouzet, *L'Economie Britannique et le Blocus Continental (1806–1813)* (2 vols., Paris, 1958) is indispensable. G.E. Mingay, *Enclosure and the small farmer in the age of the Industrial Revolution* (1968) re-examines an important theme; see also A.H. John, 'Farming in Wartime, 1793–1815', in E.L. Jones and G.E. Mingay (above, 1). For economic development in the Scottish Highlands and Islands, see Malcolm Gray, *The Highland Economy, 1750–1850* (1957), and the impassioned account in John Prebble, *The Highland Clearances* (1963). Further aspects of the iron industry are examined in A. Birch, *Economic History of the British Iron and Steel Industry, 1784–1879* (1967). A.E. Musson and E. Robinson discuss 'The Early Growth of Steam Power', in *EconHR* XI (1958–9). Michael M. Edwards, *The Growth of the British Cotton Trade, 1780–1815* (Manchester, 1967) is indispensable, and can be supplemented from S.D. Chapman, 'Fixed Capital Formation in the British Cotton Industry, 1770–1815', *EconHR* XXIII (1970–1), and *The Cotton Industry in the Industrial Revolution* (1972). Phyllis Deane, 'The output of the British Woollen Industry in the eighteenth century', *J of Economic History* XVII (1957), provides useful statistical estimates; and see D.T. Jenkins, 'Early Factory Developments in the West Riding, 1770–1850', in *Textile History and Economic History* (above, 1). For linen, see the essay by Harte in the same volume already noted. In addition to Davis, *The Industrial Revolution and British Overseas Trade*, for connections with the United States see books by Ritcheson and Combs (below, 11); for Latin America, D.B. Goebel, 'British Trade to the Spanish Colonies, 1796–1823', *AHR* XLIII (1938), and R.A. Humphreys, 'British Merchants and South American Independence', *Proceedings of the British Academy* LI (1965); for the East, C. Northcote Parkinson, *Trade in the Eastern Seas, 1793–1815* (Cambridge, 1937), *War in the Eastern Seas, 1793–1815* (1954); and, over the more general field, the essays edited by him in *The Trade Winds: A Study of British Overseas Trade during the French Wars, 1793–1815* (1948).

Chapter 7 of Arthur Redford, *Economic History of England, 1760–1860* (1931) provides a starting point for discussion of the economic effect of the French wars, and various detailed effects are very fully examined in Crouzet (above). Phyllis Deane makes points of interest in 'War and Industrialization' in *War and Economic Development. Essays in Memory of David Joslin*, edited by J.M. Winter (Cambridge, 1975). The subject has also been pursued in G. Hueckel, 'War and the British Economy, 1793–1815. A General Equilibrium Analysis', *Explorations in Economic History* XI (1973), and J.L. Anderson, 'Aspects of the effects on the British Economy of the Wars against France, 1793–1815', *Australian Economic History Review* XII (1972).

Dorothy Marshall, *The English Poor in the Eighteenth Century* (1926) is a classic, and for further material see M. Dorothy George, *London Life in the Eighteenth Century* (1925). Other valuable explorations of working men's lives are J.L. and Barbara Hammond, *The Village Labourer, 1760–1832* (1911), *The Town Labourer, 1760–1832* (1917), and *The Skilled Labourer, 1760–1832* (1919), John Rule, *The Experience of Labour in eighteenth-century Industry* (1981) and Malcolm I. Thomis, *The Town Labourer in the Industrial Revolution* (1974). Thomis, *Politics and Society in Nottingham, 1785–1835* (Oxford, 1969) adds detail on one important provincial area. For the debate on the tangled question of wages and the standard of living, see E.J.E. Hobsbawm and R.M. Hartwell, 'The Standard of Living during the Industrial Revolution: A Discussion', *EconHR* XVI (1963–4); R.M. Hartwell, 'The Standard of Living Controversy. A Summary', in *The Industrial Revolution*, edited by Hartwell (1970); *The Standard of Living in Britain in the Industrial Revolution*, edited by A.J. Taylor (1975). Duncan Bythell, *The Handloom Weavers. A Study in the English Cotton Industry during the Industrial Revolution* (Cambridge,

1969) deals with one of the largest employed groups in industry.

There are interesting, if brief, outlines on trade combinations in this period in Sidney and Beatrice Webb, *The History of Trade Unionism* (rev. edn., 1920), and H.M. Pelling, *A History of British Trade Unionism* (1963). The main source is A. Aspinall, *The Early English Trade Unions: Documents from the Home Office Papers in the Public Records* (1949). Much interesting information on this subject and on other aspects of working-class life dealt with in this chapter is gathered together in E.P. Thompson, *The Making of the English Working Class* (1963), although some of its judgments have come under critical review. See also C.R. Dobson, *Masters and Journeymen. A Prehistory of Industrial Relations, 1717–1800* (1980).

Sidney and Beatrice Webb, *English Poor Law History*, Part I: *The Old Poor Law* (1927) remains a classic account, but is now dated. Geoffrey W. Oxley, *Poor Relief in England and Wales, 1601–1834* (1974) is an excellent critical survey of the strengths and weaknesses of our knowledge as it stands at present, and the brief essay by J.D. Marshall, *The Old Poor Law, 1795–1834* (1968), has suggestive points. See also A.W. Coats, 'Economic Thought and Poor Law Policy in the eighteenth century', *EconHR* XIII (1960–61). David Owen, *English Philanthropy, 1660–1960* (Cambridge, Mass., 1964) is a standard history of charitable activity.

For problems of industrial unrest towards the end of the Napoleonic wars see, in addition to E.P. Thompson (above), F.O. Darvall, *Popular Disturbances and Public Order in Regency England* (rep. 1969); Malcolm I. Thomis, *The Luddites: Machine Breaking in Regency England* (Newton Abbot, 1970), and his *Nottingham* (above); J.R. Dinwiddy, 'Luddism and Politics in the Northern Counties', *J of Social History* IV (1979).

8 The Ascendancy of Pitt

Apart from the analyses of personality in the biographies of Pitt and Fox listed above, there are suggestive pen-portraits in *Politics and Personality, 1760–1827. Selections from History Today*, edited by M.J. Barnes (1967), and Richard Pares, *The Historian's Business and other Essays*, edited by R.A. and Elisabeth Humphreys (Oxford, 1961). Pitt's role is fully treated up to 1789 in Ehrman's biography, and there is a perceptive analysis of his administrative control in chapter 4 of Harlow, *Second British Empire*, vol. II (above, 4). J.E.D. Binney, *British Public Finance and Administration, 1774–92* (Oxford, 1958) provides more specialist discussion of fiscal policy. Important aspects of commercial policy are examined in John Ehrman, *The British Government and Commercial Negotiations with Europe, 1783–1793* (Cambridge, 1962). Various questions of empire and trade are discussed in Harlow; and see also D.L. Mackay, 'British Interest in the Southern Oceans, 1782–1794', *The New Zealand J. of History* III (1969), and 'Direction and Purpose in British Imperial Policy, 1783–1801', *HJ* XVII (1974). For the interaction of the East India Company with British politics see C.H. Philips, *The East India Company, 1784–1834* (1961). Holden Furber, *John Company at work* (1948) examines intensively British activity in India during the years 1783–93. P.J. Marshall, *The Impeachment of Warren Hastings* (1965) is a full, authoritative study.

One central problem in foreign relations in this decade, the Anglo-French rivalry in the Dutch Netherlands, has received detailed treatment in Alfred Cobban, *Ambassadors and Secret Agents. The Diplomacy of the First Earl*

of Malmesbury at the Hague (1954). T.C.W. Blanning is illuminating on
' "That Horrid Electorate" or "Ma Patrie Germanique"? George III,
Hanover, and the *Fürstenbund* of 1785', *HJ* XX (1977). On relations with
Eastern Europe Dietrich Gerhard, *England und der Aufstieg Russlands*
(Berlin, 1933) is valuable for its material drawn from European archives.
The Nootka Sound episode is discussed in J.M. Norris, 'The Policy of the
British Cabinet in the Nootka Sound Crisis', *EHR* LXX (1955). For British
relations with the United States see H.C. Allen, *Great Britain and the
United States* (1954), C.R. Ritcheson, *Aftermath of Revolution. British
Policy towards the United States, 1783–1795* (Dallas, 1969), and Jerald A.
Combs, *The Jay Treaty. Political Battleground of the Founding Fathers*
(Berkeley, 1970). McDowell (above, 4) provides a full account of Irish
affairs.

Opposition party politics are treated in detail in L.G. Mitchell (above, 2)
and in J.W. Derry, *The Regency Crisis and the Whigs, 1788–9* (Cambridge,
1963). Paul Kelly suggests a return of politics to its traditional pattern after
1784 in 'British Parliamentary Politics, 1784–1786', *HJ* XVII (1974). G.M.
Ditchfield outlines 'The Parliamentary Struggle over the Repeal of the Test
and Corporation Acts, 1787–90', in *EHR* LXXXIX(1974). For the
beginnings of the anti-slavery campaign see Roger Anstey, *The Atlantic
Slave Trade and British Abolition, 1760–1810* (1975).

For the tail-end of the county association movement see Christie, *Wilkes,
Wyvill and Reform.* Resurgent radicalism in Britain at the time of the
French Revolution is now best followed in Albert Goodwin, *The Friends of
Liberty: The English Democratic Movement in the age of the French
Revolution* (1979). The impact of the American example after 1783 on
dissenting and radical opinion is traced in Bonwick (above, 3). For Foxite
reactions to the French Revolution and radicalism see Frank O'Gorman,
The Whig Party and the French Revolution (1967).

9   War Against Revolution 1793–1796

Pending the completion of John Ehrman's work on the younger Pitt, the best
outline is J. Holland Rose, *William Pitt and the Great War* (1911). Sir
Arthur Bryant, *The Years of Endurance, 1793–1802* (1942) is well-written
and evocative, but less penetrating. Clive Emsley, *British Society and the
French Wars, 1793–1815* (1979) provides a valuable discussion of various
aspects of the home front. The disintegration of the Foxite opposition is
followed in O'Gorman and L.G. Mitchell (above). Books on the popular
movements listed for the previous chapter carry the story on through these
years. Black, *Association* (above, 6) gives a good general account of the
Loyalist associations, but see also Austin Mitchell, 'The Association
Movement of 1792–3', *HJ* IV (1961), and D.E. Ginter, 'The Loyalist
Association Movement of 1792–3 and British Public Opinion', *HJ* IX
(1966). There is a critical discussion of the government prosecution of
reformers in F. Prochaska, 'English State Trials in the 1790s: a Case Study',
J of British Studies XIII (1973).

The naval war against France is outlined in G.J. Marcus, *A Naval History
of England*, volume II: *The Age of Nelson* (1971), and for various important
episodes see Carola Oman, *Nelson* (1947). A.H. Burne, *The Noble Duke of
York* (1949) provides a sketch of the British campaign in the Low Countries.
The British attempts to mobilize allies by financial inducements are
followed in J.M. Sherwig, *Guineas and Gunpowder* (Cambridge, Mass.,

1969). For Ireland, in addition to books already listed, see A.P.F. Malcomson, *John Foster. The Politics of the Anglo-Irish Ascendancy* (1978), and E.A. Smith, *Whig Principles and Party Politics. Earl Fitzwilliam and the Whig Party, 1748–1833* (1975), which examines anew Fitzwilliam's ill-fated lord lieutenancy and its political repercussions.

10 Fight for Survival, 1796–1801

Most of the books listed for chapter 9 are relevant. The rump Foxite party is reviewed critically in R.E. Willis, 'An handful of violent people. The nature of the Foxite Opposition', in *Albion* VIII (1976). The best treatment of the Duke of York's army reforms is in Richard Glover, *Peninsular Preparation: The Reform of the British Army, 1795–1809* (Cambridge, 1963). Piers Mackesy, *Statesmen at War. The Strategy of Overthrow, 1798–9* (1974) deals exhaustively with this theme. The naval mutinies of 1797 are discussed in G.E. Manwaring and B. Dobrée, *The Floating Republic* (1935), and James Dugan, *The Great Mutiny* (1966). On the eastern theatre of war see Parkinson (above, 7), and on the Mysore War of 1799, Iris Butler, *The Eldest Brother* (1973). Geoffrey Bolton, *The Passing of the Irish Act of Union* (Oxford, 1966) provides a full account.

11 Britain faces Napoleon 1801–1807

Arthur Bryant, *Years of Victory, 1802–1812* (1944) provides a readable general narrative, and for naval campaigns see once again Marcus and Oman (above, 9). Biographies on Pitt, Fox, Addington and Castlereagh listed above should be consulted. A full but somewhat old-fashioned treatment of home affairs is presented in A.T. Fremantle, *England in the nineteenth century, 1801–1805* (1929), and *England in the nineteenth century, 1806–1810* (1930). For a good modern survey see A.D. Harvey, *Britain in the early nineteenth century* (1978), and his tart critique of 'The Ministry of all the Talents', in *HJ* XV (1972). James J. Sack, *The Grenvillites, 1801–1829. Party Politics and Factionalism in the age of Pitt and Liverpool* (Univ. of Illinois Press, 1979) is a substantial contribution to party political history. The development of British military preparations and activity is traced in two books by Richard Glover, *Peninsular Preparation* (above, 10) and *Britain at Bay. Defence against Bonaparte, 1803–1814* (1973). The classic work on the Trafalgar campaign is Sir Julian S. Corbett, *The Campaign of Trafalgar* (1910); for a recent account see Oliver Warner, *Trafalgar* (1959). Piers Mackesy gives a good account of the southern war theatre in *The War in the Mediterranean, 1803–1810* (1957).

12 Politics after Pitt and Fox 1807–1815

For outline treatment of the politics of these years see books by Fremantle, Harvey and Sack (above, 11). Spencer Walpole, *The Life of the Right Honourable Spencer Perceval* (2 vols., 1874) is a substantial and informative, if old-fashioned, treatment of the years up to 1812 by the prime minister's grandson, and there is an excellent account in Denis Gray's biography (above). C.D. Yonge, *The Life and Administration of Robert Banks, Second Earl of Liverpool* (3 vols., 1868) remains the fullest published source of information on the early career of the man who was one of Perceval's most faithful cabinet colleagues during the years 1807–12 and ultimately succeeded him as premier. Michael Roberts, *The Whig Party, 1807–1812* (1939) is an excellent survey of opposition politics. For further detail see his article, 'The leadership of the Whig Party in the House of Commons, 1807–1815', *EHR* L. (1935), and Leslie Mitchell, *Holland House* (1980). The re-emergence of radicalism in the metropolis is outlined in M.W. Patterson, *Sir Francis Burdett and his times, 1770–1844* (2 vols., 1931), and in two papers: Naomi C. Miller, 'John Cartwright and radical parliamentary reform, 1808–1819', *EHR* LXXXIII (1968), and J.R. Dinwiddy, 'Robert Waithman and the revival of Radicalism in the City of London, 1795–1818', *BIHR* XLVI (1973).

13   Britain and Napoleon: The Final Phase 1807–1815

See titles listed for chapter 11: Sherwig's contribution on British aid to continental allies is substantial for this period. Sir William F.P. Napier, *History of the War in the Peninsula and in the South of France, 1807–14* (6 vols., 1828–40) is on the grand scale, and on some points an excellent frist-hand account, but marred by prejudice. Definitive is Sir Charles W.C. Oman, *A History of the Peninsular War* (7 vols., Oxford, 1902–30). S.G.P. Ward provides a good study of administrative problems in *Wellington's Headquarters. A Study of the Administrative Problems in the Peninsula, 1809–1814* (1957), and the personality of the commander comes through well in Elizabeth Longford, *Wellington. The Years of the Sword* (1969). For the Waterloo campaign see Jac Weller, *Wellington at Waterloo* (1967). On the war against the United States see Reginald Horsman, *The War of 1812* (1969), and C.S. Forester, *The Naval War of 1812* (1957) – the classic treatment of the latter subject is A.T. Mahan, *Sea Power in its relations to the War of 1812* (2 vols., Boston, 1905). François Crouzet, *L'économie britannique et le blocus continental, 1806–1813* (2 vols., Paris, 1958) is indispensable on Anglo-French economic warfare during the period. Anglo-Austrian relations are discussed in C.S.B. Buckland, *Metternich and the British Government from 1809 to 1813* (1932). Sir C.K. Webster, *The Foreign Policy of Castlereagh, 1812–1815. Britain and the Reconstruction of Europe* (1931) is a meticulous, detailed account.

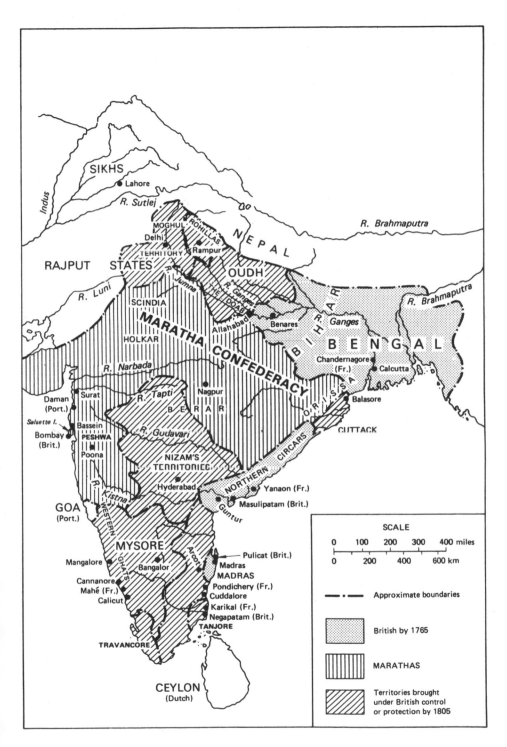

Map I India

The map contains the following labels:

SIKHS

Lahore

Indus

R. Sutlej

R. Brahmaputra

MOGHUL
ROHILLAS

Delhi

Rampur

N E P A L

TERRITORY

RAJPUT STATES

OUDH

SCINDIA

R. Luni

THE DOAB

R. Jumna

R. Ganges

Allahabad

Benares

B I H A R

Ganges

R. Brahmaputra

MARATHA CONFEDERACY

HOLKAR

R. Narbada

B E N G A L

Chandernagore
(Fr.)

Calcutta

Daman
(Port.)

Surat

R. Tapti

Nagpur

B E R A R

O R I S S A

Balasore

Salsette I.

Bassein

R. Godavari

CUTTACK

Bombay
(Brit.)

PESHWA

Poona

NIZAM'S TERRITORIES

GOA
(Port.)

Hyderabad

NORTHERN CIRCARS

Yanaon (Fr.)

R. Kistna

Guntur

Masulipatam (Brit.)

WESTERN GHATS

MYSORE

Arcot

Pulicat (Brit.)

Mangalore

Bangalor

Madras

Cannanore

MADRAS

Mahé (Fr.)

Pondichery (Fr.)

Calicut

Cuddalore

Karikal (Fr.)

Negapatam (Brit.)

TANJORE

TRAVANCORE

CEYLON
(Dutch)

SCALE

| 0 | 100 | 200 | 300 | 400 miles |

| 0 | 200 | 400 | 600 km |

━ ·— Approximate boundaries

British by 1765

MARATHAS

Territories brought
under British control
or protection by 1805

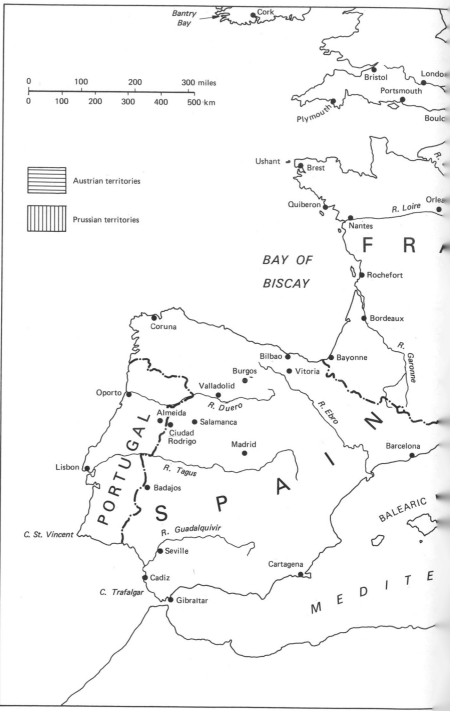

Bantry Bay
Cork
Bristol
London
Portsmouth
Plymouth
Boulo

Ushant
Brest

0   100   200   300 miles
0 100 200 300 400 500 km

Austrian territories

Prussian territories

Quiberon
R. Loire
Orlea
Nantes

F R A

BAY OF

BISCAY

Rochefort

Bordeaux

Coruna

Bilbao
Bayonne
R. Garonne
Burgos
Vitoria

Oporto
Valladolid
R. Duero
Almeida
Salamanca
Ciudad Rodrigo
Madrid
Barcelona

S P A I N

R. Ebro

Lisbon
R. Tagus

P O R T U G A L

Badajos

R. Guadalquivir

C. St. Vincent

Seville

BALEARIC

Cartagena

Cadiz

C. Trafalgar
Gibraltar

M E D I T E

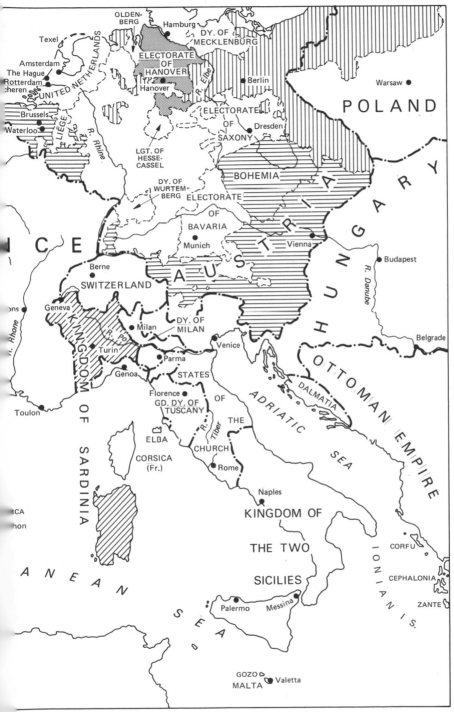

OLDEN-
BERG
Texel
Hamburg
Amsterdam
The Hague
Rotterdam
cheren
UNITED NETHERLANDS
DY. OF
MECKLENBURG
Brussels
Waterloo
LIEGE
R. Rhine
R. Elbe
Berlin
ELECTORATE
OF
HANOVER
Hanover
ELECTORATE
OF
SAXONY
Dresden
WARSAW
POLAND
Warsaw
LGT. OF
HESSE-
CASSEL
BOHEMIA
DY. OF
WURTEM-
BERG
ELECTORATE
OF
BAVARIA
Munich
AUSTRIA
Vienna
HUNGARY
R. Danube
Budapest
Berne
SWITZERLAND
Geneva
ons
KINGDOM
OF
SARDINIA
R. PO
Milan
DY. OF
MILAN
Turin
Venice
Parma
STATES
Genoa
Belgrade
OTTOMAN EMPIRE
Toulon
Florence
GD. DY. OF
TUSCANY
OF
THE
DALMATIA
ADRIATIC
SEA
ELBA
CORSICA
(Fr.)
R. Tiber
CHURCH
Rome
ICA
hon
Naples
KINGDOM OF
THE TWO
SICILIES
CORFU
IONIAN IS.
CEPHALONIA
ZANTE
ICE
R. Rhone
ANEAN
SEA
GOZO
MALTA
Valetta
Palermo
Messina

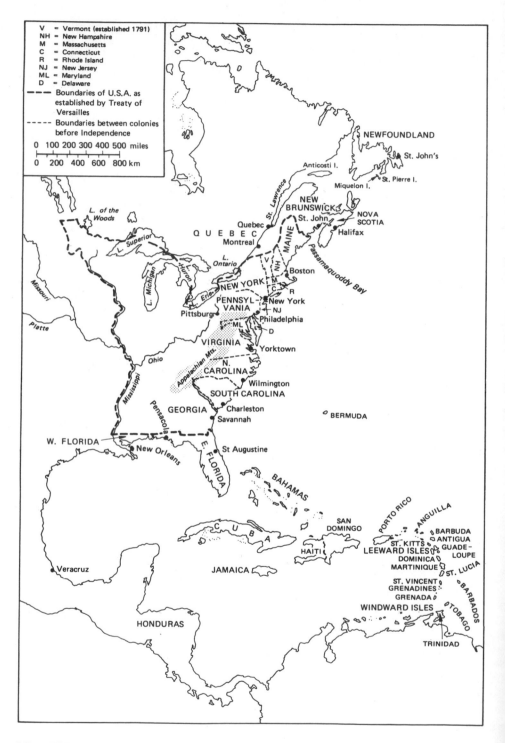

NEWFOUNDLAND

St. John's

Anticosti I.

Miquelon I.

St. Pierre I.

St. Lawrence

NEW BRUNSWICK

Quebec

St. John

NOVA SCOTIA

Halifax

QUEBEC

Montreal

MAINE

Passamaquoddy Bay

L. of the Woods

L. Superior

L. Michigan

L. Huron

L. Ontario

L. Erie

Boston

NEW YORK

V

NH

M

C

R

PENNSYL-VANIA

Pittsburg

New York

NJ

Philadelphia

ML

D

Missouri

Platte

VIRGINIA

Yorktown

Ohio

Appalachian Mts.

N. CAROLINA

Mississippi

Wilmington

SOUTH CAROLINA

Pensacola

GEORGIA

Charleston

Savannah

BERMUDA

W. FLORIDA

New Orleans

E. FLORIDA

St Augustine

BAHAMAS

CUBA

SAN DOMINGO

PORTO RICO

ANGUILLA

BARBUDA

ANTIGUA

ST. KITTS

LEEWARD ISLES

GUADE-LOUPE

HAITI

DOMINICA

MARTINIQUE

ST. LUCIA

Veracruz

JAMAICA

ST. VINCENT

GRENADINES

GRENADA

BARBADOS

WINDWARD ISLES

TOBAGO

HONDURAS

TRINIDAD

Map III North America and the West Indies

Index

(Battles, Rivers, Statutes, and Treaties are listed under these general heads)